THE LIFE

OF

MAJOR GENERAL

ZACHARY TAYLOR,

Twelfth President of the United States.

BY H. MONTGOMERY.

With Illustrations.

TWENTIETH EDITION, REVISED AND ENLARGED.

AUBURN:
DERBY, MILLER & COMPANY.

1850.

THOMAS B. SMITH, STEREOTYPER,
216 WILLIAM STREET, N. Y.

PUBLISHERS' NOTICE.

The sudden and unexpected termination of the earthly career of the lamented TAYLOR, seems to have called for a final chapter to the great Hero's Life; including the closing scene of his death.—This is incorporated in the present edition by the esteemed author; and it is now offered to the Public as the only complete record yet issued from the press, of the main incidents in the life of one who "never surrendered," but to the *Great Conqueror* of all.

AUBURN, September, 1850.

ADVERTISEMENT

TO THE REVISED EDITION.

The sale of the previous editions of the Life of Taylor, and his election to the Presidency of the United States, has induced the publishers to issue a new edition, believing that the favor which the work has thus far met with from the public, demand of them a continuance of the history. It has been undertaken by the compiler, and the chain of events in the life of the extraordinary man of whose history it treats, is brought down to the present time, including a sketch of the leading features connected with the political campaign which resulted in his election to the Presidency.. The work has therefore been much enlarged, if not improved, and it is trusted has thereby been rendered more acceptable to the public.

Auburn, 1850.

PREFACE.

The sudden splendor with which General Taylor nas burst upon the nation, has created in the public mind an anxiety, as intense as it is universal, to become acquainted, not only with the brilliant deeds which have rendered his name so illustrious, but with all the incidents of his life from his youth to his first prominent appearance before the country, as commander-in-chief of the army, destined to operate against Mexico. It was to satisfy this anxiety more fully, if possible, and in a more durable form than it had yet been done, that this work has been prepared. The compiler claims for it no other merit than this over the many sketches of this eminent man's life that have preceded it. He has labored under much embarrassment in collecting materials for a work claiming even that merit. So little had General Taylor sought public notoriety, that almost his very name was unknown to a large portion of the American people, until the victories of Palo Alto and Resaca de la Palma revived the recollection of it. Even his heroic defence of Fort

Harrison, and his services in Florida, were nearly forgotten.

The inconveniences arising from this cause were increased by the rapidity with which the materials had necessarily to be prepared. In less than seven weeks from the day the first "copy" was written and placed in the hands of the compositor, the last sheet had run through the press. In addition to its preparation, the compiler had the management of a daily and weekly paper, and the various other duties connected with them upon his hands. Though the reader has a right to hold him strictly accountable for the imperfections that may be discovered, yet he has some confidence that these circumstances will induce a less rigid exaction than he would have had any right to expect if he had possessed ampler materials, longer time to collect, and more leisure to prepare them. It is proper to say, however, that he has been careful to exclude everything not believed to be strictly authentic. Much of it has already been made public, principally through the newspaper press of the day. Some of this has been acknowledged in the appropriate place. But with the exception of Mr. Thorpe's excellent work, entitled "Our Army on the Rio Grande," the sources of his information are so various, that it would be as tedious as it is unnecessary to specify them.

AUBURN, JUNE, 1847.

CONTENTS.

CHAPTER I.

CHAPTER II.

CHAPTER III.

CHAPTER IV.

CHAPTER V.

CHAPTER VI.

CHAPTER VII.

CHAPTER VIII.

CHAPTER IX.

CHAPTER X.

CHAPTER XI.

LIFE

OF

GENERAL ZACHARY TAYLOR.

CHAPTER I.

The Taylor Family—Colonel Richard Taylor—Birth of Zachary Taylor—His youth—Early indications of Character—Education—Disadvantages he labored under—His Bold and Adventurous Disposition—Hazardous Exploit—Love of Military Display—Receives a Lieutenant's Commission in the Regular Army—Promoted to the rank of Captain—His Gallant Defence of Fort Harrison—The Account of the Engagement—Receives the Brevet of Major—Expedition against the Indians—Services in the Black Hawk War—Promoted successively to the rank of Lieutenant Colonel and Colonel—Appointed Indian Agent.

Zachary Taylor is descended from an ancient and distinguished English family, which emigrated to America and settled in the eastern part of the colony of Virginia, in the year 1692, and the name has been intimately identified and interwoven with the civil, political, and military history of Virginia, both as a weak and languishing colony, and a great and powerful commonwealth, from that day to the present. Amongst others with whom General Zachary Taylor is connected, either by the ties of consanguinity or marriage, and whose names have rendered its history illustrious, are numbered the Madisons, Lees, Barbours, Pendletons, Conways, Talafieros, Hunts, Gaineses, &c.

The father of Zachary Taylor held a colonel's commission throughout the Revolution, and served with great valor during that long and unequal struggle, much of the time with Washington himself, and retaining in all emergencies, and under every difficulty, his confidence and esteem. He was engaged in many of the most fiercely contested and bloody battles of the war, and particularly at Trenton, where he rendered distinguished and valuable aid to the commander-in-chief, in that brilliant achievement.

In 1790 Colonel Taylor emigrated to Kentucky, in company with Colonels Croghan and Bullitt, when that territory was but little more than an Indian hunting ground. It was then the scene of frequent fierce and bloody strifes between the various tribes which inhabited it, and murderous excursions against the emigrant population who had settled there. From these desperate and bloody encounters, amongst themselves and with the white man, Kentucky derived the name of the "Dark and Bloody Ground."

In many of these encounters Colonel Taylor bore a conspicuous part, and by his bold and daring conduct, and ceaseless vigilance, rendered his name a terror to the merciless foe. After peace was established, he held many honorable and responsible positions. He was one of the framers of the constitution of Kentucky; represented Jefferson county, and Louisville city for many years in both branches of the state legislature, and was a member of the electoral colleges which voted for Jefferson, Madison, Monroe, and Clay. Among the politicians of Kentucky, he is remembered as one of the few men of the Old Court party, who could be elected during the excitement of the "Old Court and New Court question."

Colonel Taylor died on his plantation near Louisville, Kentucky, leaving three sons, (his second and fourth sons, George and William, having died previously,) Hancock, Zachary and Joseph, and three daughters, Elizabeth, Sarah, and Emily.

Hancock, Elizabeth, and Emily, have died since their father, so that Joseph and Sarah are the only brother and sister of Zachary now living. The descendants of the deceased members of the family, with two exceptions, live in and near Louisville, Kentucky.

ZACHARY TAYLOR was born in Orange county, Virginia, in 1784, and was less than a year old when his father emigrated to Kentucky. His youth was therefore spent, and his character formed, amidst the dangers and difficulties of Indian warfare, and the hardships and privations ever incident to a frontier life. His boyhood was distinguished by indications of that straightforward, manly independence of character, inflexibility of purpose, frank and open disposition, foresight, decision and energy; modest and retiring demeanor, and thoughtful, inquiring mind, that have since borne him so triumphantly through difficulties and dangers before which men educated in a less severe school would have shrunk in despair, until he has wrought out a name that will fill one of the brightest pages in American history.

Many family and neighborhood anecdotes are told to illustrate his daring and adventurous character, and his love for dangerous enterprises. Night after night he was in the habit of seeing the house barricaded, and the arms prepared to repel any attack that might be made before the morning dawned. Scarcely a week passed that there was not an alarm, or an actual incursion of Indians amongst the settlements. Even on his way to school he was in danger of the tomahawk and scalping knife. On one occasion, some of his schoolmates were murdered and scalped by the Indians, within a hundred yards from the point where he and his brothers had separated from them.

When but seventeen years old he swam across the Ohio river, from the Kentucky to the Indiana shore, in the month of March, when the river was filled with floating ice, which is a feat far surpassing in danger and difficulty the far-famed exploit of swimming the Hellespont. Many other well-attested anecdotes are related of his daring adventures, and his love of bold and dangerous exploits. He took great delight in fishing and hunting, and was often absent, roaming through forests and over boundless prairies, for days and nights together, in quest of game. No obstacle would dampen his indomitable energy, or discourage him from attempting the most hazardous enterprises.

As may well be understood, young Taylor enjoyed but few advantages for acquiring a practical, much less an ornamental or classical education. The character of the schools of Kentucky, at that time, as in all other new and sparsely settled districts, were not of a very elevated character. The few schools then, were supported by private munificence, and were not of a character to lay a very broad or deep foundation for those attainments, and that useful superstructure of knowledge, which the superior facilities of the present day render so easy of access. But few as were the advantages afforded him, his ever active and inquiring mind, his great love of learning, his remarkably strong and retentive memory, and above all, his iron will and great tenacity of purpose, more that compensated, in his case, for what otherwise would have confined his acquirements to the commonest rudiments of an English education. But by the aid of these striking characteristics, he was enabled to overcome all difficulties, and to store his mind with a fund of information that few have acquired, even under the most favorable circumstances. The elegance, beauty and simplicity of his official dispatches from Mexico, stamp him as one of the chastest and most accomplished writers of the day.

Amongst Taylor's most intimate associates at school, were Col. Joseph P. Taylor, who afterwards distinguished himself at the battle of Okee-cho-bee, during the Florida war, and has now the control of the commissary department in Mexico, and Col. George Croghan, subsequently the hero of Fort Sandusky, and at present holding a high post in the army of the United States. He remained with his family, in Kentucky, until the year 1808, when the capture of the United States Frigate Chesapeake, by the British Frigate Leopard, fired the whole country with indignation, and fearfully increased the feelings of animosity that the repeated aggressions of the English nation had already raised to so high a pitch. Young Taylor partook of the general excitement to its full extent, and eagerly seized upon the occasion as a favorable moment to gratify his anxious desire to enter the army, and at the same time to assist in vindicating the outraged honor of his country's flag. Accordingly he lost no time in making his wishes known. He therefore applied to Mr. Jefferson for a commission in the army, and, by the aid of his powerful family connections, his application was successful;

and on the 3rd of May, 1808, when only eighteen years old, he received a commission as first lieutenant in the Seventh Regiment of United States Infantry. His young ambition was now satisfied, and a wide field opened before him for the gratification of his long indulged and ardent aspirations for military fame. He had almost from his earliest youth evinced a strong inclination for martial exercises, and his greatest pleasure consisted in playing the soldier and acting the mock hero at the head of an army of equally young patriots. In these mimic battles he exhibited, on a small scale, the germ of that genius for command, and military skill and talent, which have since been so eminently developed.

From the time he entered the army until the breaking out of the war with England, but little occurred in the life of the young lieutenant to break the monotonous round of every-day duty, to which soldiers are bound when not in actual service. He passed his time in the duties of his position, and in perfecting himself in a knowledge of the profession he had chosen. He brought to the task the same untiring industry and firm determination to understand the science of war, which he had ever shown in whatever pursuit or study he entered upon. It was probably during these comparatively leisure years, that he acquired that acquaintance with military tactics which is so necessary to the successful commander, and which afterwards served to place him amongst the first generals of the day.

Previous to the breaking out of hostilities, the English government, through its agents, had been unceasing in its efforts to induce the Miamies and other tribes of western Indians to take up arms against the United States, and had been unscrupulous in the use of money and means to accomplish this end. Their agents had been partially successful in enlisting several savage tribes in their plans. The threatened outbreak, however, was discovered before their schemes had quite matured, and by the promptness, energy, and vigilance of General William Henry Harrison, who was then governor of the Northwest Territory, their intentions were anticipated, and a detachment of troops under his command was marched into the enemy's country. While on this expedition Governor Harrison determined to build a fort on the Wabash, in Indiana, about fifty miles above Vincennes, which was afterwards known as Fort Harrison. Lieutenant Taylor was actively engaged in this expedition, and in overawing the Indians in other quarters. At the beginning of 1812, Lieutenant Taylor was promoted to the rank of captain, by President Madison.

On the 19th of June, 1812, a declaration of war was formally declared against Great Britain by the United States Congress, and sanctioned by the President. Captain Taylor had but a few weeks before been placed in command of Fort Harrison, a rude and weak stockade, garrisoned by only fifty soldiers, most of whom, like himself, were worn down and disabled by their long and severe service. Almost in the very midst of an enemy's country, surrounded on all sides by a sleepless and savage foe, and kept constantly on the alert, night and day, for weeks together, it is not to be wondered at that Taylor and his men should nearly have sunk under the fatigue and labor they had so long endured. While in this wretched state, with scarcely a dozen men fit for service, he was attacked, on the night of the 5th of September, 1812, after an ineffectual attempt to get possession of the fort by stratagem, by a force of four hundred and fifty Indians. But Captain Taylor had taken his measures with too much prudence to be captured either by stratagem or force, as weak as were his defences and few his men.

The attack was commenced about eleven o'clock at night, amidst the excitement and confusion occasioned by the burning of the lower block-house, which contained the property of the contractor, and which they had previously fired. The Indians, confident of victory, had completely surrounded the little garrison, and commenced firing upon it from all sides, simultaneously with the firing of the block-house. But Captain Taylor was undismayed, either by the overwhelming number of his enemy and their murderous fire, or the more dangerous element of destruction they had called to their aid. He calmly gave his orders for having the fire extinguished, but for a long time all efforts were fruitless. The fire communicated to the roof, in spite of every effort to check it. The scene at this time is represented as truly appalling. The raging of the fire, the yelling and howling of several hundred Indians, and the cries of women and children who had taken shelter there, together with the unceasing discharge of guns, must have been enough to appal the stoutest heart. Yet we find this stripling captain, only twenty-two years of age, boldly meeting them all, and giving his orders for suppressing the fire, and repelling the attack of his four hundred savage foes, with as much coolness as the oldest veteran. By his great presence of mind, and his well-directed efforts, the flames were at length arrested, and the fire finally subdued. Having extinguished the fire, and erected a temporary breastwork, the fire of the enemy was returned with redoubled vigor during the whole night, and with such success, that at six o'clock in the morning, the enemy gave up the contest in despair, and withdrew their forces. In this gallant defence, Captain Taylor only lost two men killed, and two wounded. But his letter to General Harrison, giving a graphic and detailed account of the defence of Fort Harrison, and the incidents connected with it, will obviate the necessity of any other description of that terrible night, and be far more interesting. Captain Taylor says:—

"On Thursday evening, 3rd instant, after retreat-beating, four guns were heard to fire in the direction where two young men (citizens who resided here) were making hay, about four hundred yards distant from the fort. I was immediately impressed with an idea that they were killed by the Indians, as the Miamies or Weas had that day informed me that the Prophet's party would soon be here for the purpose of commencing hostilities, and that they had been directed to leave this place, which they were about to do. I did not think it prudent to send out at that late hour of the night to see what had become of them, and their not coming convinced me that I was right in my conjecture. I waited until eight o'clock next morning, when I sent out a corporal with a small party to find them, if it could be done without running too much risk of being drawn into an ambuscade. He soon sent back to inform me, that he had found them both killed, and wished to know my further orders. I sent the cart and oxen, had them brought in and buried. They had been shot with two balls, scalped and cut in the most shocking manner. Late in the evening of the 4th instant, old Joseph Lenar, and between thirty and forty Indians, arrived from the Prophet's town, with a white flag; among whom were about ten women, and the men were composed of chiefs of the tribes which compose the Prophet's party.

"A Shawanee man that spoke good English, informed me that old Lenar intended to speak to me next morning, and try to get something to eat. After retreat-beating, I examined the men's arms, and found them all in good order, and completed their cartridges to sixteen rounds per man. As I had not been able to mount a guard of more than six privates and two non-commissioned officers for some time past, and sometimes part of them every other day, from the unhealthiness of the company, I had not conceived my force adequate to the defence of this post, should it be vigorously attacked, for some time past. As I had just recovered from a very severe attack of the fever, I was not able to be up much through the night.

"After tattoo, I cautioned the guard to be vigilant, and ordered one of the non-commissioned officers, as the sentinel could not see every part of the garrison, to walk around on the inside during the night, to prevent the Indians taking any advantage of us, provided they had any intention of attacking us. About eleven o'clock, I was awakened by the firing of one of the sentinels. I sprung up, ran out, and ordered the men to their posts, when my orderly sergeant (who had charge of the upper block-house) called out that the Indians had fired the lower block-house, (which contained the property of the contractors, which was deposited in the upper part, the lower part having been assigned to a corporal and ten privates as an alarm post.) The guns had begun to fire pretty smartly from both sides. I directed the buckets to be got ready, and water brought from the well, and the fire extinguished immediately, as it was perceivable at that time; but from debility, or some other cause, the men were very slow in executing my orders. The word fire appeared to throw the whole of them into confusion; and by the time they had got the water, and broken open the door, the fire had unfortunately communicated to a quantity of whiskey, (the *stock* having *licked* several holes through the lower part of the building, after the salt that was stored there, through which they had introduced the fire without being discovered, as the night was very dark,) and in spite of every exertion we could make use of, in less than a minute it ascended to the roof, and baffled every effort we could make to extinguish it.

"As that block-house adjoined the barracks that made part of the fortifications, most of the men immediately gave themselves up for lost, and I had the greatest difficulty in getting my orders executed; and, sir—what from the raging of the fire—the yelling and howling of several hundred Indians—the cries of nine women and children (a part soldiers' and a part citizens' wives, who had taken shelter in the fort)—and a desponding of so many of the men, which was worse than all—I can assure you that my feelings were very unpleasant; and, indeed, there were not more than ten or fifteen men able to do anything at all, the others being sick or convalescent; and to add to our other misfortunes, two of our stoutest men jumped the pickets and left. But my presence of mind did not for a moment forsake me. I saw by throwing off part of the roof that joined the block-house that was on fire, and keeping the end perfectly wet, the whole row of buildings might be saved, and leave only an entrance of eighteen or twenty feet for the Indians to enter, after the house was consumed; and that a temporary breastwork might be formed to prevent their entering even there. I convinced the men that this could be accomplished, and it appeared to inspire them with new life; and never did men act with more firmness or desperation. Those that were able, (while others kept up a constant fire from the upper block-house and the two bastions,) mounted the roofs of the houses, with Doctor Clark at their head, (who acted with the greatest firmness and presence of mind, the whole time the attack lasted, which was seven hours,) under a shower of bullets, and in less than a moment threw off as much of the roof as was necessary. This was done, with one man killed, and two wounded, and I am in hopes neither of them dangerously. The man that was killed was a little deranged, and did not get off of the house as soon as directed, or he would not have been hurt; and although the barracks were several times in a blaze, and an immense quantity of fire against them, the men used such exertion, that they kept it under, and before day raised a temporary breastwork as high as a man's head. Although the Indians continued to pour in a heavy fire of ball, and an innumerable quantity of arrows, during the whole time the attack lasted, in every part of the parade, I had but one other man killed—nor any other wounded inside the fort— and he lost his life by being too anxious. He got into one of the *gallies* in the bastions, and fired over the pickets, and called out to his comrades that he had killed an Indian, and neglecting to stoop down in an instant, he was shot.

"One of the men that jumped the pickets, returned an hour before day, and running up towards the gate, begged for God's sake for it to be opened. I suspected it to be a stratagem of the Indians to get in, as I did not recollect the voice; I directed the men in the bastion where I happened to be, to shoot him, let him be who he would, and one of them fired at him, but fortunately he ran up the other bastion, where they knew his voice, and Dr. Clark directed him to lie close to the pickets, behind an empty barrel that happened to be there, and at daylight I had him let in. His arm was broken in a most shocking manner, which he says was done by the Indians, which I suppose was the cause of his returning. I think it probable that he will not recover. The other they caught about one hundred and thirty yards from the garrison, and cut him all to pieces. After keeping up a constant fire until about six o'clock the next morning, which we began to return with some effect, after daylight they removed out of reach of our guns. A party of them drove up the horses that belonged to the citizens here, and as they could not catch them very readily, shot the whole of them in our sight, as well as a number of their hogs. They drove off the whole of the cattle, which amounted to sixty-five head, as well as the public oxen. I had the vacancy filled up before night (which was made by the burning of the block-house) with a strong row of pickets, which I got by pulling down the guardhouse. We lost the whole of our provisions, but must make out to live upon green corn, until we can get a supply, which I am in hopes will not be long. I believe the whole of the Miamies or Weas were among the Prophet's party, as one chief gave his orders in that language, which resembled Stone Eater's voice, and I believe Negro Legs was there likewise. A Frenchman here understands their different languages; and several of the Miamies or Weas that have been frequently here were recognized by the Frenchman and soldiers next morning.

"The Indians suffered smartly, but were so numerous as to take off all that were shot. They continued with us until the next morning, but made no further attempt on the fort, nor have we seen anything more of them since. I have delayed informing you of my situation, as I did not like to weaken the garrison, and I looked for some person from Vincennes, and none of my men were acquainted with the woods, and therefore I would either have to take the road or river, which I was fearful was guarded by small parties of Indians, that would not dare attack a company of rangers that was on a scout; but, being disappointed, I have at length determined to send a couple of my men by water, and am in hopes they will arrive safe. I think it would be best to send the provisions under a pretty strong escort, as the Indians may attempt to prevent their coming. If you carry on an expedition against the Prophet this fall, you ought to be well provided with everything, as you may calculate on having every inch of ground disputed, between this and there, that they can defend with advantage."

Three days after, Captain Taylor again addressed General Harrison as follows:—"I wrote you on the 10th instant, giving you an account of the attack on this place, as well as my situation, which account I attempted to send by water, but the two men whom I dispatched in a canoe after night, found the river so well guarded that they were obliged to return. The Indians had built a fire on the bank of the river, a short distance below the garrison, which gave them an opportunity of seeing any craft that might attempt to pass, and were waiting with a canoe ready to intercept it. I expect the fort, as well as the road to Vincennes, is as well or better watched than the river. But my situation compels me to make one other attempt by land, and my orderly sergeant, with one other man, sets out to night, with strict orders to avoid the road in the daytime, and depend entirely on the woods, although neither of them has ever been to Vincennes by land, nor do they know anything of the country; but I am in hopes they will reach you in safety. I send them with great reluctance, from their ignorance of the woods. I think it very probable there is a large party of Indians waylaying the road between this and Vincennes, likely about the Narrows, for the purpose of intercepting any party that may be coming to this place, as the cattle they got here will supply them plentifully with provisions for some time to come."

The same modesty and forgetfulness of himself mark this unpretending account of his heroic and successful defence of a post almost defenceless, that has characterized every act of his life, and especially that so eminently distinguished his official dispatches at a later period. Though the style of his composition is immature, and in some degree obscure and inelegant, compared with his subsequent writings, yet it is distinguished by the same vigor of thought and manly independence of manner.

Soon after this dispatch was written, Captain Taylor was reinforced by Colonel Russell, with several companies of Rangers and Indiana volunteers. At the time of the fortunate arrival of these forces the little garrison was in a most wretched condition, being out of provisions, three-fourths of them disabled from duty by sickness and fatigue, and destitute of almost every necessary for health or comfort. But for the relief brought them, they must either have abandoned the fort at once, or died with hunger. Supplies of provisions had been forwarded, but the wagons were captured, and the escort killed nearly to a man.

The Indians were greatly incensed at their disgraceful repulse, and the loss they suffered, and retaliated upon the Americans, by attacking an unarmed settlement, and murdering about twenty inhabitants. But the country was filled with the highest admiration for the gallant and noble conduct of the young captain. The repulse of four hundred Indians, by an officer only twenty-two years old, with only fifty men, three-fourths of whom were on the sick list, and arresting at the same time a destructive fire that had broken out in one of his block-houses, was looked upon as indicating the very first order of military talent, and deserving the highest commendation. For his valuable services to the country, and his daring courage on this occasion, the brevet rank of major was conferred upon Captain Taylor, being the first brevet commission conferred during the war, and the oldest one in the army. His praises were on every tongue throughout the whole western country, and the most flattering compliments were bestowed upon him. Amongst others, Major-General Hopkins spoke in the warmest terms of commendation of him, in a letter to Governor Shelby, of Kentucky. He said, "the firm and almost unparalleled defence of Fort Harrison, by Captain Zachary Taylor, has raised for him a fabric of character not to be effaced by eulogy." His victory, like all his subsequent triumphs, was won with an overwhelming odds against him, and it inspired the highest confidence amongst his superior officers, in his courage, skill, and judgment.

Shortly after the battle of Fort Harrison, Major Taylor was dispatched on an expedition against the Prophet's and Winnebago towns, under General Hopkins, in which he displayed the same vigilance and energy that had signalized his previous conduct. These towns, and also some other Indian villages, were entirely destroyed. In all these operations Major Taylor bore a conspicuous part, and his gallant conduct was favorably referred to by General Hopkins, in his official dispatches of these transactions against the Indians. By these active and efficient measures, the power of the Indians was nearly destroyed, and their strength so much broken, that the western settlers enjoyed comparative security from their incursions for many years.

Though Major Taylor, from the peculiar circumstances of his position, had no other opportunity during the war, of signalizing himself; yet he rendered equally valuable services to the country, by keeping in awe the numerous tribes of western savages, and preventing them, in a great measure, from rendering efficient aid to the British.

From the termination of the war in the beginning of 1815, to 1832, when the Black Hawk war broke out, he was stationed at various posts in the West, as the interests of the service required, always active and faithful in the performance of the duties of his profession, and scrupulously exact in requiring it from those under his command. In 1832, previous to which he had been promoted to the rank of Lieutenant-Colonel, he was assigned to the command of the regular troops in the Black Hawk war, and endured all the hardships and privations of that vexatious war. At the battle of the Bad-Axe, which resulted in the capture of Black Hawk and the Prophet, and in the overwhelming defeat of their forces, he particularly distinguished himself, and had an important agency in bringing the war to a close. He commanded the regular troops, in this fiercely contested and destructive engagement, as he had during the long and trying march through the wilderness in pursuit of the enemy.

An anecdote of Taylor, that occurred during the early scenès of the Black Hawk war, is related by C. F. Hoffman, Esq., which may here be appropriately introduced as illustrative of his character, and foreshadowing those remarkable qualities of mind that have since shone forth so brilliantly on so many trying occasions. As such it will undoubtedly prove interesting to the reader. Such incidents, indeed, of such a man are always not only interesting, but valuable and instructive as a preface or introduction to the character of the man.

Some time after Stillman's defeat by Black Hawk's band, Taylor, marching with a large body of volunteers and a handful of regulars in pursuit of the hostile Indian force, found himself approaching Rock River, then asserted by many to be the true north-western boundary of the State of Illinois. The volunteers, as Taylor was informed, would refuse to cross the stream. They were militia, they said, called out for the defence of the State, and it was unconstitutional to order them to march beyond its frontier into the Indian country. Taylor thereupon halted his command, and encamped within the acknowledged boundaries of Illinois. He would not, as the relater of the story said, budge an inch further without orders. He had already driven Black Hawk out of the State, but the question of crossing Rock River seemed hugely to trouble his ideas of integrity to the constitution on one side, and military expediency on the other. During the night, however, orders came, either from General Scott or General Atkinson, for him to follow up Black Hawk to the last. The quietness of the Regular colonel meanwhile had rather encouraged the mutinous militia to bring their proceedings to a head. A sort of town-meeting was called upon the prairie, and Taylor invited to attend. After listening for some time very quietly to the proceedings, it became Rough and Ready's turn to address the chair. "He had heard," he said, "with much pleasure the views which several speakers had expressed of the independence and dignity of each private American citizen. He felt that all gentlemen there present were his equals—in reality, he was persuaded that many of them would in a few years be his superiors, and perhaps, in the capacity of Members of Congress, arbiters of the fortune and reputation of humble servants of the Republic like himself. He expected then to obey them as interpreters of the will of the people; and the best proof he could give that he would obey them, was now to observe the orders of those whom the people had already put in the places of authority, to which many gentlemen around him justly aspired. In plain English, gentlemen and fellow-citizens, the word has been passed on to me from Washington, to follow Black Hawk, and to take you with me as soldiers. I mean to do both. There are the flat-boats drawn up on the shore, and here are Uncle Sam's men drawn up behind you on the prairie."

"Stra-anger," added the man who told the story, "the way those militia-men sloped into those flat-boats was a caution. Not another word was said. Had Zach Taylor been with Van Rensselaer at Niagara

River, in the last war, I raytber think he'd a taught him how to get militia-men over a ferry."

Taylor, as is well known, did follow Black Hawk through the prairies of northern Illinois—through the wooded gorges, the rocky fells, the plashy rice-pools, the hitherto unbroken wilderness of western Wisconsin. The militia-men gave out from day to day; the country became impassable to horses, and the volunteer settlers who had first seized arms merely to repel an Indian foray, refused to submit their backs to the necessary burdens in carrying their own supplies through the deep swamps and almost impervious forests. At last the very Indians themselves, whom Taylor thus desperately pursued from day to day, and week to week, began to sink from fatigue and exhaustion: they were found by our men stretched beside their trails, while yet the good Anglo-Norman blood of Taylor's band held out amid sufferings in the wilderness which the child of the forest himself could not endure. The battle of the Bad-Axe, and the rout of Black Hawk by Taylor, at length terminated this arduous march.

The steamer bearing Atkinson and his reinforcements, reached the junction of the Bad-Axe and the Mississippi, just as the encounter was over, and we believe brought Taylor along with his prisoners back to Fort Crawford, where, after landing the former, she passed on to St. Louis. When we remember the complimentary reception which Black Hawk met with all along our Atlantic border, how strange it seems that when the name of his captor was mentioned as the hero of Okee-cho-bee, his countrymen asked, "who is this Colonel Taylor that has just been brevetted a Brigadier?" Even as it was afterwards asked concerning the Hero of Rio Bravo, "who is this Brigadier Taylor who has so brilliantly earned the brevet of major-general?" One might now, without extravagance, venture to predict that the captor of Black Hawk is as well known as was that warrior himself; and that he would probably be received by the people in a progress throughout the country, with demonstrations of affection and respect, at least equal to those which were showered upon the wily Sauk chief, the but too successful rival of the chivalrous, and loyal, but neglected Keokuk.

By the death of Colonel Morgan, Lieutenant-Colonel Taylor received the appointment of Colonel of the first regiment of Infantry, then stationed on the Upper Mississippi. He was employed there for several years as Indian Agent, in which capacity he won their confidence, and acquired great influence over them by the wisdom, prudence and tact with which he discharged his trust, and the unvarying kindness and good faith with which all his dealings and intercourse with them was marked. He was known among them as the "Big Chief."

CHAPTER II.

Commencement of the Florida War.—Severe Battle of Okee-cho-bee.—Charge of the Missouri Volunteers.—Brave conduct of the Regular Troops.—Colonel Taylor everywhere in the Fight.—Power of the Indians broken.—Colonel Taylor Brevetted Brigadier General for his brave conduct.—Assigned the Command of the First Department of the Army.—Account of his movements at Fort Bassinger.—An amusing Anecdote.—General Taylor and the Missouri Legislature.—His Agency in the Employment of Bloodhounds in the Florida War.

At the breaking out of the Florida or Seminole war, Colonel Taylor was at Fort Crawford, Prairie du Chien, built by him, where he had been stationed for four years. In 1836 he was ordered to Florida, though he was then on furlough. He cheerfully relinquished it, however, to obey the call of his country. He was placed in command of a separate column, composed of the First, Fourth, and Sixth infantry, some artillery, and the Missouri volunteers. But notwithstanding his efforts to meet the enemy, they successfully evaded him until the 25th of December, 1837, when he discovered his vicinity to Alligator, Sam Jones and Co-o-coo-chee, at the head of seven hundred Indians, all well armed, and most skilful marksmen. They had chosen their position with great judgment, in a dense hammock, perfectly concealed and strongly fortified, and were confident of victory. Their front and one flank were protected by a low swamp, almost impassable, and the other flank rested on lake Okee-cho-bee,

COLONEL TAYLOR AT THE BATTLE OF OKEE-CHO-BEE.

December 25th, 1837.

by which it was securely protected. They had therefore the advantage of position, if not of numbers on their side, Colonel Taylor's forces amounting to about one thousand men. As soon as he ascertained where they were posted, however, he determined to attack them without delay. No considerations of danger, of numbers, or advantage of position had any powei to deter him from attacking an enemy " wherever found, or in whatever numbers." On the contrary, the dangers to be encountered but nerved him the more firmly to meet them.

The only approach to the enemy led through a swamp covered with saw-grass, in the mud of which his troops sunk knee deep. This pass, difficult as it was from this cause, was rendered tenfold more dangerous by being perfectly swept by the fire of the enemy. Colonel Taylor did not hesitate to make the attack. The engagement was brought on by the Mississippi regiment in gallant style. They dashed through a most destructive and deadly fire poured in upon them from every thicket and concealment, and from the tree tops. This murderous fire was accompanied with the most infernal yells from the savage foe. The volunteers began to stagger under the shock, and were finally seized with a panic, and broke and fled in wild disorder. The officers of the Sixth Regiment of regulars promptly and boldly threw themselves in front of their troops, and led them gallantly to the charge. They were nobly seconded by the First Regiment, commanded by Colonel Taylor himself in person, and by the Fourth, who assailed their right flank with terrible effect. The enemy could not long withstand the shock of these veterans. They were quickly thrown into disorder and dr·ven in confusion from their strong position, after a contest of three hours. The conflict was one of the fiercest and most fatal of the whole war, and so dispirited and weakened the enemy that they were never after able to collect a sufficient force to resist openly the American arms. In the engagement the Americans lost one hundred and twenty-eight officers and men in killed and wounded. Amongst the former were the brave and accomplished Lieutenant-Colonel Thompson, Captain Van Swearingen, Colonel Gentry, of the Missouri volunteers, and Lieutenants Brooke and Carter. Lieutenant Walker, who went into the engagement with twenty men, had only three left—seventeen had been killed or wounded!

Colonel Taylor was everywhere to be found in the thickest of the fight, where the balls flew fastest, and the danger the greatest, encouraging and urging on his men. Nothing could resist his onsets. His coolness and presence of mind reanimated those whose power of endurance had begun to fail, and gave new ardor to others. His presence inspired all with confidence, and gave assurance of victory. Never was there a commander who possessed the power of infusing his own indomitable spirit into his troops in a more remarkable degree than Colonel Taylor. Wherever he is found all doubt of victory disappears, and his men fight with a perfect conviction of finally triumphing: such was the case at Okee-cho-bee, and such has been the case in all his engagements since.

The description of the bloody and brilliant battle of Okee-cho-bee, and the incidents preceding and connected with it, have been designedly brief, with a view of introducing Colonel Taylor's own detailed report of the engagement. This is too minute and interesting, and paints too forcibly the terrific scene to be omitted, or to be supplied by any account drawn by those who did not witness and participate in it. The report of Colonel Taylor also contains a statement in detail of all his operations in the field, from the 19th of December to the 4th of January. On the 4th of January, succeeding the battle, Colonel Taylor thus wrote to Brigadier General Jones:

"On the 19th ultimo, I received at this place a communication from Major General Jesup, informing me that all hopes of bringing the war to a close by negotiation, through the interference or mediation of the Cherokee delegation, were at an end, Sam Jones, with the Mickasukies, having determined to fight it out to the last, and directing me to proceed with the least possible delay against any portion of the enemy I might hear of within striking distance, and to destroy or capture him.

"After leaving two officers and an adequate force for the protection of my depot, I marched the next morning, with twelve days' rations (my means of transportation not enabling me to carry more,) with the balance of my command, consisting of Captain Munroe's company of the Fourth artillery, total thirty-five men; the First infantry, under the command of Lieutenant-Colonel Foster, two hundred and seventy-four; the Sixth infantry, under Lieutenant-Colonel Thompson, two hundred and twenty-one; the Missouri volunteers, one hundred and eighty; Morgan's spies, forty-seven; pioneers, thirty; pontoneers, thirteen; and seventy Delaware Indians, making a force, exclusive of officers, of one thousand and thirty-two men; the greater part of the Shawnees having been detached, and the balance refusing to accompany me, under the pretext that a number of them were sick, and the remainder were without moccasons.

"I moved down the west side of the Kissimmee, in a south-easterly course, towards Lake Istopoga, for the following reasons: 1st. Because I knew a portion of the hostiles were to be found in that direction; 2nd. If General Jesup should fall in with the Mickasukies and drive them, they might attempt to elude him by crossing the Kissimmee, from the east to the west side of the peninsula, between this and its entrance into the Okee-cho-bee, in which case I might be near at hand to intercept them; 3rd. To overawe and induce such of the enemy who had been making propositions to give themselves up, and who appeared very slow, if not to hesitate in complying with their promises on that head, to surrender at once; and lastly, I deemed it advisable to erect block-houses and a small picket work on the Kissimmee, for a third depot, some thirty or forty miles below this, and obtain a knowledge of the intervening country, as I had no guide who could be relied on, and by this means open a communication with Colonel Smith, who was operating up the Caloosehatchee, or Sangbel river, under my orders.

"Late in the evening of the first day's march, I met the Indian chief Jumper, with his family and a part of his band, consisting of fifteen men, a part of them with families, and a few negroes, in all sixty-three souls, on his way to give himself up, in conformity to a previous arrangement I had entered into with him. They were conducted by Captain Parks and a few Shawnees. He (Parks) is an active, intelligent half-breed, who is at the head of the friendly Indians, both Shawnees and Delawares, and who I had employed to arrange and bring in Jumper and as many of his people as he could prevail on to come in. We encamped that night near the same spot, and the next morning having ordered Captain Parks to join me and take command of the Delawares, and having dispatched Jumper, in charge of some Shawnees, to this place, and so on to Fort Frazier, I continued my march, after having sent forward three friendly Seminoles to gain intelligence as to the position of the enemy.

"About noon the same day, I sent forward one battalion of Gentry's regiment, under command of Lieutenant-Colonel Price, to pick up any stragglers that might fall in his way, to encamp two or three miles in advance of the main force, to act with great circumspection, and to communicate promptly any occurrence that might take place in his vicinity important for me to know. About 10, P. M., I received a note from the colonel, stating that the three Seminoles sent forward in the morning had returned; that they had been at or near where Alligator had encamped, twelve or fifteen miles in his advance; that he (Alligator) had left there with a part of his family four days before, under the pretext of separating his relations, &c., from the Mickasukies, preparatory to his surrendering with them; that there were several families remaining at the camp referred to, who wished to give themselves up, and would remain there until we took possession of them, unless they were forcibly carried off that night by the Mickasukies, who were encamped at no great distance from them.

"In consequence of this intelligence, after directing Lieutenant-Colonel Davenport to follow me early in the morning with the infantry, a little after midnight I put myself at the head of the residue of the mounted men and joined Lieutenant-Colonel Price, proceeded on, crossing Istopoga outlet, and soon after daylight took possession of the encampment referred to, where I found the inmates, who had not been disturbed. They consisted of an old man, and two young ones, and several women and children, amounting in all to twenty-two individuals. The old man informed me that Alligator was very anxious to separate his people from the Mickasukies, who were encamped on the opposite side of the Kissimmee, distant about twenty miles, where they would fight us. I sent him to Alligator to say to him, if he were sincere in his professions, to meet me the next day at the Kissimmee, where the trail I was marching on crossed, and where I should halt.

"As soon as the infantry came up I moved on to the place designated, which I reached late that evening, and where I encamped. About 11 P. M., the old Indian returned, bringing a very equivocal message from Alligator, who, he stated, he had met accidentally; also, that the Mickasukies were still encamped where they had been for some days, and where they were determined to fight us.

"I determined at once on indulging them as soon as practicable. Accordingly, next morning, after laying out a small stockade work for the protection of a future depot, in order to enable me to move with the greatest celerity, I deposited the whole of my heavy baggage, including artillery, &c., and having provisioned the command to include the 26th, after leaving Captain Munroe with his company, the pioneer, pontoneers, with eighty-five sick and disabled infantry, and a portion of the friendly Indians, who alleged that they were unable to march farther, crossed the Kissimmee, taking the old Indian as a guide who had been captured the day before, and who accompanied us with great apparent reluctance, in pursuit of the enemy, and early the next day reached Alligator's encampment, situated on the edge of Cabbage-tree Hammock, in the midst of a large prairie, from the appearance of which, and other encampments in the vicinity, and the many evidences of slaughtered cattle, there must have been several hundred individuals.

"At another small hammock, at no great distance from Alligator's ençampment, and surrounded by a swamp impassable for mounted men, the spies surprised an encampment containing one old man, four young men, and some women and children. One of the party immediately raised a white flag, when the men were taken possession of, and brought across the swamp to the main body. I proceeded with an interpreter to meet them. They proved to be Seminoles, and professed to be friendly. They stated that they were preparing to come in; they had just slaughtered a number of cattle, and were employed in drying and jerking the same. They also informed me that the Mickasukies, headed by A-vi-a-ka, (Sam Jones,) were some ten or twelve miles distant, encamped in a swamp, and were prepared to fight.

"Although I placed but little confidence in their professions of friendship, or their intentions of coming in yet I had no time to look up their women and children, who had fled and concealed themselves in the swamp, or to have encumbered myself with them in the situation in which I then was. Accordingly, I released the old man, who promised that he would collect all the women and children and take them in to Captain Munroe, at the Kissimmee, the next day. I also dismissed the old man who had acted as guide thus far, supplying his place with the four able warriors who had been captured that morning.

"These arrangements being made, I moved under their guidance for the camp of the Mickasukies. Between two and three, P. M., we reached a very dense cypress swamp, through which we were compelled to pass, and in which our guide informed us we might be attacked. After making the necessary dipositions for battle, it was ascertained that there was no enemy to oppose us. The army crossed over and encamped for the night, it being late. During the passage of the rear, Captain Parks, who was in advance with a few friendly Indians, fell in with two of the enemies' spies, between two and three miles of our camp, one on horseback, the other on foot, and succeeded in capturing the latter. He was an active young warrior, armed with an excellent rifle, fifty balls in his pouch, and an adequate proportion of powder. This Indian confirmed the information which had been previously received from the other Indians, and, in addition, stated that a large body of Seminoles, headed by John Cohua, Co-a-coo-chee, and, no doubt, Alligator, with other chiefs, were encamped five or six miles from us, near the Mickasukies, with a cypress swamp and dense hammock between them and the latter.

"The army moved forward at daylight the next morning, and after marching five or six miles, reached the camp of the Seminoles on the border of another cypress swamp, which must have contained several hundred, and bore evident traces of having been abandoned in a great hurry, as the fires were still burning, and quantities of beef lying on the ground unconsumed.

"Here the troops were again disposed in order of

battle, but we found no enemy to oppose us; and the command was crossed over about 11 A. M., when we entered a large prairie in our front, on which two or three hundred head of cattle were grazing, and a number of Indian ponies. Here another young Indian warrior was captured, armed and equipped as the former. He pointed out a dense hammock on our right, about a mile distant, in which he said the hostiles were situated, and waiting to give us battle.

"At this place the final disposition was made to attack them, which was in two lines, the volunteers under Gentry, and Morgan's spies, to form the first line in extended order, who were instructed to enter the hammock, and in the event of being attacked and hard pressed, were to fall back in rear of the regular troops, out of reach of the enemy's fire. The second was composed of the 4th and 6th infantry, who were instructed to sustain the volunteers, the 1st infantry being held in reserve.

"Moving on in the direction of the hammock, after proceeding about a quarter of a mile, we reached the swamp which separated us from the enemy, three-quarters of a mile in breadth, being totally impassable for horses, and nearly so for foot, covered with a thick growth of saw-grass, five feet high, and about knee-deep in mud and water, which extended to the left as far as the eye could reach, and to the right to a part of the swamp and hammock we had just crossed through, ran a deep creek. At the edge of the swamp the men were dismounted, and the horses and baggage left under a suitable guard. Captain Allen was detached with the two companies of mounted infantry to examine the swamp and hammock to the right, and in case he should not find the enemy in that direction, was to return to the baggage, and in the event of his hearing a heavy firing to join me immediately.

"After making these arrangements, I crossed the swamp in the order stated. On reaching the borders of the hammock, the volunteers and spies received a heavy fire from the enemy, which was returned by them for a short time, when their gallant commander, Colonel Gentry, fell, mortally wounded. They mostly broke; and instead of forming in rear of the regulars, as had been directed, they retired across the swamp to their baggage and horses; nor could they again be brought into action as a body, although efforts were made repeatedly by my staff to induce them to do so.

"The enemy, however, were promptly checked and driven back by the 4th and 6th infantry, which in truth might be said to be a moving battery. The weight of the enemy's fire was principally concentrated on five companies of the 6th infantry, which not only stood firm, but continued to advance until their gallant commander, Lieutenant-Colonel Thompson, and his adjutant, Lieutenant Center, were killed, and every officer, with one exception, as well as most of the non-commissioned officers, including the sergeant-major and four of the orderly sergeants, killed and wounded of those companies, when that portion of the regiment retired to a short distance and were again formed, one of these companies having but four members left untouched.

"Lieutenant-Colonel Foster, with six companies, amounting in all to one hundred and sixty men, gained the hammock in good order, where he was joined by Captain Noel with the two remaining companies of the 6th infantry, and Captain Gentry's volunteers, with a few additional men, continued to drive the enemy for a considerable time, and by a change of front, separated his line and continued to drive him until he reached the great lake, Okee-cho-bee, which was in the rear of the enemy's position, and on which their encampment extended for more than a mile. As soon as I was informed that Captain Allen was advancing, I ordered the 1st infantry to move to the left, gain the enemy's right flank, and turn it, which order was executed in the promptest manner possible, and as soon as that regiment got in position, the enemy gave one fire and retreated, being persuaded by the 1st, 4th, and 6th, and some of the volunteers who had joined them, until near night, and until these troops were nearly exhausted, and the enemy driven in all directions.

"The action was a severe one, and continued from half-past twelve until three, P. M., a part of the time very close and severe. We suffered much, having twenty-six killed, and one hundred and twelve wounded, among whom are some of our most valuable officers. The hostiles probably suffered, all things considered, equally with ourselves, they having left ten dead on the ground, besides doubtless, carrying off more, as is customary with them when practicable.

"As soon as the enemy were completely broken, I turned my attention to taking care of the wounded, to facilitate their removal to my baggage, where I ordered an encampment to be formed. I directed Captain Taylor to cross over to the spot and employ every individual whom he might find there in constructing a small footway across the swamp; this, with great exertions, was completed in a short time after dark, when all the dead and wounded were carried over in litters made for the purpose, with one exception, a private of the 4th infantry, who was killed and could not be found.

"And here I trust I may be permitted to say that I

experienced one of the most trying scenes of my life, and he who could have looked on them with indifference, his nerves must have been differently organized from my own. Besides the killed, there lay one hundred and twelve wounded officers and soldiers, who had accompanied me one hundred and forty-five miles, most of the way through an unexplored wilderness, without guides, who had so gallantly beaten the enemy, under my orders, in his strongest position, and who had to be conveyed back, through swamps and hammocks, from whence we set out, without any apparent means of doing so. This service, however, was encountered and overcome, and they have been conveyed thus far, and proceeded on to Tampa Bay on rude litters, constructed with the axe and knife alone, with poles and dry hides—the latter being found in great abundance at the encampment of the hostiles. The litters were carried on the backs of our weak and tottering horses, aided by the residue of the command, with more ease and comfort to the sufferers than I could have supposed, and with as much as they could have been in ambulances of the most improved and modern construction.

"The day after the battle we remained at our encampment, occupied in taking care of the wounded, and in the sad office of interring the dead; also in preparing litters for the removal of the wounded, and collecting, with a portion of the mounted men, the horses and cattle in the vicinity belonging to the enemy, of which we found about one hundred of the former, many of them saddled, and nearly three hundred of the latter.

"We left our encampment on the morning of the 27th, for the Kissimmee, where I had left my heavy baggage, which place we reached about noon on the 28th.

After leaving two companies and a few Indians to garrison the stockade, which I found nearly completed on my return, by that active and vigilant officer, Captain Munroe, 4th artillery, I left the next morning for this place, where I arrived on the 31st, and sent forward the wounded next day to Tampa Bay, with the 4th and 6th infantry, the former to halt at Fort Frazer, remaining here myself with the 1st, in order to make preparations to take the field again as soon as my horses can be recruited, most of which have been sent to Tampa, and my supplies in a sufficient state of forwardness to justify the measure.

"In speaking of the command, I can only say, that so far as the regular troops are concerned, no one could have been more efficiently sustained than I have been, from the commencement of the campaign; and I am certain that they will always be willing and ready to discharge any duty that may be assigned them.

"To Lieutenant-Colonel Davenport, and the officers and soldiers of the First infantry, I feel under many obligations for the manner in which they have, on all occasions, discharged their duty; and although held in reserve, and not brought into battle until near its close, the eagerness it evinced to engage, and the promptness and good order with which they entered the hammock, when the order was given for them to do so, is the best evidence that they would have sustained their own characters, as well as that of the regiment, had it been their fortune to have been placed in the hottest of the battle.

"The Fourth infantry, under their gallant leader, Lieutenant-Colonel Foster, was among the first to gain the hammock, and maintained this position, as well as driving a portion of the enemy before him, until he arrived on the borders of Lake Okee-cho-bee, which was in the rear, and continued the pursuit until near night. Lieutenant-Colonel Foster, who was favorably noticed for his gallantry and good conduct in nearly all the engagements on the Niagara frontier, during the late war with Great Britain, by his several commanders, as well as in the different engagements with the Indians in this territory, never acted a more conspicuous part than in the action of the 25th ult.; he speaks in the highest terms of the conduct of brevet Major Graham, his second in command, as also the officers and soldiers of the Fourth infantry, who were engaged in the action. Captain Allen, with his two mounted companies of the Fourth infantry, sustained his usual character for promptness and efficiency. Lieutenant Hooper, of the Fourth regiment, was wounded through the arm, but continued on the field, at the head of his company, until the termination of the battle.

"I am not sufficiently master of words to express my admiration of the gallantry and steadiness of the officers and soldiers of the Sixth regiment of infantry. It was their fortune to bear the brunt of the battle. The report of the killed and wounded, which accompanies this, is more conclusive evidence of their merits than anything I can say. After five companies of this regiment, against which the enemy directed the most deadly fire, were nearly cut up, there being only four men left uninjured in one of them; and every officer and orderly sergeant of those companies, with one exception, were either killed or wounded; Captain Noel, with the remaining two companies, his own company, "K.," and Crossman's, "B.," commanded by second Lieutenant Woods, which was the left of the regiment, formed on the right of the Fourth infantry, entered the hammock with that regiment, and continued the fight and the pursuit until its termination. It is due to Captain Andrews and Lieutenant Walker, to say they commanded two of the five companies mentioned above, and they continued to direct them, until they were both severely wounded, and carried from the field; the latter received three separate balls.

"The Missouri volunteers, under the command of Colonel Gentry, and Morgan's spies, who formed the first line, and, of course, were the first engaged, acted as well, or even better, than troops of that description generally do; they received and returned the enemy's fire with spirit, for some time, when they broke and retired, with the exception of Captain Gillam and a few of his company, and Lieutenant Blakey, also with a few men, who joined the regulars, and acted with them, until after the close of the battle, but not until they had suffered severely; the commanding officer of the volunteers, Colonel Gentry, being mortally wounded while leading on his men, and encouraging them to enter the hammock, and come to close quarters with the enemy; his son, an interesting youth, eighteen or nineteen years of age, sergeant-major of the regiment, was severely wounded at the same moment.

"Captain Childs, Lieutenants Rogers and Flanagan, of Gentry's regiment, acting Major Sconce, and Lieutenants Hase and Gordon, of the spies, were wounded, while encouraging their men to a discharge of their duty.

"The volunteers and spies having, as before stated, fallen back to the baggage, could not again be formed and brought up to the hammock in anything like order, but a number of them crossed over individually, and aided in conveying the wounded across the swamp to the hammock, among whom were Captain Curd, and several other officers, whose names I do not now recollect.

"To my personal staff, consisting of first Lieutenant J. M. Hill, of the Second, and first Lieutenant George H. Griffin, of the Sixth infantry, the latter aide-de-camp to Major General Gaines, and a volunteer in Florida from his staff, I feel under the greatest obligations for the promptness and efficiency with which they have sustained me throughout the campaign, and more particularly for their good conduct, and the alacrity with which they aided me, and conveyed my orders during the action of the 25th ult.

"Captain Taylor, commissary of subsistence, who was ordered to join General Jesup at Tampa Bay, as chief of the subsistence department, and who was ordered by him to remain with his column until he (General Jesup) joined it, although no command was assigned Captain Taylor, he greatly exerted himself in trying to rally and bring back the volunteers into action, as well as discharging other important duties which were assigned to him during the action.

"Myself, as well as all who witnessed the attention and ability displayed by Surgeon Satterlee, medical director on this side the peninsula, assisted by Assistant-surgeons McLaren and Simpson, of the medical staff of the army, and Doctors Hannah and Cooke, of the Missouri volunteers, in ministering to the wounded, as well as their uniform kindness to them on all occasions, can never cease to be referred to by me but with the most pleasing and grateful recollections.

"The quartermaster's department, under the direction of that efficient officer, Major Brant, and his assistant, Lieutenant Babbitt, have done everything that could be accomplished to throw forward from Tampa Bay, and keep up supplies of provisions, forage, etc., with the limited means at their disposal. Assistant-commissaries Lieutenants Harrison, stationed at Fort Gardner, and McClure, at Fort Fraser, have fully met my expectations in discharge of the various duties connected with their department, as well as those assigned them in the quartermaster's department.

"This column, in six weeks, penetrated one hundred and fifty miles into the enemy's country, opened roads, and constructed bridges and causeways, when necessary, on the greater portion of the route, established two depots, and the necessary defences for the same, and finally overtook and beat the enemy in his strongest position. The results of which movement and battle have been the capture of thirty of the hostiles, the coming in and surrendering of more than one hundred and fifty Indians and negroes, mostly the former, including the chiefs Ou-la-too-gee, Tus-ta-nuggee, and other principal men, the capturing and driving out of the country six hundred head of cattle, upwards of one hundred head of horses, besides obtaining a thorough knowledge of the country through which we operated, a greater portion of which was entirely unknown, except to the enemy.

"Colonel Gentry died in a few hours after the battle, much regretted by the army, and will be, doubtless, by all who knew him, as his state did not contain a braver man or a better citizen.

"It is due to his rank and talents, as well as to his long and important services, that I particularly mention Lieutenant Colonel A. R. Thompson, of the Sixth infantry, who fell, in the discharge of his duty, at the head of his regiment. He was in feeble health, brought on by exposure to this climate during the past summer, refusing to leave the country while his regiment continued in it. Although he received two balls from the fire of the enemy, early in the action, which wounded him severely, yet he appeared to disregard them, and continued to give his orders with the same coolness that he would have done had his regiment been under review, or on any parade duty. Advancing, he received a third ball, which at once deprived him of life. His last words were, "keep steady, men, charge the hammock—remember the regiment to which you belong." I had known Colonel Thompson personally only for a short time, and the more I knew of him the more I wished to know; and had his life been spared, our acquaintance, no doubt, would have ripened into the closest friendship. Under such circumstances, there are few, if any, other than his bereaved wife, mother, and sisters, who more deeply and sincerely lament his loss, or who will longer cherish his memory than myself.

"Captain Van Swearingen, Lieutenant Brooke, and Lieutenant and Adjutant Center, of the same regiment, who fell on that day, had no superiors of their years in service, and, in point of chivalry, ranked among the first in the army or nation; besides their pure and disinterested courage, they possessed other qualifications, which qualified them to fill the highest grades of their profession, which, no doubt, they would have attained and adorned, had their lives been spared. The two former served with me on another arduous and trying campaign, and on every occasion, whether in the camp, on the march, or on the field of battle, discharged their various duties to my entire satisfaction."

The gallantry and good conduct of Colonel Taylor,

in this hard fought and important battle, received the highest commendation of Mr. Poinsett, the Secretary of War, General Macomb, the commander-in-chief of the army, and the country at large. General Macomb issued a general order to the army, upon the occasion of his victory, in which he especially referred to his bravery in the following terms: "To Colonel Taylor and the officers, non-commissioned officers and troops of the regular army, the Secretary of War tenders the thanks of the President of the United States for the discipline and bravery displayed by them on the occasion; as, likewise, to the officers and volunteers of Missouri, who shared in the conflict, and who evinced so much zeal and gallantry in bringing on the action." He also received the brevet rank of Brigadier General, and was given the chief command of the operations in Florida, in consideration of his valuable services, which he retained until the year 1840, having continued four years in that harassing and dangerous service.

Immediately succeeding this victory General Taylor took up his position at Fort Bassinger, in Florida. Here he remained for several months, harassing the enemy, by cutting off their small parties, capturing several of their principal chiefs, and taking their cattle and means of subsistence. On the 8th of February, 1838, an officer of high standing in General Taylor's army, stationed at Fort Bassinger, gave the following account of their operations:

"We (Colonel Taylor's army), have just returned from the everglades. These everglades are, at the northwest, termed wet prairies. They are large wet prairies, or grassy lakes, and of which the Indians know but little, and where they cannot live a month without great suffering.

"We saw but few Indians, and they fled rapidly at our approach. We took about sixty horses, and ascertained that their cattle were exhausted. Colonel Taylor has taken about six hundred head. We found on our last excursion but few cattle tracks, and only two cows were taken. The Indians are suffering for food; in all their camps we find they had subsisted on palmetto roots and the cabbage tree, which are never eaten by them except when hard run.

"One hundred and thirty Indians and Negroes have come in since the battle of Okee-cho-bee, and they say many more will come in soon, and that they are tired of the war, and destitute of provisions.

"Florida is generally a poor, sandy country. The southern portion is nearly all prairie, wet and dry alternately. Not more than one tenth, at the utmost, of Florida is fit for cultivation, and I would not give one good township of land in Illinois or Michigan for every foot of land in East Florida.

"The Indian prisoners now admit that they lost twenty in the fight with Colonel Taylor. They had a strong position, and fought well, but were terribly whipped, and have never returned near the ground since."

An anecdote is told of the general while stationed at this fort that is as amusing as it is characteristic. He had a favorite horse which he called "Claybank," a very fine animal, and much attached to his master. But he did not much fancy the musty corn often furnished the troops. The general used to partake of the same fare as his soldiers, and so did Claybank, so far as the corn was concerned, and they were both equally dainty. The general was very fond of hominy, and musty corn made anything but a pleasant diet. He would subject himself to the suspicion of "picking," to the prejudice of the soldiers, rather than eat it, when not compelled to. Finding that Claybank understood that business better than he did, he would quietly let him loose amongst the sacks of corn. After smelling very carefully, the sagacious animal would commence gnawing a hole in one that pleased him. The general would patiently watch the manœuvre until he saw that Claybank had made a choice, then calling his servants, he would direct him to have Claybank stabled immediately, for fear he might do mischief; "but," he would say, "as the animal has eaten a hole in the bag, take out a quart or so of the corn and make a dish of hominy. The trick was played for some time, but at last it became known, that whenever Claybank gnawed into a sack, sweet corn was to be found there, and the incident became a standing joke during the war, and it was enjoyed by none more heartily than by the subject of it himself.

After his resignation of this command, he was assigned to that of the First Department of the army, including the States of Louisiana, Mississippi, Alabama, Arkansas, &c., with his head-quarters at Fort Jessup, in the former State. There he remained in the quiet but vigilant attention to the duties devolving upon him, until his services should be required on a wider and more extended field.

Before accompanying General Taylor to the new theatre, upon which he is to act so glorious a part, and where his brilliant deeds are to stand out so prominently before the world, it may not be inappropriate to refer to one or two circumstances in the history of his operations in Florida, that have been the subjects of some discussion before the public, and have produced a contrariety of opinions in the public mind.

It will have been observed, that in his official account of the battle of Okee-cho-bee, General Taylor took occasion, as truth and the interests of the service required him to do, to refer to the conduct of the Missouri volunteers and spies in that engagement. He could do no less than to report to the War Department the simple fact that these troops fell into disorder and finally fled, after having gallantly attacked the enemy. This he did in as mild terms as he could well employ. But nevertheless, his report gave great offence to the people of Missouri, and General Taylor was unsparingly denounced for his injustice to the volunteers and spies of that State. Amongst other means of expressing their dissatisfaction, Mr. Atchinson, then a member of the State Legislature, and subsequently a member of the United States Senate, made a stringent report on the subject, and also introduced a string of resolutions of a very indignant character, which were appended to it. No definite action was ever had on either, however, and public opinion finally settled down into the belief that facts fully sustained General Taylor, and that if the Missouri volunteers did not evince the same unyielding courage as veteran soldiers, there was much in the circumstances of the case to palliate their conduct, especially as their first charge was made with so much courage and effect.

There is another circumstance in the history of the Florida war, with which General Taylor's name has been associated, that requires a brief reference, and that is the employment of bloodhounds to lead to the hiding places of the Indians. No event of the whole war was so severely criticized and condemned as this act of the administration. It was natural in times of high political excitement, when only the simple fact was known to the country, without any of the reasons that led to a measure that seemed so repulsive to humanity, or the particular object for which they were employed, that it should have been so. The measure is one that even now, after the passions of men have become calmed, cannot be approved, though there is much to palliate it, and much more to free General Taylor from any charge of inhumanity in advising the employment of these savage agents.

The war had been waged for several years against an invisible enemy, at an expense of many millions of money, and a vast sacrifice of life. Our soldiers were attacked and our best troops shot down at noonday, by a foe that defied all search. After discharging a deadly volley at our soldiers, they would betake themselves to impenetrable thickets, and there lay securely concealed until another opportunity presented of pouncing down upon small parties of troops, and again flee to their hiding places. It was to find these hidden enemies that General Taylor recommended to the department the employment of bloodhounds. He says, in a letter to the Adjutant General of the army, dated July 28, 1838: "I wish it distinctly understood, that my object in employing dogs, is to ascertain where the Indians can be found, not to injure them." If anything were wanted to exempt General Taylor from an implication of cruelty for his agency in the affair, this explicit avowal of his motives will be sufficient. But he has on too many occasions, both before and since, given such evidence of his humane inclinations, that however mistaken any one may be disposed to consider him, no one will do himself and a brave man the injustice to deny him that noble virtue in an eminent degree.

CHAPTER III.

Admission of Texas into the Union.—Indirect Cause of the Mexican War.—War Recognized by the American Congress.—Prominent part General Taylor has acted since its Commencement.—Orders of the War Department to him.—Texas accepts the conditions of Annexation offered by the United States.—Ultimate Views of Government.—General Taylor arrives at Corpus Christi.—Extracts of the Official Correspondence between him and the Secretary of War.—Intentions of the American Government.

On the first day of March, 1845, Texas was admitted into the Union, by a joint resolution of the Congress of the United States. Though this act was not the immediate cause of the rupture between the United States and Mexico, it led to the adoption of measures which brought the armies of the two governments into collision, and terminated in a declaration of the *existence* of war by the American government. But whether the war was declared formally or not, according to the laws of nations, having virtually been commenced, it was recognized and adopted, and the American people, with a unanimity not shown even in the last war with Great Britain, and notwithstanding there was a difference of opinion as to the necessity and justice of it, everywhere evinced their willingness to assist the government to prosecute it with vigor, or end it with honor.

Amongst those whose names are more intimately connected with the prosecution of this war than that of any other of the brave men who have added such lustre to the American arms during its continuance, by their gallant deeds, is that of General ZACHARY TAYLOR.

Soon after the annexation of Texas, General Taylor, who was then stationed at Fort Jessup, in Louisiana, received the following communication, from Mr. Marcy Secretary of War, marked "confidential," and dated "War Department, May 28, 1845:"

"SIR:—I am directed by the President to cause the forces now under your command, and those which may be assigned to it, to be put into a position where they may most promptly and efficiently act in defence of Texas, in the event it shall become necessary or proper to employ them for that purpose. The information received by the Executive of the United States warrants the belief that Texas will shortly accede to the terms of annexation. As soon as the Texas Congress shall have given its consent to annexation, and a convention shall assemble and accept the terms offered in the resolutions of Congress, Texas will then be regarded by the executive government here, so far a part of the United States as to be entitled from this government to defence and protection from foreign invasion and Indian incursions. The troops under your command will be placed and kept in readiness to perform this duty.

"In the letter addressed to you from the Adjutant General's office, of the 21st of March, you were instructed to hold a portion of the troops under your immediate command in readiness to move into Texas under certain contingencies, and upon further orders from this department. In the treaty between the United States and Mexico, the two governments mutually stipulated to use all the means in their power to maintain peace and harmony among the Indian nations inhabiting the lands on their borders, and to restrain by force any hostilities and incursions by these nations within their respective boundaries, so that the one would not suffer the Indians within its limits to attack, in any manner whatever, the citizens of the other, or the Indians residing upon the territories of the other. The obligations which in this respect are due to Mexico by this treaty, are due also to Texas. Should the Indians residing within the limits of the United States, either by themselves, or associated with others, attempt any hostile movements in regard to Texas, it will be your duty to employ the troops under your command to repel and chastise them, and for this purpose you will give the necessary instructions to the military posts on the upper Red river, (although not under your immediate command,) and, with the approbation of the Texan authorities, make such movements, and take such position, within the limits of Texas, as in your judgment may be necessary. You are also directed to open immediate correspondence with the authorities of Texas, and with any diplomatic agent of the United States, (if one should be residing therein,) with a view to information and advice in respect to the common Indian enemy, as well as to any foreign power. This communication and consultation with the Texan authorities, &c., are directed with a view to enable you to avail yourself of the superior local knowledge they may possess, but not for the purpose of placing you, or any portion of the forces of the United States, under the orders of any functionary not in the regular line of command above you.

"Should the territories of Texas be invaded by a foreign power, and you shall receive certain intelligence through her functionaries of that fact, after her con vention shall have acceded to the terms of annexation contained in the resolutions of the Congress of the United States, you will at once employ, in the most effectual manner your judgment may dictate, the forces under your command, for the defence of these territories and to expel the invaders.

"It is supposed here that, for the mere purpose of repelling a common Indian enemy, as above provided for, it may not be necessary that you should march across the Sabine or upper Red river (at least in the first instance) with more than the particular troops which you were desired in the instructions before referred to, of the 21st March, to hold in immediate readiness for the field, but it is not intended to restrict you positively to that particular amount of force. On the contrary, according to the emergency, you may add any other corps, or any number of companies within your department deemed necessary, beginning with those nearest at hand; and in the contingency of a *foreign* invasion of Texas, as above specified, other regiments from a distance may be ordered to report to you."

This order was succeeded by another, also confidential, from the Hon. George Bancroft, Acting Secretary of War, and dated June 15th, 1845. After advising General Taylor, that on the 4th of July, or very soon thereafter, the convention of the people of Texas would probably accept the proposition of annexation, and that such acceptance would constitute Texas an integral portion of the Union, he ordered him forthwith to make a forward movement with the troops under his command, and advance to the mouth of the Sabine, or such other port on the Gulf of Mexico, or its navigable waters, as in his opinion might be most convenient for an embarkation at the proper time, for the western portion of Texas. The point of his ultimate destination, he was informed in this order, was the western frontier of Texas, and he was instructed to select and occupy, on or near the Rio Grande, such a site as would consist with the health of the troops, and be the best point to repel invasion, and to protect what, in case of annexation, would be our western border. He was further instructed to limit himself to the defence of the territory of Texas, unless Mexico should declare war against the United States, and not to effect a landing on the frontier, until he had ascertained the acceptance of the proffered terms of annexation by Texas, from our minister to that government.

Not long after, the anticipated information of the acceptance of the conditions offered to Texas by the United States was received by General Taylor, and on the following day he left New Orleans, with a portion of his troops, and on the 25th of July arrived at St. Joseph's Island. In the early part of August, he took up his position at Corpus Christi, on the west side of the Neuces, and near its mouth, where he remained until the 11th day of March, 1846. Whilst in this position, he sent forward to the Rio Grande a party of observation, with the view of selecting some favorable position as a depot of military stores, and a proper position for the encampment of the army. Some time in February, 1846, this party returned, and reported in favor of Point Isabel, a few miles from the mouth of the Rio Grande, as a depot of provisions and military stores, and in favor of the position where Fort Brown was subsequently built, as a suitable position to be occupied by the army.

It may be necessary here to give such portions of the correspondence between the War Department and

General Taylor, while the latter was at Corpus Christi, as will explain the immediate and ultimate views and intentions of the government towards Mexico, the position of Taylor, and the agency he had, if any, in hastening the war. For this purpose, the part of that correspondence that throws the most light upon these subjects, is annexed. It will be observed from it, and the order of the Secretary of War already given, that General Taylor acted under positive and specific instructions in all his movements, when such instructions could, in the nature of the case, be given. In these orders, and the dispatches of Taylor, will be found all the information required, to lead to a correct under standing of the immediate steps on the part of the two governments which led to the collision between their respective armies, that ended in the existing war. On the 23rd of August, 1845, Mr. Secretary Marcy addressed to General Taylor the following order:

"The information hitherto received as to the intentions of Mexico, and the measures she may adopt, does not enable the administration here to give you more explicit instructions in regard to your movements, than those which have been already forwarded to you. There is reason to believe that Mexico is making efforts to assemble a large army on the frontier of Texas, for the purpose of entering its territory and holding forcible possession of it. Of their movements you are doubtless advised, and we trust have taken, or early will take, prompt and efficient steps to meet and repel any such hostile incursion. Should Mexico assemble a large body of troops on the Rio Grande, and cross it with a considerable force, such a movement must be regarded as an invasion of the United States, and the commencement of hostilities. You will, of course, use all the authority which has been or may be given you, to meet such a state of things. Texas must be protected from hostile invasion, and for that purpose you will of course employ, to the utmost extent, all the means you possess or can command.

"An order has been this day issued for sending one thousand more men into Texas, to join those under your command. When the existing orders are carried into effect, you will have with you a force of four thousand men of the regular army. We are not enabled to judge what auxiliary force can, upon an emergency, be brought together from Texas; and as a precautionary measure, you are authorized to accept volunteers from the States of Louisiana and Alabama, and even from Mississippi, Tennessee and Kentucky. Should Mexico declare war, or commence hostilities by crossing the Rio Grande with a considerable force, you are instructed to lose no time in giving information to the authorities of each or any of the above-mentioned states, as to the number of volunteers you may want from them respectively. Should you require troops from any of these states, it would be important to have them with the least possible delay. It is not doubted that at least two regiments from New Orleans, and one from Mobile, could be obtained and expeditiously brought into the field. You will cause it to be known in these places, what number and description of troops you desire to receive from them in the contemplated emergency. The authorities of these states will be apprised that you are authorized to receive volunteers from them, and you may calculate that they will promptly join you when it is made known that their services are required. Arms, ammunition, and camp equipage for the auxiliary troops that you may require, will be sent forward, subject to your orders. You will so dispose of them as to be most available in case they should be needed, and at the same time with a due regard to their safety and preservation. Orders have been issued to the naval force on the Gulf of Mexico to co-operate with you. You will, as far as practicable, hold communication with the commanders of our national vessels in your vicinity, and avail yourself of any assistance that can be derived from their co-operation. The Lexington is ordered into service as a transport ship, and will sail in a few days from New York, with a detachment of United States troops for Corpus Christi. She will be employed as the exigency of the public service may require. In order to keep up a proper communication between the army in Texas and the United States, the On-ka-hy-e, the Harney, and the Dolphin will be put into service as soon as they can be made ready, as dispatch vessels, to convey intelligence, supplies, &c. You will avail yourself of these vessels, and all other proper means, to keep the government here advised of your operations, and the state of things in Texas and Mexico."

Two days after, on the 25th of August, the Secretary of War addressed a circular letter to the Governors of Alabama, Mississippi, and Louisiana, and on the 28th, a similar letter to the Governors of Kentucky and Tennessee, advising them that General Taylor had been appointed to the command of the army of occupation in Texas, and that he was authorized to draw any auxiliary force he might need from that state. He advises them that General Taylor has been authorized to call on them for any additional volunteers he might consider necessary to repel the invasion of Texas by Mexico, should it be attempted. He also observes, "that the emergency rendering such assistance from the militia of your state necessary, does not appear to have been foreseen by Congress, and consequently, no appropriation was made for paying them; but it is not to be doubted that such a provision will be promptly made when Congress shall again assemble. In order to be paid, the state troops must be mustered into service. In organizing companies and regiments for that purpose, the number of officers must be proportioned to that of the privates. Inclosed I send you from the Adjutant-General, a statement of the number and rank of officers for each company of men, as well as the regimental and staff officers, should a regiment of volunteers be called for. From the known patriotism and military ardor of the militia of your state, it is presumed that volunteers, to the number that may be required, will readily tender their services to their country in the contemplated emergency. Should aid from your state be required by the commanding general in Texas, it will be of the utmost importance that the troops should be sent into that state without delay. This consideration will render it proper that they should come from such parts of the state as can most promptly furnish them."

On the 30th of August Mr. Marcy wrote to General Taylor, to urge upon him the importance of availing himself of every opportunity of communicating with the War Department, as it was desirable to have early and correct information from him, so as to enable the government to form a true judgment of the designs and movements of Mexico, founded upon ascertained facts. He then continues: "It is presumed that, in pursuance of previous instructions from this department, you have taken special pains to become acquainted with the proceedings of Mexico, particularly in regard to the number and kind of Mexican troops at Matamoras, Monterey, and other places, as well as those which are on the march towards them, and may be brought to act against your forces, or pushed across the Rio Grande, either in the vicinity of Matamoras or at distant points on that river. You will not, I trust, underrate the importance of such information, or fail to use the proper and necessary means for acquiring it. You are directed, should you deem it expedient, to employ competent and trustworthy persons to obtain such intelligence.

"The instructions heretofore issued, enjoin upon you to defend Texas from invasion and Indian hostilities; and should Mexico invade it, you will employ all your forces to repulse the invaders, and drive all Mexican troops beyond the Rio Grande. Should you judge the forces under your command inadequate, you will not fail to draw sufficient auxiliary aid from Texas, and, if there be need, from the states, pursuant to your previous instructions. It is not to be doubted, that on your notification, volunteer troops, to the number you may require, will rally with alacrity to your standard. You have been advised that the assembling a large Mexican army on the borders of Texas, and crossing the Rio Grande with a considerable force, will be regarded by the Executive here as an invasion of the United States, and the commencement of hostilities. An attempt to cross that river with such a force, will also be considered in the same light. There may be other acts on the part of Mexico which would put an end to the relations of peace between that republic and the United States. Should depredations be committed on our commerce by her public armed vessels, or privateers acting under authority, this will constitute a state of war.

"Orders have been issued to the vessels of the United States in the Gulf, to furnish you with information of any hostile proceedings of Mexico, and the state of things in that republic. You will embrace every occasion that may present, to forward to the commanders of these vessels such intelligence as you may possess concerning the movements of the military forces and the state of things in Mexico and Texas, and to suggest to them such assistance and co-operation as you may desire to receive.

"In case of war, either declared or made manifest by hostile acts, your main object will be the protection of Texas; but the pursuit of this object will not necessarily confine your action within the territory of Texas. Mexico having thus commenced hostilities, you may, in your discretion, should you have sufficient force, and be in a condition to do so, cross the Rio Grande, disperse or capture the forces assembling to invade Texas, defeat the junction of troops uniting for that purpose, drive them from their positions on either side of that river, and, if deemed practicable and expedient, take and hold possession of Matamoras and other places in the country. I scarcely need to say that enterprises of this kind are only to be ventured on under circumstances presenting a fair prospect of success."

Again, on the 16th of October, 1845, the Secretary of War informed General Taylor that no apprehension was felt at Washington, that any serious attempts would be made by Mexico to invade Texas, although she still continued to threaten it, and that in carrying out the instructions of government he would be left very much to his own judgment, as his superior knowledge of localities, and his advantages for obtaining earlier notice of the views of Mexico, and the movements of her troops, would enable him to judge much more correctly what action on his part might be necessary. He was advised that he would, in a great measure, be left to act, during the coming winter, as circumstances might seem in his judgment to require, and instructed to approach as near the western boundary of Texas, ("the Rio Grande,") as a due regard for his safety and the comfort of his army would permit.

Having given such suggestions as he considered advisable as to the movements of the army, the secretary proceeds: "Ought your present position to be changed? the forces which are, or soon will be, assembled under your command, be kept together or divided? and, if divided, what positions are to be taken, and how are they to be divided? These are questions which must be in a measure left to your judgment, or, at least, the decision upon them here, if there be time, will be influenced in no inconsiderable degree by the information and views which you may furnish the department. You need not, therefore, wait for directions from Washington, to carry out what you may deem proper to be done. Upon all the points above enumerated, and others not suggested, your reports and views in full are desired, not only with reference to the continuance of the present aspect of affairs between the United States and Mexico, but in the contingency of your selecting, or being directed to take, a position on the banks of the Rio Grande near its mouth, or places above, or even in the event of open hostilities. It is expected that the officers of the Engineer and Topographical Corps, who have been sent into Texas, will examine as far as practicable, under your direction, the country, with a view to selecting eligible positions for permanent or temporary occupation, for depots of supplies, arms, and munitions of war. It is extremely desirable that the sea-coast, or at least that part of it which will be likely to be visited by our vessels in aid of any contemplated military operations, should be better known here than it now is; as well as the character of the several rivers which may present obstacles to the movements of our forces, or furnish facilities for transporting supplies. You are requested to avail yourself of all proper occasions, and employ the means you possess to collect information in regard to matters, and forward it to this department."

The next communication from the Secretary of War to General Taylor is an explicit and peremptory order to march to the Rio Grande, and take such a position there as he might deem advisable, the season, the route by which his encampment could be approached, and the security of the army being considered. Mr. Marcy writes: "I am directed by the President to instruct you to advance and occupy, with the troops under your command, positions on or near the east bank of the Rio del Norte, as soon as it can be conveniently done with reference to the season and the routes by which your movements must be made. From the views heretofore presented to this department, it is presumed Point Isabel will be considered by you an eligible position. This point, or some one near it, and points opposite Matamoras and Mier, and in the Vicinity of Laredo, are suggested for your consideration; but you are left to your better knowledge to determine the post or posts which you are to occupy, as well as the question of dividing your forces with a view to occupying two or more positions.

"In the positions you may take in carrying out these instructions, and other movements that may be made, the use of the Rio del Norte may be very convenient, if not necessary. Should you attempt to exercise the right which the United States have, in common with Mexico, to the free navigation of this river, it is probable that Mexico would interpose resistance. You will not attempt to enforce this right without further instructions.

"You are requested to report to this department, without delay, what means you may require, if any, beyond those you now possess, to enforce and maintain our common right to navigate this river, as well as your views of the importance of this right in the defence and protection of the state of Texas.

"It is not designed, in our present relations with Mexico, that you should treat her as an enemy; but, should she assume that character by a declaration of war, or an open act of hostility towards us, you will not act merely on the defensive, if your relative means enable you to do otherwise.

"Since instructions were given you to draw aid from Texas, in case you should deem it necessary, the relations between that state and the United States have undergone some modification. Texas is now fully incorporated into our union of states, and you are hereby authorized by the President to make a requisition upon the executive of that state for such of its militia force as may be needed to repel invasion, or to secure the country against apprehended invasion."

These extracts from the instructions and orders of the Secretary of War to General Taylor, in regard to his movements in Texas, and his operations there, will render sufficiently intelligible the objects and wishes of the American government in regard to Mexico, and what was expected of the commanding General. The dispatches of General Taylor to his government during the same period, are necessary, however, to place before the reader the whole question in all its bearings, to show the condition and number of the army, with which the first great achievements of this war were accomplished, and to help to illustrate the character of the extraordinary man whose name has been so closely identified with almost every incident of it. Besides the official dispatches of Taylor that are annexed, there will be found a communication to him from the Prefect of Tamaulipas, and also one from General Ampudia, Commander-in-chief of the Mexican army on the Texan frontier, as well as General Taylor's reply to it:

"NEW ORLEANS, La., July 20, 1845.

SIR:—I respectfully acknowledge your communication of July 8th, covering the instructions of the Secretary of War of the same date, relative to the Mexican settlements on this side of the Rio Grande. Those instructions will be closely obeyed; and the department may rest assured that I will take no step to interrupt the friendly relations between the United States and Mexico. I am gratified at receiving these instructions, as they confirm my views, previously communicated, in regard to the proper line to be occupied at present by our troops.

I am, sir, very respectfully,
Your obedient servant,
Z. TAYLOR,
Brevet Brig. Gen. U. S. A., commanding.

The ADJUTANT GENERAL of the Army,
Washington, D. C.

"HEADQUARTERS, ARMY OF OCCUPATION,
Steamship Alabama, Aransas Pass,
Texas, July 28, 1845.

SIR:—I respectfully report my arrival at this place on the 25th instant, with eight companies of the Third infantry, it having been found necessary to leave two companies of that regiment to be brought over in other transports.

The troops are temporarily established on St. Joseph's Island. I am waiting the report of a boat expedition sent to Corpus Christi Bay, before I determine on the site of an encampment. I hope to receive the necessary information in the course of the day, when I shall immediately commence the removal of the Third infantry to the point selected. The position will probably be "Live Oak Point," in Aransas Bay, some ten miles from our present position. I am very anxious to establish myself at the mouth of the Nueces, but the extreme shoalness of the water will, I fear, present an insuperable obstacle, unless we can procure lighters of much lighter draught than those we have at present.

The difficulties of effecting a debarkation on this coast, and of establishing depots for supplying the army, are much greater than I anticipated, and will render our operations at once embarrassing and expensive. Between Pass Cavello and Brazos Santiago there is no entrance for vessels drawing more than seven or eight feet; and the prevailing winds render the operation of lightening extremely uncertain and hazardous. We nave been favored with fine weather, and, should it continue, the other transports, which may now be expected, will be enabled to discharge without difficulty.

We had a very favorable run from New Orleans and I am happy to state that the health of the command was greatly improved by the voyage. The eight companies have scarcely any sickness at this time.

The day before leaving New Orleans, I received from Major Donelson, a communication dated at Austin, on the 7th of July, informing me that the convention had unanimously accepted the proposition of annexation, and suggested that two companies should be posted at Austin. I still deem it best to concentrate my force until our relations with Mexico shall become settled, and until the country can be examined, and the best mode of supply ascertained.

I hear nothing important from the Mexican frontier. Some Indian depredations are committed from time to time near Corpus Christi, and will claim my first attention after I can get established.

I am, sir, very respectfully,
Your obedient servant,
Z. TAYLOR.
Brevet Brig. Gen. U. S. A., commanding.

The Adjutant General of the Army,
Washington, D. C.

"Headquarters, Army of Occupation,
Corpus Christi, Texas, Aug. 15, 1845.

Sir:—I have the honor to report that, by New Orleans papers of the 7th inst, I have received intelligence of the preparatory steps taken by Mexico towards a declaration of war against the United States. I shall spare no exertions to meet suitably this probable change in the relations between the two countries; and the additional force ordered to join me, as announced in your communication of July 30th, will, I trust, enable me to do something more than maintain a merely defensive attitude on the Nueces. This will depend upon the demonstrations made by Mexico along the Rio Grande, in regard to which the Secretary of War has solicited a report. I am enabled to say, upon information which is regarded as authentic, that General Arista was to leave Monterey on the 4th of this month for Matamoras, with one thousand five hundred men—five hundred being cavalry. I learn, from the same source, that there are five hundred regular troops at Matamoras. In regard to the force at other points on the Rio Grande, except the militia of the country, I have no information; nor do I hear that the reported concentration at Matamoras is for any purpose of invasion. I have but just arrived at this place, and hope in a few days to be able to obtain more full and precise intelligence concerning the movements of the Mexicans. I shall not fail to communicate promptly to the department all such intelligence upon which I think reliance can be placed.

I am, sir, very respectfully,
Your obedient servant,
Z. TAYLOR,
Brevet Brig. Gen. U. S. A., commanding.

The ADJUTANT GENERAL of the Army,
Washington, D. C.

"HEADQUARTERS, ARMY OF OCCUPATION,
Corpus Christi, Texas, Aug 30, 1845.

SIR:—I respectfully report the arrival at this post of seven companies of the 7th infantry, under Major Brown, and two companies of volunteer artillery under Major Gally. Major Seawell's company, I am informed, was ordered back to Baton Rouge by General Gaines, and some small detachments of that regiment were also left at several posts. I have retained one company as a guard for the depot at St. Joseph's Island.

The battalion of volunteer artillery has a fine battery of eight pieces—two twelves and six sixes, completely equipped in every respect. The officers are zealous, and the men seem to be quite well instructed in their duties. In case of need, I look for some valuable services from this battalion.

I have just received a communication from President Jones, under date of the 23rd inst., notifying me that he had taken preparatory steps towards organizing a volunteer force of one thousand men to assist me if necessary. This matter will form the subject of a special communication to your office in a few days.

Apprehending that the erroneous impressions current in New Orleans in regard to our situation, might induce General Gaines to order the muster of a battalion or brigade of infantry, I addressed a communication to his staff officer by the steamship Alabama, expressing my thanks for the reinforcement of the volunteer battalion of artillery, but with the hope that no more volunteers would be sent without a requisition from me. That communication will reach New Orleans to-night or to-morrow, in time, I trust, to stop the employment of any more volunteers.

We have no news from the Rio Grande. Idle stories are brought in from that quarter, but with the means of accurate information which we now possess, I do not deem it necessary to repeat them.

I am, sir, very respectfully,

Your obedient servant,

Z. TAYLOR,

Brevet Brig. Gen. U. S. A., commanding.

The ADJUTANT GENERAL of the Army,

Washington, D. C.

HEADQUARTERS, ARMY OF OCCUPATION,
Corpus Christi, Texas, Oct. 4 1845.

SIR:—I beg leave to suggest some considerations in relation to the present position of our force, and the dispositions which may become necessary for the more effectual prosecution of the objects for which it has been concentrated. It will be recollected that the instructions of June 15th, issued by Mr. Bancroft, then Acting Secretary of War, directed me to "select and occupy, on or near the Rio Grande, such a site as will consist with the health of the troops, and will be best adapted to repel invasion," &c. Brazos Santiago is the nearest entrance to the mouth of the Rio Grande; and Point Isabel, within that entrance, and twenty-one miles from Matamoras, would have fulfilled more completely than any other position the conditions imposed by the Secretary. But we had no artillery, no engineer force or appliances, and but a moderate amount of infantry; and the occupation of Point Isabel, under these circumstances, and with at least the possibility of resistance from the Mexicans, might have compromised the safety of the command. I therefore determined to take up the next accessible position in the rear, which is the mouth of the Nueces river. All the information which I could obtain before leaving New Orleans, seemed to point to Corpus Christi as the most suitable point for concentration; and, although before the President's instructions of July 30th reached me, I would have preferred a position on the left bank of the river, yet a careful examination of the country had already convinced me that none could be found combining so many advantages as this. Every day's experience has confirmed these impressions. Corpus Christi is healthy, easily supplied, and well situated to hold in observation the course of the Rio Grande from Matamoras to Laredo—being about one hundred and fifty miles from several points on the river. I have reason to believe, moreover, that a salutary moral effect has been exercised upon the Mexicans. Their traders are continually carrying home the news of our position and increasing numbers, and are confessedly struck by the spectacle of a large camp of well-appointed and disciplined troops, accompanied by perfect security to their persons and property, instead of the impressment and pillage to which they are subject in their own country. For these reasons, our position thus far has, I think, been the best possible; but, now that the entire force will soon be concentrated, it may well be a question whether the views of government will be best carried out by our remaining at this point. It is with great deference that I make any suggestions on topics which may become matter of delicate negotiation; but if our government, in settling the question of boundary, makes the line of the Rio Grande an ultimatum, I cannot doubt that the settlement will be greatly facilitated and hastened by our taking possession at once of one or two suitable points on or quite near that river. Our strength and state of preparation should be displayed in a manner not to be mistaken. However salutary may be the effect produced upon the border people by our presence here, we are too far from the frontier to impress the government of Mexico with our readiness to vindicate, by force of arms, if necessary, our title to the country as far as the Rio Grande. The "army of occupation" will, in a few days, be concentrated at this point, in condition for vigorous and efficient service. Mexico having as yet made no positive declaration of war, or committed any overt act of hostilities,

I do not feel at liberty, under my instructions, particularly those of July 8th, to make a forward movement to the Rio Grande without authority from the War Department.

In case a forward movement should be ordered or authorized, I would recommend the occupation of Point Isabel and Laredo, as best adapted to the purposes of observing the course of the river, and covering the frontier settlements of Texas. Point Isabel is accessible by water, and can be safely occupied by two brigades of infantry, with a suitable force of field artillery. On the arrival of the steamer Harney, I shall order a careful reconnoissance of Brazos Santiago, as a necessary preliminary measure to the occupation of Point Isabel. To occupy Laredo will require a land march from this point. Supplies may probably be transported by water as high as San Patricio, and possibly to the junction of the Rio Frio with the Nueces. I propose to establish a depot on the Nueces river, probably at the crossing of the San Antonio and Laredo road, from which to operate towards the Rio Grande. You will perceive from my "special orders" No. 24, that a reconnoissance has been ordered in that direction. A brigade of infantry, with the cavalry, and a battery or two of field artillery, will be sufficient for the occupation of Laredo. That town is on the left bank of the Rio Grande, and possesses the military advantage of holding in observation the main route from the interior of Mexico through Monterey to Matamoras.

In case it should be found impracticable to establish a suitable depot on the Nueces, the entire force, after strengthening San Antonio, might be thrown forward to Point Isabel, where it could be readily supplied, and held in readiness for any further service.

I have deemed it my duty to make the above suggestions. Should they be favorably considered, and instructions based upon them, I will thank you to send the latter in duplicate to Lieutenant-Colonel Hunt—one copy to be dispatched *direct,* without delay; the other to be sent via Galveston, should a steamer be running to that port from New Orleans.

I am, sir, very respectfully,

Your obedient servant,

Z. TAYLOR,

Brevet Brig. Gen. U. S. A., commanding.

The Adjutant General of the Army,
Washington, D. C.

P. S. It is proper to add, that should any auxiliary force be required, I propose to draw it wholly from Texas. I do not conceive that it will become necessary, under any circumstances, to call for volunteers from the United States. Z. T.

Headquarters, Army of Occupation,
Corpus Christi, Texas, Nov. 7, 1845.

Sir:—I respectfully enclose a copy of a letter from Commodore Connor, commanding the home squadron, which I received by the "Saratoga," sloop of war, on the 5th instant. The intelligence communicated by the commodore will, doubtless, reach the seat of government long before the receipt of this letter.

The communication from the Secretary of War, dated October 16th, was received and acknowledged on the 1st and 2d instant. I purposely deferred a detailed reply to the various points embraced in that communication, until I could receive an answer to mine of October 4th, which covered (at least in part) the same ground. The intelligence from Mexico, however, tends to modify, in some degree, the views expressed in that communication. The position now occupied by the troops may, perhaps, be the best while negotiations are pending, or at any rate until a disposition shall be manifested by Mexico to protract them unreasonably. Under the supposition that such may be the view of the department, I shall make no movement from this point, except for the purpose of examining the country, until further instructions are received. You will perceive, from my orders, that reconnoissances are almost constantly in the field, the officers of engineers and topographical engineers rendering valuable service on those duties. I refer you to the reports made by those officers to the chiefs of their own bureaux, for the information which is thus procured in relation to the country. An examination of the harbor of Brazos Santiago will be ordered in a few days—as soon as a proper vessel shall become disposable for that service.

In case no movement is made this season towards the Rio Grande, I may find it necessary to detach a portion of the army a short distance into the interior, where wood can be more readily procured than here. But in no case do I deem it necessary to hut the troops. Sheds, with platforms, on which to pitch the tents, were extensively used in camps of position in Florida, and will, I cannot doubt, form a sufficient protection here.

On the hypothesis of an early adjustment of the boundary, and the consequent establishment of permanent frontier posts, I cannot urge too strongly upon the department the necessity of occupying those posts before the warm weather shall set in. A large amount of sickness is, I fear, to be apprehended, with every precaution that can be taken; but the information which I obtain leads me to believe that a summer movement would be attended with great expense of health and life. As in Florida, the winter is the best season for operations in Texas.

I am, sir, very respectfully,
Your obedient servant,
Z. TAYLOR,
Brevet Brig. Gen. U. S. A., commanding

The ADJUTANT GENERAL of the Army,
Washington, D. C.

HEADQUARTERS, ARMY OF OCCUPATION,
Corpus Christi, Texas, Feb. 4, 1846.

SIR:—I respectfully acknowledge the communication of the Secretary of War, dated January, 13th, and containing the instructions of the President to move forward with my force to the Rio Grande. I shall lose no time in making the necessary preparations for carrying out those instructions.

The occupation of Point Isabel or Brazos Santiago as a depot will be indispensable. That point and a position on or near the river opposite Matamoras will I think answer all present purposes. At any rate, I shall not separate my force further until the position of affairs shall render it entirely safe to do so.

I propose to abandon this position entirely, as soon after our march as the stores, hospital, &c., can be transferred to St. Joseph's Island. It will be necessary to keep up an establishment at that point for the present, although our supplies will come to Point Isabel direct from New Orleans.

In reply to the call of the Secretary for information as to what means, if any, will be required "to enforce and maintain our common right to navigate" the Rio Grande, I would respectfully state that, until I reach the river and ascertain the condition of things in the frontier states of Mexico, temper of the people, &c., I cannot give any satisfactory answer to the question. I have every reason to believe that the people residing on the river are well-disposed towards our government Our advance to the Rio Grande will itself produce a powerful effect, and it may be that the common navigation of the river will not be disputed. It is very important to us, and will be indispensable when posts are established higher up, as must ultimately be the case.

I shall not call for any militia force in addition to what I already have, unless unforeseen circumstances shall render its employment necessary.

I beg leave again to call the attention of the department to the necessity of having our movement and position at Brazos Santiago covered by a small armed vessel. I deem this vitally important, and hope it will meet with favorable consideration.

We have no news from the interior of Mexico more recent than that derived from the New Orleans papers of the 26th of January.

I am, sir, very respectfully,

Your obedient servant,

Z. TAYLOR,

Brevet Brig. Gen. U. S. A., commanding.

The Adjutant General of the Army,
Washington, D. C.

Headquarters, Army of Occupation,
Corpus Christi, Texas, February, 26, 1846.

Sir:—I have to report that the preparations for a forward movement of this command are now nearly completed. The examinations spoken of in my report of the 16th instant have shown the practicability of both routes—by the main land and by Padre Island. The reconnoissance of Padre Island extended to its southern extremity, and included the harbor of Brazos Santiago and Point Isabel; that of the main route reached to a point near the Little Colorado. A depot, with four days' forage and subsistence for the army, will be thrown forward some forty miles, to the Santa Gertrudes. A detachment of two companies, to establish and cover this depot, will march, on the 28th, under Brevet Major Graham. In about a week thereafter, say the 7th of March, the cavalry will march, to be followed, at intervals of one day, by the brigades of infantry. By the 25th of March, at latest, I hope to be in position on the Rio Grande.

I have taken occasion to represent to some citizens of Matamoras, who were here with a large number of mules for sale, and who are represented to have considerable influence at home, that the United States government, in occupying the Rio Grande, has no motive of hostility towards Mexico, and that the army will, in no case, go beyond the river, unless hostilities should be commenced by the Mexicans themselves; that the Mexicans, living on this side, will not be disturbed in any way by the troops; that they will be protected in all their usages; and that everything which the army may need will be purchased from them at fair prices. I also stated that, until the matter should be finally adjusted between the two governments, the harbor of Brazos Santiago would be open to the free use of the Mexicans as heretofore. The same views were impressed upon the Mexican custom house officer at Brazos Santiago, by Captain Hardee, who commanded the escort which covered the reconnoissance of Padre Island.

We are entirely without news of interest from the frontier, or the interior of Mexico, our latest date from the capital being the 21st of January, and the same from Vera Cruz.

I am, sir, very respectfully,
Your obedient servant,
Z. TAYLOR,
Brevet Brig. Gen. U. S. A., commanding.

The ADJUTANT GENERAL of the Army,
Washington, D. C.

HEADQUARTERS, ARMY OF OCCUPATION,
Corpus Christi, Texas, March, 8, 1846.

SIR :—I respectfully report that the advance of the army, composed of the cavalry and Major Ringgold's light artillery, the whole under the command of Colonel Twiggs, took up the line of march this morning in the direction of Matamoras, its strength being twenty-three officers and three hundred and seventy-eight men. The advance will be followed in succession by the brigades of infantry, the last brigade marching on the 11th inst. The roads are in good order, the weather fine, and the troops in excellent condition for service.

Major Munroe will embark for Brazos Santiago in season to reach that harbor about the time the army will be in the vicinity of Point Isabel. He takes with him a siege train and a field battery. Captain Sanders, of the engineers, the officers of ordnance, and the pay department, accompany Major Munroe.

The movement by water, to Brazos Santiago, will be covered by the revenue cutter "Woodbury," Captain Foster, whose commander has kindly placed her at my disposal for this service.

All proper arrangements have been made by the staff departments for supplying the army on the route, as well as establishing a depot for its further wants at Point Isabel.

I have deemed it proper to cause my "orders" No. 30, to be translated into Spanish, and circulated on the Rio Grande. Sixty copies have already been sent in advance of the army to Matamoras, Camargo, and Mier. This form of giving publicity to the spirit which actuates our movements in occupying the country, I thought preferable to a proclamation. I trust the order itself will meet the approval of the department. A few copies of the translation are herewith enclosed.

I shall again communicate with general headquarters before I march, and I expect to do so at least once on the route.

My headquarters will march with the rear brigade, but will soon pass to the advance of the army.

I am, sir, very respectfully,

Your obedient servant,

Z. TAYLOR,

Brevet Brig. Gen. U. S. A., commanding.

The ADJUTANT GENERAL of the Army.
Washington, D. C.

[TRANSLATION—ORDER NO. 30.]

HEADQUARTERS, ARMY OF OCCUPATION,
Corpus Christi, March, 8, 1846.

The army of occupation of Texas being now about to take a position upon the left bank of the Rio Grande, under the orders of the Executive of the United States, the general-in-chief desires to express the hope that the movement will be advantageous to all concerned; and with the object of attaining this laudable end, he has ordered all under his command to observe, with the most scrupulous respect, the rights of all the inhabitants who may be found in peaceful prosecution of their respective occupations, as well on the left as on the right side of the Rio Grande. Under no pretext, nor in any way, will any interference be allowed with the civil rights or religious privileges of the inhabitants; but the utmost respect for them will be maintained.

Whatsoever may be needed for the use of the army will be bought by the proper purveyor, and paid for at the highest prices. The general-in-chief has the satisfaction to say that he confides in the patriotism and discipline of the army under his command, and that he feels sure that his orders will be obeyed with the utmost exactness.

Z. TAYLOR,
Brevet Brig. Gen. U. S. A, commanding.

HEADQUARTERS, ARMY OF OCCUPATION,
Camp at "El Sauce." 119 miles from
Corpus Christi, March 18, 1846.

SIR:—I avail myself of a chance opportunity to Corpus Christi to report that I have advanced to this point with the cavalry and 1st brigade of infantry. The 2d brigade encamps to-night about seven miles in my rear; the 3rd brigade about nineteen. I shall concentrate all my force on reaching the Little Colorado, thirteen miles in my front, so as to be prepared for any contingency. I am happy to say that all the corps of the army are in fine condition and spirits, equal to any service that may be before them.

Within the last two days, our advance has met with small armed parties of Mexicans, who seem disposed to avoid us. They were, doubtless, thrown out to get information of our advance.

I am, sir, very respectfully,

Your obedient servant,

Z. TAYLOR,

Brevet Brig. Gen. U. S. A., commanding.

THE ADJUTANT-GENERAL of the Army.
Washington, D.C.

HEADQUARTERS, ARMY OF OCCUPATION,
Point Isabel, March 25, 1846.

SIR:—I respectfully report that I marched on the morning of the 23rd inst. with the entire army from the camp near the Colorado, in the order prescribed in my order No 35, herewith inclosed. After a march of fifteen miles, we reached, on the morning of the 24th, a point on the route from Matamoras to Point Isabel, eighteen miles from the former and ten from the latter place. I here left the infantry brigades under Brigadier-General Worth, with instructions to proceed in the direction of Metamoras until he came to a suitable position for encampment, where he would halt, holding the route in observation, while I proceeded with the cavalry to this point to communicate with our transports, supposed to have arrived in the harbor, and make the necessary arrangements for the establishment and defence of a depot.

While on my way hither, our column was approached by a party on its right flank, bearing a white flag. It proved to be a civil deputation from Matamoras, desiring an interview with me. I informed them that I would halt at the first suitable place on the road, and afford them the desired interview. It was, however, found necessary, from the want of water, to continue the route to this place. The deputation halted while yet some miles from Point Isabel, declining to come further, and sent me a formal protest of the prefect of the northern district of Tamaulipas against our occupation of the country, which I inclose herewith. At this moment it was discovered that the buildings at Point Isabel were in flames. I then informed the bearer of the protest that I would answer it when opposite Matamoras, and dismissed the deputation. I considered the conflagration before my eyes as a decided evidence of hostility, and was not willing to be trifled with any longer, particularly as I had reason to believe that the prefect, in making this protest, was but a tool of the military authorities at Matamoras.

The advance of the cavalry fortunately arrived here in season to arrest the fire, which consumed but three or four houses. The port captain, who committed the act under the orders, it is said, of General Mejia, had made his escape before its arrival. We found two or three inoffensive Mexicans here, the rest having left for Matamoras.

I was gratified to find that the water expedition had exactly answered to our land movement—the steamers arriving in the harbor only two or three hours before we reached Point Isabel, with the other transports close in their rear. The "Porpoise" and "Lawrence," brigs of war, and cutter "Woodbury," are lying outside. I have thought it necessary to order Captain Porter's company in this place to reinforce Major Munroe. Our great depot must be here, and it is very important to secure it against any enterprise of the enemy. The engineer officers are now examining the ground with a view to tracing lines of defence, and strengthening the position.

As soon as a sufficient amount of supplies can be

thrown forward toward Matamoras, I shall march in the direction of that town, and occupy a position as near it as circumstances will permit.

I inclose a sketch prepared by my aide-de-camp, Lieutenant Eaton, exhibiting the route of march since leaving the Colorado, and the bearings of important points.

I am, sir, very respectfully,
Your obedient servant,
Z. TAYLOR,
Brevet Brig. Gen. U. S. A., commanding.

The ADJUTANT-GENERAL of the Army,
Washington, D. C.

[TRANSLATION.]

OFFICE OF THE PREFECT OF THE NORTHERN DISTRICT OF THE DEPARTMENT OF TAMAULIPAS, Santa Rita, March 23, 1846.

GOD AND LIBERTY!

SIR:—Although the pending question respecting the annexation of the department of Texas to the United States, is subject to the decision of the supreme government of Mexico, the fact of the advance of the army under your excellency's orders, over the line occupied by you at Corpus Christi, places me under the necessity, as the chief political authority of the northern district of Tamaulipas, to address you, as I have now the honor to do, through the commissioners, who will place this in your hands, and to inform you that the people, under this prefecture, being justly alarmed at the invasion of an army, which, without any previous declaration of war, and without announcing explicitly the object proposed by it, comes to occupy a territory which never belonged to the insurgent province, cannot regard with indifference a proceeding so contrary to the conduct observed towards each other by civilized nations, and the clearest principles of the law of nations; that, directed by honor and patriotism, and certain that nothing has been said officially by the cabinet of the Union to the Mexican government, respecting the extension of the limits of Texas to the left bank of the Rio Bravo, trusting in the well-known justice of their cause, and using their natural right of defence, they (the citizens of this district) protest, in the most solemn manner, that neither now nor at any time do they, or will they, consent to separate themselves from the Mexican republic, and to unite themselves with the United States; and that they are resolved to carry this firm determination into effect, resisting so far as their strength will enable them, at all times and places,. until the army under your excellency's orders shall recede and occupy its former positions; because so long as it remains within the territory of Tamaulipas, the inhabitants must consider that whatsoever protestations of peace may be made, hostilities have been openly commenced by your excellency, the lamentable consequences of which will rest before the world exclusively on the heads of the invaders.

I have the honor to say this to your excellency, with the object indicated, and to assure you of my consideration and esteem.

JENES CARDENAS.

JUAN JOSE PINEDA.

To General Z. TAYLOR, &c.

[EXTRACT.]

CAMP ON THE LEFT BANK OF THE RIO GRANDE,
Opposite Matamoras, March 29th, 1846.

SIR:—I have the honor to report that I arrived at this camp yesterday, with the forces under my command, no resistance having been offered to my advance to the banks of the river, nor any act of hostility committed by the Mexicans, except the capture of two of our dragoons, sent forward from the advanced guard. I deem it possible that these two men may have deserted to the enemy, as one of them, at least, bears a bad character. Our approach seems to have created much excitement in Matamoras, and a great deal of activity has been displayed since our arrival, in the preparation of batteries. The left bank is now under reconnoissance of our engineer officers, and I shall lose no time in strengthening our position by such defensive works as may be necessary, employing for that purpose a portion of the heavy guns brought round by sea.

The attitude of the Mexicans is, so far, decidedly hostile. An interview has been held, by my direction, with the military authorities in Matamoras, but with no satisfactory result.

Under this state of things, I must again and urgently call your attention to the necessity of speedily sending recruits to this army.

The militia of Texas are so remote from the border, * * * * that we cannot depend upon their aid.

The strength gained by filling up the regiments here, even to the present feeble establishment, would be of very great importance.

I respectfully inclose a field report of the force now in this camp.

I am, sir, very respectfully,

Your obedient servant,

Z. TAYLOR,

Brevet Brig. Gen. U. S. A., commanding.

The ADJUTANT GENERAL of the Army,
Washington. D. C.

While the American government was thus preparing to meet any emergency that might grow out of the annexation of Texas, as will have been gathered from this correspondence, Mexico was not idle. She had, through her minister at Washington, General Almonte, warmly and decidedly protested against that measure. His protest having been disregarded, he demanded his passports, and left the United States, thus putting an end to all diplomatic intercourse between the two governments. As soon as information was received at the capital of Mexico that Congress had admitted Texas into the American confederacy, active preparations were taken to resist what the Mexican government affected to believe a virtual dismemberment of the Mexican nation, and an encroachment upon the integrity of its soil. The step seems to have been generally regarded as a sufficient and justifiable cause of war. Loans were immediately made, and an army ordered to Texas, and the regular army was to be increased forthwith to sixty thousand men. There were already two thousand troops at Matamoras, and these were joined, in April, 1846, by twenty-two hundred more, amongst whom were two hundred cavalry.

On the 11th of March, 1846, General Taylor, with the troops that had not already preceded him, took up his line of march from Corpus Christi, and on the 28th of the same month arrived at the Rio Grande, where Fort Brown now stands, a distance of one hundred and nineteen miles from the post he had left on the Nueces. This march, at any season of the year, over a low marshy country, would have been attended with great difficulty and embarrassment. But it was especially so, at the time General Taylor, with his army, performed it. The soldiers were therefore nearly worn out with fatigue upon their arriving at their destination. Upon General Taylor's arrival at Point Isabel, on his way to Matamoras, he had defences thrown up there under the superintendence of Captain Sanders, with a view to making it a depot for his provisions and military stores. While here he was met by a deputation of fifty Mexicans, who protested against his occupying the country; but he coolly informed them he should not have time to consider their request until he reached Matamoras.

When General Taylor arrived at the Rio del Norte, the Mexican colors were flying from the headquarters of Gen. Mejia, the commander of Matamoras, troops were moving about in every direction, and everything indicated the excitement and activity of a military encampment on the eve of some great event. On the 12th of April, two weeks after General Taylor had taken up his position opposite the city, he was summoned by General Ampudia, the commander-in-chief of the Mexican forces, to evacuate his posts, and the American Consul, and all other American citizens, were ordered to leave Matamoras without delay. The summons of General Ampudia was in terms as follows:—

"To explain to you the many grounds for the just grievances felt by the Mexican nation, caused by the United States government, would be a loss of time, and an insult to your good sense; I therefore pass at once to such explanations as I consider of absolute necessity.

"Your government, in an incredible manner—you will even permit me to say an extravagant one, if the usage or general rules established and received among all civilized nations are regarded—has not only insulted, but has exasperated the Mexican nation, bearing its conquering banner to the left bank of the Rio Bravo del Norte; and in this case, by explicit and definite orders of my government, which neither can, will, nor should receive new outrages, I require you in all form, and at latest in the peremptory term of twenty-four hours, to break up your camp and retire to the other bank of the Nueces river, while our governments are regulating the pending question in relation to Texas. If you insist in remaining upon the soil of the department of Tamaulipas, it will clearly result that arms, and arms alone, must decide the question; and in that case I advise you that we accept the war to which, with so much injustice on your part, you provoke us, and that, on our part, this war shall be conducted conformably to the principles established by the most civilized nations; that is to say, that the law of nations and of war shall be the guide of my operations; trusting that on your part the same will be observed."

To this summons to General Taylor to withdraw his troops beyond the Nueces, he replied on the same day. After acknowledging the receipt of Ampudia's order, and recounting its purport, he says, "I need hardly advise you that, charged as I am, in only a military capacity, with the performance of specific duties, I cannot enter into a discussion of the international question involved in the advance of the American army. You will, however, permit me to say that the government of the United States has constantly sought a settlement, by negotiation, of the question of boundary; that an envoy was dispatched to Mexico for that purpose, and that up to the most recent dates said envoy had not been received by the actual Mexican government, if indeed he has not received his passports and left the republic. In tl e meantime, I have been ordered to occupy the cou try up to the left bank of the Rio Grande, until the boundary shall be definitely settled. In carrying out these instructions I have carefully abstained from all acts of hostility, obeying, in this regard, not only the letter of my nstructions, but the plain dictates of justice and humanity.

"The instructions under which I am acting will not permit me to retrograde from the position I now occupy. In view of the relations between our respective governments, and the individual suffering which may result, I regret the alternative which you offer; but, at the same time, wish it understood that I shall by no means avoid such alternative, leaving the responsibility with those who rashly commence hostilities. In conclusion, you will permit me to give the assurance, that on my part, the laws and customs of war among civilized nations shall be carefully observed."

General Worth was appointed to open communications with General Mejia, and bear to him this answer to General Ampudia's summons. Mejia at first declined to receive either General Worth or General Taylor's communication. He, however, finally consented to receive the latter, and sent General La Vega to meet Worth. The interview terminated in nothing decisive, except the return of two dragoons who had been captured by the Mexicans, while in advance of the main body of the army.

Matters having been brought nearly to a crisis, by the refusal of General Taylor to obey the summons of Ampudia, to withdraw his forces within twenty-four hours to the left bank of the Nueces, the Second regiment of the American troops was on the 13th removed out of the reach of the shot from the Mexican batteries, while the Third, and Duncan's and Bragg's companies of flying artillery occupied the field works. The river was also blockaded, and all communications and supplies thereby cut off with this city. Four days after, Lieutenants Porter and Dobbins, with a party of ten men, were sent in pursuit of Colonel Cross, Deputy Quartermaster General, whom it was subsequently ascertained, was murdered on the 10th of April by the Mexicans, while he was taking a ride near the American camp. While in the performance of this duty, the party fell in, on the 18th, with one hundred and fifty Mexicans, whom they fired upon and put to flight, and took possession of their camp, equipage and horses. But they were attacked by night, on their return to camp, by a large party of Mexicans, and Lieutenant Porter, a brave and gallant young officer, and son of the late Commodore Porter, was killed.

Upon ascertaining that the Rio Grande had been blockaded, Ampudia addressed a strong remonstrance to General Taylor against the measure. He informed Taylor that from various sources worthy of confidence, "I have learned that some vessels bound for the mouth of the river, have not been able to effect an entrance into that port, in consequence of your orders that they should be conducted to Brazos Santiago. The cargo of one of them is composed in great part, and of the other entirely of provisions, which the contractors charged with providing for the army under my orders had procured to fulfil the obligations of their contracts. You have taken possession of these provisions by force, and against the will of the proprietors, one of whom is vice consul of her Catholic Majesty, and the other of her Britannic Majesty; and whose rights, in place of being rigorously respected, as was proffered, and as was to be hoped from the observance of the principles which govern among civilized nations, have, on the contrary, been violated in the most extraordinary manner opposed to the guarantee and respect due to private property.

"Nothing can have authorized you in such a course. The commerce of nations is not suspended or interrupted except in consequence of a solemn declaration of blockade, communicated and established in the form prescribed by international law. Nevertheless, you have infringed these rules: and, by an act which can never be viewed favorably to the United States government, have hindered the entrance to a Mexican port, of vessels bound to it, under the confidence that commerce would not be interrupted. My duties do not allow me to consent to this new species of hostility, and they constrain me to require of you, not only that the vessels taken by force to Brazos Santiago shall be at liberty to return to the mouth of the river, but the restoration of all the provisions which, besides belonging to private contractors, were destined for the troops on this frontier. I consider it useless to inculcate the justice of this demand, and the results which may follow an unlooked-for refusal.

"I have also understood that two Mexicans, carried down in a boat by the current of the river near one of the advanced posts of your camp, were detained, after being fired upon, and that they are still kept and treated as prisoners. The individuals in question do not belong to the army, and this circumstance exempts them from the laws of war. I therefore hope that you will place them absolutely at liberty, as I cannot be persuaded that you pretend to extend to persons not military the consequences of an invasion, which without employing this means of rigor against unarmed citizens, is marked in itself with the seal of universal reprobation."

This remonstrance of the Mexican commander, seems to have made but little impression upon General Taylor; and his reply to it is so much to the point, so happily conceived, and so elegantly expressed, that it deserves careful attention. After acknowledging the receipt of Ampudia's communication, Taylor expresses his surprise that the Mexican general should complain, after all that had passed since the arrival of the American army on the Rio Grande, of a measure which is no other than a natural result of the state of war, so much insisted on by the Mexican authorities as actually existing. He then proceeds to recall to his mind circumstances that would show, in his opinion, that the state of war insisted upon by Mexico, had not been sought by the American army, but had been forced upon it, and that the exercise of the rights incident to such state, could not be a subject of complaint.

"On breaking up my camp at Corpus Christi," he continues, "and moving forward with the army under my orders, to occupy the left bank of the Rio Bravo, it was my earnest desire to execute my instructions in a pacific manner; to observe the utmost regard for the personal rights of all citizens residing on the left bank of the river, and to take care that the religion and customs of the people should suffer no violation. With this view, and to quiet the minds of the inhabitants, I issued orders to the army enjoining a strict observance of the rights and interests of all Mexicans residing on the river, and caused said orders to be translated into Spanish, and circulated in the several towns on the Bravo. These orders announced the spirit in which we proposed to occupy the country, and I am proud to say that up to this moment the same spirit has controlled the operations of the army. On reaching the Arroyo Colorado, I was informed by a Mexican officer that the order in question had been received at Matamoras; but was told at the same time, that if I attempted to cross the river, it would be regarded as a declaration of war. Again, on my march to Frontone, I was met by a deputation of the civil authorities of Matamoras protesting against my occupation of a portion of the department of Tamaulipas, and declaring that if the army was not at once withdrawn, war would result. While this communication was in my hands, it was discovered that the village of Frontone had been set on fire and abandoned. I viewed this as a direct act of war, and informed the deputation that their communication would be answered by me when opposite Matamoras, which was done in respectful terms. On reaching the river I dispatched an officer, high in rank, to convey to the commanding general in Matamoras, the expression of my desire for amicable relations, and my willingness to leave open to the use of the citizens of Matamoras the port of Brazos Santiago, until the question of boundary should be definitely settled. This officer received for reply, from the officer selected to confer with him, that my advance to the Rio Bravo was considered as a veritable act of war, and he was absolutely refused an interview with the American consul, in itself an act incompatible with a state of peace.

"Notwitnstanding these repeated assurances on the part of the Mexican authorities, and notwithstanding the most obviously hostile preparations on the right bank of the river, accompanied by a rigid non-intercourse, I carefully abstained from any act of hostility —determined that the onus of producing an actual state of hostilities should not rest with me. Our relations remained in this state until I had the honor to receive your note of the 12th instant, in which you denounce war as the alternative of my remaining in this position. As I could not under my instructions, recede from my position, I accepted the alternative you offered me, and made all my dispositions to meet it suitably. But, still willing to adopt milder measures before proceeding to others, I contented myself in the first instance with ordering a blockade of the mouth of the Rio Bravo, by the naval forces under my orders —a proceeding perfectly consonant with the state of war so often declared to exist, and which you acknowledged in your note of the 16th instant, relative to the late Colonel Cross. If this measure seem oppressive, I wish it borne in mind that it has been forced upon me by the course you have seen fit to adopt. I have reported this blockade to my government, and shall not remove it until I receive instructions to that effect, unless indeed you desire an armistice pending the final settlement of the question between the governments, or until war shall be formally declared by either, in which case I shall cheerfully open the river. In regard to the consequences you mention as resulting from a refusal to remove the blockade, I beg you to understand that I am prepared for them, be they what they may.

"In regard to the particular vessels referred to in your communication, I have the honor to advise you that, in pursuance of my orders, two American schooners, bound for Matamoras, were warned off on the 17th instant when near the mouth of the river, and put to sea, returning probably to New Orleans. They were not seized, or their cargoes disturbed in any way, nor have they been in the harbor of Brazos Santiago to my knowledge. A Mexican schooner, understood to be the "Juniata," was in or off that harbor when my instructions to block the river were issued, but was driven to sea in a gale, since which time I have had no report concerning her. Since the receipt of your communication, I have learned that two persons, sent to the mouth of the river to procure information respecting this vessel, proceeded thence to Brazos Santiago, when they were taken up and detained by the officer in command, until my orders could be received. I shall order their immediate release. A letter from one of them to the Spanish vice consul is respectfully transmitted herewith.

"In relation to the Mexicans said to have drifted down the river in a boat, and to be prisoners at this time in my camp, I have the pleasure to inform you that no such persons have been taken prisoners, or are now detained by my authority. The boat in question was carried down empty by the current of the river, and drifted ashore near one of our pickets, and was secured by the guard. Some time afterwards an attempt was made to recover the boat under the cover of the darkness; the individuals concerned were hailed by the guard, and, failing to answer, were fired upon as a matter of course. What became of them is not known, as no trace of them could be discovered on the following morning. The officer of the Mexican guard directly opposite was informed next day that the boat would be returned on proper application to me, and I have now only to repeat that assurance.

"In conclusion, I take leave to state that I consider

GENERAL ARISTA.

the tone of your communication highly exceptionable, where you stigmatize the movement of the army under my orders as 'marked with the seal of universal reprobation.' You must be aware that such language is not respectful in itself, either to me or my government; and while I observe in my own correspondence the courtesy due to your high position, and to the magnitude of the interests with which we are respectively charged, I shall expect the same in return."

In the meantime, matters were rapidly ripening for an open resort to arms, and everything indicated too surely that the Mexicans were only waiting for the most favorable time to strike a blow at our army that should annihilate it, and rid themselves of such unwelcome neighbors. They did not rely alone on the power of their arms to accomplish that object. They resorted to the less dangerous expedient of attempting to corrupt the fidelity of the American soldiers, and of inducing them to desert, by the most tempting offers of lands and promotions. Addresses were issued to them containing these flattering propositions, which they always found means to have introduced into General Taylor's camp. One of these papers, signed by Arista, who had superseded Ampudia in the command of the Mexican forces, and which will be found below, most artfully appeals to the cupidity and prejudices of those soldiers not native citizens of the United States.

"Headquarters at Matamoras,
April 26, 1846.

"Soldiers!—You have enlisted in time of peace to serve in that army for a specific term; but your obligation never implied that you were bound to violate the laws of God, and the most sacred rights of friends! The United States government, contrary to the wishes of a majority of all honest and honorable Americans, has ordered you to take *forcible* possession of the territory of a *friendly* neighbor, who has never given her consent to such occupation. In other words, while there exists a treaty of peace and commerce between Mexico and the United States, the United States, presuming on her strength and prosperity, and on our supposed imbecility and cowardice, attempts to make you the blind instruments of her unholy and mad ambition, and *force* you to appear as the hateful robbers of our dear homes, and the unprovoked violators of our dearest feelings as men and patriots. Such villany and outrage, I know, is perfectly repugnant to the noble sentiments of any gentleman, and it is base and foul to rush you on to certain death, in order to aggrandize a few lawless individuals, in defiance of the laws of God and man!

"It is to no purpose if they tell you, that the law of the annexation of Texas justifies your occupation of the Rio Bravo del Norte; for by this act they rob us of a great part of *Tamaulipas, Coahuili, Chihuahua, and New Mexico;* and it is barbarous to send a handful of men on such an errand against a powerful and warlike nation. Besides, the most of you are Europeans, and we are the *declared friends* of a majority of the nations of *Europe.* The North Americans are ambitious, overbearing, and insolent as a nation, and they will only make use of you as vile tools to carry out their abominable plans of pillage and rapine.

"I warn you in the name of justice, honor, and your own interests and self-respect, to abandon their desperate and unholy cause, and become *peaceful Mexican citizens.* I guarantee you, in such case, a half section of land, or three hundred and twenty acres, to settle upon, gratis. Be wise, then, and just, and honorable, and take no part in murdering us who have no unkind feelings for you. Lands shall be given to officers, sergeants, and corporals, according to rank, privates receiving three hundred and twenty acres, as stated.

"If in time of action you wish to espouse our cause, throw away your arms and run to us, and we will embrace you as true friends and Christians. It is not decent nor prudent to say more. But should any of you render important service to Mexico, you shall be accordingly considered and preferred."

It has already been stated that General Taylor had established a depot of provisions, arms, and munitions of war at Point Isabel. On the 24th of April, information was received by him that twenty-five hundred Mexicans had crossed the Rio Grande, part above and part below his camp, and cutting off all communication between Fort Brown and Point Isabel. Captain Ker's squadron of dragoons was immediately ordered to reconnoitre the country between the two positions, and Captain Thornton was dispatched above the Fort for the same purpose. The latter proceeded up the river for about twenty miles, when his Mexican guide refused to proceed any further, alleging as his reason that the country was filled with Mexican troops. Captain Thornton proceeded to move on, however, until he came to a farm-house and plantation, which were entirely surrounded by a thick chapparal fence. He entered the plantation with his squadron in single file, and while making inquiries at the house he was completely surrounded and taken by surprise by a Mexican force of several hundred infantry and cavalry, under the command of General Torrejon. Captain Thornton charged upon the Mexican cavalry in gallant style, and drove them back. But the infantry, from every quarter of the chapparal, poured in a destructive fire upon his command, and prevented them from reaching the opening by which they had entered. Thornton, however, succeeded in clearing the chaparral hedge and making his escape, though his noble charger was severely wounded in the act of making this extraordinary leap. His followers were less fortunate in the attempt. They immediately rallied under Captain Hardee, upon whom the command now devolved, and endeavored to escape from the snare in which they had become so fatally entangled, by escaping to the Mexican side of the river. But here they again failed, the banks of the stream being impassable. All retreat being thus rendered impossible, Captain Hardee expressed his willingness to surrender, on condition that the Mexican commander would guarantee to him and his men the treatment to which prisoners of war are entitled amongst civilized nations, and he declared their determination to sell their lives as dearly as possible, if such terms should be refused. This assurance, however, was readily given, when the Americans surrendered themselves prisoners of war, and were taken to Matamoras. This remarkable victory of three or four hundred Mexicans over twenty-five Americans, was received with unbounded delight by the Mexican army, and filled their imaginations with numerous future triumphs over the American arms. Upon the receipt of the tidings, General Arista issued the following glowing congratulatory letter to General Torrejon:—

"This has been a day of rejoicing to all the Division of the North, it having this day been known of the triumph achieved by the brigade which your excellency so worthily commands. The rejoiced country will doubtless celebrate this preliminary of glorious deeds that her happy sons will in future present to her. Your excellency will communicate to your brave soldiers that I have seen with the greatest pleasure their valiant behavior, and that I await for the detailed dispatch to elevate it to the knowledge of the supreme government, so that the nation may learn the triumph of your arms."

Captain Thornton succeeded in reaching the American camp within five miles, after almost miraculously escaping a perfect shower of Mexican bullets, while fleeing through their lines, when he was captured and taken to Matamoras. He remained there for some time, but was finally given up. In this encounter Lieutenant G. T. Mason was killed.

Captain Ker, with his detachment, after having reconnoitered the country between Fort Frown and the mouth of the Rio Grande, returned, without having fallen in with the enemy. On the 28th, however, Captain Walker, of the Texas Rangers, who was at Point Isabel, attempted a reconnoissance of the route towards General Taylor's headquarters, but was driven back with some loss, having encountered a force of fifteen hundred men. The next day he made a successful attempt to convey a message from Major Munroe, in command at Point Isabel, to General Taylor.

CHAPTER IV.

General Taylor leaves Fort Brown.—Mexicans prepare to Dispute his Passage.—Mexican estimate of their Valor.—Charge of Cowardice against General Taylor.—Bombardment of Fort Brown.—Further account of their Glorious Deeds.—Erect a Battery in the rear of the Fort.—Death of Major Brown.—The Fort Summoned to Surrender.—Refusal.—Bombardment Resumed.—Taylor starts on his return from Point Isabel.—Meets the Enemy.—Battle of Palo Alto.—The Details.

On the 1st of May, 1846, immediately after receiving the message of Major Munroe, General Taylor left his intrenchments opposite Matamoras, and took up his line of march for Point Isabel, determined to open the communication between the two positions, at all hazards, and to fight the enemy, however strong he might be. He left Major Jacob Brown, a brave and accomplished officer, in command of Fort Brown, with the Seventh regiment of infantry, and two companies of artillery, the latter commanded by Captain Lowd, and Lieutenant Bragg, respectively, making a force of about five hundred effective men. Arista mistook the movement of General Taylor towards Point Isabel for a precipitate retreat of the American forces, and forthwith dispatched a bulletin to Mexico, announcing the fact; or, if he did not himself believe our army intended to retreat, he meant to create such an impression amongst the Mexican soldiers, and in the mind of his own government. All the movements of General Taylor seem to have been well known at Matamoras, however imperfectly his motives and intentions were understood, and preparations were accordingly made for cutting him off. The designs of the Mexican generals are revealed in the following semi-official communication, taken from the El Monitor Republicano of May 4th, three days after General Taylor left Fort Brown. It is in the usual exaggerated and grandiloquent style of Mexican documents, but it reveals the feelings which they entertained towards the Americans before the breaking out of hostilities, and the large expectations of success by which they were governed :—

"On the first of this month (May) at eleven o'clock in the morning, the general-in-chief left this place (Matamoras) to join the army, who several hours before had left with the intention of crossing the river at a short distance from the camp of the enemy. In consequence of the orders given, so that this dangerous operation might be performed with due security, and according to the rules of military art, when our troops arrived at the spot designated for the crossing of the river, the left bank was already occupied by Gen. D. Anastasio Torrejon, with all the force under his command. The enthusiasm of our soldiers to conquer the obstacles which separated them from the enemy was so great, that they showed themselves impatient of the delay occasioned by the bad condition of some of the flat boats, which had been very much injured in the transportation by land, and could not be used, as they would fill up with water as soon as they were launched. In spite of that obstacle, the work went on with such activity, and so great was the ardor of the most excellent general-in-chief, whose orders were obeyed with the greatest promptness and precision, that a few hours were sufficient to transport, to the opposite bank of the Bravo, a strong division, with all its artillery and train.

"This rapid and well combined movement ought to have proved to the invaders not only that the Mexicans possess instruction and aptness for war, but that those qualities are now brought forth by the purest patriotism. The Northern Division, fearless of fatigue, and levelling all difficulties, ran to seek an enemy who, well sheltered under parapets, and defended with guns of a large calibre, could wait for the attack with indisputable advantage. With deep trenches, with a multitude of fortifications, the defence was easy against those who presented themselves with their naked breasts.

"But General Taylor dared not resist the valor and enthusiasm of the sons of Mexico. Well did he foresee the intrepidity with which our soldiers would rush against the usurpers of the national territory. Well did he know the many injuries which were to be avenged by those who had taken up arms, not to aggrandize themselves with the spoils of the property of others, but to maintain the independence of their country. Well did he know, we repeat it, that the Mexicans would be stopped neither by trenches, or fortresses, or large artillery. Thus it was that the chief of the American forces, frightened as soon as he perceived from the situation and proximity of his camp, that our army were preparing to cross the river, left with precipitation for Point Isabel, with almost all his troops, eight pieces of artillery, and a few wagons. Their march was observed from our position, and the most excellent General D. Francisco Mejia immediately sent an express extraordinary to communicate the news to the most excellent general-in-chief. Here let me pay to our brave men the tribute which they deserve. The express verbally informed some of the troops which had not yet arrived at the ford, of the escape of the Americans; in one instant, all the soldiers spontaneously crossed the river, almost racing one with another. Such was the ardor with which they crossed the river to attack the enemy.

"The terror and haste with which the latter fled to the fort, to shut themselves up in it and avoid a conflict, frustrated the active measures of the most excellent Senor General Arista, which were to order the cavalry to advance in the plain and to cut off the flight of the fugitives. But it was not possible to do so, notwithstanding their forced march during the night. General Taylor left his camp at 2 o'clock in the afternoon, and, as fear has wings, he succeeded in shutting himself up in the fort. When our cavalry reached the point where they were to detain him, he had already passed, and was several leagues ahead. Great was the sorrow of our brave men not to have been able to meet the enemy face to face; their defeat was certain, and the main body of that invading army, who thought that they inspired the Mexicans with so much respect, would have disappeared in the first important battle. But there was some fighting to be done; and the Americans do not know how to use other arms but those of duplicity and treachery. Why did they not remain with firmness under their colors? Why did they abandon the ground which they pretend to usurp with such iniquity? Thus has an honorable general kept his word. Had not General Taylor said, in all his communications, that he was prepared to repel all hostilities? Why, then, does he fly in so cowardly a manner to shut himself up at the Point? The commander-in-chief of the American army has covered himself with opprobrium and ignominy in sacrificing a part of his forces, whom he left in the fortifications, to save himself; for it is certain that he will not return to their assistance—not that he is ignorant of their peril, but he calculates that this would be greater if he had the temerity of attempting to resist the Mexican lances and bayonets in the open plain."

The Mexican general conceived that, as General Taylor had "retreated" from Fort Brown, the small detachment left to defend it must fall a very easy prey to Mexican valor and prowess. On the 3rd of May, they opened upon it a fire from a seven-gun battery, which was returned by Major Brown with great spirit and effect, silencing their guns in a very few moments. They immediately commenced another attack, however, with shot and shell, killing Sergeant Weigard while at his post, but doing little other damage. The firing upon the fort was heard by General Taylor, at Point Isabel, and he immediately dispatched Captains May and Walker to ascertain the position of affairs there. They returned with intelligence that the fort was in a condition to resist any force that could be brought against it.

The result of their first day's bombardment of Fort Brown filled the Mexicans with even greater delight, if possible, than the remarkable achievement of surprising and capturing Captain Thornton's handful of men with their overwhelming force. Great rejoicings were had in Matamoras over the brilliant achievement, and an official dispatch, in the following terms, was forwarded to the Mexican government:

"But let us relate the glorious events of yesterday. As Aurora dawned, we began to fire from our ramparts on the fortifications of the enemy, and the thunder of Mexican cannon was saluted by the reveille from every point of our line, by the bell of the parochial church, and by the *vivas* of the inhabitants of Matamoras. In a moment the streets were filled, and all were rejoiced to see at last the hour arrived, when we were to give a terrible lesson to the American camp, whose odious presence could no longer be tolerated. The enemy answered, but they were soon convinced that their artillery, although of a superior calibre, could not compete with ours. After a fire of five hours, our ramparts remained immovable, on account of the solidity of their construction, and the intelligence with which the rules of art had been observed. The same did not happen to the American fortifications, whose bastions were so completely demolished, that towards eleven o'clock in the morning their artillery ceased to play, and their fire was hushed. We continued to fire with activity during the day, without the enemy's daring to respond to us, because the parapets under which they would shelter themselves being destroyed, they had not courage to load their guns, which remained uncovered. This result shows us of what in reality consists the exalted skill of the American artillerists. They have eighteen pounders, and we have nothing larger than eight pounders; and yet the intelligence and practice of the Mexicans sufficed to conquer those who had superior arms. Unequalled glory and eternal honor to our brave artillerymen.

"The enemy, in their impotent rage, and before they concealed their shame behind the most distant parapets, had the barbarous pleasure of aiming their guns towards the city, to destroy its edifices, as it was not in their power to destroy the fortifications from which they received so much injury. This wicked revenge, which only springs from cowardly and miserable souls, did not meet with the success expected by those who so unworthily adorn themselves with the title of *savans* and philanthropists. Their stupidity was equal to their wickedness. Almost all the balls passed too high; and those which touched the houses, although they were eighteen pounders, did not cause any other mischief but that of piercing one or two walls. If those who conceived the infamous design of destroying Matamoras, had seen the contemptuous laughter with which the owners of those houses showed their indifference for the losses which they might sustain, they would have admired the patriotism and disinterestedness of the Mexicans, always ready to undergo the greatest sacrifices, when it is necessary to maintain their nationality and independence. The glorious 3rd of May is another brilliant testimony of this truth; through the thickest of the firing, one could remark the most ardent enthusiasm on all faces, and hardly had a ball fallen, when even the children would look for it, without fearing that another aimed in the same manner should fall in the same place. That, we saw ourselves in the public square, where a multitude of citizens were assembled.

"The triumph of our arms has been complete, and we have only to lament the loss of a sergeant and two artillerymen, who fell gloriously in fighting for their country. The families of those victims ought to be taken care of by the supreme government, to whose paternal gratitude they have been recommended by the most excellent senor general-in-chief. We must also be consoled by the thought that the blood of these brave men has been revenged by their bereaved companions. As many of our balls passed through the enemy's embrasures, the loss to the Americans must have been very great; and although we do not know exactly the number of their dead, the most accurate information makes it amount to fifty-six. It is probable that such is the case. Since eleven o'clock in the morning, the abandonment of their guns, merely because two of them were dismounted, and the others were uncovered; the panic-terror with which, in all haste, they took refuge in their furthest entrenchments, taking away from the camp all that could suffer from the attack of our artillery; the destruction which must have been occasioned by the bombs, so well aimed, that some would burst at a yard's distance from the ground in their descent to the point where they were to fall; everything contributes to persuade that indeed the enemy have suffered a terrible loss. If it were not the case—if they preserved some remnant of valor, why did they not dare to repair their fortifications in the night. It is true that, from time to time, a few guns were fired on them in the night, but their aim could not be certain, and cowardice alone could force them not to put themselves in an attitude to return the fire which was poured on them again at daylight. No American put out his head; silence reigned in their camp; and for this reason we have suspended our fire to-day—that there is no enemy to meet our batteries.

"To conclude, we will give a brilliant paragraph relating to the contest, by the most excellent senor general-in-chief, as to the part which he took in the events of yesterday. He says thus: 'Mexico must glorify herself, and especially the valiant men of the Division of the North, that a force inferior in its elements, and perhaps in number also, and which required nearly two months to swell itself with the auxiliaries coming from the capital, should meet in an immense plain, defying the army of the United States, and the whole power of that republic, without their opponents, who could receive succor in the space of fifty hours, daring to leave the fort to give us battle.'

"From the news which we publish to-day, it will be seen that the Northern Division, so deservedly intrusted with the first operations against the North American army, has most nobly filled its highly important mission. Not that we mean to be understood as considering its task is yet fully completed, but we anticipate, before the end of the present week, to witness the total discomfiture of the enemy, who has had the temerity to answer the fire of our batteries; of those batteries that gave them yesterday such abundant proof of that valor, so characteristic of the Mexicans: a valor rendered famous in a hundred bloody contests! It were endless to recount all the acts of patriotism performed by the troops of the garrison, and the valiant citizens who shared in the defence of the city—they courted danger with that intrepidity always inspired by a just cause.

"So rapid is the fire of our guns, that *the batteries of the enemy have been silenced.* But what is most worthy of notice, as showing the great enthusiasm of this place, is the fact that many of the inhabitants, of both sexes, in the hottest of the cannonade, remained firm in front of the enemy, filled with enthusiasm; indeed, fear is always unknown to those whose mission is to avenge an outrage upon the sacred rights of their beloved country.

"From our account of the war, the world will judge of the great superiority of our troops, in courage as well as skill, over the Americans. It is indeed wonderful to witness the dismay of the enemy: rare is the occurrence when an American ventures outside of the breastwork. There can be no doubt of this, that the Mexicans will be considered by foreign nations as the very emblems of patriotism. How evident that they inherit the blood of the noble sons of Pelayo! Happy they who have met with so glorious a death in defending the territory bequeathed to them by their fathers!

"The nation with which we are at war is most savage in its proceedings; no regard being paid to the flags of friendly nations: even those usages and customs respected by civilized nations, to divest war of some of its horrors, have been shamefully disregarded. The enemy have fired red shot against this innocent city, and we publish it to the world in proof that, with all their boasted wisdom and liberty, they are unworthy of being counted among enlightened nations.

"His excellency, the general-in-chief of the Northern Division, and his intrepid soldiers, are ready to fight the enemy in any numbers, and we are certain that our arms will be successful; but the nation against whom we have to contend is excessively proud; and it is also possessed of resources which may perhaps surpass those within our reach. Let us then make an immense effort to repel their aggressions. Let us contribute everything most dear to us, our persons, our means, to save our country from its present danger Let us oppose to the unbridled ambition of the Anglo-American, that patriotic enthusiasm, so peculiar to us. Indeed, we need only follow the glorious example of Matamoras, that noble city, which will be known in future by the name of Heroic. Its inhabitants have emulated the examples of Menamia, and Sagantum; they have determined to die at the foot of the eagle of

Anahuac, defend their fort whilst they retain the breath of life—this plan is settled. The supreme government is making strenuous exertions in order to protect the territory placed under its care by the nation, and nothing is now wanting but for the people to rush in a mass to the frontier, and the independence of Mexico is safe."

During the night of the 4th of May, a large body of Mexican troops crossed the river and erected a strong battery in the rear of Fort Brown, and on the morning of the 5th a heavy fire was opened from this battery, and the fort was assailed with great vigor. At the same time a hot fire was opened from the batteries at Matamoras, and a galling discharge of shot and shell was kept up for about an hour. The fire of the enemy from both these positions was returned with spirit and effect, by Major Brown, until they were silenced for the day. Early on the morning of the 6th, the fire from the enemy's batteries was renewed with increased vigor, their shot and shell falling in every direction, tearing tents to pieces and wounding many of the horses. But for the great size of the field-works and the very few men to defend it, the loss of life must have been very severe. As it was, the only one who fell during the bombardment, which continued throughout the day, was Major Brown, the noble, high-minded and accomplished commander of the fort. After the firing had continued for several hours, this gallant officer took his usual round to satisfy himself that every man was at his post and in the performance of his duties. While making his observations he was struck by a shell, which took off one of his legs, and dreadfully mangled him. He was immediately taken to the hospital and his leg amputated above the knee.

But he could not be saved, and after lingering until the 9th of May, he died, universally lamented, not only by the army, who best knew his worth, but by the whole country. Few men, indeed, had obtained a stronger hold upon the affection of the soldiers, or was more sincerely esteemed by his brother officers, of whatever rank, than Major Brown.

Upon leaving Fort Brown for Point Isabel, General Taylor gave orders to Major Brown to maintain his post, whatever contingency might arise, and under no circumstances to hazard his position by making a sally against the enemy. In the event of the fort being surrounded and an assault made upon him, he was ordered to warn him of the fact, by firing, at stated intervals, his eighteen pounders. On the evening of that day, accordingly, the signal guns were fired, and their warning voice informed him, though many miles distant, that the contemplated danger was threatening the gallant defenders of Fort Brown. These signal guns seemed to stimulate the enemy to still more active exertions to capture the fort, before they could call General Taylor back to its aid. So satisfied were they that they were making dreadful havoc amongst the Americans, and that Captain Hawkins, who had succeeded Major Brown in command, could not hold out against their destructive fire, that Arista summoned him to surrender, out of pure humanity. Captain Hawkins, however, was wholly insensible to this magnanimous conduct, and informed him that, as his interpreter was not skilled in Spanish, he might not have understood his communication, but if he did, he should respectfully decline to surrender the fort. This indifference to the humane proposition, brought upon the fort a more heavy fire from the Mexican batteries than they had yet suffered. Shells and shot were literally showered into the fort. This storm of iron Captain Hawkins was unable to return for want of powder, which rendered the condition of his troops extremely irksome and mortifying.

With the morning light of the 7th the enemy's batteries recommenced, but after pouring into the fort a large number of shot and shell, they suddenly ceased. About half-past seven o'clock a large number of Mexicans were discovered in and around the *Fanques del Raminero,* and the houses formerly occupied by the guards of the Second Brigade. Several rounds of canister and grape were fired into them, which caused them to make a precipitate retreat, after throwing a few shell in return. The Mexicans had theretofore used shell made of bronze; they now used iron, which they fired at intervals until noon. It was at this time discovered that the mortar battery in the rear of the fort, had been removed to the city of Matamoras. About noon some shells were thrown, which killed four of Lieutenant Bragg's horses, and broke the wheel of one of his caissons. Soon after, all their batteries opened, and kept up a steady firing of round shot and shell, which continued for nearly two hours. By one of these discharges the sentinel lost his arm, but the bomb proofs were so far advanced that the men were comparatively protected. Random shots were now fired from under the bank of the river, and the rear of the fort; it was evidently the determination of the besiegers to give the fort no rest, and induce them to expend all their ammunition, having been informed by deserters that there was little in the fort. Orders had been given to return no fire more than eighty yards distant, and as the Mexicans never approached to within twice that distance, they elicited no reply. At half-past two a regular bombardment commenced from all the batteries, howitzers, and mortars, which continued without intermission until sunset.

At dark, the indefatigable Captain Mansfield, with a small party, left the fort, and levelled the traverse thrown up by our troops when they first arrived on the banks of the river, and also cut down a large quantity of chapparel that served at times to cover the "sharp shooters" of the enemy. Everything after this remained quiet until midnight. Each man was at his post, and anxiously awaiting the assault, when the stillness was broken by volleys of musketry, and bugles "sounding the charge." The firing then ceased, but in a short time recommenced, and continued until daylight.

At noon the bombardment was resumed, and kept up about two hours. Many of the soldiers began to show symptoms of being worn down with hard labor and watching; nature was becoming exhausted, they grew indifferent about the exploding shells, and listlessly let them burst in dangerous proximity to their persons. The heavy bombardment had hardly ceased, when a *severe cannonading was heard towards Point Isabel;* so sudden did it commence, and so rapidly was it carried on, that it seemed like one continued volley of field-pieces. The soldiers in the fort sprang as one man to their feet, and listened. The sounds of artillery continued to roll on the plain; a simultaneous shout rose from the men in the fort, that must have sounded in Matamoras more terribly than our severest cannonade, for it must have told the people there that those in the fort believed that General Taylor was on the advance from Point Isabel. The enemy felt that shout, for there immediately commenced a severer bombardment than the fort had yet sustained; and a new mortar battery having been opened across the river, west of the fort, made four playing upon it from different points at the same time. The enemy's cavalry and infantry were seen above and below the fort crossing the river in masses, supposed for the purpose of reinforcing the enemy. At seven o'clock the bombardment ceased, the fort having received through the day three hundred shot and shell, with comparatively little injury.

As soon as General Taylor was satisfied by the signal guns from Fort Brown, that it had been attacked and was in danger, he made prompt preparations for opening his communication between it and Point Isabel and for relieving its gallant defenders from their perilous situation. Accordingly, on the evening of the 7th of May, he left Point Isabel with a force of about twenty-one hundred men, and a train of two hundred and fifty wagons, loaded with provisions and military stores, determined to give the enemy battle, however numerous he might be. That night his army encamped about seven miles from Point Isabel, and resumed his march early on the morning of the 8th. About twelve o'clock, his advanced guards reported that the Mexican forces were drawn up in large numbers to dispute his progress. Another report immediately followed, however, informing him that they had withdrawn their advance, and were retreating towards Fort Brown. His wagon trains and troops were therefore again put in motion, and progressed until the country opened into a broad prairie, bounded by Palo Alto, a thick grove of dwarfish trees. On both the right and left of the American army were ponds of fresh water, and beyond them, chapparal.

Upon this prairie the enemy were again drawn up, prepared for battle. On the extreme right was drawn up a division of Mexican cavalry, with their long, sharp-pointed lances glittering in the sun, and their pennants gayly waving in the breeze. Next, were posted their artillery and their heavy bodies of infantry, the whole forming a solid column of over a mile in length, with artillery, infantry and cavalry, alternately arranged, and presenting a most formidable appearance.

General Taylor's train was immediately formed into a solid square, and his army rapidly advanced until the heads of his column reached the open prairie. While thus advancing, Lieutenant J. E. Blake, of the Topographical Engineers, passed at full speed the advance guard, saying "he was going down to observe the enemy's lines." He continued on, until within one hundred and fifty yards of them, when he dismounted, and drawing out his spyglass, commenced a reconnoissance, the boldness of which, called forth admiration from the thousands who witnessed it. While thus engaged, two Mexican officers, evidently under the impression that he had some important communication to make to their commanding general, rode out from the ranks to meet him; Lieutenant Blake observing this, remounted his horse, and rode deliberately down the whole of the enemy's line; then returning, he gave to General Taylor, what was subsequently proved to be a correct account of the Mexican force, in both artillery, cavalry, and infantry.

The space between the two armies was now gradually lessening, and soon the details could be distinguished. The tall, rank grass of the prairie, deadened the heavy tramp of the cavalry, and the lumbering wheels of the artillery; and the whole moved forward so silently that the rattling of their trappings could be heard singularly plain. A space of seven hundred yards only, intervened between the two armies, when the batteries on the right of the Mexican line opened, throwing their ball and grape over the heads of the Americans, and announcing, in tones of thunder, that the contest had begun. In quick succession the whole of their artillery, from extreme right to left, poured forth volleys of ball, which made the earth tremble, and filled the air with clouds of dust and sulphurous smoke. The word was now given for the advancing columns to halt, and deploy into line. When this was done, Lieutenant Churchill's eighteen-pounders boomed above the surrounding din, announcing, in full rolling echoes, that the Americans were "in the field." Major Ringgold's and Captain Duncan's commands were now ordered forward into the open prairie, and commenced their rapid discharges. A general cannonading now raged, unparalleled, it is believed, in any fight upon an open battle-field. Duncan's battery, from its conspicuousness and nearness to our line, had often the concentrated fire of the enemy upon it. For two hours twenty or thirty pieces of artillery rent the air with their thunders; the iron hail tearing up the prairie in deep furrows, and sending the dry dust in clouds in the air. There was but little precision in the enemy's firing. The missiles almost invariably passed over the American lines. Far different was it with our own; at every discharge, the sudden opening that followed in the solid masses, marked the terrible course of death where the Mexican cavalry bit the dust. The infantry, cool spectators of the raging battle, marked with eagle eyes this havoc in the opposing ranks, and mingled their exulting shouts with the din, as they witnessed the prowess of their companions in arms. The terrible eighteen-pounders rose ever above the tumult, and seemed as if keeping time in solemn sound, as at every discharge they sent their huge masses of crushing iron into the living wall at which they were directed. As the battle thickened, the infantry, now formed in our rear, grew impatient to participate in the fight, and the Mexican cavalry, by suffering so severely by our artillery, prepared for the charge. The manœuvring of the day now commenced—the time for cool courage, quick thought, and deeds of individual heroism had arrived.

A regiment of Mexican lancers, commanded by General Torrejon, moved towards our right, as it was supposed to gain possession of our train. The Third and Fifth regiments of infantry, with a portion of Ringgold's battery, under the command of Lieut. Ridgeley, were ordered to check this movement, and turn the left flank of the enemy. They, however, still keeping up an irregular fire, continued steadily to advance toward our right and front, so as to out-flank our line, if possible. Upon their near approach, the Fifth was thrown into square, with Captain Walker, and twenty mounted men, on its right. Lieutenant Ridgeley having dashed forward, unlimbered his battery, and commenced rapid discharges of grape and canister upon the enemy's artillery, causing it to retreat; but the lancers, fifteen hundred strong, continued steadily to advance, in spite of all opposition, until the Fifth poured into them from the head of the square, a fire so deadly, that the front of the cavalry recoiled; great numbers fell dead, and those in the rear, without pressing forward on the bayonets, ready to receive them, broke into confusion. A portion, however, re-formed, and kept bravely on, in the attempt to reach the trains, when Coloned Twiggs ordered the Third infantry to the extreme right, to cut off their advance. When the enemy saw this movement, they commenced a retreat in good order, marching apparently by squadrons, when Lieutenant Ridgeley, assisted by Lieutenant French, opened his batteries, scattering them in all directions.

While Lieutenant Ridgeley was engaged in directing this fire, his horse was shot from under him, and the same ball probably that caused the death of his steed, alarmed the horses at one of his caissons, which sprang madly forward in range of the gun. Lieutenant Ridgeley, regardless of personal danger, rushed forward between the two contending fires, seized the front horses by the head, and brought them into their places; thus saving not only his horses, but the ammunition of his battery. During this time, Major Ringgold's battery was not idle; but, supported by the Fourth infantry, kept up a galling and continuous fire. On the left, and in the advance, was Duncan's battery, which, supported by the Eighth infantry and Captain Ker's squadron of dragoons, poured forth a terrible discharge. The dragoons, who, from their elevated position could witness its effects, say that horses and riders were frequently blown into the air, and long openings were often visible that it made in the columns against which it was directed; notwithstanding this, the enemy's line remained unshaken. So rapid were these discharges, that the wiry grass of the prairie, that reached nearly up to the muzzle of the pieces, dried before the sheeted flame, and burst into a blaze; the sulphurous smoke of the exploded cannon and the musket cartridges had already clouded the air, as if to veil the horrors of war from the clear blue sky above; but, when this conflagration took place, the very heavens were at times

GENERAL TAYLOR AT THE BATTLE OF PALO ALTO

May 8th, 1846.

darkened, and huge masses of smoke rolled across the plain, completely obscuring our lines from the enemy's view.

After the battle had raged two hours, the Mexican batteries began to slacken, and finally ceased altogether. They were unable longer to withstand the terrible and destructive fire of Ringgold's, Churchill's, Duncan's and Ridgeley's guns, and began to fall back for the purpose of forming a new line of battle under cover of the smoke. Our eighteen pounders were then moved forward until they occupied the position where the Mexican cavalry were posted at the beginning of the battle. The Americans also formed a new line, their right wing resting on these eighteen-pounders. The two armies were now formed in parallel lines, but the Mexicans were better protected than in their first position, by the chapparal in their rear.

Scarcely an hour elapsed before the action was resumed. It was commenced by our artillery, which was evidently more destructive than ever. But the Mexicans withstood the shock with great firmness. Soon after the action was renewed, Captain May was ordered to attack their left. He cheerfully obeyed the order, but he was unable to make much impression on the cavalry with his small force, and accordingly resumed his former position without again having an opportunity to share in the engagement. It was now nearly night, and the Mexicans resolved to make one last effort to shake the firmness of the American lines, and to silence the deadly fire of the eighteen pounders and Ringgold's battery. Accordingly, they poured in upon them almost a literal tempest of balls. Captain Page fell, mortally wounded, a cannon ball having carried away the whole of his lower jaw, and the brave

Major Ringgold had both legs nearly shot away by a ball which passed entirely through his horse. Sanguine expectations of his recovery were for a time entertained. But they were not to be realized, and on the evening of the 11th he died at Point Isabel, mourned by the army as a loss to the service and the country, not easily to be repaired.

The artillery battalion under Colonel Childs was now brought up to support the artillery on the right, when a fierce charge was made upon this part of the line by a strong body of Mexican cavalry, which continued to advance in spite of a destructive fire from our artillery. The battalion was formed into a hollow square, and calmly awaited the attack; but a severe discharge of canister from the eighteen-pounders threw them into confusion, and finally dispersed them. A heavy fire of musketry was in the meantime opened upon the square, wounding Lieutenant Luther slightly, and killing and severely wounding several soldiers. Colonel Childs, however, poured in upon them a well-directed discharge from his guns, which effectually silenced the enemy's left. But another effort was made by Arista to turn our flank, and get possession of our stores in the rear. This movement was fortunately discovered by Captain Duncan, and he was immediately ordered to hold the enemy in check until the eighth infantry could come to his assistance. This he accomplished in most gallant style, opening upon them a deadly fire before they were aware of his vicinity. Every discharge was fearfully destructive, mowing down whole ranks of the enemy. They could not long stand under this murderous fire, though they continued to advance with great firmness for a time. They were driven back in confusion, but immediately reformed

MAJOR RINGGOLD.

and again moved forward, and were again driven back in hopeless disorder, and commenced a precipitate retreat, throwing all into confusion who had yet stood firm. Thus they were driven from the field and compelled to take shelter in the chapparal. Night now put an end to the contest. Thus ended the battle of Palo Alto, after the action had continued for nearly five hours with almost uninterrupted fury. When it was ended, our soldiers sunk down wherever they chanced to be, wholly exhausted by the exertions and excitement of the day, and fell asleep with nothing but the sky above them and the earth beneath. The dragoons, however, kept watch all night, fearing an attempt would be made to surprise them by the enemy. Too much uncertainty hung over the future to allow the officers any repose. All felt that the morrow would bring forth another day of battle, and excitement, and carnage, and that the Mexicans would make another mighty effort to crown it with victory to their arms. They held a council of war, however, and after calmly considering the events of the day they had just passed, and the probabilities of the approaching contest, they unanimously resolved to move on early the next morning and give the enemy battle again, if they should be found on this side of the Rio Grande.

The force under General Taylor in this hard fought battle, but little exceeded two thousand men; while the Mexican army was, at least, six thousand strong, or about three to one against the Americans. Our loss in the engagement, was four men killed, and three officers, and thirty-seven wounded—several of the latter mortally. The loss of the Mexicans was two hundred killed and about four hundred wounded, besides the missing and desertions. It is believed, however, that their loss in killed, wounded, and missing, was but little short of one thousand men.

"Our march," says General Taylor, in his official dispatch, "was resumed the following morning. About noon, when our advance of cavalry had reached the water-hole of 'Palo Alto,' the Mexican troops were reported in our front, and were soon discovered occupying the road in force. I ordered a halt upon reaching the water, with a view to rest and refresh the men, and to form deliberately our line of battle. The Mexican line was now plainly visible across the prairie, and about three quarters of a mile distant. Their left, which was composed of a heavy force of cavalry, occupied the road, resting upon a thicket of chapparal, while masses of infantry were discovered in succession on the right, greatly outnumbering our own force.

"Our line of battle was now formed in the following order, commencing on the extreme right:—5th infantry, commanded by Lieutenant-Colonel McIntosh; Major Ringgold's artillery; 3rd infantry, commanded by Captain L. N. Morris; two eighteen-pounders, commanded by Lieutenant Churchill, 3rd artillery; 4th infantry, commanded by Major G. W. Allen; the 3rd and 4th regiments composed the Third brigade, under command of Lieutenant-Colonel Garland; and all the above corps, together with two squadrons of dragoons under Captains Ker and May, composed the right wing, under the orders of Col. Twiggs. The left was formed by the battalion of artillery commanded by Lieutenant-Colonel Childs, Captain Duncan's light artillery, and the 8th infantry, under Captain Montgomery—all forming the First brigade, under command of Lieutenant-Colonel Belknap. The train was parked near the water, under direction of Captains Crossman and Myers, and protected by Captain Ker's squadron.

"At two o'clock we took up the march by heads of columns, in the direction of the enemy—the eighteen pounder battery following the road. While the columns were advancing, Lieutenant Blake, topographical engineer, volunteered a reconnoissance of the enemy's line, which was handsomely performed, and resulted in the discovery of at least two batteries of artillery in the intervals of their cavalry and infantry. These batteries were soon opened upon us, when I ordered the columns halted and deployed into line, and the fire to be returned by all our artillery. The 8th infantry, on our extreme left, was thrown back to secure that flank. The first fires of the enemy did little execution, while our eighteen-pounders and Major Ringgold's artillery soon dispersed the cavalry which formed his left. Captain Duncan's battery, thrown forward in advance of the line, was doing good execution at this time. Captain May's squadron was now detached to support that battery, and the left of our position. The Mexican cavalry, with two pieces of artillery, were now reported to be moving through the chapparal to our right, to threaten that flank, or make a demonstration against the train. The 5th infantry was immediately detached to check this movement, and supported by Lieutenant Ridgeley, with a section of Major Ringgold's battery and Captain Walker's company of volunteers, effectually repulsed the enemy—the 5th infantry repelling a charge of lancers, and the artillery doing great execution in their ranks. The 3rd infantry was now detached to the right as a still further security to that flank, yet threatened by the enemy. Major Ringgold, with the remaining section, kept up his fire from an advanced position, and was supported by the 4th infantry.

"The grass of the prairie had been accidentally fired by our artillery, and the volumes of smoke now partially concealed the armies from each other. As the enemy's left had evidently been driven back and left the road free, the cannonade having been suspended, I ordered forward the eighteen-pounders on the road nearly to the position first occupied by the Mexican cavalry, and caused the First brigade to take up a new position still on the left of the eighteen-pounder battery. The 5th was advanced from its former position and occupied a point on the extreme right of the new line. The enemy made a change of position corresponding to our own, and after a suspension of nearly an hour the action was resumed.

"The fire of artillery was now most destructive—openings were constantly made through the enemy's ranks by our fire, and the constancy with which the Mexican infantry sustained this severe cannonade was a theme of universal remark and admiration. Captain May's squadron was detached to make a demonstration on the left of the enemy's position, and suffered severely from the fire of artillery to which it was for some time exposed. The 4th infantry, which had been ordered to support the eighteen-pounder battery, was exposed to a most galling fire of artillery, by which several men were killed and Captain Page dangerously wounded. The enemy's fire was directed against our eighteen-pounder battery, and the guns under Major Ringgold in its vicinity. The Major himself, while coolly directing the fire of his pieces, was struck by a cannon ball and mortally wounded.

"In the meantime the battalion of artillery under

CAPTAIN WALKER.

Lieutenant-Colonel Childs, had been brought up to support the artillery on our right. A strong demonstration of cavalry was now made by the enemy against this part of our line, and the column continued to advance under a severe fire from the eighteen-pounders. The battalion was instantly formed in square, and held ready to receive the charge of cavalry, but when the advancing squadrons were within close range, a deadly fire of canister from the eighteen-pounders dispersed them. A brisk fire of small-arms was now opened upon the square, by which one officer, Lieutenant Luther, 2nd artillery, was slightly wounded, but a well-directed volley from the front of the square silenced all further firing from the enemy in this quarter. It was now nearly dark, and the action was closed on the right of our line, the enemy having been completely driven back from his position, and foiled in every attempt against our line.

"While the above was going forward on our right, and under my own eye, the enemy had made a serious attempt against the left of our line. Captain Duncan instantly perceived the movement, and by the bold and brilliant manœuvring of his battery, completely repulsed several successive efforts of the enemy to advance in force upon our left flank. Supported in succession by the 8th infantry and Captain Ker's squadron of dragoons, he gallantly held the enemy at bay, and finally drove him, with immense loss, from the field. The action here and along the whole line, continued until dark, when the enemy retired into the chapparal in rear of his position. Our army bivouacked on the ground it occupied. During the afternoon the train had been moved forward about half a mile, and was parked in rear of the new position."

General Arista, in his official report of the battle, exercises the usual ingenuity of Mexican generals, in turning a disastrous defeat into a brilliant and decisive victory. The tone of his dispatch affords a remarkable contrast to the modest and unassuming account of the same battle by General Taylor. In his dispatch the Mexican commander says: "Constant in my purpose of preventing General Taylor from uniting the forces which he brought from the Fronton of Sante Isabel, with those which he left fortified opposite Matamoras, I moved this day from the Fanques del Raminero, whence I dispatched my last extraordinary courier, and took the direction of Palo Alto, as soon as my spies informed me that the enemy had left Fronton, with the determination of introducing into his fort wagons loaded with provisions and heavy artillery.

"I arrived opposite Palo Alto about one o'clock, and observed that the enemy was entering that position.

"With all my forces, I established the line of battle in a great plain, my right resting upon an elevation, and my left on a slough of difficult passage.

"Scarcely was the first cannon fired, when there arrived General D. Pedro de Ampudia, second in command, whom I had ordered to join me after having covered the points which might serve to besiege the enemy in the forts opposite Matamoras.

"The forces under my orders amounted to three thousand men, and twelve pieces of artillery; those of the invaders were three thousand, rather less than more, and were superior in artillery, since they had twenty pieces of the calibre of sixteen and eighteen pounds.

"The battle commenced so ardently, that the fire of cannon did not cease a single moment. In the course of it, the enemy wished to follow the road to Matamoras, to raise the siege of his troops; with which object he fired the grass, and formed in front of his line of battle a smoke so thick, that he succeeded in covering himself from our view, but by means of manœuvres this was twice embarrassed.

"General Taylor maintained his attack rather defensively than offensively, employing his best arm, which is artillery, protected by half of the infantry, and all of his cavalry,—keeping the remainder fortified in the ravine, about two thousand yards from the field of battle.

"I was anxious for the charge, because the fire of cannon did much damage in our ranks, and I instructed General D. Anastasio Torrejon to execute it with the greater part of the cavalry, by our left flank, with some columns of infantry, and the remainder of the cavalry.

"I was waiting the moment when that general should execute the charge, and the effect of it should begin to be seen, in order to give the impulse on the right; but he was checked by a fire of the enemy, which defended a slough that embarrassed the attack.

"Some battalions, becoming impatient by the loss they suffered, fell into disorder, demanding to advance or fall back. I immediately caused them to charge with a column of cavalry, under the command of Colonel D. Cayetano Montero; the result of this operation being that the dispersed corps repaired their fault as far as possible, marching towards the enemy, who, in consequence of his distance, was enabled to fall back upon his reserve, and night coming on, the battle was concluded,—the field remaining for our arms.

"Every suitable measure was then adopted, and the division took up a more concentrated curve in the same scene of action.

"The combat was long and bloody, which may be estimated from the calculations made by the commandant general of artillery, General D. Thomas Requena, who assures me that the enemy threw about three thousand cannon shots from two in the afternoon, when the battle commenced, until seven at night, when it terminated,—six hundred and fifty being fired on our side.

"The national arms shone forth, since they did not yield a hand's breadth of ground, notwithstanding the superiority in artillery of the enemy, who suffered much damage.

"Our troops have to lament the loss of two hundred and fifty-two men dispersed, wounded and killed,—the last worthy of national recollection and gratitude for the intrepidity with which they died fighting for the most sacred of causes.

"Will your excellency please with his note to report to his excellency the President, representing to him that I will take care to give a circumstantial account of this deed of arms; and recommending to him the good conduct of all the generals, chiefs, officers, and soldiers under my orders, for sustaining so bloody a combat, which does honor to our arms, and exhibits their discipline."

CHAPTER V.

Resaca de la Palma.—The Battle Commenced.—Character of the Mexican Troops.—May's Charge.—Capture of La Vega.—The Americans Victorious.—Lieutenant Lincoln's Heroic Conduct.—Incidents of the Engagement.—A Brave Corporal.—Colonel McIntosh.—Mexican confidence of Victory.—Taylor's Official Account.—Particulars of May's Charge.—Notice of the Battle.

Early on the morning of the 9th the enemy commenced their retreat from Palo Alto, towards Fort Brown, the cavalry being the last to leave the ground. They continued to fall back upon that post until they advanced several miles, to Resaca de la Palma, a position naturally very strong. At this point they had thrown up intrenchments and erected three batteries, so as completely to command the approach to Fort Brown. The road at the place where they had planted their batteries, crosses at right angles a ravine, which is about four rods wide, and four or five feet deep. The lowest part of it is usually filled with water, and in a wet season it forms a stagnant pond, which unites across the ridge forming the road, over which the American army had to pass. On the side of the ravine occupied by the Mexicans is a dense growth of chapparal. The enemy was formed in double line, one in the ravine, under the front bank, and the other behind the wall of chapparal. They were seven thousand strong, having been reinforced during the night, and strongly fortified, and skilfully posted. The narrow ridge of road through the ravine, already referred to, which formed the only unobstructed approach to them, was perfectly commanded by their batteries.

Soon after the enemy had withdrawn, General Taylor formed his army in line of battle and commenced his march. He moved on until he reached the edge of the chapparal, where he halted, and ordered several companies to advance and reconnoitre the enemy and ascertain their position. While they were in the performance of this duty, Lieutenant J. E. Blake, who had been on duty the whole of the night previous, and was therefore nearly exhausted, dismounted for the purpose of obtaining a few moments rest. He, unbuckled his holsters and threw them on the ground, when, from some cause, one of the pistols exploded, the ball entering his body, and producing almost immediate death.

Captain McCall, who had command of the reconnoitering forces, moved on until he reached Resaca de la Palma, when he was suddenly fired upon by one of the Mexican masked batteries, killing one of his men and wounding three others. General Taylor, upon receiving a message acquainting him with the facts, immediately ordered Lieutenant Ridgeley, with his battery, and the Third, Fourth, and Fifth infantry to engage the enemy's infantry. Captain Smith was ordered to the right and Captain McCall to the left, with instructions to bring on the engagement. Lieutenant Ridgeley immediately advanced, and when he had discovered the position of the enemy's batteries, he charged upon them at full speed, quickly followed by the Fifth regiment and a portion of the Fourth, the Third and remainder of the Fourth advancing towards the ravine on the enemy's left. In the meantime Captain McCall had gallantly attacked their right. The Eighth regiment was also now ordered to enter the engagement, which they did in gallant style, at double quick time. At the same time Lieutenant Ridgeley was hotly pressed by the enemy, but he poured in upon them such an overwhelming shower of grape and canister, that they could make no impression upon him. But for the fact of the enemy's shots going nearly all above the heads of his men, they would have been literally cut to pieces. He was supported by the Fifth regiment, under Lieutenant Colonel McIntosh; the Third regiment, under the command of Captain L. N. Morris, and the Fourth, under Major Allen, scattered by the dense chapparal, were obliged to form in the ravine. The Eighth, under the command of Captain W. R. Montgomery, with Smith's Light and other corps, faced to the right. Duncan's battery was at the edge of the ravine, but he could not use it, as the only position from which the enemy conld be engaged, without galling our troops, was in possession of Ridgeley.

The enemy fought with great valor and almost desperation. They were the best troops in Mexico; all veterans of many a hard contested field; and they seemed to have resolved upon victory or death. The contest in the ravine, therefore, was long and bloody. The Mexicans contested every inch of ground, with a bravery and determination that only the valor of American soldiers could have overcome. But the deadly discharge of artillery and musketry, and the repeated charge of our troops, was too much for flesh and blood long to endure, and they now began to waver, and at last to give way. They were finally driven from the ravine, and our troops occupied the position in it held by them at the beginning of the action. The infantry had captured one of their guns, and they frequently attempted to charge across the ravine, in the meanwhile keeping up upon our front ranks a murderous fire of artillery. But it was of no avail against the discipline and firmness of our gallant troops. They were equally resolved on victory, and had never contemplated any other result of the contest.

The enemy still retaining their strongest positions, General Taylor saw that they must be dislodged, and the batteries taken. He therefore gave orders to Captain May to take them at all events. May replied, "I will do it, sir," and immediately placing himself at the head of his dragoons, said, "men, follow me!" and dashed forward with lightning speed, his command rapidly upon his heels. As he was rushing on, he was stopped by the brave Ridgeley, who said to him, "wait, Charley, until I draw their fire," and at the same instant discharged his batteries upon the enemy. The discharge of their guns was almost simultaneously with Ridgeley's. By this great presence of mind, and noble-hearted magnanimity, he saved May from a fire that must have made dreadful slaughter amongst his men, and drew the fire upon himself. There are but few instances of equal bravery and magnanimity on record. The instant Ridgeley had thus drawn upon himself the fire of the Mexican battery, May again dashed on in advance of his command, in spite of a most destructive fire, and cleared the enemy's works at a bound, cutting down the gunners at their pieces. He was gallantly supported by his men, and the Mexicans were driven from their guns by their furious charge. They immediately rallied, however, and again got possession of them, May's command having scattered amongst the enemy. But he collected several of

COLONEL MAY.

them, and again charged the enemy. In this charge he captured General La Vega, while bravely fighting at the guns. He immediately surrendered to Captain May, and was carried to our lines in charge of Lieutenant Stevens.

But though the battery had been silenced for the time, it was not captured. The enemy re-manned their guns, and were preparing to pour their deadly fire again into our ranks. But the Fifth regiment, which had followed closely upon the heels of the dragoons, now approached the battery, and charged the enemy up to the very cannon's mouth, the enemy and our soldiers contending hand to hand for the possession of the works. The struggle was a fierce and bloody one, but the enemy were cut down at their guns, or compelled to fly, and the battery was left in possession of the Americans.

The enemy having thus been driven from their batteries, the Eighth regiment under Captain Montgomery, and the Fifth under Lieutenant-Colonel McIntosh, charged the Mexicans up the ravine, amidst a destructive fire from their right and front. Though vastly superior in numbers, the enemy were compelled to retreat after great slaughter, and were ultimately driven from the field. The battle was now nearly ended, and the victory won. In every part of the field where the contending parties met, the enemy were defeated. Whether they were only equal in numbers to the Americans, or four to one, made no difference—the result was the same. On all sides they were compelled to give way before the superior discipline, courage, and physical strength of our troops.

The further details of the action are supplied from "Our Army on the Rio Grande," the most minute and interesting account of General Taylors's operations from the time he entered Texas to the capture of Matamoras, that has been published. During the progress of the action, Lieutenant Lincoln, of the Eighth regiment, made a charge on a body of Mexicans lodged in a thicket of chapparal, who were pouring a destructive fire upon his regiment as it advanced up the road. In the midst of the conflict, he saw Lieutenant Jordan, (who had personally charged the enemy,) wounded upon the ground, with a Mexican over him, in the act of running a bayonet through his body ; Lincoln sprang forward, and the Mexican faltering, in alarm, ran his bayonet through the arm, instead of the breast of Jordan. At the same instant, Lincoln cleft his skull. This gallant officer, with his sergeant, engaged in a conflict with others of the enemy, causing them to retreat, after having slain three of them with their own hands. Lieutenant Chadbourne, also of the Eighth, after distinguishing himself for his bravery, in one of these skirmishes fell mortally wounded, at the head of his command.

The third regiment, under the command of Captain L. N. Morris, and the Fourth, under Major Allen, were conspicuous for the spirit with which they entered the contest. These two corps gallantly rivalled each other in sharing the brilliant events of the day. They fearlessly charged through the densest chapparal; and while Captain Morris, and the other officers of the Third, were overcoming what appeared to be insurmountable difficulties; to meet the enemy, the Fourth came into the ravine, opposite an intrenchment supported by a piece of artillery, that poured a most galling fire into our ranks. Captain Buchanan, being senior officer nearest the point, collected some twenty-five or thirty men, and with Lieutenant Hays and Woods charged across the lagoon, knee and waist deep in water, and after a close-quarter conflict, routed the enemy. Lieutenant Hays distinguished himself by springing forward and seizing the leading mules attached to the piece, to prevent its being driven off, while Lieutenant Woods sprang to the handspikes, and turned it in such a direction as to lock one of the wheels against a tree. A large force of the enemy's cavalry suddenly charged upon these officers, but Captain Barbour, of the third, came to the rescue, and with the point of the bayonet drove off the cavalry. Corporal Chisholm, of the Third infantry, shot the Mexican lieutenant-colonel who led the charge. As the officer fell, the corporal was seen to hand him his canteen of water, and but a moment afterwards Chisholm was lying dead on his back, with a cartridge in his hand, and the bitten-off end resting on his lips.

Buchanan's party, along with portions of the Fifth regiment, then charged on the Mexican lines. In the excitement, Lieutenant-Colonel McIntosh dashed on a wall of chapparal, although it was lined with infantry and cavalry. Under a galling fire he broke it down by repeated blows of his sword, and the weight of his horse. The instant he got through, his horse fell dead from under him; Colonel McIntosh sprang to his feet; a crowd of Mexicans, armed with muskets and lances, rushed upon him; still he gallantly defended himself. A bayonet passed through his mouth and came out below his ear; seizing the weapon, he raised his sword to cut the fiend down who held it, when another bayonet passed through and terribly shattered his arm, and another still, through his hip; borne down by superiority of force, he fell, and was literally pinned to the earth. The command of the Fifth now devolved upon Major Staniford, who conducted it with zeal and ability to the close of the engagement.

After the first charge on the enemy's lines had been made, Ridgeley was obliged to suspend his fire for fear of galling his own troops. Duncan's battery had been idle, for want of a position to act with any effect. Both batteries were now ordered across the ravine, supported by Captain C. F. Smith's light infantry, and Captain Ker's squadron of dragoons. Lieutenant Duncan came up ahead with his battery, when the Fifth was engaged with the enemy, under a heavy fire from the opposite side of the lagoon that crossed the road. Here he met Colonel McIntosh, and requested of him a party to support him, while he crossed the lagoon, and forced the enemy from their strong position. In the hurry of the moment Lieutenant Duncan did not perceive that Colonel McIntosh was wounded. The Colonel turned to Lieutenant Duncan, presenting a most terrible sight. The blood from some of his numerous wounds had clotted on his face, and he answered with difficulty, "I will give you the support you need." Lieutenant Duncan perceiving his situation, asked, with some emotion, "if he could be of any service to him?" Colonel McIntosh replied: "Yes! give me some water, and show me my regiment."

Lieutenants Woods and Hays, with a portion of the Fourth, pressed on, and came up with Leutenants Cochrane and Augur, with a few men of every regiment, when, to their surprise, they found themselves in the head-quarters of General Arista. After taking possession of it, the party still kept up the road, until reconnoitred by a Mexican officer, who was seen riding very close. He was saluted with a discharge of musketry, but he escaped unharmed. Again he was seen moving towards our party, and again he was fired upon, and again escaped. Undauntedly he moved on, held his ground, and received a volley of musketry, and most singularly he remained upon his horse, and rode off. A moment only elapsed, when he returned with a squadron of lancers, charging like a whirlwind; our soldiers delivered their fire steadily, bringing one or two to the ground, and then fell back into the chapparal. Lieutenant Cochrane remained in the open space, and received the whole charge; he nobly defended himself with his sword, but was crushed down, falling dead with seven lance wounds in his breast.

All order of battle was now lost, yet the enemy, driven from their intrenchments, and without artillery, and with their camp in our possession, still chivalrously, but unsuccessfully, disputed the onward march of our troops.

The last Mexican flag that waved over the field had struck, the tri-color of the Tampico veterans, that had so gallantly shown itself on the Palo Alto, where it was torn by our artillery, and had been defended on the Resaca de la Palma, until the regiment to which it had belonged was literally destroyed, was torn from its staff by the gallant spirit that bore it; concealing it about his person, when all hope was lost, he attempted to flee to his countrymen on the east of the Rio Grande. The poor standard-bearer, however, did not escape; rode down by our dragoons, he, with others, was taken prisoner, and the flag of the *Battallon Tampico*, hangs a trophy in our national capitol.

Both Duncan's and Ridgeley's batteries were opened on the retreating enemy, driving them from their last holds, and completely routing those who still lingered.

Cavalry and infantry were seen in confused masses, flying in every direction; many rushing towards the Rio Grande.

The camp of Arista told the perfect confidence he had in the strength of his arms. It was evident that not the least preparation had been made for a defeat—no such thought had ever been indulged in. Arista brought with him into the field an unnecessary amount of baggage. His head-quarters were just being arranged; his splendid marquee, his trunks, and private property were together, surrounded by pompously arranged walls, comprising the military wealth of the army. There were stands of small-arms, ammunition boxes, hundreds and thousands of musket ball cartridges, and nearly five hundred splendid pack-saddles; in short, almost an eastern prodigality of military equipage.

In the camp of the army were found the preparations for a great festival, no doubt to follow the expected victory. The camp-kettles were simmering over the fires, filled with savory viands, from which our troops made a plentiful evening meal. In the road were carcasses of half-skinned oxen. The hangers-on of the camp, while the battle was raging, were busy in their feast-preparing work, unconscious of danger, when, on an instant, a sudden panic must have seized them, and they fled, leaving their half-completed labors to be consummated by our own troops. Never, probably, in the history of war, had a more perfect consternation seized upon a defeated army, and seldom has one left such singularly eloquent memorials of the fact, as did the Mexicans at Resaca de la Palma.

The detailed report of this brilliant action, so glorious to the American arms, and reflecting so much honor upon our gallant army, is given below. However minutely and correctly it may have been described, the account would be imperfect without the report of the commanding officer. General Taylor seems to be everywhere and to see everything, and is therefore better prepared to give perfectly all the particulars of the engagement. He does it in this instance, as in all others, with that rare combination of modesty and good sense, and it is marked by the same beauty and elegance of style, and clearness and perspicuity of expression, that have distinguished all his dispatches:

"Early on the morning of the 9th instant, the enemy who had encamped near the field of battle of the day previous, was discovered moving by his left flank, evidently in retreat; and perhaps at the same time to gain a new position on the road to Matamoras, and there again resist our advance.

"I ordered the supply train to be strongly parked at its position, and left with it four pieces of artillery—the two eighteen-pounders which had done such good service on the previous day—and two twelve-pounders which had not been in the action. The wounded officers and men were at the same time sent back to Point Isabel. I then moved forward with the columns to the edge of the chapparal or forest, which extends to the Rio Grande, a distance of seven miles. The light companies of the first brigade, under Captain C. F. Smith, 2d artillery, and a select detachment of light troops, the whole under the the command of Captain McCall, 4th infantry, were thrown forward into the chapparal, to feel the enemy and ascertain his position. About three o'clock, I received a report from the advance, that the enemy was in position on the road, with at least two pieces of artillery. The command was immediately put in motion, and at about four o'clock I came up with Captain McCall, who reported the enemy in force in our front, occupying a ravine which intersects the road and is skirted by thickets of dense chapparal. Ridgeley's battery and the advance under Captain McCall were at once thrown forward on the road, and into the chapparal on either side, while the 5th infantry and one wing of the 4th were thrown into the forest on the left, and the 3d and the other wing of the 4th, on the right of the road. These corps were employed as skirmishers to cover the battery and engage the Mexican infantry. Captain McCall's command became at once engaged with the enemy, while the light artillery, though in a very exposed position, did great execution. The enemy had at least eight pieces of artillery, and maintained an incessant fire upon our advance.

"The action now became general, and although the enemy's infantry gave way before the steady fire and resistless progress of our own, yet his artillery was still in position to check our advance—several pieces occupying the pass across the ravine, which he had chosen for his position. Perceiving that no decisive advantage could be gained until this artillery was silenced, I ordered Captain May to charge the batteries with his squadron of dragoons. This was gallantly and effectually executed: the enemy was driven from his guns, and Gen. La Vega, who remained alone at one of the batteries, was taken prisoner. The squadron, which suffered much in this charge, not being immediately supported by infantry, could not retain possession of the artillery taken, but it was completely silenced. In the meantime, the Eighth infantry had been ordered up, and had become warmly engaged on the right of the road. This regiment and a part of the Fifth, were now ordered to charge the batteries, which was handsomely

GENERAL TAYLOR AT THE BATTLE OF RESACA DE LA PALMA

May 9th, 1846.

done, and the enemy driven from his artillery, and his position on the left of the road.

"The light companies of the First brigade, and the Third and Fourth regiments of infantry, had been deployed on the right of the road, where, at various points, they became briskly engaged with the enemy. A small party under Captain Buchanan and Lieutenants Wood and Hays, Fourth infantry, composed chiefly of men of that regiment, drove the enemy from a breastwork which he occupied, and captured a piece of artillery. An attempt to recover this piece was repelled by Captain Barbour, Third infantry. The enemy was at last completely driven from his position on the right of the road, and retreated precipitately, leaving baggage of every description. The Fourth infantry took possession of a camp where the headquarters of the Mexican general-in-chief were established. All his official correspondence was captured at this place.

"The artillery battalion (excepting the flank companies) had been ordered to guard the baggage train, which was parked some distance in rear. The battalion was now ordered up to pursue the enemy, and with the Third infantry, Captain Ker's dragoons, and Captain Duncan's battery, followed him rapidly to the river, making a number of prisoners. Great numbers of the enemy were drowned in attempting to cross the river near the town. The corps last mentioned encamped near the river; the remainder of the army on the field of battle.

"The strength of our marching force on this day, as exhibited in the annexed field report, was one hundred and seventy-three officers, and two thousand and forty-nine men—aggregate, two thousand two hundred and twenty-two. The actual number engaged with the enemy did not exceed one thousand and seven hundred. Our loss was three officers killed and twelve wounded; thirty-six men killed and seventy-one wounded. Among the officers killed, I have to regret the loss of Lieutenant Inge, second dragoons, who fell at the head of his platoon, while gallantly charging the enemy's battery; of Lieutenant Cochrane, of the Fourth, and Lieutenant Chadbourne, of the Eighth infantry, who likewise met their death in the thickest of the fight. The officers wounded were Lieutenant-Colonel Payne, inspector general; Lieutenant Dobbins, Third infantry, serving with the light infantry advance, slightly; Lieutenant-Colonel McIntosh, Fifth infantry, severely (twice); Captain Hooe, Fifth infantry, severely (right arm since amputated); Lieutenant Fowler, Fifth infantry, slightly; Captain Montgomery, Eighth infantry, slightly; Lieutenants Gates and Jordan, Eighth infantry, severely (each twice); Lieutenants Selden, Maclay, Burbank, and Morris, Eighth infantry, slightly. A statement of the killed and wounded is annexed herewith.

"I have no accurate data from which to estimate the enemy's force on this day. He is known to have been reinforced after the action of the 8th, both by cavalry and infantry, and no doubt to an extent at least equal to his loss on that day. It is probable that six thousand men were opposed to us, and in a position chosen by themselves, and strongly defended with artillery. The enemy's loss was very great. Nearly two hundred of his dead were buried by us on the day succeeding the battle. His loss in killed, wounded, and missing, in the two affairs of the 8th and 9th, is, I think, moderately estimated at one thousand men.

"Our victory has been decisive. A small force has overcome immense odds of the best troops that Mexico can furnish—veteran regiments perfectly equipped and appointed. Eight pieces of artillery, several colors and standards, a great number of prisoners, including fourteen officers, and a large amount of baggage and public property have fallen into our hands.

"The causes of victory are doubtless to be found in the superior quality of our officers and men. I have already, in former reports, paid a general tribute to the admirable conduct of the troops on both days. It now becomes my duty—and I feel it to be one of great delicacy—to notice individuals. In so extensive a field as that of the 8th, and in the dense cover where most of the action of the 9th was fought, I could not possibly be witness to more than a small portion of the operations of the various corps; and I must, therefore, depend upon the reports of subordinate commanders, which I respectfully inclose herewith.

"Colonel Twiggs, the second in command, was particularly active on both days in executing my orders, and directing the operations of the right wing. Lieutenant-Colonel McIntosh, commanding the Fifth infantry, Lieutenant-Colonel Garland, commanding the Third brigade, Lieutenant-Colonel Belknap, commanding the First brigade, Lieutenant-Colonel Childs, commanding the artillery battalion, Major Allen, Captains L. N. Morris and Montgomery, commanding respectively the Fourth, Third, and Eighth regiments of infantry, were zealous in the performance of their duties; and gave examples to their commands of cool and fearless conduct. Lieutenant-Colonel McIntosh repulsed with his regiment a charge of lancers in the action of Palo Alto, and shared with it in the honors and dangers of the following day, being twice severely wounded. Lieutenant-Colonel Belknap headed a charge of the

Eighth infantry, which resulted in driving the enemy from his guns, and leaving us in possession of that part of the field.

"Captain Duncan and Lieutenant Ridgeley deserve especial notice for the gallant and efficient manner in which they manœuvred and served their batteries. The impression made by Captain Duncan's battery upon the extreme right of the enemy's line, at the affair of Palo Alto, contributed largely to the result of the day; while the terrible fire kept up by Lieutenant Ridgeley, in the affair of the 9th, inflicted heavy losses upon the enemy. The eighteen-pounder battery, which played a conspicuous part in the action of the 8th, was admirably served by Lieutenant Churchill, Third artillery, assisted by Lieutenant Wood, topographical engineers. The charge of cavalry on the enemy's batteries on the 9th, was gallantly led by Captain May and had complete success.

"Captain McCall, Fourth infantry, rendered distinguished service with the advanced corps under his orders. Its loss, in killed and wounded, will show how closely it was engaged. I may take this occasion to say that, in two former instances, Captain McCall has rendered valuable service as a partisan officer. In this connection, I would mention the services of Captain Walker, of the Texan Rangers, who was in both affairs with his company, and who has performed very meritorious service as a spy and partisan.

"I must beg leave to refer to the reports of subordinate commanders for the names of many officers, non-commissioned officers and privates, who were distinguished for good conduct on both days. Instances of individual gallantry and personal conflict with the enemy were not wanting in the affair of the 9th, but cannot find place in a general report. The officers serving in the staffs of the different commanders, are particularly mentioned by them.

"I derived efficient aid on both days from all the officers of my staff. Captain Bliss, assistant adjutant-general, Lieutenant-Colonel Payne, inspector-general, Lieutenant Eaton, A. D. C., Captain Waggaman, commissary of subsistence, Lieutenant Scarret, engineer, and Lieutenants Blake and Meade, topographical engineers, promptly conveyed my orders to every part of the field. Lieutenant-Colonel Payne was wounded in the affair of the 9th, and I have already had occasion to report the melancholy death of Lieutenant Blake, by accident, in the interval between the two engagements. Major Craig and Lieutenant Brereton, of the ordnance department, were actively engaged in their appropriate duties, and Surgeon Craig, medical director, superintended in person the arduous service of the field-hospitals. I take this occasion to mention generally the devotion to duty of the medical staff of the army, who have been untiring in their exertions both in the field and in the hospitals, to alleviate the sufferings of the wounded of both armies. Captains Crossman and Myres of the quartermaster's department, who had charge of the heavy supply-train at both engagements, conducted it in a most satisfactory manner, and finally brought it up without the smallest loss, to its destination.

"I inclose an inventory of the Mexican property captured on the field, and also a sketch of the field of 'Resaca de la Palma,' and of the route from Point Isabel, made by my aide-de-camp, Lieutenant Eaton. One regimental color, (battalion of Tampico,) and many standards and guidons of cavalry were taken at the affair of the 9th. I would be pleased to receive your instructions as to the disposition to be made of these trophies—whether they shall be sent to Washington, &c."

There is no incident connected with this brilliant action that has created so much admiration throughout the country, and which, in reality, displayed such daring courage, as the charge of Captain May upon the Mexican batteries. Though this bold and hazardous achievement has already been incidentally referred to, it is believed the following more detailed account, by an eye witness and actor in the charge, will possess interest. It is by Sergeant Milton, an officer of May's dragoons:

"At Pálo Alto," says he, "I took my rank in the troop as second sergeant, and while upon the field my horse was wounded in the jaw by a grape-shot, which disabled him for service. While he was plunging in agony I dismounted, and the quick eye of Captain May observed me as I alighted from my horse. He inquired if I was hurt. I answered no—that my horse was the sufferer. 'I am glad it is not yourself,' replied he; 'there is another,' (pointing at the same time to a steed without a rider, which was standing with dilated eye, gazing at the strife,) 'mount him.' I approached the horse, and he stood still until I put my hand upon the rein and patted his neck, when he rubbed his head alongside of me, as if pleased that some human being was about to become his companion in the affray. He was a noble bay, which had, with a number of others, been purchased for the troop in St. Louis. I bestrode him, and we passed through the first day unharmed.

"On the second day, at Resaca de la Palma, our troop stood anxiously waiting for the signal to be given, and never had I looked upon men on whose countenances were more clearly expressed a fixed determination to win. The lips of some were pale with excitement, and their eyes wore that fixed expression which betokens mischief; others, with shut teeth, would quietly laugh, and catch a tighter grip of the rein, or seat themselves with care and firmness in the saddle, while quiet words of confidence and encouragement were passed from each to his neighbor. All at once Captain May rode to the front of his troop—every rein and sabre was tightly grasped. Raising himself and pointing at the battery, he shouted, 'Men, *follow!*' There was now a clattering of hoofs and a rattling of sabre sheaths—the fire of the enemy's guns was partly drawn by Lieutenant Ridgeley, and the next moment we were sweeping like the wind up the ravine. I was in a squad of about nine men, who were separated by a shower of grape from the battery, and we were in advance, May leading. He turned his horse opposite the breastwork, in front of the guns, and with another shout 'to follow,' leaped over them. Several of the horses did follow, but mine, being new and not well trained, refused; two others balked, and their riders started down the ravine to turn the breastwork where the rest of the troop had entered. I made another attempt to clear the guns with my horse, turning him around—feeling all the time secure at thinking the guns discharged—I put his head towards them and gave him spur, but he again balked; so turning his head down the ravine, I too started to ride round the breastwork.

"As I came down a lancer dashed at me with lance in rest. With my sabre I parried his thrust, only receiving a slight flesh-wound from its point in the arm, which felt at the time like the prick of a pin. The lancer turned and fled; at that moment a ball passed through my horse on the left side and shattered my right side. The shot killed the horse instantly, and he fell upon my left leg, fastening me by his weight to the earth. There I lay, right in the midst of the action, where carnage was riding riot, and every moment the shot, from our own and the Mexican guns, tearing up the earth around me. I tried to raise my horse so as to extricate my leg, but I had already grown so weak with my wound that I was unable, and from the mere attempt, I fell back exhausted. To add to my horror, a horse, who was careering about, riderless, within a few yards of me, received a wound, and he commenced struggling and rearing with pain. Two or three times, he came near falling on me, but at length, with a scream of agony and a bound, he fell dead—his body touching my own fallen steed. What I had been in momentary dread of now occurred—my wounded limb, which was lying across the horse, received another ball in the ankle.

"I now felt disposed to give up; and, exhausted through pain and excitement, a film gathered over my eyes, which I thought was the precursor of dissolution From this hopeless state I was aroused by a wounded Mexican, calling out to me, '*Bueno Americano,*' and turning my eyes towards the spot, I saw that he was holding a certificate and calling to me. The tide of action now rolled away from me, and hope again sprung up. The Mexican uniforms began to disappear from the chapparal, and squadrons of our troops passed in sight, apparently in pursuit. While I was thus nursing the prospect of escape, I beheld, not far from me, a villanous-looking ranchero, armed with an American sergeant's short sword, dispatching a wounded American soldier, whose body he robbed—the next he came to was a Mexican, whom he served the same way, and thus I looked on while he murderously slew four. I drew an undischarged pistol from my holsters, and, laying myself along my horse's neck, watched him, expecting to be the next victim; but something frightened him from his vulture-like business, and he fled in another direction. I need not say that had he visited me I should have taken one more shot at the enemy, and would have died content, had I succeeded in making such an assassin bite the dust. Two hours after, I had the pleasure of shaking some of my comrades by the hand, who were picking up the wounded. They lifted my Mexican friend, too, and I am pleased to say he, as well as myself, live to fight over again the sanguine fray of *Resaca de la Palma*."

The splendid victories of Palo Alto and Resaca de la Palma were received with unbounded enthusiasm in every part of the Union. Fought against such overwhelming odds as they were, they were looked upon, not only by military men in this country, but by competent and not over partial judges in Europe, as evincing the very highest order of military genius in the commander-in-chief, and great courage and discipline in his soldiers. No actions, in modern times, were ever fought under such disadvantages of numbers and position, as those under which General Taylor labored in these two engagements, with such decisive results. The following notice of these actions, from a gentleman formerly attached to the army, will give a correct view of the character of the victories, besides possessing interest to all classes of readers:

"General Taylor, in his peculiarly modest manner,

says: 'It is probable that six thousand men were opposed to us, and in a position selected by themselves, and strongly defended with artillery.' The whole tenor of the general's dispatches, proves an anxious desire not to overrate the numbers opposed to him or the character of his victories; and the concurrent testimony of the officers of both armies, leaves no question that, on the 9th of May, the enemy had actually engaged upwards of seven thousand troops, or more than *four times* the number opposed to them; and it is equally certain, that their loss greatly exceeded in killed, wounded and missing, one thousand. General Taylor accounts for four hundred buried by our troops in the two actions; and Colonel Twiggs in a letter now before us says, 'we found in the hospitals at Matamoras three hundred and eighty-two wounded soldiers and several officers, and very many wounded accompanied the retreating army.' This, it must be borne in mind, was on the 18th of May—nine days after the battle; and an officer writes that the number buried at Matamoras between the 9th and 18th must have been several hundred. Our conviction is, that in the two engagements the enemy's loss was nearer *two* than *one* thousand; and this fact is very material, as demonstrating the character of the Mexican troops, and proving that an army seldom fought better. They did not retreat on the night of the 8th, nor even on the 9th, until at least *one-seventh* of their whole army had been either killed or wounded; or, in other words, until our army had rendered *hors du combat* a number exceeding one half of its whole force.

"These facts prove that the Mexicans fought bravely. It is admitted on all hands that they were admirably disciplined, the flower of the Mexican army—and composed of officers and men who had been engaged in battle after battle, and had nobly earned for themselves the title of *veterans.* This army, commanded, as has been said, by one of the most gallant and accomplished artillery officers of the age, (Arista,) selected its position, and arranged at leisure its line of defence, composed of three batteries of artillery, supported by five thousand infantry and two thousand cavalry—whose boast is, that they are the best cavalry in the world; and that they are brave, daring, and the best horsemen on the continent is fully admitted. Thus posted, this army is assailed by the American army only *one-fourth* as strong. General Taylor reports that its artillery, with the exception of Ringgold's and Duncan's eight pieces of light artillery, was parked with his immense baggage train and provisions a great distance in the rear, and was only employed in pursuing the enemy after he had been completely routed. Thus then, the naked fact is presented to the consideration of the country, that our army attacked the Mexicans 'strongly posted in a position selected by themselves.' The forces thus posted and assailed, were composed of veterans, disciplined troops, *four times* as numerous as their assailants, with a heavier train of artillery, and nearly five times as many cavalry! They fought bravely for three hours; lost *one-seventh* of their whole number; and then were literally dispersed by the *bayonets* of our troops—throwing their muskets at our men in the spirit of desperation, swearing that they were devils incarnate!

"Such was the battle of Resaca de la Palma, and such, too, was that of Palo Alto on the day preceding it. To judge of this achievement and compare it with European battles, we need only ask ourselves, on what occasion have eighty thousand disciplined troops strongly posted, in a position selected by themselves, been driven from that position, routed and cut to pieces, by twenty thousand? When and where did any army thus conquer, rout and completely disperse, *four times its number* of brave and disciplined troops, who fought in a manner which, under ordinary circumstances, entitled them to victory? When such affairs can be found in modern history, we will yield to them the palm. But we know that there are no such battles on record; and we desire to impress upon our countrymen, that our little army, under General Taylor, has achieved for itself a reputation, such as no other army has ever won in modern times, and the scene of which will hereafter be referred to as another Thermopylæ.

"Now a few words as to the causes which produced these two victories. We said on the 12th of May, when apprehensions were very general for the fate of our army, we felt very certain, that before that day, General Taylor had met and dispersed the entire force of the enemy, *if it was not more than four times as great as his own!* We said that this opinion was based upon a knowledge, that no disciplined troops ever yet abandoned their officers; that we knew our old comrades well, knew of what material they were composed—what West Point had made them—and that they would never yield or retreat. We knew that every officer in that little army was prepared for victory or death; and that such being the case, and knowing their men were disciplined and would certainly stand by them, we felt that victory was inevitable, unless the opposing force was so great as to forbid its possibility; in which case our whole army would be cut to pieces—selling their lives dearly, but never yielding. And such, too, would have been their conduct, and such the result of this affair, if the opposing force had been English instead of Mexican.

"To this gallantry and determination on the part of our officers, we are indebted for the glorious achievements of the 8th and 9th of May; and an examination into the killed and wounded, very certainly demonstrates this fact. When in order of battle, the officers are always posted with a view to their greater security, as they are required to conduct the battle. Thus the company officers are immediately in the rear of their men in line of battle, and the field and staff, still further in the rear; and it is admitted to be a sound calculation, that when the proportion of officers to the rank and file is as one to twenty, the proportion of killed and wounded should be one officer to every forty of the rank and file, owing to the greater security of their position, intended to preserve their lives. Now let us apply this calculation to the battle of Resaca de la Palma.

"In that ever memorable affair, the proportion of officers to the rank and file, was as one to thirteen; and therefore, according to European calculation, the proportion of killed and wounded, should have been one to twenty-six. Now what are the facts? The total of killed and wounded is one hundred and twenty-two, of whom fifteen were commissioned officers, or one out of every eight!

"Here, in a few words, the country has the means of determining how it was that seventeen hundred American troops drove from their selected position, defeated and utterly routed, four times their number of disciplined Mexican cavalry, artillery, and infantry! Here is the true cause of the victories of the 8th and

9th of May, being the most wonderful in the history of modern warfare. Our officers fought in front of their men. They literally led them to the cannon's mouth; and as the history of these battles proves, when their swords were useless, threw them away, picked up the muskets and accoutrements of those who had fallen, and with these, set their men an example of coolness and daring which made every private in the little army feel himself a hero. When officers thus lead their men up to the very mouths of the enemy's cannon; when sword in hand, or with the bayonet, they drive the enemy from their guns, and then themselves perform the work of gunners; when for hours, as was the case in our flying artillery, the officers helped work the guns, and in some cases did the duty of three privates—victory is certain—inevitable.

"Such was the character of the battles of the 8th and 9th May—such the manner in which they were won—and such the conduct of such officers. Under such circumstances, our whole army might have been destroyed; but if not, then was victory absolutely certain. We care not how exalted the character of the troops opposed to them, or to what nation they belonged, in this, their first fight after years of peace and the taunts of members of Congress, it was morally and physically impossible to resist them. Honor—unfading and perpetual honor—to General Taylor, the gallant officers who so nobly sustained him, and to the army of heroes they led to victory on the 8th and 9th of May, 1846; and most fortunate for them and for the country was it, that we had no undisciplined volunteers or militia in those battles. We doubt not their courage; but no undisciplined troops could have fought those fights. It would have been morally impossible for any such to have withstood the fire of the enemy on those days and do what was required of our soldiers and officers; and had there been any faltering—had a single battalion given way, as they most assuredly would—the enemy would have been encouraged to persevere, and our whole army might have been annihilated and cut to pieces. Never was the value of disciplined men more triumphantly demonstrated than on these glorious occasions; and since we have learned that General Taylor compels the volunteers with him to receive six hours' drilling per day, and relieves them from all other duties, to make soldiers of them, we venture to predict that they, too, when they meet the enemy, will add to the reputation of our arms. 'Rough and Ready' will first make them soldiers, and then win victories with them."

The London Herald remarks: "The proceedings of the soldiers under General Taylor have been such as to do honor to the Republic. The little army, amount-to but a handful of men, at a distance of thousands of miles from any available succor, has defended itself against superior numbers, and at length has crossed the Rio Grande, and took possession of Matamoras, almost in sight of an opposing enemy—an exploit which Napoleon has pronounced to be the *perfection of generalship.*"

It is not easy to imagine the painful solicitude and anxiety that prevailed at Fort Brown during the actions of the 8th and 9th. Although within sound of the firing, the result of the contest was, of course, for many hours in doubt, however strong their confidence was that victory would, in the end, crown the American arms. But if they were in painful doubt as to the fate of the contest in which they knew their brothers in arms were engaged, without being able to aid them in the struggle, they were left in comparative quiet by the Mexicans during the memorable two days, and had time to repair the damages done to the fort by the bombardment to which they had so long been subject; and, accordingly, on the morning of the 9th, their first act was to raise the national flag. The history of the events during the action are resumed from "Our Army on the Rio Grande." On the 8th, continues this work, the halyards had become unrigged, at a time when the firing from the enemy was too intense to establish them, the staff at that time being outside of the fort. To meet this difficulty, the regimental colors were raised on a temporary substitute, erected on the parapets. An officer of the Seventh succeeded in lowering the topmast of the staff, and rigging the halyards. While engaged in this patriotic duty, the enemy opened on him from all their batteries, with round shot and shell, amidst which he coolly labored for fifteen or twenty minutes. Finding he was not strong enough to elevate the topmast to its proper place, he lashed it in its position, and gave the stars and stripes to the breeze.

At 10 o'clock, a sergeant and ten men went out, and set fire to the rancho, known by Arista's dispatches as the *Fanques del Raminero*, the buildings of which had been successively occupied by our own and the enemy's pickets. This act brought forth a heavy discharge of shell, canister, and round shot, which continued at intervals for about four hours.

Major Brown, since his wound had lingered on, his friends bestowing on him every attention that the circumstances would admit: he bore his sufferings with the greatest fortitude, and whenever he spoke, he urged his men to do their duty, and never surrender the fort. It was necessary that he should be placed in one of the bomb-proofs, to protect him from the missiles of the enemy: the weather was exceedingly warm, and the air in the bomb-proof necessarily close; this circumstance perhaps, joined with the aggravated nature of his wounds, hastened his death. He gradually sunk, and at two o'clock peacefully breathed his last. At the time of his death, everything around the fort was perfectly still; the soldiers around the dying man seemed scarcely to breathe, lest they should intrude upon his parting spirit; nor was the silence broken, until Ridgeley opened his batteries upon *Resaca de la Palma.*

No language can describe the intense interest with which the raging battle was listened to: each man was at his post, and every booming gun called forth an almost agonizing interest to learn its nationality and effects. Meanwhile the bombardment opened simultaneously with the firing on the field, and continued to increase with unprecedented severity; but it was not to the batteries of the Mexicans that attention was directed. Our eighteen-pounders were occasionally fired, to let General Taylor know that all was still well in the fort. The firing on the battle-field was now growing less and less powerful, and the discharges were becoming irregular. "They have charged on the guns!' shouted one of the officers; another, and another was silenced. "They have carried them!" shouted another in uncontrollable ecstasy. All cannonading ceased; volleys of musketry were next heard, then all was still. How eloquently the silence spoke of the hand-to-hand conflict, and how the blood in the hearts of these brave men went and came, from excitement to be engaged in it! The victorious result of our arms was now almost certain. General Taylor and his brave men would either conquer or die. No bells were now ringing in Matamoras, and the noisy music, that was wont to belabor the air, had been silenced since the evening of the 8th. This, to the heroes of the fort, was full of meaning, and the tale was soon told. At a little before six, a confused rush of cavalry and straggling infantry towards the Rio Grande, announced the victory of the Americans, at sight of which, an officer of the Seventh jumped upon the parapet, beside the regimental flag-staff, and gave three cheers, which were responded to so loudly and heartily by all in the fort, that they silenced the enemy's batteries, for from that moment they ceased firing. The news had reached Matamoras that to Mexico the day was lost.

The distance from Resaca de la Palma to the river, is about four miles. Beyond the battle-ground the road forks, leading to both the upper and lower ferries, between which is situated Fort Brown. The country here is more broken, and the chapparal of stronger and denser growth than in the interior. Into these intricate thickets a majority of the Mexicans fled after the rout became general; hundreds and thousands of troops here buried themselves, waiting for the veil of night to aid them in their escape. Along the road, however, great numbers swept, "fear lending them wings." In this flight the slightly wounded infantry fell exhausted; horses that had been shot, but able to maintain their feet until put at full speed, rolled on the earth, carrying their riders with them. The soldiers stripped themselves of every encumbrance; they threw away their muskets, cartridge-boxes, their military cloaks, with everything calculated to retard their speed, plainly marking their route by the abandoned articles. Squadrons of cavalry, finding their movements impeded by the infantry, rode over, without scruple, those whom the fate of war had spared. Our troops pursued; but their arms lost their force when directed against troops of defenceless beings, or individuals fleeing before a victorious foe.

One of the "eighteens" in the fort was now turned towards the upper ferry, sending a shower of grape among the fleeing hundreds. As our pursuing columns debouched from the chapparal that surrounds Fort Brown, and saw the flag of our country still waving in triumph from its ramparts, they raised to the glory of its defenders, a shout that made the welkin ring, and it was sent back from the fort until cheer answering cheer, reverberated along the valley of the Rio Grande. The want of a sufficient number of dragoons made it impossible immediately to extend our lines so as to cut off the enemy's retreat, and General Taylor, deficient in means to cross the river with rapidity and force, had made no previous arrangements to attempt so desirable a consummation of his victory. With the approach of night all offensive measures on our part ceased.

A part of our pursuing troops, including May's command, having drunk of the water of the Rio Grande, fell back to the battle-ground, where they, with the main army, bivouacked for the night. Duncan's and Ridgeley's commands, Lieutenant-Colone Childs' battalion, Captain Ker's dragoons, together with Captain C. F. Smith's command, bivouacked on the banks of the river, many upon the same ground they had left nine days before.

Throughout both battles, the Mexicans had kept up

a constant communication with Matamoras by means of a secret crossing above the upper ferry. By this they had sent over their wounded, and brought over their reinforcements as the contest thickened. They forced the poor wretches into sacks slung across the backs of mules, and thus the agony of their wounds increasing at every step, they were conveyed to that city they had hoped to enter so proudly as victors.

When Captain May made his charge, many of the soldiers in the rear of the Mexican army abandoned their ranks and fled; and the rancheros, who had hung about as vultures waiting for prey, finding that our train was not likely to fall into their hands, rushed into the camp of their own countrymen, robbed it of whatever loose valuables they could find, then scattered over the country and disappeared. Colonel Curasco, the "bull-dog," so called, of the Mexican army, was the first officer that fled. Early in the contest he crossed to the east of the Rio Grande, and secreted himself in the suburbs of the town. After our troops charged, and took the batteries, General Ampudia also sought safety in flight, and was the first man that appeared in Matamoras after the defeat of the army. Mad with terror, and exhausted by his narrow escape from being drowned while crossing the river, he entered the *Plaza*, and circled it several times unconscious of what he was doing, until his senses were recalled by his wondering countrymen, who learned Arista's total defeat, as Ampudia exclaimed, "All is lost!"

At their secret crossing the Mexicans had but one flat, which was entirely insufficient for the numbers who now, in terror, sought the river. While the flat swarmed with infantry, the cavalry would charge, and, filling the flat, drive the wretches who had occupied it into the river. The water was covered with the miserable beings who, confused and desperate, plunged about in the waves, calling on God to help them, or venting their impotent maledictions upon those who had forced them to a watery grave. They sunk by scores, clutching each other in the agonies of death; and the "mad river" fairly boiled with the expiring breath of those who had sunken under its dark wave!

In the midst of the panic Father Leary arrived at the bank, and by his presence restored order, in a certain degree, among the fugitives. He took his place on the flat, already crowded with troops. It was about shoving off, when down the bank swept a flying column of cavalry. Goaded by their riders, the steeds madly leaped into the boats, crushing to death scores of their victims, and driving the remainder into the river; the holy father raised his crucifix above his head, muttered an ejaculatory prayer, and disappeared with the mass of his fellow-beings under the waves.

Nothing could exceed the consternation that reigned in Matamoras on the night of the 9th. Between four and five thousand lawless soldiers were wandering, panic struck, about the streets. The chagrined and discomfited officers, formed into cabals, and speculated upon the causes of their inglorious defeat. Meanwhile, Ampudia was endeavoring to prove his own bravery by secretly denouncing Arista, and declaring, that, had he been commander-in-chief, he would have swept the Americans from off the face of the earth.

The night was made hideous by the constant arrival of the wounded in sacks; many yelled like fiends, as the rough carriage, and contracted form, started afresh their bleeding wounds; others were found dead in their sacks, having been drowned while crossing the river on swimming mules. The women of the city rushed to the ball-rooms, and tore down the festoons prepared for the great festival, to be given in honor of their victorious arms. They tore off and stamped upon their gay apparel, and mingled their cries of wild despair with those of the wounded.

The more substantial citizens hurriedly gathered together their effects and fled into the country; many of these fell by the hands of unorganized troops, and their property was divided among the murderers. Hundreds of soldiers were scattered over the country, who pillaged all within their reach, and attacked the defenceless that came in their way. Social, civil, and military order were scattered to the winds,—dark crime, and unbridled passion rioted in the confusion that followed this terrible defeat.

General Taylor's first care, after having the wounds of the living, both American and Mexican, properly attended to, was to perform the last sad rites for the dead of the two armies. His humanity to the enemy on the occasion reflects even more honor upon him than his coolness, courage and skill in battle. The same care was shown by him in every instance, for the suffering Mexican as for the American soldier. In the retreat the Mexican generals left all their dead and most of their wounded on the field of battle, either from confidence in the humane character of General Taylor, or out of a naturally cruel disposition; probably from a mingling of both considerations. They did not rely in vain upon the American commander.

Soon after the engagement an exchange of prisoners had been proposed by General Arista, to which General Taylor cheerfully assented. The American prisoners at Matamoras were, accordingly, taken across the river on the 11th, and exchanged, man for man, for Mexican prisoners of the same rank. Amongst the Americans exchanged, were Captains Thornton and Hardee, and Lieutenant Lane. On the morning of the same day General Taylor started for Point Isabel, for the purpose of securing a communication with Commodore Conner. Inmediately upon his arrival at Point Isabel, they had an interview which is thus humorously described in the work so often before quoted:—

The singular simplicity that marks General Taylor's personal appearance and habits, has become a subject of universal fame. It is curious that a soldier, so eminent in all the qualities of discipline, should be so citizen-looking in his own appearance. Commodore Conner, on the contrary, is an officer that is not only strict in his dress, but has an extra nicety about it. He appears in full and splendid uniform on all public occasions, being the exact contrast, in this particular, of General Taylor.

At the proper time, Commodore Conner sent word to General Taylor, that he would come on shore to pay him a visit of ceremony. This put "Old Rough and Ready" into a tremendous excitement. If Commodore Conner had quietly come up to his tent, and given him a sailor's grip, and sat down on a camp-chest, and talked over matters in an old-fashioned way, General Taylor would have been prepared; but to have the most carefully dressed officer in our navy, commanding the finest fleet, come in full uniform—surrounded by all the glittering pomp of splendid equipments—to pay a visit of ceremony, was more than General Taylor had, without some effort, nerve to go through with; but, ever equal to all emergencies, he determined to compliment Commodore Conner, and through him the navy, *by appearing in full uniform,* a thing his officers, associated with him for years, had never witnessed.

In the meanwhile, Commodore Conner was cogitating over the most proper way to compliment General Taylor. Having heard of his peculiar disregard of military dress, he concluded he would make the visit in a manner comporting to General Taylor's habits, and consequently equipped himself in plain white drilling, and, unattended, came ashore.

The moment General Taylor heard that Commodore Conner had landed, he abandoned some heavy work he was personally attending to about the camp, and precipitately rushed into his tent, delved at the bottom of an old chest, and pulled out a uniform coat, that had peacefully slumbered for years in undisturbed quietude, slipped himself into it, in his haste fastening it so that one side of the standing collar was three button-holes above the other, and sat himself down as uncomfortably as can well be imagined. With quiet step, and unattended, Commodore Conner presented himself at General Taylor's tent. The noble representatives of the army and navy shook hands, both in exceeding astonishment at each other's personal appearance.

The wags of the army say that the above contains the only *authentic* account of General Taylor's ever being "headed," and that since that time, he has taken to linen roundabouts of the largest dimensions with more pertinacity than ever.

COMMODORE CONNER.

CHAPTER VI.

Barita Captured.—Surrender of Matamoras.—General Taylor in Matamoras.—A Treacherous Mexican Official.—Pursuit of Arista's Army.—Some of the Horrors of War.—Sad End to Dreams of Mexican Glory.—General Taylor Reinforced.—His March to Monterey, and arrival there.—Strength of the City.—The Preparations for its defence.—Attacked by the Americans.—Stormed.—Capitulation and Terms.—Gallant Conduct of the American Officers and Soldiers.—Comparative Strength of the two Forces.—American Loss in the Attack.

Having arranged with Commodore Conner the plan of an attack on Barita, a small village near the mouth of the Rio Grande, a force consisting of four companies of United States troops, under Lieutenant-Colonel Wilson, First infantry, two companies of Louisiana volunteers, under Captains Stockton and Tobin, and one company of Alabama volunteers, under General Desha, were detached to capture that place. On the 15th of May, the command landed at Brazos and immediately took up their march, a portion of Commodore Conner's fleet co-operating with the land-force. There being no resistance on the part of the Mexicans, the place was taken possession of by the American troops. The inhabitants fled in affright, leaving everything at the mercy of the captors, upon their first approach. The town contains a custom-house, but was only important as a resting place for such of our forces as were destined for Matamoras.

On the evening of the 14th of May, General Taylor reached his camp from Point Isabel, and determined on an immediate attack upon Matamoras, or at latest by the next day. His preparations for the attack, however, were not completed until the 17th. But on the morning of that day everything was ready, Colonel Wilson having been ordered to march from Barita, so as to reach Matamoras at the same time General Taylor should make his demonstration against the city.

Orders had been given to Colonel Twiggs to cross, when General Taylor was waited on by the Mexican general, Reguena, empowered by General Arista to treat for an armistice, until the two governments finally settled the difficulties pending. This cunning, on the part of the Mexican chief, was too apparent to General Taylor; he was aware that Matamoras was filled with the munitions of war, and time was only wanted to move them off. General Taylor replied to General Reguena, that an armistice could not be granted; he recapitulated the circumstances of the preceding month, when he had himself proposed an armistice, which General Ampudia had declined. He stated that he was receiving large reinforcements—that he would not then suspend hostilities which he had not invited nor provoked; he also said that the possession of Matamoras was a "sine qua non," and that the American troops would occupy the city, at the same time giving to General Arista and his forces leave to withdraw from the town, leaving behind the public property of every description. General Taylor remarked, that "Generals Ampudia and Arista had promised that the war should be conducted agreeably to the usage of civilized nations, and yet the Mexican forces had, in the battles of the 8th and 9th, stripped our dead, and mutilated their bodies." General Reguena replied, "that the *women* (!) and rancheros did it, and that they could not be controlled." General Taylor said he would come over to Matamoras, and control such people for them.

General Reguena then left General Taylor, pledging himself that at three o'clock that evening he would come over with an answer from General Arista. General Taylor, accordingly, for the time, suspended his preparations for crossing. The answer promised by Reguena to be delivered to General Taylor, *positively* at three o'clock, did not come. General Taylor immediately ordered preparations to be made for crossing the Rio Grande; parties were sent up and down the river to secure all the boats that could be seen on either side. That night, just after dark, the army moved up the river, and encamped opposite the contemplated crossing place.

On the morning of the 18th, Captain Bliss, assistant adjutant-general of the "Army of Occupation," Major Craig, Captain Miles, and Lieutenant Britton, appeared on the banks of the Rio Grande, and sounded a parley. Lieutenant Britton then crossed the river with a white flag, and met a deputation of citizens from the *prefect,* who was the official civil representative of the city. The deputation wished to know the cause of the parley? Lieutenant Britton replied, that Captain Bliss, aid to the commanding general, wished to see the *prefect* in person, or whoever was the commanding officer of the city, as he had an official communication for him from his chief. The deputation crossed the river with Lieutenant Britton, met Captain Bliss, and invited the American deputation to Matamoras. They immediately crossed over, and met the *prefect* in his office, which was situated on the northwest side of the Plaza. Cap tain Bliss then delivered to the *prefect* a letter from General Taylor, which *demanded a surrender of the town and all the public stores therein,* stating, at the same time, that his general had commanded him to say that the rights of individuals should be protected, that their religion should be respected, and that their courts of law and justice should proceed as they had done under the Mexican government, unless interfering with the rights of our government, and the necessary operations of the commanding general. Captain Bliss asked the *prefect* to answer in positive terms, whether he could return and report to his general that the town would be given up without a blow, or whether it would be necessary to carry it at the point of the sword, as in either emergency, General Taylor was determined to have it. The *prefect* then answered, "General Taylor can march his troops into the city at any hour that may suit his convenience." Captain Bliss then said, "here let the interview terminate."

While this conversation was going on, our army was crossing above the city. The east bank was defended by two eighteen-pounders, and the three batteries of our artillery. Colonel Twiggs ordered the regimental bands to strike up Yankee Doodle. The light companies of all battalions first went over, followed by the volunteer and regular cavalry. Lieutenant Hays, of the Fourth infantry, and ten select men, with Captain Walker, of the Rangers, first crossed the river, with orders to ascertain and report the number and position of the enemy, if near the river. Immediately after Lieutenant Hays had gone over, the flank companies of the Third, Fourth, and Fifth infantry, were thrown across, commanded by Captain Buchanan and Captain Larned. These commands were followed by Captain

Smith, of the Artillery battalion, with two companies, and also by Captain Ker's squadron of dragoons. After this force had crossed, Ridgeley's artillery was dismounted, and taken over in parts. In the meantime, the infantry already over had taken possession of a strong place, to be ready for an attack. In the midst of these busy operations, Captain Bliss arrived, and informed General Taylor of his interview with the *prefect,* and of the unconditional surrender of the town. General Taylor immediately ordered that portion of the American forces that had not crossed the river, to return to Fort Brown and cross there. Captain Ker, of the Dragoons, passed below where the troops were crossing, and raised upon the walls of Fort Parades, *the star-spangled banner*, unfolding it in proud defiance upon the west side of the Rio Grande.

The different regiments already on the west side of the Rio Grande were marched to their respective places of encampment, without noise or disorder, save when the flag of our country was unexpectedly seen waving from Fort Parades; discipline then gave way to feeling, and nine hearty cheers rent the air, and announced the occupation of Matamoras by American troops. That evening a small guard was established in Matamoras, to keep the peace. No troops, except under command, visited it that night. The Matamorians slept securely under the protection of the American government, a boon ever denied them by their own. Upon inquiry, it became evident that General Reguena had been sent over to General Taylor merely to gain time; that, even while he was negotiating for the surrender of the city, Arista's troops were throwing the public stores into the river, burying pieces of artillery in wells, and concealing other portions of the public stores in out-of-the way places about the city. Arista commenced his retreat on the evening that General Reguena promised to bring a message from him to General Taylor, taking with him two pieces of artillery, and over four thousand men, leaving behind his sick and wounded.

A gloom was thrown over the brilliant events of this day by a most unfortunate accident; Lieutenant George Stevens, a graduate of West Point in 1843, and a most promising officer in the second dragoons, was swept by the swift current from his horse, while crossing the river at the head of his command. He had distinguished himself on the brilliant days of the 8th and 9th, and his untimely death was universally lamented. His friends, two days after he was drowned, had the melancholy satisfaction of recovering his body, and giving it the ceremonies of a soldier's burial within the walls of Fort Brown, beside the gallant hero that gave it his name.

Immediately upon taking possession of Matamoras our troops were distributed so as to occupy the upper and lower suburbs of the town, a small guard only being stationed in the city itself. Colonel Twiggs' command was stationed above the city along the banks of the river, his own head-quarters occupying a romantic spot directly on its brink. General Worth's command was located in the bend of the river below, having a fine view from his tent, and Lieutenant-Colonel Belknap's, of the surrounding country.

Directly opposite Colonel Belknap's, were to be seen a few torn tents, and a number of wiry-looking horses. They marked the head-quarters of Captain Walker, of the Rangers. From Colonel Twiggs' tent you could see the volunteer regiments stretching away west almost as far as the eye could reach, centering around the

Fanques del Raminero, and then scattering off in little groups. The Seventh regiment nestled beneath the walls of Fort Brown, which they had so nobly defended. General Taylor found a few trees that appeared to be higher than their neighbors, under which he pitched his "head-quarters;" they could only be recognized from the tents about them by their disposition—they were arranged for shade and not with military precision.

Colonel Twiggs was appointed "Governor of the Town," and to his especial care was intrusted the taking possession of the military stores left by the Mexican Army. Don Jose Cardenas, the *prefect* of Matamoras at the time General Taylor took possession, was distinguished among his fellow-citizens for oppression, and for his hatred to foreigners. In surrendering the city the *prefect's* only care was to know if he could retain his office. He never stipulated for any privileges for the citizens, or seemed in any way to think of their interests. Immediately upon Colonel Twiggs taking command, he sent for this notable Cardenas, and asked him for an inventory of the public property. He stated, positively, that he knew of none, and persisted in declaring that none was left by the Mexican forces wher they evacuated the city. Colonel Twiggs dismissed him, and entering the city, with information obtained from other quarters, soon began to find vast quantities of military stores, in almost all of the out-of-the-way places about the *Plaza*.

This outrageous trifling on the part of the *prefect* Colonel Twiggs was determined to notice. Accordingly he waited upon him the following morning at his office, to give the gentleman what is denominated a "plain talk." The colonel labored under one difficulty—eloquent himself, it was a great drawback to have it marred by an indifferent translator. Fortunately, an American citizen by the name of Dugden, a very intelligent gentleman of Matamoras, and an object of the prefect's *special* oppression, offered his services as an interpreter. "I wish to give the falsifying *prefect* a proper notion of his conduct," said the colonel, with a variety of explicatures. "Can you, Mr. Dugden, do justice to what I say?" Mr. Dugden assented, and the "Governor" laid down the first paragraph of his lecture in English. Dugden did justice to what was said, and, it was thought, added a *little* on his own responsibility, much to the gratification of the governor.

The *prefect*, bearded in his own den, began to turn a variety of colors: his consternation increased, as the citizens of the town crowded into his office, and, by the wildest expressions of delight, testified their pleasure at what was going on. The *prefect* literally trembled in his shoes, and promised to act better, and honestly point out the hidden treasures. But he prevaricated so constantly, that he was finally dismissed, and ejected from the shadow of the office he still held, and he left the city, it was supposed to join Arista or some other general in the interior.

The day following the taking of Matamoras, Lieutenant-Colonel Garland, with all the regular and irregular cavalry of the army, about two hundred and fifty dragoons and rangers, started in pursuit of the retreating Mexicans, with orders to harass their rear, and to capture prisoners and baggage. On the 22d, Colonel Garland returned from his pursuit. He succeeded in capturing a small rear party, after a slight show of resistance on their part, in which two Mexicans were killed, twenty-two taken prisoners, and one wagon with ammunition and clothing of an artillery company captured. Two of our own troops were slightly wounded. The scarcity of water, the barrenness of the country, and the condition of the horses, compelled Colonel Garland to return to Matamoras, after having penetrated over sixty miles into the enemy's country.

The army of the Mexicans, under General Arista, was but twenty-four hours ahead of our cavalry, retreating in good order—our officers stopping at the *ranches* where the enemy had, the night previous. A ranchero, at one of these stopping places, inquired with great simplicity of Captain Graham, where the Americans were going. He was told in pursuit of the retreating Mexican army. "Retreating army!" said the fellow, with astonishment; "why, General Ampudia stopped at my house last night, and said that his troops had conquered the Americans, and that he was now on his way to Mexico to take the news." The man was confounded, for it was impossible for him to believe his nation had been whipped in battle, and still more incomprehensible that a small number of American dragoons should seriously, and for purposes of war, really drive before them over three thousand troops.

For several successive days after the precipitate retreat of the Mexicans, the bodies of drowned Mexican soldiers were thrown ashore by the current of the river. Among the mass, were distinguishable several officers. Arista, in his official dispatch, mentions two who thus met their death. The body of Father Leary was taken out of the water near the fort, his canonicals still on, and his cross clutched tightly in his hand. As the Rio Grande fell, it left suspended to the overhanging trees, the bodies caught in the meshes of their branches; thus they hung in the air, until they dropped piecemeal into the water below. The very river itself, for a while, became offensive; mutilated corpses floated along, attacked by the voracious catfish, causing them to twitch and roll about, as if still in the agonies of death.

On the battle-fields, more glaringly horrible effects of war were presented; in the lone places in the deep chapparal, lay the mouldering bodies of those of the wounded who had crawled away to die. Buzzards and carrion crows wheeled in eccentric circles over these unmade graves; beetles and foul insects burrowed beneath them; jackals, at night, dug their way into the mounds of the dead, exposing the interior corruption to the passer-by. The descending rains would beat down the arch made by these desecrations, and the pile marking where a hundred Mexicans lay, gradually sunk, until it seemed as if the remains of so many human beings scarcely disfigured the surface of the earth. When a few months, or years shall have passed away, all vestiges will be gone. The result of so great a sacrifice, will be the memory of a few glorious deeds; the suffering, the sin, the dreadful offences in the sight of heaven, will only have permanent record in another world.

With the return of Lieutenant-Colonel Garland's command from the pursuit of the fugitive Mexican army under General Arista, ended the first great act in the history of the operations of our army on the Rio Grande, and with the capture of Matamoras, terminated all immediate prospect of fighting. The Mexican army was almost literally annihilated, and the broken fragments were fleeing for safety from our victorious troops. That proud and confident army of more than eight thousand of the best troops of Mexico, which but a few days before, had marched into Matamoras without a doubt that the Americans would fall an easy prey to their arms, and whose victory magnificent preparations for celebrating had been made in advance—this army, so certain of victory, and so superior to General Taylor's, had been cut to pieces, and driven in confusion from the Rio Grande. The country had been completely subdued in a little more than six weeks from the day our army reached the point opposite Matamoras now occupied by Fort Brown. The condition of Matamoras and the state of affairs immediateiy following the occupancy of the city, by General Taylor, is thus described by an American who visited the scene of operations:—

"I arrived here yesterday morning, on the steamer Florida, after a passage of eight days, and find that the news of the taking of Matamoras was carried from here a week ago. There is nothing occurring here now of stirring interest, the fighting having ceased, for some weeks to come at least, and I am inclined to think that there will be no more of it on the Rio Grande. Our army must seek the enemy in their own country if they desire to meet them in any considerable bodies. Ampudia's defeat on the 8th and 9th, has ruined the Mexican army now in the north. They have lost everything, mules, pack-saddles, ammunition, arms, and men enough to strike terror to their hearts. Fort Polk, as this point is now called, is a complete museum at the present moment, with its Mexican booty—Mexican prisoners, mules, lances, saddles curiously wrought, leather pack-saddles, huge saddle-bags, muskets, ordnance, drums, copper cannon balls, grape-shot, letters, and all kinds of documents picked up on the ground where Ampudia was encamped. One of the officers, who was in the two engagements, says that the supper which the Mexicans had, in their confidence prepared for themselves, and which they were obliged so suddenly to abandon, afforded a rich repast to our tired and hungry officers and men. He pronounces their liquors, chocolate, soups, roast beef, &c., to have been first rate. Ampudia's plate, which was valuable, was promptly returned to him. Most of the wounded have been sent to Corpus Christi, but there are still enough here to represent most painfully the sad results of war. Captain Page, whose under jaw was completely shot away, is in a fair way of recovering. Captain Hooe is walking about with the stump of his right arm dangling by his side, and appears to be in excellent humor. Colonel McIntosh, who was badly wounded, was stretched out yesterday in a Mexican wagon, trying to read. He was stabbed in the throat, or rather down the throat, in the neck, and in other parts of the body, and was repeatedly knocked down in the fight. Lieutenant Maclay, who was wounded in the action of the 9th, is here, with an awfully sore shin, across which a Mexican grape-shot passed, shaving a *little* closer than was safe, as it carried with it a slice of bone and sinew. Instances of individual heroism occurred at those two engagements which would have immortalized a Spartan.

"Volunteers are gathering here in crowds. Yesterday the Ondiaka, Mary Kingsland, Florida, and Orleans arrived with troops from New Orleans. A company of Texas rangers came down to Padre Island, and were crossing over last evening. Some are encamped near the fort, on the prairie, and six companies of Louisiana volunteers are encamped on the Point, three miles and a half distant, at the bar. I had the pleasure, yesterday, of meeting General Memucan Hunt, of the Texan volunteers. The general looks well, and is anxious to be on the field. His men are hardy-looking fellows. All they pray for is to be permitted to go out through the interior, as our army marches on towards Mexico, and to take such towns as they can reach. Their knowledge of the country, their hardihood and experience in fighting Mexicans, fit them peculiarly for such service.

"There are more than twenty vessels lying here, inside and outside of the bar—one frigate of war, and the balance transports and trading vessels. The Florida drew less than seven feet, and bumped heavily on the bar as she came over yesterday morning. The sutlers put the screws to the poor soldiers here at a cruel rate, in the way of charges. It is really outrageous, and should be looked to by those in power."

But owing to General Taylor's deficiencies in troops, supplies and means of transportation, he was unable to follow up his advantages by a prompt movement upon Monterey, before the enemy had time to recover from the effects of their late disastrous defeat, and recruit another army sufficiently strong to dispute his further progress. He was consequently compelled to remain in comparative inactivity at Matamoras, waiting for reinforcements and wagons, until the 5th of August, nearly three months after the defeat of the Mexican army. He had, however, received by the end of June large reinforcements, but not the means of transportation. If it had been in the power of Taylor to have marched to Monterey and attacked it while the Mexicans were panic struck by their recent decisive overthrow, that important city would have fallen into his hands almost without resistance. But circumstances beyond his control rendered this impossible, and he was left no other alternative than quietly to wait for the means of making a forward movement. Small expeditions, however, were sent against several Mexican towns. Amongst others, Captain McCulloch captured Camargo, Mier and Reynosa.

While the Mexicans were suffering defeat abroad, they were threatened with a more serious enemy at home, and they seemed on the eve of another of those periodical revolutions which have distracted that wretched country for the last twenty years. Misfortune being considered a crime by her rulers, Parades, the President, superseded and recalled the defeated generals, with the view of punishing them for not wringing a victory from the Americans in spite of fate. But Arista was determined not to trust himself in the hands of his government, and began to organize an insurrectionary army, with which to dispute the authority of the President of the Republic. Parades was re-elected, however, on the 16th of June, 1846, which put an end, for a time, to the rebellious symptoms of the refractory general. Upon the re-organization of the new government, Aravalo was sent to Monterey to supersede Arista, and Ampudia to San Luis Potosi.

Active preparations were at once entered into for strongly fortifying Monterey upon the arrival of the new commander, and even before. Expecting that it would be the next to be attacked after the fall of Matamoras, every means were immediately put in requisition to place it in a complete state of defence. It was naturally one of the very strongest places in Mexico. During the war for the independence of Mexico from the Spanish yoke, this city was held by few Mexican troops for ten years, against the whole Spanish power. These natural advantages had been greatly improved by artificial defences, and the town was considered impregnable. The only access to the city for an invading army, is up steep and rugged acclivities, every inch of which could be swept by the guns of the fortifications. And it seemed like walking into the very jaws of death to attempt to storm it. Yet all these things did not for an instant deter General Taylor from his contemplated attack upon this strong-hold of Mexico.

Near the end of August, accordingly, General Worth was ordered to advance to Seralvo, and there await further instructions. Having ascertained at this place that Monterey had been reinforced by three thousand men under the command of General Ampudia, he advised General Taylor of the movement. This reinforcement increased the force of the garrison to ten thousand men, and decided him in his determination to move on without further delay to Monterey, and attack it at once. He therefore marched from Matamoras on the 7th of September, leaving General Patterson in command of that city, and all the forces between it and Camargo.

Leaving behind everything not absolutely necessary in the proposed attack, and calculated to impede his movements, he sent forward to Seralvo such supplies as were immediately required for the subsistence of his troops, and then hastened rapidly forward himself to the same place. He did not long wait for reinforcements, however, notwithstanding his army was considered by those who knew the strength of Monterey, so inadequate to the dangerous and difficult enterprise. His force did not much exceed six thousand men, while the city was garrisoned by ten thousand men at least. But hastily completing his arrangements, he moved on towards the devoted city of his destination, with all possible speed. Occasional attempts were made to obstruct his passage by small skirmishing parties. But no serious opposition was offered. He ascertained from deserters from Monterey, that preparations for a desperate resistance were going on with much activity, and everything indicated that the city would be defended with great resolution. This information, however, only had the tendency to hasten his movements, not only from the eagerness of himself and men to signalize themselves after so long a period of comparative inactivity, but to make the attack before the enemy had time to complete their defences.

After a march of twelve days, from the time he left Matamoras, he arrived at the Walnut Springs, a delightful position, within three miles of the city, and encamped there on the morning of the 19th of September. From this position he had an unobstructed view of the city of Monterey. It is situated in a beautiful valley, a part of which is extremely fertile, and highly cultivated. Almost all tropical fruits grow there in abundance. It is situated amidst lofty mountains on three sides and an open valley on the other, "and fortified with thick stone walls in the old Spanish style, with ditches and bastions, and bristling with cannon. The flat-roofed houses were all converted into fortifications, every street was barricaded, and every house was bristling with musketry." On one side was the Bishop's Palace, an extremely strong and well fortified fort; on the other were redoubts, and in the rear a river. Besides its garrison of ten thousand men, it contained a population of fifteen thousand, which could supply nearly three thousand volunteers. Thus the Mexican force was, in reality, but little if any short of thirteen thousand men for its defence, whilst the force of General Taylor was less than seven thousand men; when in reality the besieging force should at least be double the beseiged, in order to approach near an equality of strength. The reader will understand from this brief description of the city which the American force under Taylor were about to attack, the dangers of the attempt, and the almost overwhelming disadvantages which he had to fight against.

After establishing his camp at Walnut Springs, the nearest suitable position to Monterey, General Taylor ordered a reconnoissance of the ground in question, which was executed on the evening of the 19th, by the engineer officers, under Major Mansfield. A reconnoissance of the eastern approaches was at the same time made by Captain Williams, topographical engineers. The examination made by Major Mansfield proved the entire practicability of throwing forward a column to the Saltillo road, and thus turning the position of the enemy. Deeming this to be an operation of essential importance, orders were given to Brevet-Brigadier-General Worth, commanding the Second division, to march with his command on the 20th; to turn the hill of the Bishop's Palace; to occupy a position on the Saltillo road, and carry the enemy's detached works in that quarter, where practicable. The First regiment of Texan mounted volunteers, under command of Colonal Hays, was associated with the Second division on this service. Captain Sanders, engineers, and Lieutenant Meade, topographical engineers, were also ordered to report to General Worth, for duty with his column.

At two o'clock, P. M. on the 29th, the Second division took up its march. It was soon discovered, by officers who were reconnoitring the town, and communicated to General Worth, that its movement had been perceived, and that the enemy was throwing reinforcements towards the Bishop's Palace, and the height which commands it. To divert his attention, as far as practicable, the First division, under Brigadier-General Twiggs, and field division of volunteers, under Major-General Butler, were displayed in front of the town, until dark. Arrangements were made at the same time to place a battery, during the night, at a suitable distance from the enemy's main work, the citadel,—two twenty-four pounders and a ten inch mortar, with a view to open a fire on the following day, when General Taylor proposed to make a diversion in favor of General Worth's movement. The Fourth infantry covered this battery during the night. General Worth had in the meantime reached and occupied, for the night, a defensive position just without range of a battery above the Bishop's Palace, having made a reconnoissance as far as the Saltillo road.

Early on the morning of the 21st, General Taylor received a note from General Worth, written at half-past nine o'clock the night before, suggesting a strong diversion against the centre and left of the town, to favor his enterprise against the heights in rear. The infantry and artillery of the First division, and the field division of volunteers, were ordered under arms, and took the direction of the city, leaving one company of each regiment as a camp guard. The Second dragoons, under Lieutenant-Colonel May, and Colonel Wood's regiment of Texas mounted volunteers, under the immediate direction of General Henderson, were directed to the right to support General Worth, if necessary, and to make an impression, if practicable, upon the upper quarter of the city. Upon approaching the mortar battery, the First and Third regiments of infantry, and battalion of Baltimore and Washington volunteers, with Captain Bragg's field battery—the whole under the command of Lieutenant-Colonel Garland—were directed towards the lower part of the town, with orders to make a strong demonstration, and carry one of the enemy's advance works, if it could be done without too heavy loss. Major Mansfield, engineer, and Captain Williams and Lieutenant Pope, topographical engineers, accompanied this column, Major Mansfield being charged with its direction, and the designation of points to attack.

In the meantime, the mortar, served by Captain Ramsay, of the ordnance, and the howitzer battery under Captain Webster, First artillery, had opened their fire upon the citadel, which was deliberately sustained, and answered from the work. General Butler's division had now taken up a position in rear of this battery, when the discharges of artillery, mingled with a rapid fire of small-arms, showed that Lieutenant-Colonel Garland's command had become warmly engaged. General Taylor now deemed it necessary to support this attack, and he accordingly ordered the Fourth infantry, and three regiments of General Butler's division, to march at once, by the left flank, in the direction of the advance work at the lower extremity of the town, leaving the First regiment of Kentucky volunteers to cover the mortar and howitzer battery. By some mistake, two companies of the Fourth infantry did not receive this order, and consequently, did not join the advance companies, until some time afterwards.

Lieutenant-Colonel Garland's command had approached the town in a direction to the right of the advance work, at the north-eastern angle of the city, and the engineer officer, covered by skirmishers, had succeeded in entering the suburbs and gaining cover. The remainder of this command now advanced and entered the town under a heavy fire of artillery from the citadel and the works on the left, and of musketry from the houses and small works in front. A movement to the right was attempted, with a view to gain the rear of this advance work and to carry it, but the troops were so much exposed to a fire which they could not effectually return, and had sustained such severe loss, particularly in officers, that it was deemed best by General Taylor to withdraw them to a more secure position. Captain Backus, of the First infantry, however, with a portion of his own and other companies, had gained the roof of a tannery, which looked directly into the gorge of the enemy's advance battery, and from which he poured a most destructive fire into that work, and upon the strong building in its rear. This fire happily coincided, in point of time, with the advance of a portion of the volunteer division upon the same battery, and contributed largely to the fall of that strong and important work.

The three regiments of the volunteer division, under the immediate command of Major-General Butler, had in the meantime advanced in the direction of this work. The leading brigade, under Brigadier-General Quitman, continued its advance upon that work, preceded by three companies of the Fourth infantry, while General Butler, with the First Ohio regiment of volunteers entered the town to the right. The companies of the Fourth infantry had advanced within short range of the work, when they were received by a fire that almost in one moment struck down one-third of the officers and men, and rendered it necessary to

BATTLE OF MONTEREY.

The Americans forcing their way to he Main Plaza. Sept. 23d, 1846

retire and effect a conjunction with the two other companies then advancing. General Quitman's brigade, though suffering most severely, particularly in the Tennessee regiment, continued its advance, and finally carried the work in handsome st[illegible] as well as the strong building in its rear. Five pieces of artillery, a considerable supply of ammunition, and thirty prisoners, including three officers, fell into our hands.

Major-General Butler, with the First Ohio regiment, after entering the edge of the town, discovered that nothing was to be accomplished in his front, and at this point, yielding to the suggestions of several officers, General Taylor ordered a retrograde movement; but learning almost immediately from one of his staff that the advance battery had been taken, the order was countermanded, and he determined to hold the battery and defences already gained. General Butler, with the First Ohio regiment, then entered the town at a point further to the left, and marched in the direction of the second battery. While making an examination with a view to ascertain the possibility of carrying this second work by storm, General Butler was severely wounded, and soon after compelled to quit the field. As the strength of the battery, and the heavy musketry fire flanking the approach, rendered it impossible to carry it without great loss, the First Ohio regiment was withdrawn from the town.

Fragments of the various regiments engaged were now under cover of the captured battery, and some buildings in its front, and on the right. The field battery of Captains Bragg and Ridgeley was also partially covered by the battery. An incessant fire was kept upon this position from the second battery, and other works on its right, and from the citadel on all our approaches. General Twiggs joined General Taylor at this point, and was instrumental in causing the artillery captured from the enemy to be placed in battery, and served by Captain Ridgeley, against the Mexicans, until the arrival of Captain Webster's howitzer battery, which took its place. In the meantime, the commanding general directed such men as could be collected of the First, Third and Fourth regiments and Baltimore battalion, to enter the town, penetrating to the right, and carry the second battery if possible. This command, under Lieutenant-Colonel Garland, advanced beyond the bridge "Purisima," when, finding it impracticable to gain the rear of the second battery, a portion of it sustained themselves for some time in that advanced position; but as no permanent impression could be made at that point, and the main object of the general operation had been effected, the command, including a section of Captain Ridgeley's battery, which had joined it, was withdrawn to the first battery. During the absence of this column, a demonstration of cavalry was reported in the direction of the citadel. Captain Bragg, who was at hand, immediately galloped with his battery to a suitable position, from which a few discharges effectually dispersed the enemy. Captain Miller, First infantry, was dispatched with a mixed command to support the battery on this service. The enemy's lancers had previously charged upon the Ohio and a part of the Mississippi regiments, near some fields at a distance from the edge of the town, and had been repulsed with considerable loss. A demonstration of cavalry on the opposite side of the river was also dispersed in the course of the afternoon by Captain Ridgeley's battery, and the squadrons returned to the city. At the approach of evening, all the troops that had been engaged were ordered back to the camp, except Captain Ridgeley's battery and the regular infantry of the First division, who were detained as a guard for the works during the night, under command of Lieutenant-Colonel Garland. One battalion of the First Kentucky regiment was ordered to reinforce this command. Intrenching tools were procured, and additional strength was given to the works, and protection to the men, by working parties during the night, under the direction of Lieutenant Scarritt, engineers.

The main object proposed in the morning had been effected. A powerful diversion had been made to favor the operations of the Second Division, one of the enemy's advance works had been carried, and we now had a strong foot-hold in the town. But this had not been accomplished without a very heavy loss, embracing some of our most gallant and accomplished officers. Captain Williams, topographical engineers; Lieutenants Terrett and Dilworth, First infantry; Lietenant Woods, Second infantry; Captains Morris and Field, Brevet-Major Barbour, Lieutenants Irwin and Hazlitt, Third infantry; Lieutenant Hoskins, Fourth infantry; Lieutenant-Colonel Watson, Baltimore battalion; Captain Allen and Lieutenant Putnam, Tennessee regiment, and Lieutenant Hett, Ohio regiment, were killed, or have since died of wounds received in this engagement, while the number and rank of the officers wounded gives additional proof of the obstinacy of the contest, and the good conduct of our troops. The number of killed and wounded incident to the operations in the lower part of the city, on the 21st, is three hundred and ninety-four.

Early in the morning of the 21st, the advance of the

Second division had encountered the enemy in force, and after a brief but sharp conflict, repulsed him with heavy loss. General Worth then succeeded in gaining a position on the Saltillo road, thus cutting the enemy's line of communication. From this position the two heights south of the Saltillo road were carried in succession, and the guns taken in one of them turned on the Bishop's Palace. These important successes were fortunately obtained with comparatively small loss; Captain McKavett, Eighth infantry, being the only officer killed.

The 22nd day of September passed without any active operations in the lower part of the city. The citadel and other works continued to fire at parties exposed to their range, and at the work now occupied by our troops. The guard left in it the preceding night, except Captain Ridgeley's company, was relieved at mid-day by General Quitman's brigade. Captain Bragg's battery was thrown under cover in front of the town, to repel any demonstration of cavalry in that quarter. At dawn of day the height above the Bishop's Palace was carried, and soon after meridian the Palace itself was taken, and its guns turned upon the fugitive garrison. The object for which the Second division was detached had thus been completely accomplished, and all felt confident that with a strong force occupying the road and heights in his rear, and a good position below the city in the possession of the Americans, the enemy could not possibly maintain the town.

During the night of the 22d the enemy evacuated nearly all his defences in the lower part of the city. This was reported to General Taylor early in the morning of the 23d, by General Quitman, who had already meditated an assault upon those works. He immediately sent instructions to that officer, leaving it to his discretion to enter the city, covering his men by the houses and walls, and advance carefully so far as he might deem it prudent.

After ordering the remainder of the troops as a reserve, under the orders of Brigadier-General Twiggs, General Taylor repaired to the abandoned works, and discovered that a portion of General Quitman's brigade had entered the town, and were successfully forcing their way towards the principal plaza. He then ordered up the Second regiment of Texas mounted volunteers, who entered the city dismounted, and, under the immediate orders of General Henderson, co-operated with General Quitman's brigade. Captain Bragg's battery was also ordered up, supported by the Third infantry, and after firing for some time at the Cathedral, a portion of it was likewise thrown into the city. The American troops advanced from house to house, and from square to square, until they reached a street but one square in rear of the principal plaza, in and near which the enemy's force was mainly concentrated. This advance was conducted vigorously, but with due caution, and although destructive to the enemy, was attended with but small loss on our part. Captain Ridgeley, in the meantime, had served a captured piece in the first battery taken by the enemy, against the city, until the advance of our men rendered it imprudent to fire in the direction of the Cathedral. General Taylor was satisfied that his troops could operate successfully in the city, and that the enemy had retired from the lower portion of it to make a stand behind his barricades. As General Quitman's brigade had been on duty the previous night, General Taylor determined to withdraw the troops to the evacuated works, and concert with General Worth a combined attack upon the town. The troops accordingly fell back deliberately, in good order, and resumed their original positions, General Quitman's brigade being relieved after nightfall by that of General Hamer. On his return to camp, he met an officer with the intelligence that General Worth, induced by the firing in the lower part of the city, was about making an attack at the upper extremity, which had also been evacuated by the enemy to a considerable distance. He received a note from General Worth, written at eleven o'clock P. M., informing him that he had advanced to within a short distance of the principal plaza, and that the mortar which had been sent to his division in the morning was doing good execution within effective range of the enemy's position. Desiring to make no further attempt upon the city without complete concert as to the lines and mode of approach, General Taylor instructed that officer to suspend his advance, until he could have an interview with him on the following morning at his head-quarters.

Early in the morning of the 24th he received, through Colonel Moreno, a communication from General Ampudia proposing to evacuate the town. He arranged with Colonel Moreno a cessation of fire until twelve o'clock, at which hour he would receive the answer of the Mexican general at General Worth's head-quarters, to which he soon repaired. In the meantime, General Ampudia had signified to General Worth his desire for a personal interview with Taylor, to which he acceded, and which finally resulted in a surrender of the city upon the following conditions:

Terms of Capitulation of the city of Monterey, the

capital of Nuevo Leon, agreed upon by the undersigned commissioners, to wit: General Worth, of the United States army, General Henderson, of the Texas volunteers, and Colonel Davis, of the Mississippi riflemen, on the part of Major General Taylor, commanding-in-chief the United States forces, and General Requena, and General Ortega, of the army of Mexico, and Senor Manuel M. Llano, governor of Nuevo Leon, on the part of Senor General Don Pedro Ampudia, commanding-in-chief the army of the north of Mexico.

ART. 1. As the legitimate result of the operations before this place, and the present position of the contending armies, it is agreed that the city, the fortifications, cannon, the munitions of war, and all other public property, with the undermentioned exceptions, be surrendered to the commanding general of the United States forces now at Monterey.

ART. 2. That the Mexican forces be allowed to retain the following arms, to wit: the commissioned officers their side-arms, the infantry their arms and accoutrements, the cavalry their arms and accoutrements, the artillery one field battery, not to exceed six pieces, with twenty-one rounds of ammunition.

ART. 3. That the Mexican armed forces retire within seven days from this date, beyond the line formed by the pass of the Rinconada, the city of Linares and San Fernando de Presas.

ART. 4. That the citadel at Monterey be evacuated by the Mexican, and occupied by the American forces, to-morrow morning at 10 o'clock.

ART. 5. To avoid collisions, and for mutual convenience, that the troops of the United States will not occupy the city until the Mexican forces have withdrawn, except for hospital and storage purposes.

Art. 6. That the forces of the United States will not advance beyond the line specified in the 2d [3d] article before the expiration of eight weeks, or until the orders or instructions of the respective governments can be received.

Art. 7. That the public property to be delivered shall be turned over and received by officers appointed by the commanding generals of the two armies.

Art. 8. That all doubts as to the meaning of any of the preceding articles shall be solved by an equitable construction, and on principles of liberality to the retiring army.

Art. 9. That the Mexican flag, when struck at the citadel, may be saluted by its own battery.

Done at Monterey, September 24, 1846.

Upon occupying the city, it was discovered to be of great strength in itself, and to have its approaches carefully and strongly fortified. The town and works were armed with forty pieces of cannon, well supplied with ammunition, and manned with a force of at least seven thousand troops of the line, and from two to three thousand irregulars. The force under General Taylor's orders before Monterey, as exhibited by the returns accompanying his official report, was four hundred and twenty-five officers, and six thousand two hundred and twenty men. His artillery consisted of one ten inch mortar, two twenty-four pounder howitzers, and four light field batteries of four guns each—the mortar being the only piece suitable to the operations of a siege. His loss is twelve officers and one hundred and eight men killed; thirty-one officers and three hundred and thirty-seven men wounded. That of the enemy is not known, but is believed considerably to exceed our own.

In his detailed account of the capture, he warmly

GENERAL TWIGGS.

commended to the government the good conduct of the troops, both regulars and volunteers, which he declared had been conspicuous throughout all his operations against the city, and he bore testimony to their coolness and constancy in battle, and the cheerfulness with which they submitted to exposure and privation. To the general officers commanding divisions—Major-Generals Butler and Henderson, and Brigadier-Generals Twiggs and Worth—he expressed himself under many obligations for the efficient aid which they rendered him in their respective commands. He expressed himself unfortunate in being deprived, early on the 21st, of the valuable services of Major-General Butler, who was disabled by a wound received in the attack on the city. Major-General Henderson, commanding the Texan volunteers, rendered important aid in the organization of his command, and its subsequent operations. Brigadier-General Twiggs rendered important services with his division, and, as the second in command, after Major-General Butler was disabled. Brigadier-General Worth was intrusted with an important detachment, which rendered his operations independent of General Taylor's. These operations were conducted with ability, and crowned with complete success. Brigadier-Generals Hamer and Quitman, commanding brigades in General Butler's division: Lieutenant-Colonels Garland and Wilson, commanding brigades in General Twiggs' division; Colonels Mitchell, Campbell, Davis and Wood, commanding the Ohio, Tennessee, Mississippi, and Second Texas regiments, respectively; and Majors Lear, Allen, and Abercrombie, commanding the Third, Fourth and First regiments of infantry; all of whom served under his immediate direction, and conducted their commands with so much coolness and gallantry against the enemy as to entitle themselves to his most favorable notice.

Colonel Mitchell, Lieutenant-Colonel McClung, Mississippi regiment, Major Lear, Third infantry, and Major Alexander, Tennessee regiment, were all severely wounded, as were Captain Lamotte, First infantry, Lieutenant Graham, Fourth infantry, Adjutant Armstrong, Ohio regiment, Lieutenants Scudder and Allen, Tennessee regiment, and Lieutenant Howard, Mississippi regiment, while leading their men against the enemy's position on the 21st and 23rd. After the fall of Colonel Mitchell, the command of the First Ohio regiment devolved upon Lieutenant-Colonel Weller; that of the Third infantry, after the fall of Major Lear, devolved in succession upon Captain Brainbridge and Captain Henry, the former being also wounded. The following named officers were favorably noticed by their respective commanders: Lieutenant-Colonel Anderson and Adjutant Heiman, Tennessee regiment; Lieutenant-Colonel McClung, Captains Cooper and Downing; Lieutenants Batterson, Calhoun, Moore, Russel, and Cook, Mississippi regiment; also Sergeant-Major Hearlan, Mississippi regiment; and Major Price and Captain J. R. Smith, unattached, but serving with it. General Taylor also called attention to the good conduct of Captain Johnson, Ohio regiment, and Lieutenant Hooker, First artillery, serving on the staff of General Hamer, and of Lieutenant Nichols, Second artillery, on that of General Quitman. Captains Bragg and Ridgeley served with their batteries during the operations under the general's own observation, and in part under his immediate orders, and exhibited distinguished skill and gallantry. Captain Webster, First artillery, assisted by Lieutenants Donaldson and Bowen, rendered good service with the howitzer battery, which was much exposed to the enemy's fire on the 21st.

From the nature of the operations, the Second dragoons were not brought into action, but were usefully employed, under the direction of Lieutenant-Colonel May, as escorts, and in keeping open our communications. The First Kentucky regiment was also prevented from participating in the action of the 21st, but rendered highly important services, under Colonel Ormsby, in covering the mortar battery, and holding in check the enemy's cavalry during the day.

Besides these officers, whose conduct fell under his own immediate observation, he particularly referred to the reports of division commanders, for a notice of other officers, and warmly approved their recommendations.

To the officers of his personal staff and of the engineers, topographical engineers, and ordnance, associated with him, he expressed himself under many obligations for the valuable and efficient assistance he derived from them during the operations. Colonel Whiting, assistant quartermaster-general, Colonels Croghan and Belknap, inspectors-general, Major Bliss, assistant adjutant-general, Captain Sibley, assistant quartermaster, Captain Waggaman, commissary of subsistence, Captain Eaton and Lieutenant Garnett, aides-de-camp, and Majors Kirby and Van Buren, pay department, were also favorably noticed for their promptness in communicating his orders and instructions. He also expressed his particular obligations to Brevet-Major Mansfield and Lieutenant Scarritt, corps of engineers. They both rendered most important services in reconnoitring the enemy's positions, conducting troops in attack, and strengthening the works captured from the enemy. Major Mansfield, though wounded on the 21st, remained on duty during that and the following day, until confined by his wound to camp. Captain Williams, topographical engineers, was, to the great regret of General Taylor and loss of the service, mortally wounded while fearlessly exposing himself in the attack of the 21st. Lieutenant Pope, of the same corps, was active and zealous throughout the operations. Major Munroe, chief of the artillery, Major Craig, and Captain Ramsey, of the ordnance, were assiduous in the performance of their proper duties. The former superintended the mortar service on the 22nd, as particularly mentioned in the report of General Worth.

Surgeon Craig, medical director, was actively employed in the important duties of his department, and the medical staff generally were unremitting in their duties with the regular regiments, being rendered uncommonly arduous by the small number serving in the field.

Little need be added to this authentic account of the brilliant operations of our army against this strongly fortified and powerfully defended city, and of the glorious termination of the long and bloody struggle against it. The details of the capture are almost literally the language of General Taylor himself, and may, therefore, be relied upon as official. That it is eloquent from the very simplicity and modesty with which it describes one of the most brilliant achievements of modern times, need not be told the reader. But yet, as all may well imagine, there must necessarily have been numerous incidents and personal adventures of deeply exciting interest, that could not be related in an official dispatch. Many of these are supplied by the following memorandum of events during the progress of the siege and storming of the city, by a correspondent of the New Orleans papers. This supplies whatever of interest has been omitted, and gives a perfect history of the transactions of the American army before Monterey, and of the capture of the strongest city in Mexico, with the exception of Vera Cruz.

September 19, 1846. This has been a day of excitement and interest to our isolated little army. The general left the camp at San Francisco this morning at sunrise, and by eight o'clock the whole column was in motion, the Texas Rangers, and Colonel May with a squadron of dragoons, in advance. The men started off briskly, and the road was fine. After two hours' march, a bridge was found broken up by the Mexicans. A cornfield near at hand afforded materials for filling up the place, and the army proceeded over the first corn-stalk bridge I ever heard of. When within about four or five miles of the city, we heard a brisk cannonading. Some of the men had just previous to this begun to lag, some suffered from blistered feet, and others from the intensity of the heat, but no sooner did the sound of cannon reach their ears, than they straightened themselves up and pressed forward with an eagerness which showed that their sufferings were all forgotten. Captain Scott, (the veritable,) or rather now Major Scott, who commands the Fifth infantry, marched immediately before us, and the moment the brave old soldier heard the enemy's cannon, he drove his spurs into his horse and pranced about his regiment as if he would give a liberal portion of his life to be at Monterey.

Captain Miles, commander of the Seventh infantry, by whose side I was riding at the moment, likewise rose in his stirrups, with his keen black eyes sparkling, and his nostrils slightly dilated, and gave orders to his regiment to close up; but his orders were useless, for the noble fellows were already pressing on the staff, to the very rumps of the horses. Again, again and again, the noise of the twelve-pounders reverberated through the lofty mountains which rose before us and upon each side, and a buzz, a suppressed hurrah, ran through the line. The officers ran their eyes over their commands with looks of pride and confidence, and the men returned the glance, as if to say "we are ready," and pressed on still more eagerly. I rode out of the column and fell back to look at the Louisiana boys. Every eye among them was bright with eager excitement. Captain Blanchard, and Lieutenants Tenbrink and the two brothers Nicholls, wore a peculiar smile upon their countenances, an expression that I shall never forget. I translated its meaning thus: "Now we are about to be rewarded for all sacrifices and toils, and we will show old Louisiana that we can represent her worthily, though our numbers are small." They regretted the absence of their fellow-citizens who had returned to their quiet homes, for they well knew how many a brave heart would burn with bitter disappointment and laudable envy, could their returned friends but see them and know their feelings at that moment.

On reaching the place of encampment we came up with General Worth, riding his horse in beautiful style. A handsomer officer than he appeared then I never saw. Every one marked the change that had suddenly come over him. From the somewhat dejected air, and saddened countenance that he is said to have worn of late, Richard was now himself again—and the gallant soldier, forgetting all his cares, now appeared before us, the personification of an accomplished military chieftain. His handsome face was lighted up with a proud, but affable smile, as he motioned gracefully to his officers, pointing out to them the direction they were to take with their respective commands, and not a man who saw him, but what would at that moment have followed him to the cannon's mouth. Such is the feeling manifested by the whole army—which renders this body of men invincible.

This evening the enemy's batteries have been opened again upon a reconnoitring party of ours. Generals Taylor, Worth, Twiggs, and others, have been out, looking at their works.

Nine o'clock. P. M. An attack is expected, and every man in the army will rest to-night on his arms. A night attack is what a soldier dislikes very much, because it is then difficult to distinguish friend from foe.

September 20. Everything remained quiet last night. To-morrow an attempt will be made to take Monterey. A stout resistance is expected, for the town is strongly fortified, as well as the heights that command it, and the enemy has troops and ammunition enough there to defend it. A movement will no doubt be made to-night. No one expects an easy victory; on the other hand, all have made up their minds to see much blood shed. It is believed that a large number of the enemy is in our rear—in fact there is little doubt on the subject.

September 24. This is the fourth day since the battle of Monterey commenced. On the 20th at noon, General Worth marched from the camp east of the town in the direction of the heights west of the town, McCullough's and Gillespie's companies of rangers forming the reconnoitring party. At night the division bivouacked almost within range of the guns stationed upon the highest point of the hill, on which the Bishop's Palace is situated. At daylight of the 21st, the column was again in motion, and in a few moments was turning the point of a ridge which protruded out towards the enemy's guns, bringing us as near to them as their gunners could desire. They immediately opened upon the column with a howitzer and twelve-pounder, firing shell and round shot as fast as they could discharge their pieces.

The road now wound in towards a gorge, but not far enough to be out of range of their guns, which still played upon us. Another ridge lay about three-fourths of a mile beyond the first, around the termination of which the road wound, bringing it under the lofty summit of a height which rises between Palace Hill and the mountains which rise over us on the west. When the head of the column approached this ridge, a body of Mexican cavalry came dashing around the point to charge upon our advance. Captain Gillespie immediately ordered his men to dismount and place themselves in ambush. The enemy evidently did not perceive this manœuvre, but the moment they came up, the Texans opened upon them a most effective fire, unsaddling a number of them. McCullough's company now dashed into them—Captain C. F. Smith's camp and Captain Scott's camp of artillery, (acting as infantry,) and Lieutenant Longstreet's company of the Eighth infantry, with another company of the same regiment, likewise charged upon the enemy. The Texan horsemen were soon engaged with them in a sort of hand-to-hand skirmish, in which a number of tho enemy fell, and one Texan was killed and two wounded.

Colonel Duncan now opened upon them with his battery of light artillery, pouring a few discharges of grape among thom, and scattering them like chaff.

Several men and horses fell under this destructive fire. I saw one horse and rider bound some feet into the air, and both fell dead and tumbled down the steep. The foot companies above named then rushed up the steep and fired over the ridge at the retreating enemy, a considerable body of whom were concealed from our view, around the point of the hill. About thirty of the enemy were killed in this skirmish, and among them a captain, who, with two or three others, fell in the road. The captain was wounded in three places, the last shot hitting him in the forehead. He fought gallantly to the last, and I am sorry that I cannot learn his name.

The light batteries, one of which is commanded by Lieutenant Mackall, were now driven up on the slope of the ridge, and the howitzers opened upon the height of Palace Hill. A few shells only were thrown before the enemy commenced firing with a nine-pounder from the height immediately over the right of the column, aiming at Duncan's batteries. The several regiments took positions, and a few more shells were thrown towards Palace Hill, but did no execution. The nine-pounder continued to throw its shot, with great precision, at our batteries, one ball falling directly in the midst of the pieces, but fortunately hitting neither men nor guns. Finding his batteries thus exposed, and unable to effect anything, Colonel Duncan removed his command to a rancho about half a mile farther up the Saltillo road, where General Worth took up his position, after ordering the foot regiments to form along the fence, near the point of the ridge. The artillery battalion, Fifth, Seventh, and Eighth infantry, and the Louisiana volunteers, remained in this position about two hours, directly under the fire of the enemy's guns, (now two.) The balls fell directly in their midst all this time without wounding a man! To begin with, the Mexicans manage their artillery in battery as well as the Americans do—this, I believe is now conceded by every officer.

At half-past ten the column moved towards the general's position. At this time, Captain McKavett, of the Eighth infantry, was shot through the heart by a nine-pound ball, and a private of the Fifth infantry was severely wounded in the thigh, and he died the next morning. About fifty Mexicans now appeared upon the side hill, over the moving column, and fired at our troops some hundred musket shot, without doing any harm. The division deployed into the position pointed out, and remained an hour or two, when Captain C. F. Smith of the artillery battalion, with two companies (his own and Captain Scott's,) and four companies of Texas rangers on foot, were ordered to storm the second height. This the gallant officer cheerfully undertook, and was followed with enthusiasm by the officers and men of his command. It was considered on all sides to be a dangerous undertaking, and his party was considered most emphatically a forlorn hope. That the height would be taken, no one doubted, but that many brave fellows would fall in the attempt, seemed inevitable. The distance to be climbed after reaching the foot of the hill, was about a quarter of a mile; a part of the way was almost perpendicular, and through thorn-bushes and over sharp pointed rocks and loose sliding stones.

The Seventh infantry commanded by Captain Miles, was ordered to support Captain Smith's party, and by marching directly to the foot of the height, arrived before Captain Smith, who had been ordered to take a circuitous route. Captain Miles sent up Lieutenant

Gantt with a detachment of men, upon the hill side, to divert the attention of the enemy from Captain Smith's command, which could not yet be seen. The Seventh had already sustained a heavy fire of grape and round shot, as they forded the San Juan, which winds around the foot of the height, which fell like a shower of hail in their ranks, without killing a man. Lieutenant Gantt's party were greeted with grape and round shot, which cut the shrubs and tore up the loose stones in the ranks without killing any one; but the gallant young officer came within an inch of being killed by a cannon ball, which ran down the steep and filled his face with fragments of rock, dust and gravel. The fire was accompanied by a constant discharge of musketry, the enemy covering the upper part of the hill side, but the detachment continued to move up, driving the Mexicans back, until they were recalled.

Captain Smith's party now arrived and moved up the hill, the rangers in advance, and did not halt for an instant until the Mexicans were driven from the summit. Whilst this was going on, Colonel Persifer F. Smith, who commanded the Fifth and Seventh infantry—the Fifth, with Blanchard's Louisiana boys, under Major Martin Scott, had been ordered to support the whole—gave orders for these commands to pass around on each side and storm the fort, which was situated about half a mile back of the summit on the same ridge, and commanded the Bishop's Palace. Such a foot-race as now ensued, has seldom, if ever been seen; the Louisiana boys making tremendous strides to be in with the foremost. Captain Smith had the gun which he took upon the height run down towards the breastwork, and fired into it. Then came Colonel P. F. Smith's men, with a perfect rush, firing and cheering—the Fifth and Seventh, and Louisianians, reaching the ridge above nearly at the same time.

The Mexicans fired at them with grape, but it did not save them, or cause an instant's hesitation in our ranks. Our men run, and fired, and cheered, until they reached the work, the foremost entering at one end, whilst the Mexicans, about one thousand in number, left the other in retreat. The colors of the Fifth infantry were instantly raised, and scarcely were they up before those of the Seventh were alongside. The three commands entered the fort together, so close was the race—the Fifth, however, getting an advance, were in first. J. W. Miller, of Blanchard's company, was among the first four or five who entered. The three commands may be said to have come out even in the race, for the Seventh was not five seconds behind. In less than five minutes the gun found in the fort was thundering away at the Bishop's Palace!

More ammunition was found than our troops will use, with the three guns which were captured. One of the guns was found concealed. They are nine-pound brass pieces. Several mules and half a dozen beautiful tents were likewise captured. Killed, none. Wounded, in Seventh infantry, Lieutenant Potter, bullet through the calf of the leg; Orderly Sergeant Hurdle, of company K; Corporal S. P. Oakley, seriously, in the thigh. Corporal Oakley is from New York city, and a very intelligent, well-educated man, as well as a good soldier. Private White—the same who captured the Mexican officer's trunk at Marin, and who received it and its contents from General Taylor—wounded in the head. Fifth infantry, killed. none; wounded—Lieutenant Russell, in the arm: Sergeant-major Brand, badly, in the mouth, with a musket ball. Privates McManus and Grubb, slightly wounded—Sergeant Uptergraph, color-bearer, distinguished himself by his gallantry.

Thus was this brilliant *coup de main* made almost without bloodshed. I have not time to give the particulars of this glorious affair. Captain C. F. Smith, was in the advance, with McCall, at the battle of Resaca de la Palma, and is one of the most gallant and accomplished officers in the army—so say all his fellow-officers whom I have heard speak of him. Colonel P. F. Smith—General Smith, of Louisiana—distinguished himself on that occasion, as did Major Scott and Captain Miles, and in truth every officer and man did his duty nobly.

The gallant conduct of Captain Blanchard and Lieutenant Tenbrink, and the two brothers Nicholls, are praised by all the officers who were there. In truth, the Louisiana boys have fought every day for four days, and I assure you, as General Worth's report will bear me out in saying, and as every officer in the Second division will testify, that this corps has distinguished itself on every occasion where they have been called on. The sons of Judge Nicholls, of Donaldsonville, have stood fire four or five hours at a time, driving the enemy—under their battery—from bush to bush, and rock to rock, and at last were among the foremost to rush into the Bishop's Palace and take it by storm. Captain Blanchard and his company have already made a reputation that will not soon be forgotten. S G. Allen, private of this company, was mortally wounded in this fight, and died next morning. Captain Smith had no one killed or wounded in his party of regulars—two Texans were wounded, viz.: William Carley and B. F. Keese.

September 24. I date both my letters on one day, because I am obliged to foot up the news of the last four days, having had no writing materials along. Even now, though I write in a *palace*, I am obliged to hold the sheet of paper in one hand on my knee, for want of a desk. But I have no time for extra remarks —a chance offers to send you the news, and I must hurry to give you a glance at what has been done here, before the express goes off. On the morning of the 21st, Colonel Childs, of the artillery battalion, with three of his companies—one commanded by Captain Vinton, another by Captain J. B. Scott, and the third by Lieutenant Ayres, and three companies of the Eighth infantry—company A. commanded by Lieutenant Longstreet and Lieutenant Wainright; company B, Lieutenant Holloway commanding and Lieutenant Merchant; company D, Captain Scrivner and Lieutenant Montgomery—was ordered to take the summit of Palace Hill.

The colonel left the camp at three o'clock, A. M., and climbed the mountain through the chapparal and up the steep rocks, with such secrecy, that at daybreak he was within one hundred yards of the breastwork of sand-bags before he was discovered. Three of the artillerymen, having rushed ahead too fast, found themselves in the hands of the Mexicans. They surrendered: the Mexicans took their muskets, and shot them down with the very pieces they had given up. I saw the poor fellows lying there.

I have but a few moments left to write in, and must therefore defer the particulars of the storming of the palace until I have more time. Colonel Staniford went up at daylight with the balance of the Eighth, and Major Scott led up the Fifth. The Louisiana boys were on the hill with the Fifth, at eight o'clock, A. M. One of Duncan's howitzers, in charge of Lieutenant Rowland, was dragged up, or rather *lifted* up, and opened on the Palace, which was filled with troops. The Mexicans charged on the howitzer, but were driven back. A constant firing was kept up for several hours, particularly by Blanchard's men, who left a dozen Mexicans dead upon the hill side. At length a charge was ordered, and our men rushed down upon the Palace, entered a hole in a door that had been blocked up, but opened by the howitzer, and soon cleared the work of the few Mexicans that remained. Lieutenant Ayres was the lucky one who first reached the halyards and lowered the flag. One eighteen-pound brass piece, a beautiful article, manufactured in Liverpool in 1842, and a short brass twelve-pound howitzer, were captured, with a large quantity of ammunition, and some muskets and lances.

The fort adjoining the Palace walls is not complete, but is very neatly constructed, as far as it is built. The killed on our side, in taking the Palace, were seven—wounded, twelve. Lieutenant Wainwright was wounded in the side and arm by a musket-ball, but will soon recover, it is hoped. Mr. John Francis, of New Orleans, belonging to Blanchard's company, was killed. Colonel Childs, Captain Vinton, Captain Blanchard, Lieutenant Longstreet, Lieutenant Clark (adjutant of the Eighth,) Lieutenant Ayres, Lieutenant McCown, and the two Nicholls, seem to have been the heroes of the day. The two latter performed prodigies, and not only Judge Nicholls, but old Louisiana may well be proud of such sons. The Mexicans lost at least thirty killed—twenty-one had been buried this morning, and I have seen a number lying on the hillside, that were not discovered by our men when they brought in the dead.

Yesterday morning the whole division under General Worth entered the town on this side, and have been fighting there ever since. The heart of the city is nothing but one fortification, the thick walls being pierced for muskets and cannon, and placed so as to rake the principal streets. The roofs being flat, and the front walls rising three or four feet above the roof, of course every street has a line of breastworks on each side. A ten-inch mortar came round from General Taylor last evening, and it is now placed in the largest plaza, to which our troops have fought step by step, and from house to house. Duncan's batteries are in town, and the present impression is that the place will soon be taken. General Worth has gained all the strongholds that command the city, and has pushed the enemy as far as they can go without falling into General Taylor's hands on the other side of the city. All this has been done with the loss of only about seventy killed and wounded.

The achievement is a glorious one—sufficient to satisfy the ambition of any man on earth. I was expecting to see General Worth rushing his men into unnecessary danger, in order to win for them and himself great military fame, but his conduct has been very different from this. His great study has been to gain these commanding points with the least possible sacrifice of life. At first it seemed totally impossible to storm these heights—it looked like charging upon the clouds—but it has been done. The Bishop's Palace, which is as strong as it has been represented to be, has been stormed and taken by our brave soldiers. I should have stated that Colonel Hays, with a body of

GENERAL WORTH.

his troops, and Captains Gillespie and McCulloch, were at the taking of the Palace. Captain Gillespie was mortally wounded, and died yesterday morning regretted by the whole army.

I cannot keep up, at all, with the rangers. Their services have been invaluable to General Taylor, from the commencement of the campaign. They fight with all the steadiness of old soldiers—and are constantly on the move. The country owes them much for their noble conduct. I say nothing, as yet, about General Taylor's proceedings on the other side of the town, because the information I have received is not well authenticated. Mr. Kendall and I both came out with this division, neither knowing that the other was coming with it, until it was too late to return, and there is no communication between the divisions except by armed bodies of men. The general has, however, taken three batteries near the town, on the other side, in doing which he has lost about *three hundred men*, killed and wounded! I do not know the exact number killed, but will be able to ascertain before this letter goes—and will try to give other particulars.

General Taylor has arrived at General Worth's headquarters to-day, and is now engaged in town with Ampudia's messengers, considering the enemy's proposals for surrendering the town and the large fort at the north-east side of it. That fort is very strong, and is believed to contain at least twenty guns. Hostilities have ceased until the conference shall be concluded. There must be an immense quantity of property in town, particularly arms and ammunition.

I should have mentioned that the Second division marched from camp with only two days' rations, and no tents. A large majority of the officers, and many of the men, worked and climbed mountains, chased the enemy, and fought forty-eight hours, with nothing to eat but raw corn. Much of the two days' rations were spoiled by the rains, and as the troops were frequently ordered off at an instant's notice, they left their haversacks behind.

There have been from ten to fifteen thousand troops at this place ever since we have been here, but they are leaking out, in citizens' clothes, as fast as they can dodge off. As soldiers, there is no escape for them.

September 25. The city has capitulated. Many persons, particularly the Texan volunteers, who fought so bravely, are displeased at these terms. The town was all but in our hands, and, could they be believed, would have been taken in three hours. I believe that it would have required much more hard fighting to have taken it, but this was not the question with General Taylor. He and his officers knew perfectly well, of course, that the town could soon be taken, but he wanted no prisoners to take up his time and eat up his substance; but he did have an object in view which will be reached by the terms of this capitulation, and that object will lead to a result most beneficial to our government, under whose advice or orders General Taylor acted in agreeing to these terms. As I have a few moments to spare before the express goes out this morning, (he was detained last night by the slow progress of business with Ampudia,) I will speak of the operations of General Taylor on his side of the town.

Major Mansfield, of the Engineers, reconnoitred the enemy's works on the night of the 19th, but could obtain no very accurate information, although he approached very near to some of them on the heights. On the 20th, Lieutenant Scarritt and Lieutenant Pope were sent out to reconnoitre the works, Scarritt on the right and Pope on the left of the town. The latter approached and discovered the position of a battery on the extreme left, and was exposed to a fire of cannon and musketry from lancers, from which, after finishing his observations, he retired in safety. On the night of the 20th, the mortar and howitzer batteries were placed in a position to play on the strong holds around the citadel. The action commenced on the morning of the 21st, by the opening of these two batteries. Colonel Garland's brigade was ordered to move to the left for the purpose of storming the battery discovered by Lieutenant Pope the day before, and to occupy, if possible, the lower part of the city. Major Mansfield, Captain Williams, and Lieutenant Pope were ordered in advance, to select the most available point of attack, and to direct the movements of the column upon it. Three companies were thrown forward as skirmishers, and advanced rapidly towards the works, followed by the brigade in line of battle, under a cross fire of artillery from the citadel and fort, and a heavy fire of musketry.

The column charged into a street about two hundred yards to the right of the battery, passed the works entirely, and effected an entrance into the tower. After advancing rapidly about four hundred yards beyond the battery, they came immediately in front of a masked battery of artillery and musketry, which swept the street completely by its range. The barricades of the streets at sixty yards distance from the head of the column, were lined with Mexican troops, who, entirely covering themselves, opened a murderous discharge of grape and musketry upon the advancing column. Every house in the street was pierced for musketry, and enfiladed the street in every direction. Under this fire the following officers were killed or mortally wounded: Major Barbour, Third infantry, by grape shot in the abdomen; Captain Williams, topographical engineers, shot through the body by a musket ball, fell into the street, and was carried into the doorway of a house by Lieutenant Pope, amidst a shower of balls that covered him with dust. The gallantry of this young officer, now in his first battle, is spoken of in admiration by the army. Captain Williams died the next day, and was buried with the honors of war by the Mexican troops, into whose hands he had fallen. Lieutenant Merritt, First infantry, shot through the body, and died the next day.

Wounded—Major Mansfield, ball through calf of the leg. This brave officer would not leave on account of his wound, but rode about, behaving in the most gallant manner, all day. Captain Bainbridge, Third infantry, slightly wounded in the hand. Major Lear, dangerously wounded in the mouth, the ball passing out at the back of his head. Major Abercrombie, First infantry, severely wounded. Lieutenant R. Graham, Fourth infantry, severely wounded in both legs and body; hopes are entertained of his recovery. A great number of men killed and wounded—number not known.

It being impossible, in the opinion of the engineer officers, to effect anything in attacking the barricades in front, the column moved rapidly up a street to the right, with the intention of turning them. Being reinforced by the Ohio regiment, a second charge was made, under the direction of General Butler, which, owing to the tremendous fire of musketry and grape from the barricades and stone houses, likewise proved ineffectual. The troops were then ordered by General Taylor to retire in good order, and get under cover from the enemy's fire, which order was handsomely executed.

During the engagement in town, of Garland's brigade, the forts that were passed on the left, in entering the town, were gallantly carried by the Mississippi and Tennessee regiments—the first commanded by Colonel Campbell, and the second by Colonel Davis. Colonel McClung, of the Mississippi regiment, was dangerously wounded. These regiments sustained a great loss of killed and wounded, but I cannot, in the short time left me, ascertain the names or the number of those who fell. Captain Bragg's battery of light artillery was brought into action, but it being impossible to use it effectively, it was withdrawn. Several pieces of artillery were captured. The forts that were taken were occupied by Ridgeley's light artillery company, who turned the captured pieces against the Mexican works, and the cannonade was kept up the rest of the day. There were many skirmishes, and gallant deeds, which I will mention more minutely at a future time.

On the night of the 22d, the enemy abandoned the two works which had proved so destructive to the Third and Fourth infantry, and they were occupied early next morning by the Mississippi and Tennessee regiments, under General Quitman. About eight o'clock the same morning, these two regiments advanced on the town, and a sharp engagement commenced. These troops were supported by a body of Texan rangers dismounted for the occasion, under General Henderson, and by the Third regiment of infantry. The fight was kept up until four o'clock, P. M., during which time our troops drove the enemy from house to house, almost to the main plaza. The loss of life on our side was not severe during this day. On the morning of the 24th, a flag of truce was sent in, which resulted in the capitulation of the town.

During the whole of the engagement on the 21st, Colonel Kinney was exceedingly useful in carrying orders, and in giving advice in matters with which his thorough acquaintance with Mexican customs rendered him familiar. He was in the thickest of the fight, moving about from point to point, and doing good execution with his rifle. This gentleman's services have been valuable to General Taylor in the movements of the army from Matamoras to this place. He has been everywhere reconnoitring the country and procuring information—riding day and night, and exposing his life in a thousand ways. The colonel never flinched from any duty required of him, and, had General Taylor ordered him to go and bring him Ampudia's portfolio, he would have undertaken it. I devote a paragraph to a mention of this gentleman's services because he deserves much from the public, for whom he has labored so arduously and so efficiently. Our killed and wounded in taking Monterey amounted to about five hundred—nearly three hundred killed. Some time will elapse before the number will be known accurately, but it is well known that few prisoners were taken by the Mexicans.

September 27, 12 *o'clock, night.* Didn't I tell you, on the 20th, that we should have a "fight at Monterey, and have a hard one?" Well, on the 21st the ball opened, when our troops approached within one thousand four hundred yards of Monterey. Our troops advanced steadily and firmly, fighting every inch of the ground, until they drove the Mexicans into the plaza, but this took them until the evening of the 24th, (three days,) when the Mexicans surrendered the city.

On the morning of the 24th (half-past eleven o'clock,) General Ampudia sent Colonel Moreno to General Taylor, with a proposition, which General Taylor would not accept. He (General Ampudia) wanted to march out with all his men, arms, ammunition, &c. General Ampudia then requested an interview in person, which was granted, and they discoursed until half-past four, when General Taylor gave to General Ampudia his last and final proposition, and told him he would give him one hour to answer. Before the hour was up, the answer was returned that General Ampudia accepted the terms proposed by General Taylor, which were in substance these:

The Mexican army to evacuate the city, and it to be delivered up to the Americans. They should march out with their muskets and twenty rounds of cartridges, and six pieces of cannon That the Mexican force should not appear this side of a line from Riconada running through Linares and terminating at Riconada: and the Americans should not advance beyond it. This gives us Monterey and about thirty miles beyond, and puts us in possession of about thirty pieces of cannon.

It would be useless for me now to attempt to tell you of the many brilliant feats of our little army, but I will leave it to other times and perhaps to other men, (the boat leaves in three minutes,) but will add—both regulars and volunteers did all and everything that their country could expect. Some things which could be done, but ppeared almost impossible, were done quickly.

Our loss is reported—killed and wounded about five hundred—Mexican loss about the same. American force six thousand; Mexican twelve thousand, and the advantage of fortifications, and the city fortified at every point, even to the tops of the houses.

The capture of Monterey has been described in eloquent terms by a thousand pens, both in prose and poetry, and has excited the admiration of Europe as well as America. Few military enterprises display more cool, determined bravery on the part of soldiers, or more true generalship and chivalric bearing than did the conduct of General Taylor and his officers, in the storming of this city. It is therefore natural that the enthusiasm the brilliant event has inspired should have found utterance in eloquent verse as well as in sober prose. Among the many attempts to give coloring and life to the exciting and novel incidents connected with the capture of Monterey, the following is probably the most heart-stirring and eloquent:

STORMING OF MONTEREY

We were not many—we who stood
  Before the iron [illegible] that day—
Yet many a gallant spirit would
Give half his head if he but could
  Have been with us at Monterey.

Now here, now there, the shot it hailed
  In deadly drifts of fiery spray,
Yet not a single soldier quailed
When wounded comrades round them wailed
  Their dying shout at Monterey.

And on—still on our column kept
  Through walls of flame its withering way;

Where fell the dead, the living stept
Still charging on the guns which swept
  The slippery streets of Monterey.

The foe himself recoiled aghast,
  When, striking where the strongest lay,
We swooped his flanking batteries past,
And braving full their murderous blast,
  Stormed home the towers of Monterey.

Our banners on those turrets wave,
  And there our evening bugles play;
Where orange boughs above their grave
Keep green the memory of the brave
  Who fought and fell at Monterey.

We are not many—we who pressed
  Beside the brave who fell that day;
But who of us has not confessed
He'd rather share that warrior rest,
  Than not have been at Monterey.

The only act of General Taylor's during his whole operations in Mexico, and indeed, from the day he encamped at Corpus Christi, which has not received the approbation of his government, as even this has, of the country, is the terms of capitulation granted to Mexico in the surrender of Monterey. It was thought by the administration that he should have insisted upon the unconditional surrender of the Mexican army. His course was not only condemned by the President and on the floor of Congress by prominent friends of the administration, but an indirect vote of censure was passed by the lower house of Congress for his granting too liberal conditions to the enemy. The general opinion prevails amongst military men, however, and those best competent to judge of the power of General Taylor to enforce more favorable terms, that they were highly honorable to the American arms, and advantageous to the government; and further, that they were such as humanity and a proper regard for the lives of his soldiers dictated. He might have insisted, and possibly have forced an unconditional submission; but it would have been at a sacrifice that the advantages thus acquired, would not have warranted. The best explanation, however, of Taylor's motives, and the best defence of his conduct, will be found in the following reply to the letter of the Secretary of War:

"In reply to so much of the communication of the Secretary of War, dated October 13th, as relates to the reasons which induced the convention resulting in the capitulation of Monterey, I have the honor to submit the following remarks:

"The convention presents two distinct points. *First*, the permission granted the Mexican army to retire with their arms, &c. *Secondly*, the temporary cessation of hostilities for the term of eight weeks. I shall remark on these in order.

"The force with which I marched on Monterey was limited by causes beyond my control to about six thousand men. With this force, as every military man must admit, who has seen the ground, it was entirely impossible to invest Monterey so closely as to prevent the escape of the garrison. Although the main communication with the interior was in our possession, yet one route was open to the Mexicans throughout the operations, and could not be closed, as were also other minor tracks and passes through the mountains. Had we, therefore, insisted on more rigorous terms than those granted, the result would have been the escape of the body of the Mexican force, with the destruction of its artillery and magazines, our only advantage being the capture of a few prisoners of war, at the expense of valuable lives and much damage to the city. The consideration of humanity was present to my mind during the conference which led to the convention, and outweighed in my judgment the doubtful advantages to be gained by a resumption of the attack upon the town. This conclusion has been fully confirmed by an inspection of the enemy's position and means since the surrender. It was discovered that his principal magazine, containing an immense amount of powder, was in the Cathedral, completely exposed to our shells from two directions. The explosion of this mass of powder, which must have ultimately resulted from a continuance of the bombardment, would have been infinitely disastrous, involving the destruction not only of Mexican troops, but of non-combatants, and even our own people, had we pressed the attack.

"In regard to the temporary cessation of hostilities, the fact that we are not at this moment, within eleven days of the termination of the period fixed by the convention, prepared to move forward in force, is a sufficient explanation of the military reasons which dictated this suspension of arms. It paralyzed the enemy during a period when, from the want of necessary means, we could not possibly move. I desire distinctly to state, and to call the attention of the authorities to the fact, that, with all diligence in breaking mules and setting up wagons, the first wagons in addition to our original train from Corpus Christi, (and but one hundred and twenty-five in number,) reached my head-quarters on the same day with the secretary's communication of October 13th, viz: the 2nd inst. At the date of the surrender of Monterey, our force had not more than ten days' rations, and even now, with all our endeavors, we have not more than twenty-five. THE TASK OF

FIGHTING AND BEATING THE ENEMY IS AMONG THE LEAST DIFFICULT THAT WE ENCOUNTER—the great question of supplies necessarily controls all the operations in a country like this. At the date of the convention, I could not of course have foreseen that the Department would direct an important detachment from my command without consulting me, or without waiting the result of the main operation under my orders.

"I have touched the prominent military points involved in the convention of Monterey. There were other considerations which weighed with the commissioners in framing and with myself in approving the articles of the convention. In the conference with General Ampudia, I was distinctly told by him that he had invited it to spare the further effusion of blood, and because General Santa Anna had declared himself favorable to peace. I knew that our government had made propositions to that of Mexico to negotiate, and I deemed that the change of government in that country since my last instructions, fully warranted me in entertaining considerations of policy. My grand motive in moving forward with very limited supplies had been to increase the inducements of the Mexican Government to negotiate for peace. Whatever may be the actual views or disposition of the Mexican rulers or of General Santa Anna, it is not unknown to the Government that I had the very best reason for believing the statement of General Ampudia to be true. It was my opinion at the time of the convention, and it has not been changed, that the liberal treatment of the Mexican army and the suspension of arms, would exert none but a favorable influence in our behalf.

"The result of the entire operation has been to throw the Mexican army back more than three hundred miles to the city of San Luis Potosi, and to open the country to us as far as we choose to penetrate it up to the same point.

"It has been my purpose in this communication not so much to defend the convention from the censure which I deeply regret to find implied in the secretary's letter, as to show that it was not adopted without cogent reasons, most of which occur of themselves to the minds of all who are acquainted with the condition of things here. To that end I beg that it may be laid before the General-in-Chief and Secretary of War."

No farther justification of the conduct of General Taylor, for the terms of the capitulation, will be required, it is confidently believed, than this plain, but dignified and unanswerable statement of the reasons that influenced him in not demanding more rigid conditions from an enemy yet greatly superior to his own force, and capable of a long and bloody resistance, or of cutting their way from the city. He gained all the advantages of a substantial victory, and only submitted to an armistice of eight weeks because he had not the power to prosecute further operations in his then weakened condition. And while he consented to suspend hostilities until he should be able to resume them, he tied the hands of his enemy during the same time. If, therefore, he conceded to the Mexicans certain advantages, he did so because he had not the ability to withhold them.

In reference to the concluding sentence of the foregoing letter, it is proper to remark, that the correspondence of General Taylor is addressed to the "Adjutant-General of the army," at head-quarters in Washington. On the day after it bears date, General Taylor again wrote to the Department, saying: "I have formally notified the Mexican general-in-chief that the temporary suspension of arms agreed upon in the convention of Monterey will cease on the 13th instant, the date at which the notice will probably reach San Luis Potosi. This notification was sent by Major Graham, topographical engineer, who left on the 6th instant.

"You will perceive from my 'orders' No. 139, what arrangements have been made for the occupation of Saltillo at the earliest moment by our troops. Whether our operations are pushed forward towards San Luis or not, the occupation of Saltillo is important—politically, as the capital of Coahuila, and, in a military view, as covering an important region from which we may draw supplies.

"Brigadier-General Wool, with a portion of his force, arrived at Monclova on the 29th of October, and is now joined by the rear division. He reports no practicable route to Chihuahua, except the one by Parras, which will bring him within a few leagues of Saltillo. He inquires what is to be gained by going to Chihuahua? And I am free to answer, nothing at all commensurate with the excessive length of his line of operations. Chihuahua, moreover, is virtually conquered, and can be occupied at any moment, while we hold Saltillo and Santa Fe. I shall instruct General Wool to remain at Monclova, where there are supplies, until I can determine what disposition to make of his column, which cannot be done until I visit Saltillo.

"I have taken the first steps towards organizing the expedition on Tampico, and propose to accompany it, for the purpose at least of commanding a covering force. There will be some delay for the want of means of land transport.

"The information received since my communication

of October 15th, relative to the route hence to San Luis, renders it more than probable that, from the want of permanent water, it will be impossible to march a large force from Saltillo to that city. I hope to acquire certain information on this point in a few days."

General Taylor wrote from his camp near Monterey, on the 12th of November, as follows: "The communication of the Secretary of War of October 22, with its inclosures, by the hands of Major McLane, was received this morning. You will have seen by my orders, and my dispatch of the 9th, what measures have been taken to conclude the armistice and to occupy Saltillo. Being advised by special express from Matamoras of Major McLane's approach, I had postponed my intended departure this day for Saltillo, until his arrival. As I deem it still important to occupy that position, for reasons to be explained below, I shall march thither to-morrow, according to my first intention. On my return—say by the 20th instant—I shall probably be able to inform the Department more fully on certain important points connected with our operations; but I now avail myself of the return of Major McLane to Washington, to state briefly my views on some of the topics embraced in the secretary's communication.

"Without active operations towards San Luis Potosi from this quarter, I still deem the occupation of Saltillo important for three reasons: *First,* as a necessary outpost of the main force at Monterey, covering as it does the important defile which leads from the low country to the table land, and also the route to Monclova: *Secondly,* as controlling a region from which we may obtain considerable supplies of breadstuffs and cattle, viz.: the fertile country around Parras: and, *Thirdly,* as the capital of Coahuila, which renders it very important in a political point of view.

"I have already represented to the department the difficulties to be encountered in a forward movement upon San Luis, and the amount of force which would be necessary to insure success. Those reasons only apply to the country beyond Saltillo. I consider the occupation of that point as a necessary complement to our operations, and to the policy of holding a defensive line, as the Sierra Madre, and trust the Department will concur with me in this view.

"As already reported, Brigadier-General Wool is now at Monclova, having found no practicable route to Chihuahua, save the well-known but very circuitous one by Parras. I fully agree with the Department that no commensurate benefit is likely to result from the march on Chihuahua of General Wool's column, and shall accordingly direct him to suspend his movement in that direction. The occupation of Saltillo in force renders it still less necessary that Chihuahua should be occupied. I cannot yet determine specifically what disposition to make of General Wool's column. Meanwhile I have directed him to remain in his present position until further orders.

"In regard to the expedition against Vera Cruz after a good deal of reflection upon the subject, I feel bound to express my conviction that four thousand men will be a force quite too small for the purpose contemplated. In my dispatch of October 15th, I stated twenty-five thousand troops, of which ten thousand were to be regulars, as the least force that should make a descent in that quarter, with the view of marching on the capital. I now consider that, simply to invest and take Vera

Cruz, and of course hold the position, we should have ten thousand troops, of which four thousand, if possible, should be regulars. It is quite probable that a smaller force, even four thousand, might effect a landing and carry the town; but could they sustain themselves till the castle of San Juan de Ulloa should be reduced by famine? The country lying between Vera Cruz and the city of Mexico is populous, and at least one portion (Puebla) understood to be very loyal. Would not a force be brought against us, before the castle could be reduced, sufficiently strong to endanger our safety, cut off as we should be from succor? When to these considerations we add the uncertainty of weather during the winter season, rendering our communications with the fleet liable to interruption, I think it will be seen that the force should be large enough not only to land and invest the town, but also to hold itself secure against any attack from the interior, and for such purpose I consider ten thousand men quite as small a force as should be ventured.

"A force of ten thousand men cannot be spared from the occupation of the line of the Sierra Madre; four thousand may be diverted from that object; and if to these six thousand fresh troops from the United States were added at the proper time, the expedition might be undertaken with a promise of success. I propose therefore, to proceed with the preparation for a movement on Tampico, and, after accomplishing everything that is to be done in that quarter, I will, if the Department approve, hold four thousand men, of which perhaps three thousand regulars, ready to embark at some point on the coast, and effect a junction with the additional force from the States. The movement towards Tampico will not produce any delay if my views are adopted; and I consider it quite important to occupy Victoria and the lower portion of Tamaulipas, after securing properly the line to be held in this quarter.

"I conceive it all important, having in view the Mexican character, that as little should be left to accident as possible, and that we should be careful, as far as human foresight can provide, to avoid the smallest liability to disaster. A descent upon a hostile coast, notoriously dangerous, and in an inclement season of the year, is an operation requiring the most careful preparations and exact management, and possessing, under the most favorable circumstances, more or less elements of failure. It seems the part of prudence, therefore, to take a sufficient force to meet any contingency that may arise.

"Being pressed for time I have given my views briefly, and perhaps somewhat crudely, on the most important points presented in the dispatch of the secretary. There are other topics which will probably claim my attention, but which must be now passed over. I would only suggest that, in the event of an expedition to Vera Cruz, the heavy ordnance, engineers, stores, &c., should be shipped direct from the North."

After the reduction of Montery, General Taylor took up his headquarters in that city, and remained there during the armistice, or until it should be terminated by the orders of either the American or Mexican governments, awaiting reinforcements, and re-organizing and disciplining his forces, preparatory to his contemplated movement upon San Louis Potosi. He was also actively employed in establishing and keeping open a line of communication between Monterey and the

Rio Grande. On the 13th of November, General Taylor marched to Saltillo in company with General Worth's command, which was designed to operate against that city. They took possession of it without resistance. General Worth, with a force of eight hundred men, was left in command, and General Taylor returned to Monterey. General Wool, who was at Monclova, with a force of two thousand four hundred men, was ordered, by General Taylor, to take possession of Parras.

In the meantime Santa Anna, who had returned from exile, at Havana, had assembled an army of twenty-two thousand men, and concentrated it upon San Louis Potosi. This city he strongly fortified, and made it a depot for all kinds of provisions and military stores. After waiting in vain for many weeks for the advance of this powerful army to attack him at Monterey, General Taylor resolved to make a demonstration towards San Louis, with a view of drawing him out, and obtaining a battle. On the 15th of December, therefore, he left Monterey with two regiments of volunteers, having three days previously dispatched General Twiggs, with the main body of the regulars, to form a junction with General Patterson at Victoria. On arriving at Montemorales, however, a messenger reached him from Saltillo, informing him that General Worth, the commander at that place, was hourly expecting an attack from Santa Anna, at the head of his whole army. He therefore immediately gave orders for countermarching, and falling back upon Monterey, and from thence took up his line of march for Saltillo on the 20th, accompanied by General Twiggs' division of regulars. But here again be was doomed to be disappointed in meeting the enemy. Before he reached Saltillo, he learned that General Worth had been reinforced, by the arrival of General Wool's command, and that Santa Anna had retreated to his old quarters at San Louis Potosi. General Taylor, in consequence of this new aspect of affairs, again started for Victoria, and reached there on the 30th of December.

While at this place, he received information that General Scott had been ordered to Mexico with the view of commanding in person the troops destined for the reduction of Vera Cruz. Being the commander-in-chief of the army, this act would, as a matter of course, place General Taylor in a subordinate position to him. But it was understood that it was at the request of Taylor that Scott was sent to Mexico. Upon receiving orders to repair to Mexico, General Scott wrote the following letter to his old friend and companion in arms, for the purpose of informing him of his object and intention. The letter was marked confidential, but was published with the correspondence between General Taylor and the Secretary of War, called for by Congress. It is dated at New York, November 23, 1846, after Scott had departed from Washington for Mexico:

"I left Washington late in the day yesterday, and expect to embark for New Orleans the 20th inst. By the 12th of December I may be in that city, at Point Isabel the 17th, and Camargo, say the 23d—in order to be within easy corresponding distance from you. It is not probable that I may be able to visit Monterey, and circumstances may prevent your coming to me. I shall much regret not having an early opportunity of felicitating you in person upon your many brilliant achievements; but we may meet somewhere in the interior of Mexico.

"I am not coming, my dear general, to supersede you in the immediate command on the line of operations rendered illustrious by you and your gallant army. My proposed theatre is different. You may imagine it; and I wish very much that it were prudent, at this distance, to tell you all that I expect to attempt or hope to execute. I have been admonished that dispatches have been lost, and I have no special messenger at hand. Your imagination will be aided by the letters of the Secretary of War, conveyed by Mr. Armistead, Major Graham, and Mr. M'Lane.

But, my dear general, I shall be obliged to take from you most of the gallant officers and men, (regulars and volunteers,) whom you have so long and so nobly commanded. I am afraid that I shall, by imperious necessity—the approach of yellow fever on the Gulf coast—reduce you, for a time, to stand on tne aefensive. This will be infinitely painful to you, and for that reason distressing to me. But I rely upon your patriotism to submit to the temporary sacrifice with cheerfulness. No man can better afford to do so. Recent victories place you on the high eminence; and I even flatter myself that any benefit that may result to me, personally, from the unequal division of troops alluded to, will lessen the pain of your consequent inactivity.

"You will be aware of the recent call for nine regiments of new volunteers, including one of Texas horse. The president may soon ask for many more; and we are not without hope that Congress may add ten or twelve to the regular establishment. These, by the spring, say April, may, by the aid of large bounties, be in the field—should Mexico not earlier propose terms of accommodation; and, long before the spring

(March,) it is probable you will be again in force to resume offensive operations.

"It was not possible for me to find time to write from Washington, as I much desired. I only received an intimation to hold myself in preparation for Mexico, on the 18th instant. Much has been done towards that end, and more remains to be executed.

"Your detailed report of the operations at Monterey, and reply to the secretary's dispatch, by Lieutenant Armistead, were both received two days after I was instructed to proceed south."

This letter, it will be seen, indicates to General Taylor the probability that he will be compelled to take from him a considerable portion of his troops, as well volunteers as regulars. The necessity for this act he alleges to be the importance of taking Vera Cruz before the approach of the season for the yellow fever, or vomito, to make its appearance on the Gulf. The following extract from a letter of the Secretary of War to General Taylor, dated October 22, 1846, a short time before General Scott departed for Mexico, will show that in withdrawing so large a number of General Taylor's forces from him, he was but carrying out the wishes of the administration, and was acting under instructions from the War Department:

"I informed you in my last dispatch, that in connection with an invasion of Tamaulipas and attack on Tampico, an expedition against Vera Cruz was then under advisement. Upon a more full consideration of the subject, it is believed that Vera Cruz may be taken, and having possession of that city, the castle of San Juan de Ulloa might probably be reduced or compelled to surrender. If the expedition could go forth without the object being known to the enemy, it is supposed hat four thousand troops would be sufficient for the enterprise, receiving as they would the co-operation of our naval force in the Gulf; but *at least fifteen hundred or two thousand of them should be of the regular army, and under the command of officers best calculated for such an undertaking.* In looking at the disposition of the troops, *it appears to be scarcely possible to get the requisite number of regulars without drawing some of those now with you at Monterey,* or on the way to that place. Should you decide against holding military possession of any place in Coahuila or Chihuahua, and order the troops under General Wool to join you, it is presumed that the requisite force for the expedition to Vera Cruz could be detached without interfering with your plans of operation.

"You will therefore, unless it materially interferes with your own plan of operations, or weakens you too much in your present position, make the necessary arrangements for having four thousand men, of whom fifteen hundred or two thousand should be regular troops, ready to embark for Vera Cruz, or such other destination as may be given them, at the earliest practicable period. The place of embarkation will probably be the Brazos Santiago, or in that vicinity."

Accordingly, about the first of January, the divisions of Generals Patterson and Pillow, and also the brigades of Generals Quitman and Twiggs, as well as General Worth, were all detached from him for the purpose of acting under General Scott, against Vera Cruz and such other points as might dispute his march to the capital. Of the policy or necessity of thus withdrawing from General Taylor so large a portion of his troops, it is difficult to form a correct judgment at this distance from the scene of operations, and with the imperfect knowledge of the views of government that everyone must possess not in the immediate confidence of the administration. But it is certain that it placed him in a most embarrassing and even dangerous position. Upon taking leave of his veteran soldiers, the heroes of Palo Alto, Resaca de la Palma, and Monterey, he addressed them in the following brief, but manly and feeling terms:

"It is with deep sensibility that the commanding general finds himself separated from the troops he so long commanded. To those corps, regular and volunteer, who have shared with him the active services of the field, he feels the attachment due to such associations, while to those who are making their first campaign, he must express his regret that he cannot participate with them in its eventful scenes. To all, both officers and men, he extends his heartfelt wishes for their continued success and happiness, confident that their achievements on another theatre will redound to the credit of their country and its arms."

General Taylor continued at Victoria until about the last of January, 1847, when he returned to Monterey. His force now consisted of volunteers, with the exception of about four hundred and fifty regular troops, including Colonel May's dragoons. In the beginning of February he was reinforced by new volunteers, which increased his army to about six thousand men. With this small force, composed mostly of men who had never faced an enemy, and comparatively destitute of discipline, but longing to prove by their conduct that volunteers know how to fight, and can as steadily resist the attack of the foe, or as successfully charge upon him, as even veteran soldiers, General

Taylor must garrison Monterey, and hold in check the overwhelming army of Santa Anna.

Immediately after arriving at Monterey, General Taylor received information that a party of observation, consisting of about one hundred picked men, under Colonel May, had been surprised at Encarnacion, while attempting to gain some intelligence of the enemy, and that Captain Cassius M. Clay, and Majors Borland and Gaines had been taken prisoners by a Mexican force, under General Minon, of fifteen hundred men. This unwelcome intelligence, together with the belief that Santa Anna might make an attempt to re-conquer some of the posts between Monterey and the Rio Grande, and thus cut off his communication with Matamoras, determined General Taylor to march at once to Saltillo, with the view of giving him battle. He accordingly took up his march from Monterey on the 31st of January, leaving a force of about fifteen hundred men to garrison that city, and arrived at Saltillo on the 2d of February. He had been reinforced, in the meantime, by the arrival of five hundred more volunteers, which made the effective force under his command five thousand strong. Two days after he marched to Agua Nueva, a strong position, twenty miles from Saltillo, on the San Luis side of that city, and encamped there, for the purpose of disciplining his troops, and to observe the movements of the enemy. He remained in this position until the 21st of February, examining the situation of the country, the passes through the mountains, and the best point at which to await an attack from Santa Anna, should he resolve to fight on any terms. On the 21st, information was brought him that Santa Anna was advancing at the head of his whole army, and was then within a short distance. Believing Buena Vista, a point twelve miles nearer to Saltillo, and eight miles from that city, to be a much more favorable position at which to make a stand against such overwhelming odds as Santa Anna was bringing against him, he fell back to that place, and formed his army in order of battle, and calmly awaited the approach of the enemy. The account of the battle from eye witnesses, and General Taylor's official dispatch of the brilliant event, will be found in the next chapter.

N. ORR & RICHARDSON. N.Y.

American Army 4,500 men.
Mexican Army 20,000 men.

BATTLE OF BUENA VISTA,

Fought February 23d, 1847.

The American Army under Gen. Taylor Completely Victorious

American Loss, 264 Killed.
450 Wounded
26 Missing.
Mexican Loss, estimated in Killed
and Wounded 2000 men.

CHAPTER VII.

Battle of Buena Vista.—Taylor's Position.—General Taylor's Line of Battle formed.—A Summons to Surrender.—The Battle Commenced. —An Attempt to Outflank Taylor.—Flight of the Indiana Regiment. —Great Slaughter amongst the Enemy.—Mexican Stratagem.—Almost a Defeat.—Gallant Charge of the Kentucky Regiment.—Excitement of Taylor.—Death of Colonels McKee and Hardin and Lieutenant-Colonel Clay.—Taylor's Official Account of the Battle.

On the morning of the 21st, our army being encamped at Agua Nueva, information was received that the enemy was advancing, when General Taylor ordered the troops to fall back upon Buena Vista. Early on the 22nd, the clouds of dust towards Agua Nueva told that the Mexican army was on the advance. At about eleven o'clock the long roll of the drum summoned us to the field. Our regiments were formed, artillery posted, and we availed ourselves of every advantage that could be taken of the ground. In a few minutes, the leading columns of the enemy were distinctly seen, at a distance of two miles, steadily advancing in the most perfect order. Some two thousand lancers with the artillery, fourteen pieces of different calibre, from twenty-fours down, composed the leading division; then such a host of infantry and lances as never was seen together in Mexico before, I suppose, came into full view and filed into position. It was the most grand and gorgeous spectacle I ever witnessed; the sun glancing from the bright lances and bayonets of the twenty-one thousand men—the rattling of their artillery carriages—the prancing of their richly caparisoned horses, and the continued sound of their bugles, swelling through the air, made up a scene never to be described or forgotten.

The armies in line of battle were drawn up in a mountain pass. On our right was a deep ravine, impraticable to be turned by cavalry or artillery, whilst on our left the mountains of "Sierra Madre," towered two thousand feet in the skies. A spur of continuous hills, running from the mountain nearly to the ravine, was occupied by our troops—whilst the space between the spur of hills and the ravine, over which the San Luis road runs, was occupied by five pieces of light artillery commanded by Captain Washington. This was our centre, and was most gallantly defended by the captain, upon whose battery the enemy played four hours with six twenty-four-pounders, planted within point-blank range, and out of reach of his sixes, without making the slightest impression on them. Between the two armies were immense ravines, some of them nearly fifteen feet deep, the sides covered with loose pebbles, and the bottom extremely precipitate and serpentine from the heavy washing rains. A smooth piece of ground next the mountain, and between it and the head of the ravine, some three hundred yards in depth, was the most accessible point for turning our left flank, if, indeed, an army of five thousand two hundred men, displayed over two miles of ground, in the presence of such a host, could be considered as having a flank. Overlooking Washington's battery, and within near musket shot, is a high hill, on the crown of which was posted the First regiment of Illinois volunteers, to cover the battery and save the centre.

As soon as he received intelligence of Santa Anna's approach, General Taylor moved forward with May's squadron of dragoons, Sherman's and Bragg's batteries of artillery, and the Mississippi regiment of riflemen, under Colonel Davis, and arrived at the position which he had selected for awaiting the attack of the enemy. The time and the place, the hour and the man, seemed to promise a glorious celebration of the day. It was the 22nd of February, the anniversary of that day on which the God of battles gave to freedom its noblest champion, to patriotism its purest model; to America a preserver, and to the world the nearest realization of human perfection—for panegyric sinks before the name of Washington.

The morning was bright and beautiful. Not a cloud floated athwart the firmament, or dimmed the azure of the sky, and the flood of golden radiance which gilded the mountain tops, and poured over the valleys, wrought light and shade into a thousand fantastic forms. A soft breeze swept down from the mountains, rolling into graceful undulations the banner of the Republic, which was proudly streaming from the towers and battlements of Saltillo. The omens were all in our favor.

In the choice of his position, General Taylor had exhibited the same comprehensible sagacity and masterly *coup de' œil*, which characterized his dispositions at Resaca de la Palma, and which crowned triumphantly all his operations amid the blazing lines of Monterey. The mountains rise on either side of an irregular and broken valley, about three miles in width, dotted over with hills and ridges, and scarred with broad and winding ravines. The main road lies along the course of an arroyo, the bed of which is now so deep as to form an almost impassible barrier, while the other side is bounded by precipitous elevations, stretching perpendicularly towards the mountains, and separated by gullies, until they mingle into one at the base of the principal range. On the right of the narrowest point of the road-way, a battalion of the First Illinois regiment, under Lieutenant-Colonel Weatherford, was stationed in a small trench, extending to the ravine, while, on the opposite height, the main body of the regiment, under Colonel Hardin, was posted, with a single piece of artillery from Captain Washington's battery. The post of honor on the extreme right, was assigned to Bragg's artillery, his left supported by the Second regiment of Kentucky foot, under Colonel McKee, the left flank of which rested upon the arroyo. Washington's battery occupied a position immediately in front of the narrow point of the road-way, in rear of which and somewhat to the left, on another height, the Second Illinois regiment, under Colonel Bissel, was posted. Next, on the left, the Indiana brigade, under General Lane, was deployed, while on the extreme left the Kentucky cavalry, under Colonel Marshall, occupied a position directly under the frowning summits of the mountains. The two squadrons of First and Second dragoons, and the Arkansas cavalry under Colonel Yell, were posted in rear, ready for any service which the exigencies of the day might require.

The dispositions had been made for some time, when the enemy was seen advancing in the distance, and the clouds of dust which rolled up before him, gave satisfactory evidence that his numbers were not unworthy the trial of strength upon which we were about to enter. He arrived upon his position in immense masses, and with force sufficiently numerous to have commenced his attack at once, had he been as confident of success as it subsequently appeared he was solicitous for our safety. The first evidence directly afforded us of the presence of Santa Anna, was a white flag, which was dimly seen fluttering in the breeze, and anon Surgeon General Lindenberg, of the Mexican Army, arrived, bearing a beautiful emblem of benevolent bravado and Christian charity. It was a missive from Santa Anna, suggested by considerations for our personal comfort, which has placed us under lasting obligations, proposing to General Taylor terms of unconditional surrender, promising good treatment; assuring us that his force amounted to upwards of twenty thousand men, that our defeat was inevitable, and that to spare the effusion of blood, his proposition should be complied with. Strange to say, the American General showed the greatest ingratitude; evinced no appreciation whatever of Santa Anna's kindness, and informed him that whether his force amounted to twenty thousand or fifty thousand, it was equally a matter of indifference: the terms of adjustment must be arranged by gunpowder.

The messenger returned to his employer, and we waited in silence to hear the roar of his artillery. Hours rolled by without any movement on his part, and it appeared that the Mexican commander, grieved at our stubbornness, was almost disposed to retrace his steps, as if determined to have no further intercourse with such ungrateful audacity. At length, he mustered resolution to open a fire from a mortar, throwing several shells into our camp without execution. While this was going on, Captain Steene, of the First dragoons, with a single man, started towards a hill on which the Mexican general seemed to be stationed with his staff, but before he completed the ascent, the party vanished and when he reached the top, he discovered that two regiments had thrown themselves into squares to resist his charge. The captain's gravity was overcome by this opposition, and he returned.

The Kentucky cavalry and Arkansas troops were posted near the mountain, and as skirmishers, having been first dismounted, brought on the action, at half-past four o'clock, on the 22d, by engaging about fifteen hundred of the enemy's light troops, who had been deployed on the top of the mountain to turn our left. Our riflemen advanced up the side of the mountain, extending their line to prevent the enemy's flanking them, and fighting as they toiled up the almost perpendicular ascent, until the whole side of the mountain, from base to summit, was one sheet of fire. The sight was a splendid one, and our hearts warmed towards home and country, as we lay upon the field, contemplating the scene two thousand feet above us, and resolving that the next day should witness a noble victory, or a disastrous and terrible defeat. The firing continued until after dark, when our riflemen retired, the enemy remaining in possession of the heights. We slept upon our arms, on what was to be, the next day, a ghastly field of carnage. The Second Illinois regiment, which has suffered so severely, was posted about eight hundred yards from the base of the mountain; the Second Indiana on the left, and three pieces of light artillery, commanded by Lieutenant O'Brien, between us and the Indianians. Our position was that upon which the enemy would advance, it was supposed, with the heaviest force of his infantry, and was to be desperately defended. The first gun on the 23d was fired at daylight, and the firing continued until darkness put an end to the effusion of blood. No adequate description of the fight can be given; it was a succession of brilliant advances and disastrous retreats all day—our regiments advancing to attack five times their numbers, driving them with great loss, until the enemy, reinforced by fresh regiments, rallied, and in their turn, with overwhelming numbers, compelled us to fall back.

As we expected, the Mexican infantry advanced upon us in three columns, composed of eight regiments. Advancing steadily to the brow of the hill, the first line came down the hill a few paces; the second not quite so low, and the third upon the summit of the ravine bank; the most distant line about two hundred yards from us. Our regiment was kneeling, awaiting their advance, expecting that they would cross the ravine, and would have but two regiments to fight at once; but the instant they were formed, a terrific fire was opened upon us by the entire force, in our part of not less than four thousand regular troops. We were here ordered to open upon them, and for thirty minutes we poured into them as galling a fire as ever was witnessed—our men discharging their pieces not less than twenty times within point blank. Here we had about sixty officers and men killed and wounded. The Indianians on our left giving way early in the fight, enabled the lancers to cross the ravine, and come down upon our left flank, when we fell back some two hundred and fifty yards, where those that could be rallied halted and were again formed.

The Second Kentucky, commanded by Colonel McKee, were ordered to our support, as well as Colonel Hardin's First Illinoisians. Poor Hardin, with his gallant regiment, advanced upon them to our relief, and drove back the enemy to our left. By the time the Second Kentucky came up, we were again rallied, and with them made as fine a charge as ever was made, driving back four times our number, killing and wounding an immense number of the enemy, and capturing the standard of the First battalion of Cuanahuoto, which was taken by Captain Raith, of St. Clair county, and after remaining in our possession all day, was unfortunately lost in the last charge, which robbed the nation of Hardin, McKee and Clay.

During the night the Mexicans had established a twelve-pounder on a point at the base of the mountain, which commanded any position which could be taken by us. To counteract the effect of this piece, Lieutenant O'Brien, Fourth artillery, was detached with three pieces of Washington's battery, having with him Lieutenant Bryan, of the Topographical Engineers, who, having planted a few shells in the midst of the enemy's gunners, for the time effectually silenced his fire.

From the movements, soon perceptible, along the left of our line, it became evident that the enemy was attempting to turn that flank, and for this purpose had concentrated a large body of cavalry and infantry on his right. The base of the mountain around which these troops were winding their way, seemed girdled with a belt of steel, as their glittering sabres and polished lances flashed back the beams of the morning sun. Sherman's and Bragg's batteries were immediately ordered to the left: Colonel Bissell's regiment occupied a position between them, while Colonel McKee's Kentuckians were transferred from the right of our line, so as to hold a position near the centre. The Second Indiana regiment, under Colonel Bowles, was placed on our extreme left, nearly perpendicular to the direction of our line, so as to oppose, by a direct fire, the flank movement of the enemy. These dispositions having been promptly effected, the artillery of each army opened its fire, and, simultaneously, the Mexican infantry commenced a rapid and extended discharge upon our line, from the left to McKee's regiment. Our artillery belched forth its thunders with tremendous effect, while the Kentuckians returned the fire of the Mexican infantry, with great steadiness and success; their field officers, McKee, Clay and Fry, passing along their line, animating and encouraging the men, by precept and example. The Second Illinois regiment also received the enemy's fire with great firmness, and returned an ample equivalent. While this fierce conflict was going on, the main body of Colonel Hardin's regiment moved to the right of the Kentuckians, and the representatives of each state seemed to vie with each other in the honorable ambition of doing the best service for their country. Both regiments gallantly sustained their positions, and won unfading laurels. The veterans of Austerlitz could not have exhibited more courage, coolness and devotion.

In the meantime, the enemy's cavalry had been stealthily pursuing its way along the mountain, and though our artillery had wrought great havoc among its numbers, the leading squadrons had passed the extreme points of danger, and were almost in position to attack us in the rear. At this critical moment, the Indiana regiment turned upon its proper front, and commenced an inglorious flight. The efforts of Colonel Bowles to bring it into position were vain, and over hills and ravines they pursued their shameful career, to the great delight of the enemy, who rent the air with shouts of triumph. Several officers of General

Taylor's staff immediately dashed off, to arrest, if possible, the retreating regiment, and restore it again to reputation and to duty. Major Dix, of the Pay Department, formerly of the Seventh infantry, was the first to reach the deserters, and seizing the colors of the regiment, appealed to the men, to know whether they had determined to desert them. He was answered by three cheers, showing, that though the men had little disposition to become heroes themselves, they were not unmindful of an act of distinguished gallantry on the part of another. A portion of the regiment immediately rallied around him, and was re-formed by the officers. Dix, in person, then led them towards the enemy, until one of the men volunteered to take the flag. The party returned to the field, and though not in time to repair the disaster which their flight had created, to retrieve in a slight degree, the character of the state. While the day, however, by this disgraceful panic, was fast going against us, the artillery was advanced, its front extended, and different sections and pieces under Sherman, Bragg, O'Brien, Thomas, Reynolds, Kilburn, French, and Bryan, were working such carnage in the ranks of the enemy as to make his columns roll to and fro, like ships upon the billows. His triumph at the Indiana retreat was but for a moment, and his shouts of joy were soon followed by groans of anguish, and the shrieks of expiring hundreds.

Washington's battery on the right, had now opened its fire, and driven back a large party of lancers, advancing in that direction. Along the entire line the battle raged with great fury. Twenty-one thousand of the victims of Mexican oppression and the myrmidons of Mexican despotism, were arrayed against five thousand Americans, sent forth to conquer a peace.

The discharges of the infantry followed each other more rapidly than the sounds of the Swiss bell-ringers in the fierce fervor of a finale, and the volleys of artillery reverberated through the mountains like the thunders of an Alpine storm.

The myriads of Mexican cavalry still pressed forward on our left, and threatened a charge upon the Mississippi rifles under Colonel Davis, who had been ordered to support the Indiana regiment, and had succeeded in preserving a fragment of it in position. Colonel Davis immediately threw his command into the form of a V, the opening towards the enemy, and awaited his advance. On he came, dashing with all the speed of Mexican horses, but when he arrived at that point from which could be seen the whites of his eyes, both lines poured forth a sheet of lead that scattered him like chaff, felling many a gallant steed to the earth, and sending scores of riders to the sleep that knows no waking.

While the dispersed Mexican cavalry were rallying, the Third Indiana regiment, under Colonel Lane, was ordered to join Colonel Davis, supported by a considerable body of horse. About this time, from some unknown reason, our wagon train displayed its length along the Saltillo road, and offered a conspicuous prize for the Mexican lancers, which they seemed not unwilling to appropriate. Fortunately, Lieutenant Rucker, with a squadron of the First dragoons, (Captain Steene having been previously wounded, and Captain Eustis confined to his bed by illness,) was present, and by order of General Taylor, dashed among them in a most brilliant style, dispersing them by his charge, as effectually as the previous fire of the Mississippi riflemen. May's dragoons, with a squadron of Arkansas cavalry, under Captain Pike, and supported by a single piece of artillery, under Lieutenant Reynolds, now claimed their share in the discussion, and when the Mexicans had again assembled, they had to encounter another shock from the two squadrons, besides a fierce fire of grape from Reynolds' six-pounder. The lancers once more rallied, and directing their course towards the Saltillo road, were met by the remainder of Colonel Yell's regiment and Marshall's Kentuckians, who drove them towards the mountains on the opposite side of the valley, where, from their appearance when last visible, it may be presumed, they are still running. In this precipitate movement, they were compelled to pass through a rancho, in which many of our valiant comrades had previously taken refuge, who, from this secure retreat, opened quite an effective fire upon them. Several hundreds of the Arkansas cavalry were so well satisfied with the result of this single effort, that they deemed it unnecessary to make another, and accordingly kept on their way to town, and there reported General Taylor as in full retreat.

About two o'clock in the day, the Second Kentucky and Second Illinois, who had never retired more than three hundred yards from where we had received the enemy's first fire, were lying in the head of two ravines, under cover from the enemy's artillery, who had taken post upon the ground abandoned by the Indiana regiment, and were driving a torrent of round shot, grape and canister amongst us, when suddenly the firing ceased, and four officers, at their utmost speed, came galloping towards us. Colonels McKee, Clay, Bissell and myself, advanced some sixty yards from our cover to meet them. With the greatest difficulty our men were restrained from firing upon them as they came up, alleging that as they brought no white flag, it was a *ruse*. They asked for General Taylor. Colonel Clay accompanied one of them, the Aid of General Santa Anna, to General Taylor, who was sitting with his right leg over his horse's neck, just behind us, as unconcerned at the danger he was in, and as composed as man possibly could be. Whilst the aid was delivering his message to the general, we took the liberty of quizzing the other three a little. I asked one of them who appeared highest in rank, "What is the object of your mission?" He replied, by pointing to our men, who were, the most of them, lying on their faces, at full length, about forty paces from him, "Those are troops of the line, are they?" To which we re plied, "Six hundred of them are." I then resumed my questions, when he answered in Spanish, and as we did not appear to comprehend him, repeated in French, that "General Santa Anna wishes to know what General Taylor wants." He said it with such an air of unconcern, that we all broke out into a loud laugh.

I understand that when the aid reached the General, he repeated the same thing to him, when the old "war hero" told the interpreter to tell him, "he wanted the Mexican army to surrender; tell him that I will treat Santa Anna and his army like gentlemen." The fact is, that at this time the right wing of the Mexican forces had been entirely cut off, and near four thousand lancers and infantry were at the mercy of Captain Bragg's battery of light artillery, which had been advanced so close to their line, that with canister they would rake a deep ravine, through which they were compelled to pass to rejoin the main body of the Mexican force, which they were on the full retreat to re-unite with, having been driven back by the cavalry, Mississippians and Sherman's light battery, which poured a most destructive fire upon them. At the same time that the messenger came from Santa Anna, to whom I have alluded, a white flag was sent in from the right wing under retreat. Mr. Crittenden, General Taylor's aid, I think, returned with it to the enemy's lines, where they closed round him, and under protection of the flag, with Mr. Crittenden in their midst, passed Bragg's battery within point-blank canister range. Thus, but for their duplicity, the entire right wing of their army would have been taken, the victory won, and the terrible loss we sustained in the last charge, saved the nation.

The craft of Santa Anna had restored his courage, and with his reinforcement of cavalry, he determined to charge our line. Under cover of their artillery, horse and foot advanced upon our batteries. These, from the smallness of our infantry force, were but feebly supported, yet by the most brilliant and daring efforts nobly maintained their position. Such was the rapidity of their transitions, that officers and pieces seemed empowered with ubiquity, and upon cavalry and infantry alike, wherever they appeared, they poured so destructive a fire as to silence the enemy's artillery, compel his whole line to fall back, and soon to assume a sort of *sauve qui peut* movement, indicating anything but victory. The two wings re-united (near where the Second Indiana were posted in the morning) under the most blazing and effective fire from our light batteries, that cannon ever poured into columns of men. They fell by scores, and on this spot I saw, the next day, as many as five men killed by the same round shot—legs were knocked in one direction, arms in another—horses, lancers and infantry, in rich profusion strewed the ground. The enemy retired under this most withering fire, and if we had been content with a victory only, we had won one never to be forgotten whilst our history lasts; but, unfortunately, we here pursued it too far. The gallant and lamented Hardin—the soul of bravery—advanced with his regiment to charge the enemy's cannon, under cover of which he was rapidly retiring. But while we were negotiating with the white flags, the enemy's reserve of nearly five thousand chosen infantry, who were fresh, and had not participated in the day, were advanced, and placed in the immense ravine which separated the two armies in the morning. They must have extended down the ravine, towards the San Louis road, for six hundred yards. The ground was cut to pieces with these ravines running parallel to each other, and not more than one hundred and fifty yards apart. In advancing upon the enemy's battery, the First regiment soon came under a most galling fire from the right of the enemy's reserve, and was immediately ordered to cover itself by the deep ravine, around the head of which it was filing, when the fire opened upon it.

As we had fought side by side so long, our regiment with one will and heart advanced to their relief, crossed the deep ravine, and taking position on the right of the First Illinois regiment, commenced a hot fire upon the enemy's right, which soon would have brought them to a right-about. After exchanging some dozen rounds, a perfect forest of bayonets made their appearance over the brow of the hill right in our front, and gave us as much to do as we could to return their fire.

At this critical point of the battle, when it became

necessary to sustain one of our columns, which was staggering under a charge made by the Mexicans in overwhelming numbers, General Taylor dispatched Mr. Crittenden to order Colonel McKee, of the Second Kentucky regiment, to bring his men into immediate action. Mr. Crittenden found the regiment, men and officers, eager for the fray, delivered the order and rode back to the general, by whose side it was his duty to keep. The Kentuckians moved forward in gallant style, led by McKee and Clay, both of whom, alas! fell in a subsequent part of the day. It so happened that before reaching a position from which they could deliver an effective fire, the regiment had to cross a valley which was broken up by ravines and masses of stone. While crossing this valley, the heads only of the men could be seen from the point which General Taylor and Mr. Crittenden occupied, and these were bobbing up and down and crosswise in such confusion as to impress both with the idea that the regiment had fallen into disorder. The Mexicans were annoying them at the same moment by a fire, which helped to confirm the opinion of the general that the Kentuckians were thrown into dismay. It was one of those decisive crises which occur in every contested field, when the issue of the day depended, for the time being, upon the gallantry of a particular corps.

General Taylor, who, as before said, could only see the heads of the troops, and misled by their motions in getting across gullies and going around rocks and other obstructions, into the belief that they were about to falter, turned to Mr. Crittenden, (who is a Kentuckian,) and with a countenance indicating deep mortification, for the general is a Kentuckian too, and an eye fierce with emotion, exclaimed: "Mr. Crittenden, this will not do—this is not the way for Kentuckians to behave themselves when called upon to make good a battle—it will not answer, sir;" and with this he clenched his fist, and knit his brow, and set his teeth hard together. Mr. Crittenden, who was mistaken by the same indications that deceived the general, could scarcely make a reply, from very chagrin and shame. In a few moments, however, the Kentuckians had crossed the uneven places, and were seen ascending the slope of the valley, shoulder to shoulder, and with the firm and regular step of veterans of a hundred fields.

On they moved until they reached the crest of the hill, where they met the enemy before the flush of a temporary advantage had subsided. Here they delivered their fire by companies with such regularity and deadly aim that the decimated phalanx of Mexico gave way and retreated precipitately. As the Kentuckians emerged from the valley, the countenance of the old general, who was regarding them with the intensest interest, gradually relaxed the bitterness of its expression. A glow of pride supplanted the deep mortification which fixed his muscles, and enthusiasm qualified the fierce glances of his eye. Forward they moved under his riveted gaze, whose feelings became more and more wrought up as they approached the scene of carnage. When they opened their fire the old general could no longer restrain his admiration, but broke forth with a loud huzza. "Hurrah for old Kentuck," he exclaimed, talking as it were to himself and rising in his saddle—"That's the way to do it; give it to 'em," and the tears of exultation rolled down his cheeks as he said it. Having got rid of this exultation of state pride, he went about looking after other parts of the field.

This regiment, too, had as much to do in front as one regiment could attend to, whilst about one thousand infantry on their right ran across the level ground between the two ravines, to cut off our retreat to the San Luis road, down which, under cover of Washington's guns, we could only reach the redoubt on the hill, where the First Illinois were posted in the early part of the action.

Again our spirits rose. The Mexicans appeared thoroughly routed, and while their regiments and divisions were flying before us, nearly all our light troops were ordered forward, and followed them with a most deadly fire, mingled with shouts which rose above the roar of artillery. In this charge the First Illinois regiment and McKee's Kentuckians were foremost. The pursuit was too hot, and as it evinced too clearly our deficiency in numbers, the Mexicans, with a suddenness which was almost magical, rallied and returned upon us. They came in myriads, and for a while the carnage was dreadful on both sides. We were but a handful to oppose the frightful masses which were hurled upon us, and could as easily have resisted an avalanche of thunderbolts. We were driven back, and the day seemed lost beyond redemption. Victory, which a moment before appeared within our grasp, was suddenly torn from our standard. There was but one hope, but that proved an anchor sure and steadfast.

While our men were driven through the ravines, at the extremities of which a body of Mexican lancers was stationed to pounce upon them like tigers,—Brent and Whiting, of Washington's battery, gave them such a torrent of grape as to put them to flight, and thus saved the remnants of those brave regiments, which had long born the hottest portion of the fight. On the other flank, while the Mexicans came rushing on like legions of fiends, the artillery was left unsupported, and capture by the enemy seemed inevitable.

I soon discovered that the odds against us was so great, that we must be overpowered, and having witnessed, during the day, the barbarities committed upon our wounded officers, resigned myself to die. The right wing of the enemy's reserve had crossed over, and were turning our left flank—our men were too tired and broken down to bring them to the bayonet, and our only salvation was in retreat. I turned my eyes down the ravine, and the distance sickened me; and when I thought, but for one instant, upon how many gallant men would die there—murdered, butchered, even after surrender—my brain reeled: the order was given to retreat—no possible order could be observed, the banks were precipitate, rocky, and covered with loose rolling pebbles—five colonels were, with their regiments, at the head of the ravine where the order was given—three of them, John J. Hardin, Colonel KcKee, and Lieutenant-Colonel Henry Clay, fell wounded, and were inhumanly lanced to death, and stripped of their clothing. I think the lance was run through poor Clay as often as ten times; his men carried him some two hundred yards, but to save their own lives, were compelled to abandon him; the wound which disabled him, was slight one through the legs. The same was poor Hardin's case. Colonel Bissell and myself escaped untouched, but a horrible massacre of our men took place here. Besides a large number of privates, there fell in this fatal ravine, Captain Zabriskie, First Illinois volunteers; Captain William T. Willis, Kentucky volunteers; Lieutenants T. Kelly, Rodney Ferguson, Edward F. Fletcher, Lauriston Robbins, Allen B. Rountree, and James C. Steele, of Second Illinois volunteers; Lieutenant Hoten, First Illinois, and Lieutenant Ball, Second Kentucky volunteers.

But Bragg 'and Thomas rose with the crisis, and eclipsed even the fame they won at Monterey, while Sherman, O'Brien and Bryan, proved themselves worthy of the alliance. Every horse with O'Brien's battery was killed, and the enemy had advanced to within range of grape, sweeping all before him. But here his progress was arrested, and before the showers of iron hail which assailed him, squadrons and battalions fell like leaves in the blast of autumn. The Mexicans were once more driven back with great loss, though taking with them the three pieces of artillery which were without horses.

The lancers who had dashed down the road to cut off our retreat, were driven back by Washington's artillery, which opened a well directed fire upon them; but for which, not one of us would have gotten out—the banks on each side of the ravine were very steep, at least fifty feet, and it was impossible to rally a man under the desolating fire which poured upon us from several thousand fresh troops. When we reached the redoubt it was nearly night; we had been in the engagement since daylight, and nature, unable to bear under greater burdens, yielded, officers and men sinking down upon the rocks and earth, completely exhausted. Thus, thrice during the day, when all seemed lost but honor, did the artillery, by the ability with which it was manœuvred, roll back the tide of success from the enemy, and give such overwhelming destructiveness to its effect, that the army was saved and the glory of our arms maintained.

The battle had now raged with variable success for

DEATH OF LIEUT. COLONEL CLAY.

nearly ten hours, and by a sort of mutual consent, after the last carnage wrought among the Mexicans by the artillery, both parties seemed willing to pause upon the result. Night fell, and the American general, with his troops, slept upon the battle-ground, prepared, if necessary, to resume operations on the morrow. But ere the sun rose again upon the scene, the Mexicans had disappeared, leaving behind them only their dead and dying, whose bones are to whiten their native hills, and whose moans of anguish were to excite in their enemies that compassion, which can have no existence in the bosoms of their friends.

Throughout the action, General Taylor was where the shot fell hottest and thickest, two of which passed through his clothes. He constantly evinced the greatest quickness of conception, fertility of resource, and a cool, unerring judgment, not to be baffled. General Wool was wherever his presence was required, stimulating the troops to activity and exertion. The operations of General Lane were confined to his own brigade, and his efforts were worthy of better material for their application. Major Bliss bore himself with his usual gallantry, having his horse, as at Palo Alto, shot in the head. Mr. Crittenden, a son of the senator from Kentucky, was conspicuous in the field, as volunteer aid to General Taylor, and the medical director' assistant surgeon, Hitchcock, could be sometimes seen where the balls fell fastest, binding up a wound or dressing a broken leg, with true professional zeal; and, anon, galloping with the ardor of an amateur knight, conveying orders to different commanders.

I could recount a thousand acts of individual courage worthy of record, but when all behaved so well, it would be invidious almost to record them. Captain

Lincoln was waving us on with his sword, when he fell dead into the arms of Captain Raith, of Belleville. Captain Steene, of the Dragoons, was on every part of the field, animating the volunteers by his presence and words; where the bullets were thickest his towering black was seen, until the gallant rider fell, severely wounded. Colonel Churchill has won an imperishable reputation for coolness and bravery. He rode along the lines but a minute before the enemy opened upon us, remarking, "My brave Illinoisians, you did not make this long march to be defeated now, did you?" and retired, his horse receiving four wounds.

General Wool behaved most gallantly, and has earned all the country can do for him, besides the respect, esteem and admiration of his brigade, who, before the battle, had a long account of what they considered petty annoyances treasured against him.

What can be said of "Old Rough and Ready?" He was everywhere at the same time, animating, ordering, and persuading his men to remember the day and their country, and strike home for both. The breast of his coat was pierced by a canister shot. "These balls are growing excited," was his cool remark.

I give you a list of killed and wounded of our regiment; it is the highest, though bloodiest eulogium that can be passed upon it. I have extended this letter to an alarming length, I am aware, but your readers will excuse it—the theme is a mighty one—my heart is full, and my pen could not be controlled. Major Mansfield, for self-possession and cool courage, was unequalled by any officer on the field. General Taylor's staff, among whom is Lieutenant Pope, of our state, bore orders through every part of the field.

In this, as in every case of arbitrament by the sword,

GENERAL WOOL

the laurel is closely entwined with the cypress, and the lustre of a brilliant victory is darkened by the blood with which it has been purchased. I am unable to state our loss, but it has been very severe, and proves the battle of Buena Vista to have been, by far, the most terrible conflict in which our troops have been engaged. Captain Lincoln, assistant adjutant-general to General Wool, fell early in the action, while proudly distinguished by his efforts to bring the flying regiment back to their position, and with his last breath bore testimony against Indiana cowardice. Colonel Yell was pierced by a lance, while gallantly leading his regiment against the Mexican cavalry. The noble Hardin met his death gloriously, while conducting the last terrible charge. Colonel McKee, after having gallantly sustained the honor of Kentucky, throughout the action, fell in the foremost rank, and Lieutenant-Colonel Clay was cut down at almost the same moment with Hardin and McKee, while giving his men the most brilliant example of noble daring and lofty chivalry. Others have fallen, but their names are not known to me; nor is it for me to pronounce the eulogy of those whose names I have recorded. Other and abler pens will do justice to the character and memory of the illustrious dead, whose devotion to the republic they have written with their blood and sealed with their lives. Lincoln was a gallant officer and accomplished gentleman, of pure heart and generous impulses, and worthy of his revolutionary lineage. Yell was a warm friend and gallant man, quick to see the right, and ready to pursue it. Hardin was one of Nature's noblest spirits, a soldier tried and true, a rare union of the best qualities of the head and heart. McKee was wise in council and brave in the field, with a heart moved by the tenderest sympathies and most noble impulses. And what shall I say of Clay—the young, the brave, the chivalrous—foremost in the fight—the soul of every lofty sentiment? Devoted to his friends and generous to his enemies, he fell in the flower of his age and usefulness, and has left no worthier name behind him. If he was not the "noblest Roman of them all,' few will deny that in him—

"Were the elements
So mixed, that Nature might stand up and say
To all the world—THIS WAS A MAN."

As General Taylor's own account of his brilliant achievements always presents the clearest conception of them to the mind, and affords the best index to his character, his detailed official report of this most splendid of all his military deeds, is given at length below. There are many incidents in such a battle as this, that must escape the attention of every one but the commanding general himself; and though his account is, of necessity, less exciting, as it is confined more to mere detail, than the graphic description already given, yet it presents facts in an authentic shape, and is therefore not only most sought after, but composes a necessary part of the history of the war. It is a monument, too, to the patriotism of the brave men who sacrificed their lives for their country on the bloody field of Buena Vista, no less than to his own genius, gallantry and patriotism, and as such must be preserved:

"I have the honor to submit a detailed report of the operations of the forces under my command, which resulted in the engagement of Buena Vista, the repulse of the Mexican army, and the re-occupation of this position.

"The information which reached me of the advance and concentration of a heavy Mexican force in my front, had assumed such a probable form as to induce a special examination far beyond the reach of our pickets to ascertain its correctness. A small party of Texan spies, under Major McCullough, dispatched to the hacienda of Encarnacion, thirty miles from this, on the route to San Luis Potosi, had reported a cavalry force of unknown strength at that place. On the 20th of February, a strong reconnoissance, under Lieutenant-Colonel May, was dispatched to the hacienda of Hecliondo, while Major McCullough made another examination of Encarnacion. The result of these expeditions left no doubt that the enemy was in large force at Encarnacion, under the orders of General Santa Anna, and that he meditated a forward movement and attack upon our position.

"As the camp at Agua Nueva could be turned on either flank, and as the enemy's force was greatly superior to our own, particularly in the arm of cavalry, I determined, after much consideration, to take up a position about eleven miles in rear, and there await the attack. The army broke up its camp and marched at noon on the 21st, encamping at the new position a little in front of the hacienda of Buena Vista. With a small force I proceeded to Saltillo, to make some necessary arrangements for the defence of the town, leaving Brigadier-General Wool in the immediate command of the troops.

"Before those arrangements were completed, on the morning of the 22d, I was advised that the enemy was in sight, advancing. Upon reaching the ground, it was found that his cavalry advance was in our front, having marched from Encarnacion, as we have since learned, at eleven o'clock the day previous, and driving in a mounted force left at Agua Nueva to cover the removal of public stores. Our troops were in position, occupying a line of remarkable strength. The road at this point becomes a narrow defile, the valley on its right being rendered quite impracticable for artillery by a succession of deep and impassable gullies, while on the left a succession of rugged ridges and precipitous ravines extends far back toward the mountain which bounds the valley. The features of the ground were such as nearly to paralyze the artillery and cavalry of the enemy, while his infantry could not derive all the advantage of its numerical superiority. In this position we prepared to receive him. Captain Washington's battery (Fourth artillery) was posted to command the road, while the First and Second Illinois regiments, under Colonels Hardin and Bissell, each eight companies, (to the latter of which was attached Captain Conner's company of Texas volunteers,) and the Second Kentucky, under Colonel McKee, occupied the crests of the ridges on the left and in rear. The Arkansas and Kentucky regiments of cavalry, commanded by Colonels Yell and H. Marshall, occupied the extreme left near the base of the mountain, while the Indiana brigade, under Brigadier-General Lane, (composed of the Second and Third regiments, under Colonels Bowles and Lane,) the Mississippi riflemen, under Colonel Davis, the squadrons of the First and Second dragoons, under Captain Steene and Lieutenant-Colonel May, and the light batteries of Captains Sherman and Bragg, Third artillery, were held in reserve.

"At eleven o'clock I received from General Santa Anna a summons to surrender at discretion, which, with a copy of my reply, I have already transmitted. The enemy still forebore his attack, evidently waiting for the arrival of his rear columns, which could be distinctly seen by our look-outs as they approached the field. A demonstration made on his left caused me to detach the Second Kentucky regiment and a section of artillery to our right, in which position they bivouacked for the night. In the meantime the Mexican light troops had engaged ours on the extreme left, (composed of parts of the Kentucky and Arkansas cavalry dismounted, and a rifle battalion from the Indiana brigade, under Major Gorman, the whole commanded by Colonel Marshall,) and kept up a sharp fire, climbing the mountain side, and apparently endeavoring to gain our flank. Three pieces of Captain Washington's battery had been detached to the left, and were supported by the Second Indiana regiment. An occasional shell was thrown by the enemy into this part of our line, but without effect. The skirmishing of the light troops was kept up with trifling loss on our part until dark, when I became convinced that no serious attack would be made before the morning, and returned, with the Mississippi regiment and squadron of Second dragoons, to Saltillo. The troops bivouacked without fires, and laid upon their arms. A body of cavalry, some fifteen hundred strong, had been visible all day in rear of the town, having entered the valley through a narrow pass, east of the city. This cavalry, commanded by General Minon, had evidently been thrown in our rear to break up and harass our retreat, and perhaps make some attempt against the town, if practicable. The city was occupied by four excellent companies of Illinois volunteers, under Major Warren, of the First regiment. A field-work, which commanded most of the approaches, was garrisoned by Captain Webster's company, First artillery, and armed with two twenty-four pound howitzers, while the train and headquarter camp was guarded by two companies of Mississippi riflemen, under Captain Rogers, and a field-piece, commanded by Captain Shover, Third artillery. Having made these dispositions for the protection of the rear, I proceeded on the morning of the 23rd to Buena Vista, ordering forward all the other available troops. The action had commenced before my arrival on the field.

"During the evening and night of the 22nd, the en emy had thrown a body of light troops on the mountain side, with the purpose of outflanking our left; and it was here that the action of the 23rd commenced at an early hour. Our riflemen, under Colonel Marshall, who had been reinforced by three companies under Major Trail, Second Illinois volunteers, maintained their ground handsomely against a greatly superior force, holding themselves under cover, and using their weapons with deadly effect. About eight o'clock, a strong demonstration was made against the centre of our position, a heavy column moving along the road. This force was soon dispersed by a few rapid and well-directed shots from Captain Washington's battery. In the meantime the enemy was concentrating a large force of infantry and cavalry, under cover of the ridges, with the obvious intention of forcing our left, which was posted on an extensive plateau. The Second Indiana and Second Illinois regiments formed this part of our line, the former covering three pieces of light artillery under the orders of Captain O'Brien

—Brigadier-General Lane being in the immediate command. In order to bring his men within effective range, General Lane ordered the artillery and Second Indiana regiment forward. The artillery advanced within musket range of a heavy body of Mexican infantry, and was served against it with great effect, but without being able to check its advance. The infantry ordered to its support had fallen back in disorder, being exposed, as well as the battery, not only to a severe fire of small-arms from the front, but also to a murderous cross-fire of grape and canister, from a Mexican battery on the left. Captain O'Brien found it impossible to retain his position without support, but was only able to withdraw two of his pieces, all the horses and cannoneers of the third piece being killed or disabled. The Second Indiana regiment, which had fallen back as stated, could not be rallied, and took no farther part in the action, except a handful of men, who under its gallant colonel, Bowles, joined the Mississippi regiment, and did good service, and those fugitives who, at a later period in the day, assisted in defending the train and depot at Buena Vista. This portion of our line having given way, and the enemy appearing in overwhelming force against our left flank, the light troops which had rendered such good service on the mountain were compelled to withdraw, which they did, for the most part, in good order. Many, however, were not rallied until they reached the depot at Buena Vista, to the defence of which they afterwards contributed.

"Colonel Bissell's regiment (Second Illinois,) which had been joined by a section of Captain Sherman's battery, had become completely outflanked, and was compelled to fall back, being entirely unsupported. The enemy was now pouring masses of infantry and cavalry along the base of the mountain on our left, and was gaining our rear in great force. At this moment I arrived upon the field. The Mississippi regiment had been directed to the left before reaching the position, and immediately came into action against the Mexican infantry which had turned our flank. The Second Kentucky regiment, and a section of artillery under Captain Bragg, had previously been ordered from the right to reinforce our left, and arrived at a most opportune moment. That regiment, and a portion of the First Illinois, under Colonel Hardin, gallantly drove the enemy, and recovered a portion of the ground we had lost. The batteries of Captains Sherman and Bragg were in position on the plateau, and did much execution, not only in front, but particularly upon the masses which had gained our rear. Discovering that the enemy was heavily pressing upon the Mississippi regiment, the Third Indiana regiment, under Colonel Lane, was dispatched to strengthen that part of our line, which formed a crotchet perpendicular to the first line of battle. At the same time Lieutenant Kilburn, with a piece of Captain Bragg's battery, was directed to support the infantry there engaged. The action was for a long time warmly sustained at that point—the enemy making several efforts both with infantry and cavalry against our line, and being always repulsed with heavy loss. I had placed all the regular cavalry and Captain Pike's squadron of Arkansas horse under the orders of Brevet Lieutenant-Colonel May, with directions to hold in check the enemy's column, still advancing to the rear along the base of the mountain, which was done in conjunction with the Kentucky and Arkansas cavalry, under Colonels Marshall and Yell.

"In the meantime our left, which was still strongly threatened by a superior force, was further strengthened by the detachment of Captain Bragg's and a portion of Captain Sherman's batteries to that quarter. The concentration of artillery fire upon the masses of the enemy along the base of the mountain, and the determined resistance offered by the two regiments opposed to them, had created confusion in their ranks, and some of the corps attempted to effect a retreat upon their main line of battle. The squadron of the First dragoons, under Lieutenant Rucker, was now ordered up the deep ravine which these retreating corps were endeavoring to cross, in order to charge and disperse them. The squadron proceeded to the point indicated, but could not accomplish the object, being exposed to a heavy fire from a battery established to cover the retreat of those corps. While the squadron was detached on this service, a large body of the enemy was observed to concentrate on our extreme left, apparently with the view of making a descent upon the hacienda of Buena Vista, where our train and baggage were deposited. Lieutenant-Colonel May was ordered to the support of that point, with two pieces of Captain Sherman's battery under Lieutenant Reynolds. In the meantime, the scattered forces near the hacienda, composed in part of Majors Trail and Gormon's commands, had been to some extent organized under the advice of Major Munroe, chief of artillery, with the assistance of Major Morrison, volunteer staff, and were posted to defend the position. Before our cavalry had reached the hacienda, that of the enemy had made its attack; having been handsomely met by the Kentucky and Arkansas cavalry under Colonels Marshall and Yell. The Mexican column immediately divided, one portion sweeping by the depot, where it received a destructive fire from the force which had collected there, and then gaining the mountain opposite, under a fire from Lieutenant Reynolds' section, the remaining portion regaining the base of the mountain on our left. In the charge at Buena Vista, Colonel Yell fell gallantly at the head of his regiment; we also lost Adjutant Vaughan, of the Kentucky cavalry—a young officer of much promise. Lieutenant-Colonel May, who had been rejoined by the squadron of the First dragoons and by portions of the Arkansas and Indiana troops, under Lieutenant-Colonel Roane and Major Gorman, now approached the base of the mountain, holding in check the right flank of the enemy, upon whose masses, crowded in the narrow gorges and ravines, our artillery was doing fearful execution.

"The position of that portion of the Mexican army which had gained our rear was now very critical, and it seemed doubtful whether it could regain the main body. At this moment I received from General Santa Anna a message by a staff officer, desiring to know what I wanted? I immediately dispatched Brigadier General Wool to the Mexican general-in-chief, and sent orders to cease firing. Upon reaching the Mexican lines, General Wool could not cause the enemy to cease their fire, and accordingly returned without having an interview. The extreme right of the enemy continued its retreat along the base of the mountain, and finally, in spite of all our efforts, effected a junction with the remainder of the army.

"During the day, the cavalry of General Minon had ascended the elevated plain above Saltillo, and occupied the road from the city to the field of battle, where they intercepted several of our men. Approaching the town, they were fired upon by Captain Webster, from the redoubt occupied by his company, and then moved off towards the eastern side of the valley, and obliquely towards Buena Vista. At this time, Captain Shover moved rapidly forward with his piece, supported by a miscellaneous command of mounted volunteers, and fired several shots at the cavalry with great effect. They were driven into the ravines which lead to the lower valley, closely pursued by Captain Shover, who was farther supported by a piece of Captain Webster's battery, under Lieutenant Donaldson, which had advanced from the redoubt, supported by Captain Wheeler's company of Illinois volunteers. The enemy made one or two efforts to charge the artillery, but was finally driven back in a confused mass, and did not again appear upon the plain.

"In the meantime the firing had partially ceased upon the principal field. The enemy seemed to confine his efforts to the protection of his artillery, and I had left the plateau for a moment, when I was recalled thither by a very heavy musketry fire. On regaining that position, I discovered that our infantry (Illinois and Second Kentucky) had engaged a greatly superior force of the enemy—evidently his reserve—and that they had been overwhelmed by numbers. The moment was most critical. Captain O'Brien, with two pieces, had sustained this heavy charge to the last, and was finally obliged to leave his guns on the field—his infantry support being entirely routed. Captain Bragg, who had just arrived from the left, was ordered at once into battery. Without any infantry to support him, and at the imminent risk of losing his guns, this officer came rapidly into action, the Mexican line being but a few yards from the muzzles of his pieces. The first discharge of canister caused the enemy to hesitate ; the second and third drove him back in disorder and saved the day. The Second Kentucky regiment, which had advanced beyond supporting distance in this affair was driven back and closely pressed by the enemy's cavalry. Taking a ravine which led in the direction of Captain Washington's battery, their pursuers became exposed to his fire, which soon checked and drove them back with loss. In the meantime the rest of our artillery had taken position on the plateau, covered by the Mississippi and Third Indiana regiments, the former of which had reached the ground in time to pour a fire into the right flank of the enemy, and thus contribute to his repulse. In this last conflict we had the misfortune to sustain a very heavy loss. Colonel Hardin, First Illinois, and Colonel McKee and Lieutenant-Colonel Clay, Second Kentucky regiment, fell at this time, while gallantly leading their commands.

"No farther attempt was made by the enemy to force our position, and the approach of night gave an opportunity to pay proper attention to the wounded, and also to refresh the soldiers, who had been exhausted by incessant watchfulness and combat. Though the night was severely cold, the troops were compelled for the most to bivouac without fires, expecting that morning would renew the conflict. During the night the wounded were removed to Saltillo, and every preparation made to receive the enemy, should he again attack our position. Seven fresh companies were drawn from the town, and Brigadier-General Marshall, with a reinforcement of Kentucky cavalry and four heavy guns, under Captain Prentiss, First artillery, was near at hand, when it was discovered that the enemy had abandoned his position during the night. Our scouts soon ascertained that he had fallen back upon Agua Nueva. The great disparity of numbers, and the exhaustion of our troops, rendered it inexpedient and hazardous to attempt pursuit. A staff officer was dispatched to General Santa Anna, to negotiate an exchange of prisoners, which was satisfactorily completed on the following day. Our own dead were collected and buried, and the Mexican wounded, of which a large number had been left upon the field, were removed to Saltillo, and rendered as comfortable as circumstances would permit.

"On the evening of the 26th, a close reconnoissance was made of the enemy's position, which was found to be occupied only by a small body of cavalry, the infantry and artillery having retreated in the direction of San Luis Potosi. On the 27th, our troops resumed their former camp at Agua Nueva, the enemy's rearguard evacuating the place as we approached, leaving a considerable number of wounded. It was my purpose to beat up his quarters at Encarnacion early the next morning, but upon examination, the weak condition of the cavalry horses rendered it unadvisable to attempt so long a march without water. A command was finally dispatched to Encarnacion, on the 1st of March, under Colonel Belknap. Some two hundred wounded, and about sixty Mexican soldiers were found there, the army having passed on in the direction of Matehuala, with greatly reduced numbers, and suffering much from hunger. The dead and dying were strewed upon the road and crowded the buildings of the hacienda.

"The American force engaged in the action of

Buena Vista is shown, by the accompanying field-report, to have been three hundred and thirty-four officers, and four thousand four hundred and twenty-five men, exclusive of the small command left in and near Saltillo. Of this number, two squadrons of cavalry, and three batteries of light artillery, making not more than four hundred and fifty-three men, composed the only force of regular troops. The strength of the Mexican army is stated by General Santa Anna, in his summons, to be twenty thousand; and that estimate is confirmed by all the information since obtained. Our loss is two hundred and sixty-seven killed, four hundred and fifty-six wounded, and twenty-three missing. Of the numerous wounded, many did not require removal to the hospital, and it is hoped that a comparatively small number will be permanently disabled. The Mexican loss in killed and wounded may be fairly estimated at one thousand and five hundred, and will probably reach two thousand. At least five hundred of their killed were left upon the field of battle. We have no means of ascertaining the number of deserters and dispersed men from their ranks, but it is known to be very great.

"Our loss has been especially severe in officers, twenty-eight having been killed upon the field. We have to lament the death of Captain George Lincoln, assistant adjutant-general, serving in the staff of General Wool—a young officer of high bearing and approved gallantry, who fell early in the action. No loss falls more heavily upon the army in the field, than that of Colonels Hardin and McKee, and Lieutenan-Colonel Clay. Possessing in a remarkable degree the confidence of their commands, and the last two having enjoyed the advantage of a military education, I had looked particularly to them for support in case we met the enemy. I need not say that their zeal in engaging the enemy, and the cool and steadfast courage with which they maintained their positions during the day, fully realized my hopes, and caused me to feel yet more sensibly their untimely loss.

"I perform a grateful duty in bringing to the notice of the Government the general good conduct of the troops. Exposed for successive nights, without fires, to the severity of the weather, they were very prompt and cheerful in the discharge of every duty; and finally displayed conspicuous steadiness and gallantry in repulsing, at great odds, a disciplined foe. While the brilliant success achieved by their arms releases me from the painful necessity of specifying many cases of bad conduct before the enemy, I feel an increased obligation to mention particular corps and officers, whose skill, coolness and gallantry, in trying situations, and under a continued and heavy fire, seem to merit particular notice.

"To Brigadier-General Wool my obligations are especially due. The high state of discipline and instruction of several of the volunteer regiments was attained under his command, and to his vigilance and arduous service before the action, and his gallantry and activity on the field, a large share of our success may justly be attributed. During most of the engagement he was in immediate command of the troops thrown back on our left flank. I beg leave to recommend him to the favorable notice of the government. Brigadier-General Lane (slightly wounded,) was active and zealous throughout the day, and displayed great coolness and gallantry before the enemy.

"The services of the light artillery, always conspicuous, were more than usually distinguished. Moving rapidly over the roughest ground, it was always in action at the right place, and the right time, and its well-directed fire dealt destruction in the masses of the enemy. While I recommend to particular favor the gallant conduct and valuable services of Major Munroe, chief of artillery, and Captains Washington, Fourth artillery, and Sherman and Bragg, Third artillery, commanding batteries, I deem it no more than just to mention all the subaltern officers. They were nearly all detached at different times, and in every situation exhibited conspicuous skill and gallantry. Captain O'Brien, Lieutenants Brent, Whiting, and Couch, Fourth artillery, and Bryan, topographical engineers, (slightly wounded,) were attached to Captain Washington's battery. Lieutenants Thomas, Reynolds, and French, Third artillery, (severely wounded,) to that of Captain Sherman; and Captain Shover and Lieutenant Kilburn, Third artillery, to that of Captain Bragg. Captain Shover, in conjunction with Lieutenant Donaldson, First artillery, rendered gallant and important service in repulsing the cavalry of General Minon. The regular cavalry, under Lieutenant-Colonel May, with which was associated Captain Pike's squadron of Arkansas horse, rendered useful service in holding the enemy in check, and in covering the batteries at several points. Captain Steene, First dragoons, was severely wounded early in the day, while gallantly endeavoring, with my authority, to rally the troops which were falling to the rear.

"The Mississippi riflemen, under Colonel Davis, were highly conspicuous for their gallantry and steadiness, and sustained throughout the engagement the reputation of veteran troops. Brought into action against an immensely superior force, they maintained themselves for a long time unsupported, and with heavy loss, and held an important part of the field until reinforced. Colonel Davis, though severely wounded, remained in the saddle until the close of the action. His distinguished coolness and gallantry at the head of his regiment on this day, entitle him to the particular notice of the government. The Third Indiana regiment, under Colonel Lane, and a fragment of the Second, under Colonel Bowles, were associated with the Mississippi regiment during the greater portion of the day, and acquitted themselves creditably in repulsing the attempts of the enemy to break that portion of our line. The Kentucky cavalry, under Colonel Marshall, rendered good service dismounted, acting as light troops on our left, and afterwards, with a portion of the Arkansas regiment, in meeting and dispersing the column of cavalry at Buena Vista. The First and Second Illinois, and the Kentucky regiments, served immediately under my eye, and I bear a willing testimony to their excellent conduct throughout the day. The spirit and gallantry with which the First Illinois and Second Kentucky engaged the enemy in the morning, restored confidence to that part of the field, while the list of casualties will show how much these three regiments suffered in sustaining the heavy charge of the enemy in the afternoon. Captain Conner's company of Texas volunteers, attached to the Second Illinois regiment, fought bravely, its captain being wounded and two subalterns killed. Colonel Bissell, the only surviving colonel of these regiments, merits notice for his coolness and bravery on this occasion After the fall of the field-officers of the First Illinois and Second Kentucky regiments, the command of the former devolved upon Lieutenant-Colonel Weatherford; that of the latter on Major Fry.

"Regimental commanders and others who have rendered reports, speak in general terms of the good conduct of their officers and men, and have specified many names, but the limits of this report forbid a recapitulation of them here. I may, however, mention Lieutenants Rucker and Campbell of the dragoons, and Captain Pike, Arkansas cavalry, commanding squadrons; Lieutenant-Colonel Field, Kentucky cavalry; Lieutenant-Colonel Roane, Arkansas cavalry, upon whom the command devolved after the fall of Colonel Yell; Major Bradford, Captain Sharpe (severely wounded,) and Adjutant Griffith, Mississippi regiment; Lieutenant-Colonel Hadden, Second Indiana regiment, and Lieutenant Robinson, aide-de-camp to General Lane; Lieutenant-Colonel Weatherford, First Illinois regiment; Lieutenant-Colonel Morrison, Major Trail, and Adjutant Whiteside, (severely wounded,) Second Illinois regiment; and Major Fry, Second Kentucky regiment, as being favorably noticed for gallantry and good conduct. Major McCulloch, quartermaster in the volunteer service, rendered important services before the engagement, in the command of a spy company, and during the affair was associated with the regular cavalry. To Major Warren, First Illinois volunteers, I feel much indebted for his firm and judicious course, while exercising command in the city of Saltillo.

"The medical staff, unde[illegible] able direction of Assistant Surgeon Hitchcock, [illegible] assiduous in attention to the wounded on the field, and in their careful removal to the rear. Both in these respects, and in the subsequent organization and service of the hospitals, the administration of this department was everything that could be wished.

"Brigadier-General Wool speaks in high terms of the officers of his staff, and I take pleasure in mentioning them here, having witnessed their activity and zeal upon the field. Lieutenant and Aide-de-camp McDowell, Colonel Churchill, inspector general, Captain Chapman, assistant quartermaster, Lieutenant Sitgreaves, topographical engineers, and Captains Howard and Davis, volunteer service, are conspicuously noticed by the General for their gallantry and good conduct. Messrs. March, Addicks, Potts, Harrison, Burgess, and Dusenbery, attached in various capacities to General Wool's headquarters, are likewise mentioned for their intelligent alacrity in conveying orders to all parts of the field.

"In conclusion, I beg leave to speak of my own staff, to whose exertions in rallying troops and communicating orders I feel greatly indebted. Major Bliss, assistant adjutant-general, Captain J. H. Eaton, and Lieutenant R. S. Garnett, aides-de-camp, served near my person, and were prompt and zealous in the discharge of every duty. Major Munroe, besides rendering valuable service as chief of artillery, was active and instrumental, as were also Colonels Churchill and Belknap, inspectors general, in rallying troops and disposing them for the defence of the train and baggage. Colonel Whiting, quartermaster-general, and Captain Eaton, chief of the subsistence department, were engaged with the duties of their departments, and also served in my immediate staff on the field. Captain Sibley, assistant quartermaster, was necessarily left with the headquarter camp near town, where his services were highly useful. Major Mansfield and Lieutenant Benham, engineers, and Captain Linnard and Lieutenants Pope and Franklin, topographical engineers, were employed before and during the engagement in making reconnoissances, and on the field were very active in bringing information and in conveying my orders to distant points. Lieutenant Kingsbury, in addition to his proper duties as ordnance officer, Captain Chilton, assistant quartermaster, and Majors Dix and Coffee, served also as extra aides-de-camp, and were actively employed in the transmission of orders. Mr. Thomas L. Crittenden, of Kentucky, though not in service, volunteered as my aide-de-camp on this occasion, and served with credit in that capacity. Major Craig, chief of ordnance, and Surgeon Craig, medical director, had been detached on duty from headquarters, and did not reach the ground until the morning of the 24th—too late to participate in the action, but in time to render useful services in their respective departments of the staff."

The following is the summons of Santa Anna to General Taylor to surrender. It evinces much more humanity for the American troops than the Mexican general had ever shown for his own, and is a model of that assurance for which he is far more celebrated than for his military talent or courage.

"You are surrounded by twenty thousand men, and cannot, in any human probability, avoid suffering a rout, and being cut to pieces with your troops; but as you deserve consideration and particular esteem, I wish to save you from a catastrophe, and for that purpose give you this notice, in order that you may surrender at discretion, under the assurance that you will be treated with the consideration belonging to the Mexican character; to which end you will be granted an hour's

GENERAL SANTA ANNA.

time to make up your mind, to commence from the moment when my flag of truce arrives in your camp."

To this characteristic document General Taylor immediately returned the following laconic and modest reply:

"In reply to your note of this date, summoning me to surrender my forces at discretion, I beg leave to say that I decline acceding to your request."

Having now given the sober facts of one of the most decisive as well as the most remarkable victories ever won by American arms, it is appropriate to present some of the romance of history connected with an event which is the source of so much just pride in America, and of admiration in Europe. The official report of the battle by General Santa Anna, supplies this embellishment. This report of the wily Mexican commander, however, is important in another point of view; for while it claims a victory over the American forces, it virtually sustains General Taylor's account, and proves that the Mexican army was almost literally cut to pieces. No one can question this fact after having read the artful and ingenious attempt to cover the disasters he had suffered, and justify to his government his failure to redeem the just expectations that had been created by his magnificent preparations and his more magnificent promises. He says:

"In my dispatch from the battle-field of Angostura, dated the 23d, I promised to give you details of the action of the 23d, so soon as I should effect the movement which our entire lack of water and of all supplies made indispensable. In those engagements the army and the nation have restored the lustre of their arms, by overcoming obstacles inconceivable to all save those who witnessed them. These arose, not only from the difficulties of this contest, and of our own situation, but also from the rigor of the season, and the exhaustion of the country along an almost desert route of over fifty leagues, that was destitute of good water, and of all save the most limited supplies.

"The supreme government was informed by communications made before my leaving San Luis, that the army under my command would not commence its operations till the end of winter, as I knew by experience the severe climate of the region, which was also scant of habitations, provisions, shelter, and even of fuel. I therefore resolved to go on organizing, drilling, arming and clothing the army; and, in a word, to put into a military shape the forces which had just been assembled. My intentions, however, could not be maturely realized.

"The want of pecuniary resources embarrassed all my dispositions. The soldiers, though well disposed to combat with the enemy, had been badly supplied for a month, and would soon have been in want even of food, but that the exertions of the commanders of corps prevented that destitution from driving them from their ranks. While those meritorious men were suffering all kinds of privation, certain writers, from ignorance, want of reflection, party spirit, or, perhaps, from mistaken patriotism, were zealously engaged in thwarting the plans which might otherwise have proved successful. This they did by unjust charges against the army and particular individuals, whom they abused for not marching to the conflict, accusing them of want of decision, and asserting that the position of the army at San Luis was more threatening to our liberties than to the enemy. In the clubs of that capital they labored with assiduity to make the army the instrument of a revolt; but I frustrated their intrigues by timely steps. There was one writer who had the audacity to intimate that I was in collusion with the enemy. Yes, I, to whom they may attribute errors, but whose whole previous course has shown the most elevated patriotism! Traitors are they who seek not only to traduce me, but, by their detraction of the army, to unnerve its vigor for the service of the country. It seems as if a fatality directs the destinies of this nation, and interdicts a unanimity of the public will for its defence; and from this fatal blindness, the moment when every heart and every aspiration should be directed to one object, is the very juncture when division and distrust are disseminated. Behold me, then, compelled by every circumstance to change my plans. Desertion had already commenced to a shameful extent; and I was fully persuaded that if the scarcity should continue, the army would be dishonorably frittered away. I therefore resolved that, if annihilated, it should be with glory. Having no supplies, I, to obtain them, compromitted my private fortune and the credit of myself and friends. All this procured me the sum of one hundred and eighty thousand dollars, with which I was able to furnish the needful supplies to the army for twelve days. I knew well the country we had to cross, and the necessity there would be for carrying provisions; and I sympathized in anticipation with the soldier for what he would endure from the rigor of the season; but to render good service to the country, and save its honor, I had to overlook all this.

"The army moved from San Luis by brigades, so as to render available the scanty resources afforded by the country we were to cross. The force consisted of thirteen thousand four hundred and thirty-two infantry, divided into twenty-eight battalions; four thousand three hundred and thirty-eight cavalry, in thirty-nine squadrons; and a train of artillery of three twenty-four pounders, three sixteen-pounders, five twelve-pounders, five eight-pounders, and a seven-inch howitzer, all served by four hundred and thirteen artillerymen—the total being eighteen thousand one hundred and thirty-three men. Of this force there remained behind, the garrison of the works of San Luis, and others which I allotted to the towns on the route; as also two squadrons to escort our small and only reserve of ammunition; a brigade of infantry, of two battalions, under General Don Ciriaco Vasquez, which remained as a corps of reserve in Matehuala, and of observation upon Tula; as also a brigade of cavalry, under General Don Jose Urrea. The latter was intended to pass Tula, and move through Tamaulipas to the neighborhood of Monterey, so as to call the enemy's attention to that quarter. The point of concentration for the brigades ought necessarily to be near this place, so that in the region through which they had to move, many troops might not be at once thrown together. I therefore fixed on the hacienda of Encarnacion for that point, it being, as I calculated, the last stage but one of my march. I there held a review of the army, which had already lost a thousand men by sickness and desertion. The former was caused by the scantiness and bad quality of food, and still more of water, which was brackish as well as scarce, as also by snow storms and the exposure of the troops, who had always to be in bivouac and without fuel. These snow storms obliged me to suspend the march two days, till the weather became more settled; for the cold had already caused the death of several men and horses, and I felt bound by every means to diminish the losses we were incurring. These hardships will account for the number of desertions which occurred up to our arrival at Encarnacion, and which afterwards even increased. It must also be remembered, that almost the whole army had been recently formed, and, as is well known, of men taken by violence from their homes.

"We had advices that the enemy were fortified in the hacienda of Agua Nueva, with six thousand men and thirty pieces, resolved to defend the defiles known by the names of the passes of Canero and Agua Nueva. The Americans did not know the precise point on which our march was directed; for, though they exchanged some shots with our advance in Encarnacion, and had frequently small skirmishes with us in the above passes, they supposed our troops to be scouting parties of the first brigade of cavalry, under Don Jose V. Minon, whom I had advanced as far as the hacienda of Potosi. These were the impressions when I made my dispositions.

"It was my intention to place my forces between the enemy and Saltillo, so as to oblige him to fight under the disadvantage of having his communication cut off, or, if he would not leave his works, to enable me to besiege him in Agua Nueva. The plan might be carried out in three different ways. One was by marching twenty leagues by the direct road; another by moving to the right by La Hedionda, so as to occupy Buena Vista; and the third, by moving to the left by La Punta de Santa Elena, so as to occupy the hacienda of La Banqueria, and thereafter the road to Saltillo. The two last movements were at this time impracticable, for they would either of them require three or four days' march, while we were without provisions, forage, or water. I therofore resolved to operate by the direct road, force the positions, and, after passing the last defile, make a diversion by the left, and occupy the rancho of Encantada, with the view of obtaining water, none of which was to be had for more than eighteen leagues. All this was favored by the enemy's ignorance of our march; but misfortune still followed us. A deserter from the regiment of Coraceras, a native of Saltillo, named Francisco Valdes, passed over from Encarnacion to the enemy, and gave him information of the movement. The execrable treason of this infamous wretch frustrated the best combinations.

"On the 21st, at noon, I ordered the march to commence, the four light battalions, under General Don Pedro Ampudia, forming the vanguard. I had not hesitated to allow that general, and other officers who had been court-martialled for the affair of Monterey, to participate in these operations, not only because I did not consider them culpable, but also on account of the zeal they manifested. This brigade was followed by one of artillery, of sixteen-pounders, with the regiments of engineers and their train, and those by the park of the regiment of hussars. Then came the First division, commanded by General Don Manuel Lombardini, with four twelve-pounders and the park. The second division, under General Don Francisco Pacheco, followed next, with four eight-pounders and their park; after these the whole of the cavalry, under Don Julian Juvera; and then the remainder of the general park and baggage, the rear being covered by a brigade of cavalry under General Don Manuel Andrade.

"In this order of march the troops were ordered to make the first fourteen leagues, between Encenada and a plain called De la Guerra, which is in front of the first defile called the pass of the Pinones; and to pass the night on that plain in the same order of column. The troops having eaten their rations, order was given for carrying water, as none could be met with till the day following, after having overcome the enemy at Agua Nueva, three leagues beyond the aforesaid pass. I, with my staff and the regiment of engineers, occupied the front, a little behind the light troops. On arriving at the plain De la Guerra, I continued the march in order to pass the defile of Pinones, which was accomplished; and I ordered the light brigade to take a position in the pass of Carnero, where it had a skirmish with an advance of the enemy. Under these dispositions we passed the night.

"At dawn on the 22d the army continued its march, with the idea of carrying by force of arms the pass of Agua Nueva which I supposed would be defended by the enemy; but I found to my surprise that it had been abandoned. I then concluded that the American forces had retired to their fortifications in the hacienda, to concentrate their defence under cover of the intrenchments which I had heard they had there thrown up. Under this idea I continued the march, in order to turn by the right to the rancho of Encantada, which, as I have before mentioned, is on the Saltillo road, being between that city and Agua Nueva, and four or five leagues from each. Till that time no one had appeared to give me information, nor did any one after, except a servant from Agua Nueva, who told me that the enemy had been evacuating his position since the day previous, and falling back towards Saltillo; and that on that same morning, the hacienda had been wholly abandoned, by the retreat of a small detachment which escorted a large quantity of munitions. By this movement my first plans and dispositions, founded on an expected resistance, were rendered abortive; but I still did not despair of a successful result, for I had in anticipation directed General Minon, with his cavalry brigade, twelve hundred strong, to occupy, on the morning of the 22d, the hacienda of Buena Vista, distant three short leagues from Saltillo. This force might arrest the enemy's march, or, at least, make a diversion that would give time for the army to come up. I therefore continued my march, without losing more time than would allow the soldiers to drink water on the road. The light brigade came within sight of the enemy's rear-guard, and I ordered them to charge in conjunction with the hussar regiment. I had reason to believe the enemy were making a precipitate retreat, as they left several articles on the road, such as carts, forge implements, extra wheels, and other things, which we gathered while marching. In consequence of the different reports I received, I ordered the cavalry to advance; I thought we would be able to reach their rear-guard, and placed myself at the head of those troops.

"On arriving at a place called Angostura, I found the main body of the enemy awaiting me in position. The road from the pass of Pinones to Saltillo runs between two chains of mountains, which form that pass and those of Carnero and Agua Nueva. The ridges open beyond the hacienda, and approach each other again at Angostura, where the road turns to the right. At this place there is a succession of ridges, which run out toward the line of our route, and at right angles with it, and between them are ravines which form the drains of the mountains on the right. They are more or less passable, but all very difficult. The enemy's position was in front and in rear of the road, his right and front being covered by ravines that were impassable, even for infantry, and a battery of four pieces being planted on the highest point. His battalions were formed on the heights with two other batteries, one of which was in a low part of the road, betwen two hills; and, to my view, their forces appeared to be about eight thousand men, with twenty pieces; but the prisoners taken from them report twenty-six pieces, and upwards of eight thousand combatants.

"I reconnoitred the position and situation of the enemy, and ordered the director of engineers, General Don Ignacio de Mora y Villamil, to do the same. After ascertaining the force of the invader, it was necessary either to await the infantry, to take position, or to fight, as might seem most advisable. At this interval, I observed that the enemy had neglected to occupy a height on his left flank; and, without losing a moment, I ordered General Ampudia's light brigade to take possession of, and hold it at every cost. As the brigade came up, I formed them in two lines on a rising ground that fronted the enemy, there being another eminence between our two positions; the first division of infantry was under the command of General Lombardini, and the second under the command of General Pacheco. I directed that General Mora y Villamil, in conjunction with the commanding general of artillery, Don Antonio Corona, should find a position for a battery of sixteen-pounders, to be sustained by the regiment of engineers. Two other batteries of twelve and eight-pounders, were located by me. The cavalry, commanded by General Juvera, were placed on the right of our rear, and on our left flank. The regiment of hussars was also posted in the rear, and on the left flank aforesaid was a height which I ordered the battalion of Leon to occupy. The general park was in the rear, covered by the brigade of General Andrade, and between this park and the lines of battle I took my own position.

"The making of these dispositions, as may be supposed, occupied some time, for the troops arrived at their positions after a march of more than twenty leagues. It was therefore not an hour for combat, and the army lay on its arms. The enemy, however, so soon as he perceived that we had occupied the height that flanked his left and our right, dispatched two bat talions to dislodge us, which led to a warm engagement, that lasted all the afternoon and till after dark, when he was repulsed with the loss of four hundred men, according to the report of the prisoners. Ours was much less, as we had the advantage of the ground.

"At dawn on the 23rd I mounted my horse; the enemy had not changed his previous dispositions, and was ready to receive us. I observed but one difference, which was, that on his right, and at some distance from his position, he had formed two bodies of infantry, with a battery of four pieces, as if with the intent of threatening our left flank, but I at once believed this to be a mere demonstration, for he would never have left in his rear the difficult ground which gave strength to that position, being the web of impassable ravines before referred to. I, therefore, gave no attention to this disposition of his forces, and resolved to move mine by the right. With this intention, I advanced the divisions of General Lombardini and General Pacheco in that direction. I ordered General Don Manuel Micheltorena to plant the battery of eight-pounders on our right flank, so as to rake obliquely the enemy's line, and to remain with the staff of which he was chief, and await my orders. I directed that General Ampudia, with the light brigade, should charge by our left flank on the enemy's right, and that General Mora y Villamil should form a column of attack composed of the regiment of engineers, the 12th battalion, the *fijo de Mexico*, and the companies of Puebla and Tampico, commanded by Colonel Don Santiago Blanco. At the same time, I directed General Corona, commanding the artillery, to place the battery of twelve-pounders in a more commanding position, while the Third division remained in reserve, Under Brevet-General Don Jose Maria Ortega.

So soon as the enemy perceived our movements, he commenced the action at all points, attacked our troops with intrepidity, and maintained the conflict with great vigor. Our men received them with proper energy, driving back and following up the assailants. At this time my horse was disabled by a grape shot, and it was some time before I could mount another. As the enemy had yielded ground, I ordered the cavalry to advance and charge, which was done with vigor. Suitable orders had been sent to the generals of division and brigade, among the rest to General Don Angel Guzman; but, though the officers and troops acted with great resolution. it was impossible to overcome the difficulties of the ground; and after a struggle which did them honor, they were obliged to fall back to their positions. After various alternations, the same occurred with the infantry.

"The battle which commenced at seven in the morning, was prolonged for many hours, our loss every moment accumulating. Many officers and soldiers had already been killed, and a number of commanders and distinguished officers wounded, among whom were General Lombardini, Lieutenant-Colonels Brito, Galloso, and others. Among the slain were Lieutenant-Colonels Asonos, Berra, and other meritorious officers, whose loss the country will ever lament. The enemy maintained his ground with the utmost obstinacy, insomuch that some of our troops faltered in their attacks, and many of the raw recruits dispersed. This, however, ought to exalt the merit of those whose intrepidity was never paralyzed, and may also be cited to show how hotly contested was the action.

"Things were in this situation when I concluded to make the final effort. With this view I ordered that a battery of twenty-four pounders should be mounted; that the column of attack then posted on our left flank, where it had no object of operation, should be transferred to our right, and there be joined by the remains of the Eleventh regiment, the battalion of Leon, and the reserves, all under the command of Brevet-General Don Francisco Perez. I executed this in person, and afterwards sent for General Mora y Villamil, and made him acquainted with my final disposition. I had already directed Generals Perez and Pacheco, each with his command, to be prepared for an extreme struggle, and had ordered the battery of eight-pounders to advance and take the enemy's line in flank. The charge was made with daring valor, and was resisted with animated vigor, with a fire so heavy and rapid as to cause admiration; but the Americans could not sustain themselves—they were driven back and overcome, with the loss of three pieces of cannon and as many stands of colors. I sent two of the latter to the government with my last dispatch; the other, which I then omitted to notice, will be presented to the honorable congress of the state of San Luis Potosi, as a testimonial of the army's gratitude for the patriotic services they had rendered, and the generous sacrifices they had made for its benefit. We moreover captured a travelling forge, and some smaller articles, which I will not enumerate. Our cavalry, which so bravely executed the order to charge, reached the enemy's rearmost positions; but, owing to the nature of the ground and the fatigue of the men and horses, I did not think it prudent to attempt to dislodge them from those. The battle closed at six in the evening, our troops being then formed on the ground which the Americans had occupied. Our last effort would have been decisive, if General Minon had done his part by attacking the enemy in the rear; but he omitted to do it, and I am under the painful necessity of subjecting his conduct to a court-martial, that he may explain it. An action thus contested necessarily involved considerable loss. Ours in killed and wounded amounted to more than fifteen hundred men, and that of the enemy was much greater, for we had time to take a view of the great number of their dead.

"The plans of these two actions, and of the route from Agua Nueva to Saltillo, and the reports of the generals of division and brigade, which I send with this to your excellency, will give the supreme government an idea of such details as I have not dwelt on without making this report more diffuse; but this will still serve to attest the bravery of our troops, and the glory acquired by the nation during these days of action.

"In the order of the day, I expressed, as in duty bound, my satisfaction with the conduct of the officers, commanders of corps, and generals, and gave them thanks for it in the name of the republic. I could wish to announce in this report the names of many commanding officers, that their memory may be engraved on the gratitude of the nation, not only for their resolute and honorable deportment in both actions, but for the constancy with which they have overcome so many privations, sufferings and fatigues, and given therein an example both of civic and military worth. Anxious to do this justice, I adopt, as my own, the authorship of those eulogies which the generals of brigade and division have bestowed on their subordinates. I would moreover, place in view of the government, the merit manifested by the director-general of engineers, Don Ignacio Mora y Villamil, who fulfilled, to my entire satisfaction, all the duties I assigned to him, for which I consider him worthy of the highest praise, and of such remuneration as the supreme government may be pleased to award to his distinguished services. General Ampudia, to whom, from the favorable opinion which I had of him, I intrusted the command of the four light battalions, acquitted himself with gallantry. General Lombardini, who commanded the First division of infantry, conducted himself with valor, and was wounded. General Pacheco, commanding the Second division of infantry, came up to my orders and his duties, and fought to my satisfaction. General Juvera comported himself honorably, and had his horse killed under him. Brevet General Torrejon received a contusion, and General Guzman displayed the gallantry for which he was already distinguished, and was wounded. Brevet-General Micheltorena, as head of the staff, duly performed all that belonged to his station; and I also confided to his special charge the battery of eight-pounders, which was the most in advance. General Perez acted as might be expected from his accustomed gallantry, and for this I intrusted to his command the troops I have before mentioned, with which he contributed to disorder the line of the enemy at five in the evening. I would also commend General Ortega, who commanded the Third division of foot, and performed his duties to my satisfaction, as also Brevet-General Uraga, and Generals Parrodi, Portilla, Vasquez, Jauregui, Terres, and Sanchez.

"It is entirely due to the commanding general of artillery, Don Antonio Corona, that I should commend him for carrying out my dispositions, as might be expected from him, and for laboring assiduously at San Luis, in the heaviest duties of his branch of service; and it is a pleasing duty for me to laud the merit acquired by Colonel Banencli, and Colonel Brito, who was wounded; Colonel Aldrede, of the hussars, who, to my satisfaction, evinced his usual bravery; Colonel S. Blanco, who commanded a column of attack on the left, and acted well, and Colonel M. Blanco—both of the last being of the engineers—as also Colonel Obando, of the flying artillery, and Colonel Garay.

"The report of the killed and wounded, which I also send, will show what has been our loss. I should be lacking in justice, and not express my own feelings were I not most earnestly to request that attention be paid, as is by law provided, to the cases of the widows, orphans, and such of the wounded as may be permanently disabled.

"The formidable position which the enemy occupied, was all that saved him; the victory would otherwise have been decisive, notwithstanding his obstinate resistance. Still this triumph will have favorable results to the national cause, as it will show to every one what can be accomplished when all hearts are united, and with one aim.

"The army has done more than could be expected under the laws of nature. It had just been formed, and as yet had not acquired discipline or military habits; yet in marching to the combat, it overcame difficulties which might have subdued the stoutest heart. After a march of twenty leagues, sixteen of them without water, and without other food than a single ration, which was dealt out at Encarnacion, it endured the fatigue of combat for two days, and finally triumphed. With all this its physical powers were exhausted. My knowledge of this, and the duty I felt in attending to such a number of wounded, constrained me, after remaining a few hours on the field of battle, to fall back upon Agua Nueva, for the relief and refreshment of the troops.

"From the impression we had made on the enemy, he did not appear before us for three days. The bearer of a flag of truce, however, arrived with a proposition from General Taylor for an exchange of prisoners, and for our sending for the wounded who had remained on the field. He also expressed to me the desire which the Americans felt for the re-establishment of peace. I replied, in order that he might say the same to his general, that we sustained the most sacred of causes—the defence of our territory, and the preservation of our nationality and rights; that we were not the aggressors, and that our government had never offended that of the United States. I observed that we could say nothing of peace while the Americans were on this side of the Bravo, or occupied any part of the Mexican territory, or blockaded our ports; and that we were resolved to perish or vindicate our rights; that fortune might not be always favorable to the enemy, and their experience of the 22nd and 23rd should convince them that it could change; I added, that the Americans waged against us a war of vandalism, whose excesses outraged those sentiments of humanity which one civilized nation ought to evince towards another; and that if he would go outside of the apartment he would still see smoking, which was the fact, the dwellings of Agua Nueva, recently a flourishing, though a small settlement; that the same vestiges of desolation marked the route of his retreat; and that if he would go a little further on, to Catana, he would hear the moans of the widows and orphans of innocent victims who had been sacrificed without necessity.

"With respect to the wounded, whom I was invited to send for, I replied that there could be none save those who had been too much hurt to rise from the field, or those most in the advance, who had remained in the ravines; and that as I had not means for their conveyance, the enemy might take them to Saltillo, under the protection of the laws of nations. As for the prisoners which he offered to exchange, I told him I did not know who they could be, unless it were some of our dispersed troops, or some who, from the fatigue of the two previous days, had remained asleep when we moved. In answer to the courtesy the enemy's general had shown with respect to our wounded, I consented, in the name of the nation, to release all the prisoners we had—those taken both in the battle and at Encarnacion. At the same time I allowed the bearer of the flag, who was a superior officer, of prepossessing appearance and manners, to take the bandage from his eyes, and informed him that it was for him personally that the honor of this concession was meant. I did it also that he might see our camp and our troops.

"As I have said in the preceding paragraph, we remained at the hacienda three days; but the only supply we could obtain was ninety beeves, and these were consumed on the 25th. The horses were also without forage, and notwithstanding all the efforts or provisions that I could make, many of the wounded had been but once attended to, and some not at all. From the rigor of the climate, the badness and scantiness of the sustenance, the entire want of bread, and the bad quality of the water used in our former bivouacs, a bowel complaint had broken out in the army, and rendered ineffective at least one-half of it. I knew that a retrograde movement to our former positions had become inevitable; but though everything around me proclaimed this necessity, my feelings revolted against it, solely because I foresaw that from ignorance, malice, or presumption, the countermarch would be condemned, and that those who did not witness our situation would imagine the possibility of the army's continuing its operations.

"Six days before, when the troops had not suffered so much, nor fought for two successive days, nor been embarrassed with sick and wounded, but were still sound in morale and in health, I had not deemed it prudent to augment the labors and difficulties of the army by moving to the right or to the left; how then would it have been possible to go on operating after all that subsequently occurred? But let detractors say what they will, the army as well as myself will always answer by an appeal to our conduct, our wishes, and the notorious impossibility of carrying them out. Notwithstanding my conviction, I wished to hear the opinion of the generals and some of the commanders of corps, and to ascertain if they could point out any resource which had not occurred to me; without disclosing my own ideas on the subject I listened to theirs, and they all unanimously, and each one, by his opinion separately expressed, showed and demonstrated in various ways, that however good their will to remain, the countermarch of the army had become indispensable, but that this necessity was not forced upon us by the enemy. It was not till I had heard their opinions that I announced my own accordant resolution, and the proceedings of the council being drawn up, I had the honor of remitting them to your excellency on the 25th.

"On the 26th, after I had ordered General Minon to follow the movement, the army commenced its retreat with the view of occupying the first peopled localities, where resources might be obtained, such as Vanegas Catorce, El Cadral and Matehuala, as also Tula; but I doubt if in those places proper attention can be given to the sick and wounded—or the losses we have sustained in those laborious movements be remedied.

"The nation, for which a triumph has been gained at the cost of so many sufferings, will learn that, if we were able to conquer in the midst of so many embarrassments, there will be no doubt as to our final success in the struggle we sustain, if every spirit but rallies to the one sacred object of common defence. A mere determined number of men will not, as many imagine, suffice for the prosecution of war: it is indispensable that they be armed, equipped, disciplined, and habituated, and that a systematized support for such an organized force be provided. We must bear in mind that we have to combat in a region deficient of all resources, and that everything for subsistence has to be carried along with the soldiery: the good will of a few will not suffice, but the co-operation of all is needed; and if we do not cast aside selfish interests, and petty passions, we can expect nothing but disaster. The army, and myself who have led it, have the satisfaction of knowing that we have demonstrated this truth."

The following heart-stirring description of the battle of Buena Vista will be read with absorbing interest by every American. Captain Pike is a poet of no mean reputation, and he proved by his daring and chivalrous conduct on the bloody field he so well describes, that if his commanding general can "*write* as well as fight." he can *fight* as well as write. Captain Pike commanded a company of Arkansas cavalry in the engagement.

BUENA VISTA.

From the Rio Grande's waters, to the icy lakes of Maine,
Let all exult for we have met the enemy again:
Beneath their stern old mountains we have met them in their pride,
And rolled from Buena Vista back the battle's bloody tide:
Where the enemy came surging, like the Mississippi's flood;
And the reaper, Death, was busy with his sickle red with blood.

Santa Anta boasted loudly, that before two hours were past,
His lancers through Saltillo should pursue us thick and fast:
On came his solid infantry, line marching after line;
Lo! their great standards in the sun like sheets of silver shine!
With thousands upon thousands, yea, with more than four to one,
A forest of bright bayonets gleamed fiercely in the sun!

Lo! Guanajuato's regiment!—Lo! Puebla's boasted corps!—
And Guadalajara's chosen troops!—all veterans tried before;
And galloping upon the right, four thousand lances gleam,
Where, waving in the morning light, their blood-red pennons stream:
And there, his stern artillery climbs up the broad plateau—
To-day he means to strike at us an overwhelming blow.

Now hold on strongly to the heights!—for lo! the mighty tide
Comes thundering like an avalanche, deep, terrible, and wide;
Now, Illinois! stand ready!—Now, Kentucky, to their aid!
For a portion of our line, alas! is broken and dismayed;
A regiment of fugitives is fleeing from the field,
And the day is lost if Illinois and brave Kentucky yield.

One of O'Brien's guns is gone!—on, on their masses drift,
And their infantry and lancers now are passing round our left—
Our troops are driven from the hills, and flee in wild dismay,
And round us gathers, thick and dark, the Mexican array.
Santa Anna thinks the day is gained;—and riding yet more near,
Minon's dark cloud of lancers sternly menaces our rear.

Now Lincoln, gallant gentleman! lies dead upon the field,
Who strove to stay those men that in the storm of bullets reeled.
Now, Washington! fire fast and true!—Fire, Sherman! fast and far!
Lo! Bragg comes thundering to the front, to breast the adverse war!
Santa Anna thinks the day is gained—on, on his masses crowd,
And the roar of battle rises up more terrible and loud.

Not yet!—our brave old general comes to regain the day.
Kentucky, to the rescue!—Mississippi, to the fray!
Now charge, brave Illinoisans! Gallant Davis drives the foe,
And back before his rifles the red waves of lancers flow;
Upon them yet once more my braves! The avalanche is stayed;
Back rolls the Mexique multitude, all broken and dismayed.

Ho! May!—to Buena Vista! for the enemy are near,
And we have none there who can stop their vehement career:
Still swelling, downward comes the tide; Porter and Yell are slain!
Marshall before him drives a part; but still they charge in vain;—
And now, in wild confusion mixed, pursuers and pursued,
On to Saltillo wildly drifts a frantic multitude.

Upon them with your squadrons, May!—Out leaps the flashing steel!
Before his serried column, how the frightened lancers reel!
They flee amain.—Now to the left, to stay their triumph there,
Or else the day is surely lost in horror and despair:
For their hosts are pouring swiftly on, like a river in the spring—
Our flank is turned, and on our left their cannon thundering.

Now, brave artillery! Bold dragoons!—Steady my men, and calm!
Through rain, cold, hail, and thunder;—now nerve the gallant arm!

What though their shot falls round us here, still thicker than the hail!
We'll stand against them, as the rock stands firm against the gale.
Lo!—their battery is silenced now: our iron hail still showers:
They falter, halt, retreat!—Hurra! the glorious day is ours!

In front, too, has the fight gone well, where upon gallant Lane,
And on stout Mississippi, the bold lancers charged in vain.
Ah! brave Third Indiana! ye have nobly wiped away
The reproach that, through another corps, befell your state to-day:
Like corn before the tempest crushed, before your storm of fire,
Santa Anna's boasted chivalry a shattered wreck retire.

Now charge again, Santa Anna! or the day is surely lost;
For back, like broken waves, along our left your hordes are tossed.
Still louder roar two batteries—his strong reserve moves on;—
More work is there before you, men, ere the good fight is won;
Now for your wives and children stand! steady, my braves once more!
Now for your lives, your honor, fight! as you never fought before.

Ho! Hardin breasts it bravely!—McKee and Bissell there,
Stand firm before the storm of balls that fills the astonished air.
The lancers are upon them, too!—the foe swarms ten to one—
Hardin is slain—McKee and Clay the last time see the sun;
And many another gallant heart, in that last desperate fray,
Grew cold, its last thoughts turning to its loved ones far away.

Still sullenly the cannon roared—but died away at last;
And o'er the dead and dying came the evening shadows fast,
And then above the mountains rose the cold moon's silver shield,
And patiently and pityingly looked down upon the field;—
And careless of his wounded, and neglectful of his dead,
Despairingly and sullen, in the night Santa Anna fled.

And thus, on Buena Vista's heights, a long day's work was done—
And thus our brave old general another battle won;
And still our glorious banner waves unstained by flight or shame,
And the Mexicans among their hills still tremble at our name.
So honor unto those that stood! Disgrace to those that fled!
And everlasting honor to the brave and gallant dead!

The annexed description of the same battle, is attributed, whether truly or not it is difficult to say, to Don Jose Ho Ace de Saltillo, a Mexican of some celebrity. It may be proper to state that the poet calls his own country Aztec, its ancient name, while he gives to the Americans the name of Alleghan or Alleghanian. The "sun" of Aztec and the "stars" of Alleghan are the banners of the respective combatants. The "patriot chief" is Santa Anna, the President of the Mexican Republic, and commander of the Mexican troops:

We saw their watch-fires through the night,
  Light up the far horizon's verge;
We heard at dawn the gathering fight,
  Swell like the distant ocean surge—
The thunder-tramp of mounted hordes
  From distance sweeps a boding sound,
As Aztec's twenty thousand swords
  And clanking chargers shake the ground.

A gun!—now all is hushed again—
  How strange that lull before the storm!
That fearful silence o'er the plain—
  Halt they their battle-line to form?
It booms again—again—again—
  And through its thick and thunderous shock
The war-scream seems to pierce the brain,
  As charging squadrons interlock.
Columbia's sons—of different race—
  Proud Aztec and brave Alleghan,
Are grappled there in death-embrace,
  To rend each other, man to man!

The storm-clouds lift, and through the haze,
  Dissolving in the noontide light,
I see the sun of Aztec blaze
  Upon her banner, broad and bright!
And on—still on, her ensigns wave,
  Flinging abroad each glorious fold:
While drooping round each sullen stave
  Cling Alleghan's but half unrolled.

But stay! that shout has stirred the air,
  I see the stripes—I see the stars—

O God! who leads the phalanx there,
Beneath those fearful meteor bars?
"OLD ZACK"—"OLD ZACK"—the war-cry rattles,
Amid those men of iron tread,
As rung "Old Fritz," in Europe's battles,
When thus his host great Frederick led!

And where, O where is Aztec?—where,
As now the rush of Alleghan
Resistless tramples to despair
The ranks of our victorious van?
Still charging onward, ever—ever,
They shatter now our central might,
Where half our bravest lances shiver,
Still struggling to maintain the fight!

Still struggling, from the carnage dire
To snatch our patriot chief away—
Who, crushed by famine, steel and fire,
Yet claims as his the desperate day;
That day whose sinking light is shed
O'er Buena Vista's field, to tell
Where round the sleeping and the dead,
Stalks conquering TAYLOR's sentinel.

CHAPTER VIII.

The Dark Features of War.—General Taylor's Order.—Letter to Mr. Clay and Governor Lincoln.—His private Letter to E. G. W. Butler.—His Reference to the Presidency.—Particulars of the Battle of Buena Vista.—Notice of Clay, Hardin, McKee and Yell.—Anecdotes of General Taylor.—Incidents of the Battle.—Character and Personal Appearance of General Taylor.

Although the triumph of our arms over an enemy four times more numerous than the forces under Taylor, was received with universal enthusiasm by all parties and classes throughout the country, yet it was purchased at a sacrifice of life that filled the land with mourning, and brought desolation and despair to the homes and hearts of hundreds and thousands of wives, and parents, and children, and brothers, and sisters. Many of the noblest spirits of the nation fell a sacrifice on that blood-stained field, and the reflection that so much misery and heart-rending distress was spread over the land with the news that another glorious victory had crowned our arms, moderated the joy, and subdued the feelings which otherwise would have filled every breast. None felt more keenly this dreadful sacrifice to the country than the heroic Taylor himself. Everything that a kind and humane heart could suggest to soothe the afflictions of those whose friends had fallen in the battle, was done. His order to the army upon the result of this victory, and his letter to Mr. Clay, which are annexed, exhibit this fine trait of his character in its true light.

On the 26th of February, General Taylor issued the following order. It is written in fine taste. It alludes in the most modest terms which he could employ, to the brilliant victory which our troops have won over immense superiority of Mexicans, headed by their most distinguished military leader. It pays due honor to the brave officers and troops who live to receive the gratitude of their country. It pays a brief but affecting tribute to those gallant spirits who have gloriously fallen in the battle, but whose "illustrious example will remain for the benefit and admiration of the army," and as a monument of glory in the eyes of Europe. It treats as delicately as possible all those inexperienced soldiers who ingloriously fled, to whom he administers the warning lesson of seeking to retrieve their reputation by future exertions. It is impossible to read the various descriptions of this remarkable battle, where the skill of the commanding general in seizing his ground and manœuvring his troops, vied with the chivalry of his men, without the deepest emotions.

"1. The commanding general has the grateful task of congratulating the troops upon the brilliant success which attended their arms in the conflicts of the 22nd and 23rd. Confident in the immense superiority of numbers, and stimulated by the presence of a distinguished leader, the Mexican troops were yet repulsed in efforts to force our lines, and finally withdrew with immense loss from the field.

"2. The general would express his obligations to the officers and men engaged, for the cordial support which they rendered throughout the action. It will be his highest pride to bring to the notice of the government the conspicuous gallantry of different officers and corps whose unwavering steadiness more than once saved the fortunes of the day. He would also express his high satisfaction with the conduct of the small command he left to hold Saltillo. Though not so seriously engaged as their comrades, their services were very important and efficiently rendered. While bestowing this just tribute to the good conduct of the troops, the general deeply regrets to say that there were not a few exceptions. He trusts that those who fled ingloriously to Buena Vista, and even to Saltillo, will seek an opportunity to retrieve their reputation, and to emulate the bravery of their comrades who bore the brunt of the battle, and sustained, against fearful odds, the honor of our flag.

"The exultation of success is checked by the heavy sacrifice of life which it has cost, embracing many officers of high rank and rare merit. While the sympathies of a grateful country will be given to the bereaved families and friends of those who nobly fell, their illustrious example will remain for the benefit and admiration of the army."

Glorious as have been General Taylor's military exploits, they have reflected less real honor upon his name than the humanity he has on all occasions shown, as well for his own soldiers as for the enemy, and the kindness of heart and remarkable delicacy of feeling that characterize all his acts. The following letter of condolence to Mr. Clay on the death of his son, Lieutenant-Colonel Clay, who fell at Buena Vista, is fraught with sentiments warm from the heart, and is conceived in language as beautiful as it is feeling. It has been as it deserved to be, printed in letters of gold.

My Dear Sir:—You will no doubt have received

before this can reach you, the deeply distressing intelligence of the death of your son in the battle of Buena Vista. It is with no wish of intruding upon the sanctuary of parental sorrow, and with no hope of administering any consolation to your wounded heart, that I have taken the liberty of addressing you these few lines; but I have felt it a duty which I owe to the memory of the distinguished dead, to pay a willing tribute to his many excellent qualities, and while my feelings are still fresh, to express the desolation which his untimely loss, and that of other kindred spirits, has occasioned.

I had but a casual acquaintance with your son, until he became for a time, a member of my military family, and I can truly say that no one ever won more rapidly upon my regard, or established a more lasting claim to my respect and esteem. Manly and honorable in every impulse, with no feeling but for the honor of the service and of the country, he gave every assurance that in the hour of need I could lean with confidence upon his support. Nor was I disappointed. Under the guidance of himself and the lamented McKee, gallantly did the sons of Kentucky, in the thickest of the strife, uphold the honor of the state and the country.

A grateful people will do justice to the memory of those who fell on that eventful day. But I may be permitted to express the bereavement which I feel in the loss of valued friends. To your son I felt bound by the strongest ties of private regard, and when I miss his familiar face, and those of McKee and Hardin, I can say with truth, that I feel no exultation in our success

With the expression of my deepest and most heart-felt sympathies for your irreparable loss,

I remain,

Your friend,

Z. TAYLOR.

Equally honorable to the illustrious hero of Resaca de la Palma, Monterey and Buena Vista, is the following letter to Ex-Governor Lincoln, of Massachusetts, the life of whose son, like Colonel Clay's, is part of the price paid by the country for the glory won by our arms in Mexico. The letter to which this is an answer, was written immediately upon receipt of the painful tidings of the death of Captain Lincoln, and of course before any certain and responsible information had been received from officers in the army.

The letter is in the soothing and delicate strain that pervades other similar communications from the great and amiable general, showing, that while he has courage for a thousand battles, his noble heart is more deeply touched by the fall of one brave and accomplished officer than by all the triumphs of the war.

Sir:—Your letter of the 4th ult., in relation to the remains and effects of your much lamented son, Captain George Lincoln, has safely reached me. I beg leave to offer my heart-felt sympathies with you in the heavy affliction which has befallen you in the death of this accomplished gentleman. In his fall, you have been bereaved of a son of whom you might be most justly proud, while the army has lost one of its most gallant soldiers. It is hoped, however, that your deep grief will be assuaged in some degree in the proud reflection that he fell nobly upon the field of battle, while gallantly discharging the duties of his profession.

I learn upon inquiry that the body of your son was carefully removed from the field, immediately after his death, and that it was decently interred by itself. Its identity is therefore a matter of certainty. His effects are understood to have been collected with due care, and are now under the direction of General Wool.

I shall take an early occasion to convey your wishes on this subject to that officer, with the request that he will be kind enough to put the remains and effects, carefully prepared for transportation, en route for New York or Boston, by the first safe opportunity, and that he give you, at the same time, due notice thereof.

I am, Sir, with great respect,

Your ob't serv't,

Z. TAYLOR.

Everything that serves to throw any light upon the character and opinions of a man whose name has recently been rendered illustrious by deeds which find few parallels in the history of the world, or that relates to any of his military achievements, will be read with avidity by the American people. With this view, the following private letter to a friend in Louisiana is given. It will be perceived that he refers to the movement of the people in various parts of the country in favor of his nomination for the presidency, with the delicacy of a truly great mind, and also relates some of the events of the battle of Buena Vista, that have not previously been dwelt upon. He does not profess, however, to give a minute description of the battle; but he presents in a clearer and more authentic shape, the grandeur of the resistance made to the overwhelming forces of the enemy, and the vastness of the responsibility assumed in giving and maintaining the battle. Stripped of his most effective men, surrounded by armies four times larger than his own, and in the heart of the enemy's country, the gallant old soldier maintained his ground and obtained a victory when even his own officers counselled a retreat. It is dated at Agua Nueva, on the 4th of March, eight days after his decisive victory over the Mexican legions:

My Dear General:—Your very acceptable and interesting letter of the 15th November last, reached me on the 24th of December, while on the march from Monterey to Tampico; but the nature of my duties since then (being most of the time in the saddle,) in addition to other matters, has prevented me from replying to it till the present moment. Be assured, my dear sir, I have not since then lost sight of it or yourself; and I feel highly gratified for the flattering manner in which you have noticed the conduct of the officers and soldiers who marched with me from the Rio Grande to Monterey, and compelled that place to surrender after much hard fighting, as they fully merited the handsome encomiums you have thought proper to bestow on them. For this you have my sincere thanks.

I was aware of the report, as well as statements in a few of the public journals, that it was intended by certain individuals to bring General Butler forward as the successor to Mr. Polk, which gave me no concern, and would not, even had it been the case, which I did not credit, and which had been forgotten. I doubt if the subject would have again crossed my mind, had it not been brought to my notice by you or some one else. I have never heard him or his friends allude to this matter. He (the general), in consequence of his wound not healing, which gave him so much pain as to render him unfit for duty, left a short time since, by advice of his medical attendant, for New Orleans, where I hope he has arrived in safety, and where I truly hope he will very soon recover so as to be able to take the field once more.

I may observe that I have been also named as a candidate for that high office, the presidency, by a few newspaper editors and others, which has been done without my knowledge, wishes, or consent. This I have assured all who have written me on the subject; assuring them I had no aspirations for that or any other civil office; that my whole energies, mental and physical, were, and had been absorbed in such a way as I thought best calculated to bring this war to a speedy and honorable close, believing it was for the interest of both countries—at any rate so far as ours was concerned; and that president making should be lost sight of until this was accomplished.

I retraced my steps to Monterey, where I arrived towards the latter part of the month of January, and where I expected to remain some time to recruit myself and horses; but a few days after my arrival I received information from the command in my front, at Saltillo, sixty-five miles in the direction of San Luis Potosi from Monterey, that the command—between four and five thousand strong—under General Wool, had become very much alarmed in consequence of about one hundred picked men and horses, belonging to the Kentucky and Arkansas regiments of mounted men, who were sent out towards San Luis to gain intelligence respecting the enemy, and watch their movements, having been taken; being surrounded in the night, and all made prisoners, by a large force of cavalry, about fifty miles in advance of Saltillo. So said one of the party who succeeded in making his escape the next night, and getting back to Saltillo; also that the Mexican army was advancing in great numbers towards Saltillo.

These reports induced me to join my advance immediately. Leaving Monterey on the 31st January, I reached Saltillo on the morning of the 2nd February, with a small reinforcement, which increased my force to five thousand, when I lost no time in moving forward and establishing a camp at this place, for the purpose of carrying on a system of instruction, as well as to watch the movements of the enemy, and where I expected to fight him should he move on Saltillo. Here I remained until the 21st, examining the several passes through the mountains—at which time I ascertained that General Santa Anna was advancing and near to hand with an overwhelming force.

Not exactly liking my position, having ascertained that he could gain my rear by two roads on my right and one on my left, and not deeming it prudent to divide my forces, and having apprehensions about my supplies, which were in Saltillo, I determined at once to fall back towards that place about twelve miles, and occupy a strong position between two spurs of a mountain with a narrow valley between them, where at one point the road is so narrow as to permit the passage of only one wagon at a time, with deep gullies running up to the mountains, washed by the rains so as to prevent horses or carriages from passing them without great difficulty. Said position had been closely examined by the topographical engineers, under the eye of General Wool, before my arrival, who deemed it admirably adapted to resist a large army with the small force which composed our strength. We therefore fell back and occupied it on the evening of the 21st, and at once made the necessary preparations for giving battle.

The next day the enemy made his appearance early in the day, and, after reconnoitring our position for some time, at 2 o'clock, P. M., I received by a staff officer with a flag, a communication from General Santa Anna, requiring me to surrender at discretion; stating that in the event of my doing so we should be well treated; that he had surrounded me with more than twenty thousand men; that resistance was out of the question—and if I attempted it, my command would be put to rout and must be destroyed. In reply, I stated I could not comply with his demand, and he was at liberty to commence operations whenever he was inclined to do so. Soon after this, the action was commenced with his skirmishers on our left, which was promptly met by our left, and continued without intermission, on the side of the mountain, until dark.

In the morning at sunrise he renewed the contest with an overwhelming force—with artillery, infantry and dragoons—which lasted with slight intermissions until dark. A portion of the time the conflict was much the severest I have ever witnessed, particularly towards the latter part of the day, when he (Santa Anna) brought up his reserve, and in spite of every effort on our part, after the greatest exertions I have ever witnessed on both sides, drove us by an immense superiority of numbers for some distance. He had at least five to one at that point against us. Fortunately, at the most critical moment, two pieces of artillery which I had ordered up to support that part of our line, met our exhausted men retreating, when they were brought into battery and opened on the enemy, then within fifty yards in hot pursuit, with canister and grape, which brought him to a halt and soon compelled him to fall back. In this tremendous contest we lost three pieces of artillery, nearly all the men having been killed or crippled, which put it out of our power to bring them off; nor did I deem it advisable to attempt to regain them.

The enemy made his principal efforts against our flanks. He was handsomely repulsed on our right, but succeeded early in the day in gaining our left, in consequence of the giving way of one of the volunteer regiments, which could not be rallied, with but few exceptions, the greater portion retiring about a mile to a large rancho or farm-house, where our wagons and a portion of our stores were left. These were soon after attacked by the enemy's cavalry, who were repulsed with some loss.

For several hours the fate of the day was extremely doubtful; so much so that I was urged by some of the most experienced officers to fall back and take a new position. This I knew it would never do to attempt with volunteers, and at once declined it. The scene had now become one of the deepest interest. Between the several deep ravines, there were portions of level land from one to four hundred yards in extent, which became alternately points of attack and defence, after our left was turned, by both sides. These extended along and near the base of the mountain for about two miles, and the struggle for them may be very appropriately compared to a game of chess. Night put a stop to the contest, and strange to say, both armies occupied the same positions they did in the morning before the battle commenced. Our artillery did more than wonders.

We lay on our arms all night, as we had done the two previous ones, without fires, there being no wood to be had, and the mercury below the freezing point, ready and expecting to renew the contest the next morning; but we found at daylight the enemy had retreated during the night, leaving his killed and many of his wounded for us to bury and take care of—carrying off everything else, and taking up a position at this place. We did not think it advisable to pursue, not knowing whether he would renew the attack, continue his retreat, or wished to draw us from our strong position; but contented ourselves with watching his movements closely. Finding, on the 26th, he had renewed his retreat, early in the morning of the 27th the army was put in motion for this place, where we arrived about 3 P. M., their rear-guard, consisting of cavalry, leaving as our advance got in sight.

I at once determined on harassing his rear; but on examining the state of the men and horses, I found that five days and nights marching, incessant watching, and sixteen hours hard fighting, had so exhausted the first and broken down the latter, it was next to impossible to accomplish anything without rest. We remained quiet here until the 2nd instant, when I pushed a command on the San Luis road to a large plantation called Encarnacion, where we found between two and three hundred wounded in the most wretched condition, besides those they carried with them and left here and on the field. Here we took about ten prisoners, the main part of their army having proceeded on in the direction of San Luis in a very disorganized condition.

On the 22nd the enemy threw in our rear, through the passes of the mountains, two thousand cavalry, and early in the morning of the next day, the 23rd, made demonstrations against Saltillo, and throughout the day. They succeeded at one time in cutting off the communication between the city and battle ground, and making several prisoners, but were driven away by the officer commanding in the city, with two pieces of artillery, covered by about sixty men. They, however, while in possession of the road, prevented a good many from running off to the city, to which place about two hundred of our men had succeeded in getting, previously to the cavalry occupying the road—they, the runaways, reporting that our army was beaten and in full retreat.

The loss on both sides was very great, as you may suppose—enough so on ours to cover the whole country with mourning, for some of the noblest and purest of the land have fallen. We had two hundred and forty killed and five hundred wounded. The enemy has suffered in still greater numbers, but as the dead and wounded are scattered all over the country, it is difficult to ascertain their number. The prisoners who have fallen into our hands, between two and three hundred—enough to exchange for all that have been taken from us,—as well as some medical officers left behind to take care of the wounded, say that their killed and wounded is not less than fifteen hundred, and they say perhaps more.

I hope the greater portion of the good people of the country will be satisfied with what we have done on this occasion. I flatter myself that our compelling a Mexican army of more than twenty thousand men, completely organized and led by their chief magistrate, to retreat, with less than five hundred regulars and about four thousand volunteers, will meet their approval. I had not a single company of regular infantry; the whole was taken from me.

I was truly gratified to learn that the chief magistrate of your state had conferred on you the rank of brigadier-general of the militia, and had hoped that the President of the United States would have called you into service as such with the new regiments, and hope he may yet do so, as I need hardly repeat the pleasure it would give me to be associated with you in carrying on this war. The road to the city of Mexico from here is now open, and we only want a few thousand regulars, in addition to the volunteers, to enable us to reach that place. What effect our late battle will have on Santa Anna and the Mexican Congress, time must determine; but I sincerely hope it will lead to peace. One thing is certain; their principal army has become demolished, and it will be very difficult for them to raise and equip another.

I much fear I have spun out this long, and to you uninteresting epistle, beyond your patience even to wade through it; but I have the consolation to know that you are not compelled to read the whole or any part of it. I will conclude by desiring you to present me most respectfully to your excellent lady, as well as to my friend Colonel Nicholas, and accept my sincere wishes for the continued health and prosperity of you and yours through a long life.

With respect and esteem,

Your friend,

Z. TAYLOR.

The loss of officers in General Taylor's gallant division, in the battle of Buena Vista, sixty-five in number, exhibits a proportion and result unparalleled in any battle on record, which we can now call to mind. General Taylor's effective force was about five thousand rank and file; and allowing one commissioned officer to twenty men, the startling conclusion is arrived at, that our loss of commissioned officers in this sanguinary engagement, amounted to one-fourth of the whole number on the field. If the loss of the rank and file had been proportioned to that of officers, it would exceed one thousand two hundred men. This immense loss of officers indicates the most chivalrous daring on their part. Colonel Clay was a graduate at West Point, where he distinguished himself by every quality demanded by his profession. He was about forty years of age; and was in every way worthy the glorious stock from which he sprung. Accomplished, gentle, generous, and brave, he added to those merits the highest moral qualities, and was regarded by all who knew him with esteem, and by his relatives and friends with the warmest and proudest affection.

Colonel J. J. Hardin was a nephew of Henry Clay, and known throughout the nation as an active and able member of Congress, from Illinois. He declined a re-election from a desire to join the armies of his country; and whether as a civilian or a soldier, won, by his noble qualities, the confidence and esteem of all parties. Colonel Yell was also a member of Congress, representing Arkansas. He was a true patriot, and resigned his seat for the higher privilege of fighting the battles of his country. His letters from the seat of war have excited much attention. Colonel McKee, commanding the regiment to which Mr. Clay was attached, was extensively connected and highly esteemed in Kentucky. His loss will be generally lamented in the west, where he was justly cherished. Captain Lincoln, of Massachusetts, was of the regular army, and acted in the staff of General Wool at the time of his death. He was breveted for his courage and conduct at Resaca de la Palma, and was an officer of great daring and merit. He was with Taylor in his successful charge upon the Mexicans after the force of General Wool had been thrown into confusion; and was slain by a spent ball.

A writer from Saltillo describes the following scene: The first view that we caught of the enemy was when they had turned the left flank of our lines, and were pursuing the flying infantry and horsemen. Column after column succeeded until they formed a dense mass, numbering something like twelve thousand men. No words can convey to you even a faint idea of their imposing appearance. Their arms, brilliantly burnished, reflected a million of times the dazzling rays of the sun—their rich and gaudy uniforms stood out in bold relief against the soiled and tattered garments of the "suffering volunteers"—their lancers, drawn up in beautiful style, numbering from two to three thousand, and in lines, the beauty of which the most accurate military observer could have found no fault with; and, added to this, that they were, for the time, victors, I assure you we did not look upon them with contempt. But when the quick, sharp ringing of our rifles sounded the death-knell of score after score of them, three hearty Mississippi cheers told full well that no cowardly fear paralyzed that little band. Rushing on, our small force would have scattered the retreating foė in all directions over the death-strewn field, had not our watchful leader, Colonel Davis, perceived that we were about to be surrounded by an overpowering force, and ordered us to retire and rally.

Here an amusing circumstance took place. Major Bradford—who is probably the most impetuously brave officer who ever drew a sword—perceived us retiring, and thought we were defeated. He dismounted from his horse and followed on slowly after us, exclaiming—"*Shoot me! Shoot me!*" Some one called out—

"What the d—l's the matter, major?"

"*Ah, kill me! The Mississippi regiment has run, and I don't want to live another minute!*"

But the gallant major was quickly undeceived, for we soon re-formed, and although our ranks were terribly thinned by the killed and wounded, yet again was heard the deep voice of the noble Davis, "*Forward! Guide centre! March!*" The command was repeated by fifty voices, and with more steadiness and precision than the careless fellows were ever known to evince on a drill, they returned to the bloody contest.

What a contrast the humane conduct of General Taylor presents, when compared with the bloody atrocities of the Mexicans. His kindness to the wounded among his enemies, is equal to that which he manifested towards his soldiers. It occurred that a body of Mexican infantry, about a thousand strong, had become detached from Santa Anna's army, and were being mowed down with terrible slaughter. General Taylor sent Mr. Crittenden with a flag, to say to them if they would surrender he would stop killing them. When Mr. Crittenden got among them, he was taken by them to Santa Anna with his eyes blindfolded. This he remonstrated against without effect. When he was brought to Santa Anna, he was asked his mission. He said he had no message for him; that he was sent to ask a detached force to surrender, to save the effusion of blood, and as his errand was unsuccessful, he demanded to be sent back to his general.

As an instance of the desperation with which both armies fought, Mr. Crittenden, when asked 'whether' the Mexicans had taken three pieces of ordnance from us, as Santa Anna reported, replied in the affirmative; and said that the guns were not given up until every man at them was shot down, and every horse killed near them; and, moreover, that in bearing them off, the Mexicans suffered a loss of some six hundred men. They interfered madly between the retreating guns and our men, seeking to regain them. These guns were a part of Captain Washington's battery, under the command of Lieutenant O'Brien. Lieutenant O'Brien was wounded before his guns were taken, and, when reporting his loss to General Taylor, was complimented for his bravery—it was no fault of his. Captain Washington was in another part of the field, and sustained himself with great coolness and intelligence, as did Captains Bragg and Sherman, with their respective batteries—in all but fourteen guns.

After the battle, says an eye-witness, I rode over the whole field. Parties were engaged in burying the dead—but there were still hundreds of bodies lying stiff and cold, with no covering save the scanty remnant of clothing which the robbers of the dead found too valueless to take from them. I saw the human body piercea in every place. I saw expressed in the faces of the dead almost every expression and feeling. Some seemed to have died execrating their enemies, and cursing them with their last breath—others had the most placid and resigned expression and feeling. Some seemed to have died defending their lives bravely to the last, while others evidently used their last words in supplicating for mercy. Here lay youth and mature age calmly reposing in untimely death.

Passing on from this part of the bloody ground, I went over to the plain literally covered with the dead bodies of those who had so recently been our foes. This scene was horrible enough, God knows—but was divested of some of its horrors by the fact, that not one of the Mexican soldiers was either robbed or stripped of his clothing, nor was there the least appearance of the bodies having been abused after having been wounded. This, indeed, speaks much for the "barbarous volunteers of the United States of the North," as the Mexicans style us.

Among the hundreds of dead whom I saw there, I was much touched by the appearance of the corpse of a Mexican boy, whose age I should think, could not have exceeded fifteen years. A bullet had struck him full in the breast, and must have occasioned almost instant death. He was lying on his back, his face slightly inclined to one side, and although cold, yet beaming with a bright and sunny smile, which eloquently told the spectator that he had fallen with his face to his country's foe. Saltillo is one vast hospital. Besides our own wounded, (four or five hundred in number,) General Taylor *has collected all the wounded Mexicans who were left by their army, and put them in the hospital.*

Lieutenant Corwine gives the following interesting sketch of General Taylor on the battle field of Buena Vista: By way of illustrating an important characteristic of General Taylor, to wit, determination, I will briefly relate a scene that occurred on the battle ground of Buena Vista, during the action of the 23d. At the time when the fortunes of the day seemed extremely problematical—when many on our side even despaired of success—old Rough and Ready, as he is not inaptly styled, whom you must know, by-the-bye, is short, fat and dumpy in person, with remarkably short legs—took his position on a commanding height, overlooking the two armies. This was about three, or perhaps four o'clock in the afternoon. The enemy, who had succeeded in gaining an advantageous position, made a fierce charge upon our column, and fought with a desperation that seemed for a time to insure success to their arms. The struggle lasted for some time. All the while, General Taylor was a silent spectator, his countenance exhibiting the most anxious solicitude, alternating between hope and despondency. His staff, perceiving his perilous situation, (for he was exposed to the fire of the enemy,) approached him and implored him to retire. He heeded them not. His thoughts were intent upon victory or defeat. He knew not at that moment what the result would be. He felt that that engagement was to decide his fate. He had given all his orders, and selected his position. If the day went against him, he was irretrievably lost; if for him, he could rejoice in common with his countrymen, at the triumphant success of our arms.

Such seemed to be his thoughts—his determination. And when he saw the enemy give way, and retreat in the utmost confusion, he gave vent to his pent up feelings. His right leg was quickly disengaged from the pommel of the saddle, where it had remained during the whole of the fierce encounter—his arms, which were calmly folded over his breast, relaxed their hold—his feet fairly danced in the stirrups, and his whole body was in motion. It was a moment of the most intense interest. His face was suffused with tears.

The day was won—the victory complete—his little army saved from the disgrace of a defeat, and he could not refrain from weeping for joy at what had seemed to so many, but a moment before, as an impossible result. Long may the noble and kind-hearted old hero live to enjoy the honors of his numerous brilliant victories, and many other honors that a grateful country will ere long bestow upon him.

After the battle of Buena Vista, many of the Mexicans who were taken prisoners stated that they had not eaten anything for three days previous to the battle; that the army of Santa Anna was in a state of utter destitution; and that unless he could get supplies in four days, his army would disband, or that they must inevitably starve. Paymaster J. B. Butler says: "General Santa Anna is really to be pitied. His men are a wretched set. He had twice, during the battle, to interpose his lancers to prevent desertion, and they shot down some fifty at each time, before he could prevent the flight of his infantry. The information comes from prisoners who deserted as soon as exchanged, and came into General Taylor's camp. They report that Santa Anna is destitute of all kinds of provisions, and that he cannot keep them together."

It may be recollected that some time since a correspondent at Saltillo, informed us of a great excitement, occasioned there by the arrival of two Mexican officers from San Luis, with dispatches to General Taylor. They were supposed to be propositions for peace, but turned out to be solemn inquiries whether it was the general's intention "to conduct the war according to the manner adopted by the Camanches." The wrath of General Taylor at this preposterous insolence of the Mexicans was described as ludicrous, but we have never seen his reply till now. In the Mexican papers lately received the whole correspondence is given in Spanish. The letter to General Taylor was from General Moray Villamil, and dated the 10th of May. The letter is long, and we have no idea of translating it, and the impudence of it was not a whit exaggerated. The nature of it will be sufficiently disclosed by General Taylor's reply, which we translate, although we feel what injustice his terse and manly style will suffer by the double translation. The letter is said to be dated:

HEADQUARTERS, NEAR MONTEREY,
May 19, 1847.

SIR—I received yesterday your communication of the 20th instant, which informs me that you are instructed by the President Substitute of the Republic to address me, with a view to demand from me a categorical reply—"whether my wishes and my instructions are to prosecute the war in conformity to the laws of nations, and as war is conducted by civilized countries, or as barbarous tribes carrying it on among themselves, it being understood, that Mexico is disposed and resolved to accept the manner which is proposed or carried out, and awaits the result in order to dictate its measures accordingly."

If these instructions were not communicated to me through an authority as highly respectable as yourself, I should refuse to believe they emanated from the Chief Magistrate of the Republic, containing, as in fact they do contain, in my judgment, an implied but not less deliberate insult towards me and towards the government which I have the honor to represent. Viewing them in this light, I shall decline giving the categorical reply which is demanded of me, which I do with the respect due to his Excellency the President.

As you have thought fit to communicate to me the instructions of your government at some length, upon the manner in which the war has been carried on upon my part, I improve this opportunity to make some remarks upon the subject.

The outrages to which especial reference is made, came to my knowledge after they had been perpetrated, and I can assure you that neither yourself nor the President of the Republic can have felt deeper pain, than that which I felt on the occasion. All the means at my disposal, within the limits of our laws, were employed, but in the greater number of cases fruitlessly, to identify and punish the delinquents. I cannot suppose that you have been so ill-informed, as to believe that such atrocities were committed by my connivance, order, or consent, or that they, by themselves, give an idea of the manner in which the war has been prosecuted in this part of Mexico. They were in truth unfortunate exceptions, caused by circumstances which I could not control.

It appears to me in point, to inform you, that from the moment the American army set foot upon the territory of Mexico, it has suffered, individually, the loss of officers and soldiers, who have been assassinated by Mexicans, sometimes almost in sight of their own camp. An outrage of this character preceded the melancholy affair of Catana. I do not mention these truths with a view of justifying in any manner, the practice of retaliation, because my government is sufficiently civilized to make a distinction between the lawless acts of individuals, and the general policy which governs the operations of an enemy; but you have endeavored to make a comparison between our respective governments in regard to the manner in which they conduct the war, which I cannot pass without remark. In this connection, it should be borne in mind that the Mexican troops have given to the world the example of killing the wounded upon the field of battle.

As you have adverted to the requisition which I have made upon the people of these States to make indemnity for the losses incurred by the destruction of one of our trains, I take the liberty of informing you that this was not the act of the Mexican troops exclusively, but that the rancheros of the country were chiefly concerned in it; and that the subsequent assassination and mutilation of the unarmed teamsters were marked by an atrocious barbarity unparalleled in the present war.

It is with pain that I find myself under the necessity of addressing you in a manner to which I am little accustomed; but I have been provoked to do so by the object and the manner of your communication, which is objectionable, in my estimation, as well in its insinuations as in its tone. With respect to the implied threat of retaliation, I beg you to understand that I hold it at its true worth, and that I am at all times prepared to act accordingly, whatever may be the policy or mode of carrying on the war which the Mexican government or its generals may think it proper to adopt. I am, sir, with much respect, your obedient servant.

The following anecdotes are told of the old general's coolness at Monterey: The first shot fired at Monterey was from one of the long culverines, aimed at General

Taylor himself, whilst reconnoitring. It struck a short distance in front of him and bounded over his head. "There! I knew it would fall short of me," he calmly remarked. One anecdote of General Taylor at Monterey, told by his staff, has never appeared in print. In traversing the field of battle, it was necessary to cross a bridge which was constantly swept by the Mexican artillery. When approaching it, it was agreed that they (the general and his staff) should cross it singly at a gallop. Four had crossed thus, when it came the general's turn. Just as he reached the middle of the bridge, and when the balls were showering around him, something going wrong in another part of the field attracted his attention. Stopping his horse, much to the discomfiture of those following him, he deliberately took out and arranged his spy-glass, satisfied himself, and then closing it, rode on.

When General La Vega was introduced to General Taylor on the battle field, the latter shook him warmly by the hand, and addressed to him the following handsome remarks: "General, I do assure you I deeply regret that this misfortune has fallen upon you. I regret it sincerely, and I take pleasure in returning you the sword which you have this day worn with so much gallantry;" handing him at the same time the sword which General Vega had yielded to Captain May.

The following anecdote illustrating the simple habits and republican tastes of this heroic, unassuming, and excellent man, is related by the committee who bore to him the sword presented by the citizens of New Orleans: "We presented ourselves at the opening of one of the tents, before which was standing a dragoon's horse, much used by hard service. Upon a camp-stool at our left, sat General ——, in busy conversation with a hearty-looking old gentleman, sitting on a box, cushioned with an Arkansas blanket, dressed in Attakapas pantaloons and a linen roundabout, and remarkable for a bright flashing eye, a high forehead, a farmer look, and 'rough and ready' appearance. It is hardly necessary for us to say that this personage was General Taylor, the commanding hero of two of the most remarkable battles on record, and the man who, by his firmness and decision of character, has shed lustre upon the American arms.

"There was no pomp about his tent; a couple of rough blue chests served for his table, on which was strewn, in masterly confusion, a variety of official documents; a quiet-looking, citizen-dressed personage made his appearance upon hearing the significant call of 'Ben,' bearing, on a tin salver, a couple of black bottles and shining tumblers, arranged around an earthen pitcher of Rio Grande water. These refreshments were deposited upon a stool, and we 'helped ourselves,' by invitation. We bore to the general a complimentary gift from some of his fellow-citizens of New Orleans, which he declined receiving for the present, giving at the same time a short but 'hard sense' lecture on the impropriety of naming children and places after men before they were dead, or of his receiving a present for his services 'before the campaign, so far as he was concerned, was finished.'

"With the highest possible admiration of the republican simplicity of the manners and character of General Taylor, we bade him good day, with a higher appreciation of our native land, for possessing such a man as a citizen, and of its institutions for moulding such a character."

Nothing, it is said, annoys General Taylor more than

to have Mexicans come to him and address him in Spanish. During the year he has been in this country, he has learned but one word of Spanish, and that is *vamos;* the imperative plural of *go—begone.* One day, while encamped at Saltillo, being very busy in his tent, a Mexican came up and commenced uttering a long complaint in Spanish. The old general turned to Major Bliss and asked—"What in heaven's name does the man want?" Major Bliss explained that the Mississippians appeared to be taking wood from his house. Now, the Mississippi regiment was a favorite of the general's, and as they had always conducted themselves well, he was in an unfortunate mood to hear complaints against them. So, waving his hand towards the Mexican, he told him to "*huebos, huebos, huebos;*" [eggs, eggs, eggs!] He had heard some one use the word, a minute before, and took it for his favorite word *vamos.* When General Taylor, in January last, arrived here from Monterey, he encamped near town, but was not pleased with the location for an encampment. So speaking on the subject with a number of officers that had called to pay their respects to him, he told them that in a few days he should move the whole army to *agua ardiente,* (the Mexican word for brandy.) He meant *Agua Nueva.*

The general had occasion to visit Point Isabel, after the battle of Buena Vista; and the captain of the steamboat had reserved a suit of state-rooms for the general's accommodation. There were several sick and wounded volunteers on the boat, en route for New Orleans, who had to take the wayfare incident to a crowded boat, and particularly so on this occasion. General Taylor soon saw all this, and at once ordered these men to be placed *in his state-rooms* and proper attention paid them. It was rather a cold rainy day when this occurred. The deck hands and many others on the boat, did not know General Taylor. The wind blew high, and the firemen had raised a sail in front of the boilers to protect themselves from the rain; and under this sail there were some old mattresses: here General Taylor laid down and went to sleep. At supper-time great inquiries were made for the general, and servants sent off to look him up. But he could not be found! At last some one going below inquired of a fireman if he had seen such and such a man. The fireman said no, but added, " there is a clever old fellow asleep there under the sail in front of the fire!" It was General Taylor. Yes, sweet indeed must be the sleep of such a man, who has the heart to *change places* with the poor sick soldier, as Taylor did on this occasion;—such humanity stands out in bold relief, and greatly mitigates the evils incident to war.

A correspondent of the Pennsylvania Inquirer relates the following anecdote of the commander of the army: "This morning I heard a little incident respecting General Taylor, which, at the present time, will be interesting. During the Florida campaign, a certain young officer, after receiving his commission, was ordered to join the army in that quarter. His first duty was, of course, to report himself to General Taylor. After a very tedious journey, however, through the woods, our officer arrived at a small shanty called a tavern, about fifty miles from head-quarters, where he thought proper to stay three days. There were only two visitors there besides himself. One of them, an oldish, shabby-looking man, with a black hat, minus part of the crown, and a piece of twine for a ribbon, was very inquisitive, and among other things asked our officer what excuse he intended to make for his delay in reporting himself to the general.

"'Oh,' said the officer, 'they say Taylor is a very easy old soul, and I can easily make up an excuse.' On going to bed that night, the officer asked the landlord who that impudent, inquisitive old fellow was? 'Why,' said the host, 'don't you know General Taylor?' About an hour afterwards, at midnight, the tramp of a horse's feet was heard, making large tracks towards head-quarters."

The night of the 23d of February last was one of most intense anxiety to the participators in the bloody fight of Buena Vista. After twelve hours of obstinate fighting, with final result yet unknown, nothing but water having passed the lips of those gallant men for the last twelve hours, the flower of their respective corps dead or wounded, and the certainty of a renewal of the onslaught the next day, it is hard to imagine a period more calculated to "try men's souls" than that night. After the cessation of the fight, came the lassitude superinduced by the extraordinary excitement of the day; men fell exhausted, and bivouacked in the line—"the weary to rest and the wounded to die." The depression of physical energy was so great, that neither hunger nor danger could incite them; that bloody field was at 8 o'clock as silent as the grave. It can hardly be surmised what were the feelings of that "great old man" upon contemplating the results of that day's work. No officer sought repose, and the camp fires, which on other occasions had been the scene of jest and merriment, were now still, and the deep anxiety depicted on the faces of the various groups of officers, impressed you with a solemnity foreboding ill, that was truly painful. All eyes were turned ever and anon to the tent of one upon whom all their hopes were placed, but not a light, not a movement could be discerned. The occasion made that single tent an object of intense solicitude. Some wondered if he was alone; others would have given their earthly wealth to have known the thoughts, the hopes, the wishes, the intentions of the old hero; but all was dark and silent as the tomb. Captain L., of the topographical engineers, had visited the battle-ground at night. He had made some discoveries he thought important to be communicated immediately to the commander-in-chief. On approaching the general's quarters, he overtook his servant, who had been attending to his master's *cavalry*, and inquired if the "old man" was alone and awake. "*I 'spec he fast asleep, captain, for he eat a monstrous hearty supper, and when he eat a big supper he sleep berry hard and sound, and I reckon you won't see de old hos' 'fore* 4 *o'clock in de mornin'. Listen, you hear him snore clean out here.*" When the captain made a report of this last reconnoissance, joy and satisfaction were diffused through the camp. They knew that all was safe.

Among the volunteers was a "gentleman's son"—a full private, who, heartily sick of rainy weather, mud, and no shelter, first went to his captain with his complaints; but meeting with no particular sympathy, resolved to have a talk with General Taylor himself. Arrived at the commander's quarters, the general was pointed out to him, but he was rather incredulous. "*That* old fellow General Taylor? Nonsense!" Satisfied, however, that such was even the case, he marched up, and rather patronizingly opened his business.

"General Taylor, I believe."

"Yes, sir."

"Well, general, I'm devilish glad to see you—am, indeed." The general returned the civility.

"General, you'll excuse me, but since I've been here I've been doing all I could for you—have, indeed; but the fact is, the accommodations are very bad—they are, indeed; mud, sir! *bleeged* to lie down in it, actually; and the fact is, general, I'm a *gentleman's son*, and not used to it!"

The general, no doubt deeply impressed with the fact of having a *gentleman's* son in his army, expressed his regret that such annoyance should ever exist, under any circumstances, in a civilized army.

"Well—but, general, what am I to do?"

"Why, really, I don't know, unless you take my place."

"Well, now, that's civil—'tis, indeed. Of course don't mean to *turn you out*, but a few hours' sleep—a cot, or a bunk, or anything—would be so refreshing! Your place—where is it, general?"

"O, just drop down—*anywhere about here*—any place about camp will answer!"

The look which the "gentleman's son" gave the general was rather peculiar.

"Well, no wonder they call you 'Rough and Ready,'" said he; and, amid the smiles of all but "Rough and Ready" himself, the "gentleman's son" returned to take his chance of the weather.

It having been insinuated by some that Major Bliss was the author of General Taylor's dispatches, the Hagerstown, (Md.) Torch Light, administers a quietus to that idea, by the following fact, which the editor obtained from a gentleman who was a graduate of West Point, and a class and room-mate of Governor Davis, of Mississippi. General Taylor, without doubt, writes his own dispatches, and a blessed time it will be for the printers, as well as everybody else, when the direct, concise, comprehensive missives of "Z. Taylor" issue from the White House:

In conversation with General G——, of the U. S. Army, now stationed at Washington, our friend asked the question, if Major Bliss did not write the dispatches. The old general's eye sparkled with indignation, and he replied that he had served with General Taylor upon thirteen courts-martial, and that he (General Taylor) had been selected by each court to draw up its report, because of his superior ability in composition—that all were willing to accede to him the faculty of expressing in the clearest, strongest, and most forcible manner, the views of the court, and hence he was uniformly selected for this purpose. General G—— also stated, that in Florida a misunderstanding arose between General Twiggs and General Taylor, from a remark made by the latter in regard to some military operations of the former. A correspondence ensued, which proved perfectly satisfactory to General Twiggs. One of General Taylor's communications, in which he gave at large his views of the matter in dispute, reached Washington, and, General G—— remarked, was regarded by the gentlemen of the army as one of the most powerful military productions they had ever seen. This communication seems to have foreshadowed the dispatches, whose fame has spread over Europe and our country. One of the peculiarities of General Taylor's style of writing was also noted. Instead of having, as is customary, a margin at the side of the sheet, General Taylor commences at the extreme limit, and fills the sheet so completely, that, as our informant observed, it is impossible to crowd in anywhere, even a little *i*. This seems to be one of the many peculiarities of "Rough and Ready."

It has been the happy fortune of few men, of any age or any country, to have won so brilliant a military career by such a rapid succession of splendid and glorious achievements of arms; and to have established a fame upon so firm a basis, by a series of victories which throw so far into the shade the deeds of many of the most renowned warriors of ancient or modern times, as General Taylor has, by the rare wisdom, prudence, coolness and sagacity exhibited in all his operations in Mexico; and especially, by the gallantry, heroism, and chivalric courage displayed on the fields of Palo Alto, Resaca de la Palma, Monterey and Buena Vista. In all these fiercely contested battles he has fought under such unfavorable circumstances, and against such overwhelming odds, always in number, and generally in discipline and military appointments, as no other general has ever encountered with such uniformly decisive success.

No superiority of numbers, strength of position, or advantages in equipments and discipline, has ever, for a moment, deterred him from giving the enemy battle, or prevented him from marching straight onward to the object towards which all his energies have been bent, since he first encamped on the Rio Grande. And the country fully appreciates his almost superhuman efforts to sustain the honor of our arms. The public press of the nation has, with a unanimity never before exceeded, resounded with his praises, and the people of the whole Union vie with each other in doing him honor. Congress, too, as well as the legislative bodies of most of the states, have passed votes of thanks for his remarkable services, and several of them have presented him with other testimonials of their admiration for his character and gratitude for his efforts in defence of the nation. The legislature of the state of New York, amongst others, passed resolutions, tendering to him, and his officers and men, on behalf of their constituents, the thanks of the people of the state for their gallant conduct. They were transmitted to him by the governor, and elicited an appropriate acknowledgment.

Soon after the battles of Palo Alto and Resaca de la Palma, he also had conferred upon him the rank of Brevet Major-General, and on the 27th of June he received the appointment of Major-General, which was unanimously confirmed by Congress, and was constituted commander-in-chief of all the American forces in Mexico; and that position he held until Major-General Scott was ordered to that country, in November, 1846.

An intimate personal friend, one who has known him long and well, Colonel Humphrey Marshall of Kentucky, has, in the following extract of a speech delivered by him, at a barbecue given to the Kentucky volunteers, given the following discriminating sketch of General Taylor's character. Coming from such a source it cannot but prove highly interesting, as it may be relied on as authentic. After reading it, none will be surprised that a man possessing such high, rare and admirable traits of character as General Taylor does, should be so honored and loved by all brought into personal relations with him:

"My service in Mexico frequently brought me near to General Taylor, and I was industrious in my examination of the actual character of the man whenever opportunity was presented. I have no motive to deceive you, and you must take the impressions I received for what they are worth. The manner in which politicians, in this our day, are accustomed to speak of men, and especially of such as may be elevated to political power, is so utterly extravagant, so profusely hyperbolical, that after they take hold of the character of General Taylor, no description I could give would be recognized as bordering on truth. Glowing oratory will seize the achievements of the general, and dress them off in all the frippery of metaphor, and I doubt whether *the man* will be regarded, or whether he would know his own likeness.

"I have seen the pictures of him in books, and pamphlets, and in prints. Some have the head of Napoleon, others that of Cæsar, and some are unlike any original I have ever beheld, but none like the general I know. So it will be with the pictures the politicians will execute. If I tried to express in the fewest words what manner of man General Taylor is, I should say, that, in his manners and his appearance, *he is one of the common people of this country.* He might be transferred from his tent at Monterey to this assembly, and he would not be remarked among this crowd of respectable old farmers as a man at all distinguished from those around him. Perfectly temperate in his habits; perfectly plain in his dress; entirely unassuming in his manners, he appears to be an old gentleman in fine health, whose thoughts are not turned upon personal appearance, and who has no point about him to attract particular attention. In his intercourse with men, he is free, frank, and manly. He plays off none of the airs of some great men whom I have met. There is an artificial dignity some men wear, to add to a moral stature which conscience whispers to them may need support from *mannerism*. Some, who *would be deemed great*, preserve their reputation by studied gravity, which seems to say—

> "I am Sir Oracle ;
> When I ope my mouth let no dog bark."

But a close and critical examination of these always discovers fissures in the character fatally blemishing the perfection which they pretend to, and preserve the appearance of, by keeping at a distance from their peers. General Taylor is not of this class of great men. Any one may approach him as nearly as can be desired, and the more closely his character is examined the greater beauties it discloses.

1. *He is an honest man.* I do not mean by that merely that he does not cheat nor lie. I mean that he is a man who never dissembles and who scorns all disguises. He neither acts a part among his friends for effect, nor assumes to be what he is not. Whenever he speaks you hear what he honestly believes, and, whether right or wrong, you feel assured that he has expressed his real opinion. His dealings with men have been of a most varied character, and I never heard his honest name stained by the breath of the slightest reproach.

2. *He is a man of rare good judgment.* By no means possessed of that brilliancy of genius which attracts by its flashes, yet, like the meteor, expires even while you gaze upon it; by no means enjoying that combination of talent which penetrates instantly the abstrusest subject, and measures its length and breadth as if by intuition; General Taylor yet has that order of intellect, which more slowly but quite as surely, masters all that it engages and examines all the combi-

nations of which the subject is susceptible. When he announces his conclusions, you feel confident that he well understands the ground upon which he plants himself, and you rest assured that the conclusion is the deduction of skill and sound sense faithfully applied to the matter in hand.

It is this order of mind which has enabled him, unlike many other officers of the army, to attend to the wants of his family, by so using the means at his disposal as to surround himself in his old age with a handsome private fortune, and to be blessed with an almost perfect constitution. I would to-day prefer his advice in any matter of private interest—would take his opinion as to the value of an estate—would rather follow his suggestions in a scheme where property or capital was to be embarked, would pursue more confidently his counsel where the management of an army was involved, or the true honor of my country was at stake, than that of any other man I have ever known. I regard his judgment as being first rate at everything, from a horse trade up to a trade in human life upon the field of battle.

3. *He is a firm man and possessed of great energy of character.* It were a waste of time to dwell upon these traits of his character, for his military career has afforded such abundant examples of his exercise of these qualities, as to render them familiar to every citizen who has ever read or heard of the man. In his army they are daily exhibited, and stand conspicuously displayed in every order which emanates from his pen.

4. *He is a benevolent man.* This quality has been uniformly displayed in his treatment of the prisoners who have been placed in his power by the vicissitudes of war. No man who had seen him after the battle

of Buena Vista, as he ordered the wagons to bring in the Mexican wounded from the battle-field, and heard him as he at once cautioned his own men that the wounded were to be treated with mercy, could doubt that he was alive to all the kinder impulses of our nature.

The indiscretions of youth he chides with paternal kindness, yet with the decision which forbids their repetition, and the young men of his army feel that it is a pleasure to gather around him, because they know that they are as welcome as though they visited the hearthstone of their own home, and they are always as freely invited to partake of what he has to offer as if they were under the roof of a father. His conduct in sparing the deserters who were captured at Buena Vista, exhibited at the same time in a remarkable manner his benevolence and his judgment. "Don't shoot them," said he; "the worst punishment I will inflict is to return them to the Mexican army." When Napoleon said to one of his battalions, "inscribe it on their flag: 'No longer of the army of Italy,'" he used an expression which was deemed so remarkable, that history preserved it for the admiration of future ages; yet it was not more forcible as an illustration of his power in touching the springs of human action, than is that of General Taylor illustrative of the manner in which he would make an example for the benefit of the army.

5. *He is a man of business habits.* I never have known General Taylor to give up a day to pleasure. I have never visited his quarters without seeing evidences of the industry with which he toiled. If his talented adjutant was surrounded by papers, so was the general. And though he would salute a visitor kindly, and bid him with familiar grace to amuse him-

self until he was at leisure, he never would interrupt the duties which his station called him to perform. When these were closed for the day, he seemed to enjoy to a remarkable degree the vivacity of young officers, and to be glad to mingle in their society. As a conversationist, I do not think General Taylor possesses great power. He uses few words, and expresses himself with energy and force, but not fluently. His language is select. I would say, however, from my knowledge of the man, that he is entirely capable of producing anything in the shape of an order or letter, which has ever appeared over his signature; and in saying so much, I understand myself as asserting that he is master of his mother tongue, and can write about as effectively and handsomely as he can fight.

Such then is the picture of the man—not of the general—who won upon my esteem. I am not in the habit of eulogizing men, and have indulged on this occasion, because I desire to describe to you, with the exactness of truth, those qualities which, combined in General Taylor, made him appear to me *as a first rate model of a true American character.* Others will dwell upon the chivalry he has so often displayed, and his greatness so conspicuously illustrated upon the field of battle; I formed my ideas of the man when he was free from duty, and had no motive to appear in any other light than such as was thrown upon him by nature, education, and principles.

In personal appearance, General Taylor is described to be about five feet eight inches high, very thick set, rather inclining to corpulency, and slightly stoop-shouldered. He weighs about two hundred pounds, and has remarkably short legs in proportion to the length of his body, in consequence of which, he looks like a much taller man than he really is, when in a sitting position. He has a fine head, high forehead, light, keen, penetrating eye, indicating uniform good-humor, and firm, compressed lips. His hair is almost white, his face care-worn, but extremely intelligent, and almost uniformly lit up with a benevolent smile. When speaking to any one he is in the habit of partly closing one eye, is extremely fond of a joke, and ever ready with a witty repartee, or a kind word for all who address him. He dresses, at all times, with great simplicity, utterly eschewing tight clothes, and even a military coat. He has an unconquerable dislike for a uniform, and generally is seen with a linen roundabout, cotton pantaloons, and a straw hat, in warm weather, and his celebrated brown overcoat, that protected him, during his Florida campaigns, in cold or rainy seasons.

The most remarkable traits of General Taylor's character are the wisdom and foresight with which he lays his plans, the energy and promptness with which he executes them, and his firmness, decision and self-possession in the hour of trial. No emergency, however unlooked-for or sudden, no danger, however imminent and threatening, and no contingency, of whatever nature, are ever able to throw him off his guard, or disturb his evenly balanced mind. He always proves himself equal to every emergency, and rises as the dangers that beset him increase; and the resources of his mind are as inexhaustible as his will is indomitable and his courage unyielding. All his movements are characterized by the highest qualities of a soldier. Calm, sagacious, resolute, ready;—with a boldness which never falters, a watchfulness never at fault, and a comprehensiveness of plan embracing all contingencies, he has won for himself the very highest military renown which it has ever been the fortune of an American soldier to reach. His letters and dispatches are models of military writing, not surpassed by the justly renowned "Wellington Dispatches." His manly assertion of his rights as the commanding general, shows him to be possessed of moral courage in as eminent a degree as he is of physical. It affords some relief to the horrors of this war, that it has brought out to the knowledge of the country, and the world, the fact that we possess a man and a soldier of such extraordinary merits.

Great emergencies, it is said, produce great men. If they do not produce them, they at least bring them to light. So it has been in the unhappy war between us and a sister republic. A man of simple and unostentatious habits—who, though possessing great wealth chose to follow the profession of arms, and was satisfied with the common routine of military life, never thrusting himself into notice, but simply doing his duty in a quiet way—is by the force of circumstances brought prominently before the public, and is found to possess the highest military talents, and every other quality which men are accustomed to admire. In early life, and in humble rank, he successfully defended a Western fort against a superior force of the enemy. His modest dispatch recording the defence, had almost faded from remembrance. At a later period, a brilliant victory was won by him in the Florida war, and even with that we had almost ceased to be conversant. There was no crisis of public affairs, or essential risk of the national honor, to make these events of historical or political importance. In comparative retirement, or at most in the command of distant posts, the unaffected, though successful commander, passed away years of obscurity. We cannot tell whether this was congenial to his feelings or not; but be this as it may, he knew how to "bide his time," and the want of such knowledge destroys the prospects and usefulness of many a really great man.

How many of our most gifted public servants, impatient of delay, have endeavored to control destiny itself, and create the events upon which their advancement depended. How many bright spirits have been shrouded in darkness, before they have reached even a mid-day career. General Taylor, fortunate in his philosophy as in his temperament, permitted events to take their course, tranquil in retirement, and calm even when forgotten. But all at once he develops the qualities of a great general. In the most critical situations his judgment foresees what his valor wins. No matter what may be the difficulties around him, he meets and overcomes them all. In strategy as well as hand to hand, he evinces superior skill, and when the nation almost gives him up for lost, again and again he sends back to it intelligence that he has conquered. In no page of our history do we find recorded four such hard fought battles, fought at such fearful odds, as those which have placed such laurels on the brow of General Taylor, and the brave troops under his command. The country is astonished to find it possesses such a man!

CHAPTER IX.

General Taylor at Monterey—Punishment of Banditti—Lawlessness of Texan Rangers—Expedition against Huejutla—General Taylor's Force—Letter to Mr. Marcy—Departure from Mexico—Attachment of his Soldiers—His Reception in the United States—His Political Opinions—Presidential Question.

After the dreadful defeat of the Mexicans at Buena Vista, the army under Santa Anna precipitately fell back upon San Luis Potosi, claiming, in the mean time, the honor of a triumphant victory over General Taylor, but making no further attempt to molest the American forces in that quarter. General Taylor retired to his camp at Monterey, where he was compelled to remain, and repose upon the laurels he had won. He was too much crippled by the severe losses he had suffered at Buena Vista, weakened as his forces had previously been by the large drafts made upon them to strengthen the line of operations on the Capital of Mexico by the way of Vera Cruz, to deem it safe to attempt to march upon the Capital from the Rio Grande. But he kept a vigilant eye upon the movements of the marauding parties of the enemy who were hovering in his vicinity, under the command of Generals Urrea and Canales, who had learned sufficient wisdom from former experience not to attempt to molest the lion in his lair, or to venture within the reach of one who had proved so prompt and able to punish their presumption.

The ranchos between Meir and Monterey had long been the resort of armed bands of the enemy who had obstructed General Taylor's line of communication. He found it necessary, therefore, to his own safety, to give orders for destroying these means of annoyance. They were accordingly laid waste, and an indemnity required of the local Mexican authorities for all the property destroyed by these marauding parties. These rigid measures secured his wagon trains in a great degree from future attacks. Occasional attempts were made, however, upon his trains by the banditti, when they were not well guarded and the prospect of plunder was sufficiently tempting. But by the prompt and energetic measures adopted by General Taylor, comparative security was obtained and the enemy effectually subdued in that quarter.

While General Taylor was encamped at Monterey, thus guarding the interests of his country, General Villamil, who succeeded in the command at San Luis Potosi upon the return of Santa Anna to Mexico, addressed to him, in reply to the requisition for indemnity already referred to, a communication couched in the most offensive and even insulting language. He desired to know of General Taylor whether his intentions were to prosecute the war in conformity to the laws of nations, and as wars were conducted by civilized countries, or as barbarous tribes carry it on amongst themselves. He also very ostentatiously demanded satisfaction for several acts of violence and outrage that had been perpetrated by a portion of the Texan Rangers, under the command of Colonel Hays, and threatened to retaliate upon the Americans, should a prompt compliance with his demands be neglected. General Taylor peremptorily declined to give a direct reply to this inquiry of General Villamil, alleging as the ground of his refusal, that it was grossly insulting to himself personally as well as to his Government. He assured the Mexican general that "every possible effort had been made to discover the perpetrators of these outrages, in order to bring them to trial and punishment, but without success." In regard to the important threat of retaliation, he treated it with contempt, and stated that he was ready for any course of policy the Mexican authorities might decide to adopt. It was with pain, he said, that he found himself under the necessity of addressing General Villamil in a manner to which he was so little accustomed. But he had been provoked to do so by the object and manner of the communication, which was objectionable, in his estimation, as well in its insinuations as in its tone. With respect to the implied threat of retaliation, he begged General Villamil to understand that he held it at its true worth, and that he was at all times prepared to act accordingly, whatever might be the policy or mode of carrying on the war, which the Mexican Government or its generals might think it proper to adopt.

During the ensuing summer, General Taylor found himself unable to control the lawlessness of the Rangers; and so many unprovoked outrages were committed, the authors of which could very rarely be ascertained, that, as an act of justice to himself and to his country, he ordered a number of the more turbulent and refractory among them to be summarily dismissed from the service, regarding them as being wholly unworthy to belong to the American army. Collisions, growing out of these outrages, frequently took place; but the departments of Tamaulipas and New Leon, with this exception, were generally quiet. The active operations of the war were carried on upon a different theatre, and General Taylor remained strictly on the defensive.

Thus General Taylor remained at Monterey until November, 1847, faithfully and vigilantly watching and protecting the interests and honor of his country; maintaining his previous conquests, and keeping in subjection the turbulent bands of the enemy, who were seeking every opportunity to murder and plunder small parties of Americans, and feebly guarded wagon trains, especially when accompanied with American traders with articles of merchandise. He was able to engage in no enterprise commensurate with his former brilliant achievements, from causes already adverted to. Necessity, therefore, doomed him to comparative inactivity, while the campaign was carried on in another quarter under the command of General Scott.

An expedition against Huejutla, however, was ordered to be fitted out, which left Tampico in July, under the command of Colonel DeRussey. Learning that a large body of Mexicans lay in ambush at a narrow gorge, when but a few miles from his destination, and meeting with unexpected resistance from the enemy, he deemed it advisable to retreat, which he did in good order, though not without the loss of twenty-eight in killed, wounded and missing. The loss of the enemy was very severe, being about two hundred in killed and wounded.

"In the expectation of being ordered to advance into the interior, General Taylor directed a camp of instruction to be formed at Mier, early in the summer, in order to have his troops ready for active duty in the field. The camp was organized by General Hopping, who was placed in command of the upper district on the Rio Grande—Colonel Davenport, of the 1st infantry, being assigned to the lower district. Colonel Belknap, of the 8th infantry, was ordered to take the immediate charge of the camp, but before it had fairly gone into operation, General Taylor received orders to detach a large portion of his troops to reinforce the column under General Scott. The brilliant results which had attended the operations of the General-in-chief on the line of the National Road, and the necessity of opening his communications with the sea-coast, rendered it as necessary as it was advisable to strengthen his column without delay. Several new volunteer regiments had previously joined General Taylor, together with three regiments of infantry raised under the ten regiment bill, and a part of the 3d dragoons.

"Instructions were received by General Taylor, in August, to send all his disposable troops to Vera Cruz; and in accordance therewith, General Cushing, with his brigade, consisting of the 13th infantry, Colonel Echols, and the Massachusetts volunteers, Colonel Wright; and General Lane, with the 4th Ohio, Colonel Brough, and 4th Indiana, Colonel Gorman, forming the brigade under his command; together with five companies of Texan rangers, under Colonel Hays, were ordered to embark forthwith from the Rio Grande. General Marshall was also directed to join General Scott, with two regiments of Kentucky volunteers, recently enrolled, and on their way to Vera Cruz.

"After the departure of these troops, General Taylor had about 6,000 men under his command, including ten companies of regular dragoons, belonging to different regiments, and nine companies of regular artillery, also belonging to different regiments, serving with batteries, or garrisoning the forts on the Rio Grande. Besides the regular cavalry, there were five companies of Texan horse, and four companies of mounted volunteers from different States. The 10th infantry, Colonel Temple, was ordered to garrison Matamoras and Camargo. Colonel Butler, with the companies of the 3d dragoons, was also stationed on the Rio Grande. Colonel Tibbatts garrisoned Monterey with six companies of the 16th infantry, and the remaining four companies of his regiment occupied Seralvo. Lieutenant Colonel Fauntleroy, with his squadron of the 2d dragoons, and the battery of Lieutenant Colonel Bragg, were stationed at General Taylor's camp at Walnut Springs. At Buena Vista and Saltillo, were the Virginia and North Carolina regiments, under Colonels Hamtranck and Paine, and the 2d Mississippi rifles, Colonel R Davis, with the heavy battery of Captain Prentiss, the light battery of Captain Deas, and several companies of regular and volunteer cavalry, all under the orders of General Wool."

The idea of marching upon the Mexican capital from the line of the Sierra Madre, having now been definitely abandoned for the more feasible plan of carrying on operations through Vera Cruz, General Taylor, seeing no hope of his again being engaged in active service during the war, began to grow restless under the inactive life he was compelled to lead. Believing, therefore, that his further services for the present could be dispensed with, and finding that his private affairs were severely suffering by his long absence from his native country, he asked permission of the government to return to the United States. This request being complied with, General Taylor made all necessary arrangements for taking a final leave of his associates in arms in Mexico.

Before following the victorious General to the United States, however, and recording his brilliant reception there, it may not be out of place here to refer to some of the embarrassments under which General Taylor had labored, in consequence of the inexplicable coolness and want of confidence with which he had been treated by his government, almost ever since he crossed the Rio Grande. The censure he received from the Administration, for granting to the enemy, at the capture of Monterey, terms which they were pleased to designate as too lenient, in not requiring an unconditional capitulation, was looked upon with surprise in the United States, and pronounced by all parties as unjust and undeserved. It was not strange, therefore, that General Taylor should have deeply felt this rebuke, nor that he should have sought an opportunity to explain the motives which influenced his conduct in agreeing to the terms of capitulation which were made the occasion for this censure. If he had appealed from the Administration to the public, he would have been justified in the eyes of the American people, however wide a departure it may have been from the rules and regulations of the army. But he did not resort to this remedy for the injustice that had been done him. He was content to explain his motives for the comparatively liberal terms he had conceded to the enemy, to his old military friend, General E. P. Gaines. This he did in the freedom of a private and confidential correspondence, yet entirely avoiding all discourtesy to the Administration. It found its way, however, into the public press, and was made the justification for reviving an obsolete army regulation, designed to prohibit officers and soldiers in the United States service from writing letters for publication, detailing the movements of our army, in time of war. This was understood to be designed as a still further censure upon General Taylor; and this impression was confirmed by the consideration, that a slip containing the letter to General Gaines was forwarded to him by the President together with the order reviving the army regulation in question. This implied, if not direct, censure for an act so unobjectionable in itself as writing a private letter of the character of the one to General Gaines, drew from General Taylor the following characteristic reply to Honorable Wm. L. Marcy, Secretary of War, which was transmitted to the United States House of Representatives, in accordance with a resolution of that body, calling upon the President for the correspondence. The letter is written in that bold, manly, and independent tone, and vigor of style, for which all his correspondence is so remarkable. It displays a consciousness of rectitude, and an honesty and purity of purpose, which, aside from its unanswerable defence of his conduct, must carry conviction to every candid mind. It is dated Head Quarters, Army of Occupation, Agua Neuva, March 3d, 1847, but was not published until the February ensuing, and is as follows:

"I have the honor to receive your communication of January 27, enclosing a newspaper slip, and expressing the regret of the Department that the letter copied in that slip, and which was addressed by myself to Major Gen. Gaines, should have been published. Although your letter does not convey the direct censure of the Department and the President; yet, when it was taken in connection with the revival of the paragraph in the regulations of 1825, touching the publication of private letters concerning operations in the field, I am not permitted to doubt that I have become a subject of Executive disapprobation. To any expression of it, coming with the authority of the President, I am bound by my duty and by respect for his high office, patiently to submit; but lest my silence should be construed into a tacit admission of the grounds and conclusions set forth in your communication, I deem it a duty which I owe to myself, to submit a few remarks in reply.

"I shall be pardoned for speaking plainly. In the first place, the published letter bears upon its face the most conclusive evidence that it was intended only for private perusal, and not at all for publication. It was published without my knowledge and contrary to my wishes. Surely, I need not say that I am not in the habit of writing for the newspapers. The letter was a familiar one, written to an old military friend, with whom I have been for many years interchanging opinions on professional subjects. That he should think proper, under any circumstances, to publish it, could not have been foreseen by me. In the absence of proof that the publication was made without my knowledge, I may be permitted to say, the quotation of your letter of the 650th paragraph of the superseded regulations of 1825, in which the terms 'mischievous and disgraceful' are employed to characterize certain letters or reports, conveys, though not openly, a measure of rebuke, which to say the least, is rather harsh, and which many think not warranted by the premises.

"Again, I have carefully examined the letter in question, and I do not admit that it is obnoxious to the objections urged in your communication. I see nothing in it which, under the same circumstances, I would not write again. To suppose that it will give the enemy valuable information touching our posts or respective line of operations, is to know very little of the Mexican sources of information, or of their extraordinary sagacity and facilities in keeping constantly apprized of our movements. As to my particular views in regard to the general policy to be pursued towards Mexico, I perceive from the public journals that they are shared by many distinguished statesmen; also, in part, by conspicuous officers of the navy, the publication of whose opinions is not, perhaps, obstructed by any regulations of the department. It is difficult, then, to imagine how the diffusion of mine can render any peculiar aid to the enemy, or especially disincline him to enter into negotiations for peace.

"In conclusion, I would say, it has given me great pain to be brought into the position in which I now find myself in regard to the department of war, and the government. It has not been of my own seeking. To the extent of my abilities and the means placed at my disposal, I have sought faithfully to serve the country, by carrying out the rules and instructions of the Executive; but it cannot be concealed, that since the capitulation of Monterey, the confidence of the department, and, I too much fear, of the President, has been gradually withdrawing, and my consideration and usefulness correspondingly diminished. The apparent determination of the department to place me in an attitude antagonistical to the government, has an apt illustration in the well-known fable of Æsop. I ask no favor, and I shrink from no responsibility, while entrusted with the command in this quarter. I shall continue to devote all my energies to the public good, looking for my reward to the conscientiousness of pure motives, and to the final verdict of impartial history."

Having obtained leave from his government to return to the United States, General Taylor, early in November took his departure from Monterey. His separation from his brothers in arms—from those who had shared with him so many hardships and dangers, and whose brilliant achievements had reflected so much glory upon themselves and their country, was deeply interesting and affecting. Soldiers as well as officers shared equally in the feelings of regret which he himself experienced upon relinquishing his command of the noble little army whose gallantry had filled the world with its fame.

He had, from the day he took command of the army of occupation until the final and most glorious of his military achievements at Buena Vista, shared every privation and participated in every danger, with the common soldier. He required no service from them that he was not willing to participate in, and had proved to them by his whole life that he never lost sight of their interests, nor ever wantonly disregarded their feelings. By this constant paternal solicitude for their welfare, so far as the nature of the service and the interests of the country would permit, he had warmly attached to him every soldier as well as every officer under his command, and had inspired so much confidence by his disinterested acts of kindness, his coolness, self-possession and firmness under all circumstances, that his final separation from them was more like that of a kind parent taking leave of his family, than a great and successful general bidding farewell to his soldiers.

The same feeling of attachment and regret on the part of the army, and of warm sympathy on the part of General Taylor, were shown upon his arrival at Matamoras, where there were still stationed a detachment of American forces. He remained at this post a day or two previous to his final withdrawal from his command in Mexico, during which time he reviewed the troops there, and issued such orders and made such preparations as the exigencies of the case and the safety of his conquests seemed to require. After making these necessary arrangements he took his departure for the United States, and arrived at his residence in Baton Rouge towards the last of November, 1847.

There are few military chiefs, perhaps none, in any age or any country, with the exception of THE FATHER OF HIS COUNTRY, who had acquired so deep a hold upon the hearts of his soldiers as General Taylor had upon those whom it was his happy fortune to command, in his brilliant campaign against Mexico. In thus uniting all hearts to him in the midst of the necessarily rigorous discipline of the camp during an active campaign in the heart of an enemy's country, he displayed no less the characteristics of a great general, than he did by his consummate skill, his remarkable prudence, his great bravery and astonishing coolness and self-reliance in the hour of danger. Indeed, his success as a commander resulted as much from the implicit confidence and deep-rooted attachment he was so wonderful for inspiring amongst his troops, as it did from his own great talents. Though with mere military skill and ability, he might have exacted strict obedience from his soldiers, and under the force of a rigid discipline, they might have fought bravely and obstinately, yet without the confidence and esteem which he never failed to inspire, they never would have shown the same cheerful promptness to die rather than yield, at his command.

Upon General Taylor's arrival in the United States, he was everywhere received with the most remarkable popular demonstrations that ever before greeted an American commander, since the days of Washington. His grateful countrymen, wherever he made his appearance, were assembled in immense multitudes, to welcome his return, and to evince their gratitude for his brilliant services, as well as to attest the high respect his private virtues and his lofty bearing as a man, no less than as a general, had inspired. Public bodies, too, as well as the people at large, vied with each other in doing honor to the hero of Mexico. Invitations from town, city and State authorities, were showered upon him from every quarter, pressing him to visit their States. With the modesty and refined taste which had so distinguished his whole life, however, he declined all, or nearly all, these intended civilities, preferring the comparative seclusion and pleasures of his own quiet home, to all the honors that had been so liberally tendered him.

New Orleans was made an exception to this studied determination to avoid all public receptions and display, and there he was received with the most enthusiastic demonstration, by a public procession, bonfires, and other evidences of popular feeling. At a casual visit to Pas Christian, too, he was received by a public welcome and address. On this occasion, he replied in a neat and feeling speech, which does so much honor to his heart that an extract is here given:

"Sir, I find myself overwhelmed with emotions that defy expression on this occasion. In tendering to me the hospitalities of the residents of Pas Christian, permanent as well as temporary, you have been pleased to allude in flattering terms to my career in Mexico. I lay no claim to praise for the success which crowned my exertions in the trying and sanguinary struggles in which it was my lot to be engaged, between the forces under my command and the common enemy of my country. I but tried to discharge my duty to that country, whose servant I was proud to be. Sir, the manner in which you have alluded to my brothers in arms, on both lines of our army, has filled my heart with gratitude, and my eyes with tears. It was not due to me that the enemy with which I contended was vanquished, but to the brave soldiers that stood by and sustained me in times of peril. To them belongs the glory, and to them I frankly yield all claim to the laurels that adorn their brows.

"Sir, I feel sensibly the kindness and honor done me this night; and while I cannot command language suitable to express my emotions, I beg to thank you and my friends around me for such a flattering manifestation."

With the exception of an occasional visit to New Orleans, on business connected with his long-neglected private affairs, he confined himself closely to Baton Rouge. Here he seemed to be as little disturbed by the enthusiasm his name had excited throughout the Union, and the renown which his achievements had won him throughout Europe, as the most indifferent spectator. General Taylor of course was not insensible to these evidences of the admiration and respect of his countrymen. He would have been more or less than human, if he were. But they did not unsettle his well-regulated and thoroughly disciplined mind. He was none the less grateful for them, because he did not permit them to turn him aside from that course of strict propriety and manly bearing which had been so admirable and striking a feature of his character during his forty years of public life. He was the same plain, unassuming, dignified gentleman, now that the land rung with his praises, that he was when his name, but a few months before, was scarcely known beyond the limits of his own State. In this, too, he displayed the elements of a great and noble mind. But General Taylor was not destined long to remain in retirement.

Immediately after the battles of Palo Alto and Resaca de la Palma, his name began to be mentioned in connection with the Presidential question, in different parts of the Union, and as early as the June or July following those brilliant victories, he was formally nominated for the Presidency by a meeting of the people, irrespective of party politics, held at Newark, New Jersey. This movement was soon imitated by the people in other sections of the country; and as the splendor of his subsequent achievements at Monterey and Buena Vista reached the United States, they became more general. Nearly or quite up to the time of his departure from Mexico, these nominations had been tendered him almost indiscriminately by Whigs, Democrats, and Independents. Though it was well understood by the intimate personal friends of General Taylor that his political predilections were moderately but decidedly Whig, yet, from the nature of his profession, he had necessarily become so little identified with either of the parties of the country, that his views upon the various questions of national policy which divided the people, were comparatively but very little known to the American people at large. It is not singular therefore, that all parties should have sought to avail themselves of his great and growing popularity, and that he should have been nominated not only by independent bodies of the people, but by regularly organized county and State conventions, and legislative caucuses in several of the States. There seemed, indeed, to be almost one universal voice from one end of the Union to the other in favor of his nomination; and numerous letters were addressed to him in Mexico, by individuals and public meetings, urging upon him the acceptance of a nomination for the Presidency. Although a formal reply to all of these letters imposed upon him an amount of labor that few men in his position, and with the great responsibilities it necessarily devolved upon him, could have performed, he replied to them with that directness and candor which was so peculiar a part of his character. In these replies, he frankly avowed himself a Whig, whenever circumstances seemed to require or justify a declaration of his political sentiments. One of the earliest, and indeed the first of his letters on the Presidential question, is annexed, as an illustration of his manly frankness, as well as to show the political bias of his mind. It was addressed to the Editor of the New Lisbon, (Ohio,) Palladium, and was written at Matamoras, but little more than two months after his victories on the Rio Grande.

HEADQUARTERS, ARMY OF OCCUPATION,
Matamoras, July 21, 1846.

DEAR SIR:—By yesterday's mail, I received your letter of the 19th June, and have given the subject to which it refers some serious reflection and consideration. I feel very grateful to you, sir, and to my fellow-citizens, who with you have expressed the very flattering desire to place my name in nomination for the Presidency, but it becomes me sincerely and frankly to acknowledge to you that for that office I have no aspirations whatever. Although no politician, having always held myself aloof from the clamors of party politics, I am a Whig, and shall ever be devoted in individual opinion to that party.

Even if the subject which you have in your letter opened to me, were acceptable at any time, I have not the leisure to attend to it now: the vigorous prosecution of the war with Mexico, so important to the interests of my country, demands every moment of my present time, and it is my great desire to bring it to a speedy and honorable termination.

With my best wishes for your health and prosperity, I am sincerely yours,
Z. TAYLOR,
Major General U. S. A.

There are no concealments in this letter. He states with his accustomed frankness that he is a Whig in principle, and shall ever be devoted in individual opinion to that party. This explicit avowal, it would naturally have been supposed, would have left no one in doubt in respect to his political sentiments. Yet such was not its effect. Wide-spread and general as the determination amongst the people to make him a candidate for the Presidency evidently was before his return from Mexico, that determination was strengthened by his arrival in the United States. The enthusiasm which before seemed to have reached its highest point, was greatly increased by this event, and it soon became apparent amongst leading Whig politicians in different parts of the country, that he not only would become a candidate, but that no other name could be brought forward with equal chances of success. It is true, there was a strong opposition to him in several of the free States, principally on the ground of his supposed prejudices in favor of the institution of Slavery. But though he was a Southern man by birth and education, he had given evidence by his life and public services, and inspired sufficient confidence by his enlarged and liberal mind, as well as by his high character, that he was an *American* in feeling—that his views were not circumscribed by mere State or sectional boundaries, and that if called to preside over the destinies of the nation, he would be the President of the whole people. There were again another class, also confined principally to the North and to the Whig party, who seemed to entertain doubts upon the policy of nominating General Taylor, on the ground that he was not known, or believed by them not to be strongly enough identified with the principles and policy of the Whig party. The evidences of his decided Whig preferences multiplied so rapidly during the progress of the Presidential canvass, that these doubts, in a great measure, gradually wore away. But in proportion as the knowledge of his Whig predilections lessened opposition from that quarter, it increased amongst the Democratic party, until he was finally abandoned as a candidate by the Democrats in every instance where he had been formally nominated; and all intention of making him the Democratic nominee was relinquished long before the time for selecting a candidate had arrived. General Taylor, therefore, in the end, became to be only urged as a candidate by members of the Whig party, and by one or two independent organizations in particular States.

Many letters from General Taylor upon the subject of the Presidency had in the mean time been published, each of which contributed more or less to change, in some degree, his relation to the two great parties of the country. Amongst others which had an important influence upon the public mind, was one written at an early stage of the canvass to the Hon. Joseph R. Ingersoll, a distinguished member of Congress from Pennsylvania, but the explicit avowals of which, in regard to his political opinions, had been nearly lost sight of until General Taylor's prominence as a candidate, and the doubts already mentioned in relation to his political preferences, were the cause of bringing it again more directly before the public. It is here placed on record as the most direct avowal of his principles that had yet been made public, and the most explicit expression of his views and feelings upon the possible contingency of becoming a candidate for the Presidency. The same generous frankness and shrinking modesty, (if such a term may be applied to a man of General Taylor's character,) that so pre-eminently distinguish all his official despatches, will be remarked in every sentence. It was written at Monterey, three months before his withdrawal from the army in Mexico, and bears evidence of the freedom of a confidential correspondence. But it nevertheless displays the sentiments of a sound head, an honest heart, and a great mind.

MONTEREY, MEXICO, August 3d, 1847.

DEAR SIR:—I have the pleasure to acknowledge the receipt of your esteemed letter of the 7th ult., which has just reached me, in which you say:

"I had the honor of being called upon last evening to address a mass meeting of the Whigs of the city and county of Philadelphia. At that meeting, your name was frequently mentioned in connection with the office of chief magistrate. I stated in that meeting, as I had before stated in my place in the House of Representatives at Washington, that you were a Whig; not indeed an ultra partisan Whig, but a Whig in principle."

All of which is entirely correct; and after the discussion which occurred in both Houses of Congress, at the last session, growing out of the capitulation of Monterey, in which discussion you thought proper to defend my conduct in regard to that transaction, when assailed somewhat, if not entirely, on party grounds, I can hardly imagine how any one who was present and heard the speeches on that occasion, or read them after they were published, could well mistake the complexion of my politics. At the last Presidential canvass, it was well known to all with whom I mixed, Whigs and Democrats—for I had no concealments in the matter—that I was decidedly in favor of Mr. Clay's election, and would now prefer seeing him in that office to any individual in the Union.

I must say, I have no wish for the Presidency, and cannot consent to be exclusively the candidate of a party; and if I am one at all, or to be so at the coming election, it must be borne in mind that I have been, or will be so by others, without any agency of mine in the matter. Independent of my wishes, I greatly doubt my qualifications to discharge the duties properly of an office which was filled and adorned by a Washington, a Jefferson, as well as several others of the purest, wisest, and most accomplished statesmen and patriots of this or any other age or country. I almost tremble at the thoughts of the undertaking. Yet if the good people think proper to elevate me, at the proper time, to the highest office in their gift, I will feel bound to serve them, if not from inclination, from a principle of duty; and will do so honestly and faithfully, to the best of my ability, in accordance with the principles of the Constitution, as near as I can do so, as it was construed and acted on by our Presidents, two of whom, at least, acted so conspicuous a part in framing and completing that instrument, as well as in putting it in operation.

But very many important changes may take place at home and abroad, between now and the time for holding the election for our next Chief Magistrate—so much so, as to make it desirable, for the general good, that some one with more experience in state affairs, should be selected as a candidate, than myself. And could he be elected, I will not say I would yield my pretensions, for I have not the vanity to believe I have any for that distinguished station; but would acquiesce not only with pleasure in such an arrangement, but would rejoice that the Republic had one citizen more worthy and better acquainted than I am, to discharge the important duties appertaining to that position; and no doubt there are thousands. Be this as it may, if I ever occupy the White House, it must be by the spontaneous movement of the people, without any action of mine in relation to it, without pledges other than I have previously stated—a strict adherence to the provisions of the Constitution, so I could enter on the arduous and responsible duties appertaining to said office, untrammelled; so that I could be the President of the country, and not of a party.

With considerations of great respect and esteem,

I am your obedient servant,

Z. TAYLOR.

To J. R. INGERSOLL, Esq., Philadelphia.

But notwithstanding all thought of nominating General Taylor had been abandoned by the Democratic party, and it had been conceded on every side that he was identified in principle and feeling with the Whig party, he had never been claimed as an ultra partisan. In every communication he had made to the public, upon the subject of the Presidency, he uniformly declared, that though a Whig, he should, if elected, go into the Presidential chair untrammelled by any pledges whatever, aud must be permitted to maintain a position of perfect independence of all parties, claiming to look only to the Constitution, in the spirit and mode in which it was acted upon by the earlier Presidents, and the best interests of the whole country, as the guide for his conduct. An admirable and comprehensive declaration of his doctrines, however, and the principles upon which he should administer the government, if promoted to the office of Chief Magistrate of the nation, is contained in the celebrated "Allison letter." The sentiments avowed in this letter are such as would have done honor to the noblest patriot of the Revolution, and it embodies as perfect a political chart as the wisdom of man ever devised. If the doctrines it lays down are taken as his political guide, as the lofty character General Taylor has established by forty years of public service gives assurance they will be, the original purity of the government will be restored, and the "golden age" of the Republic will date from his inauguration as President of the United States, on the fifth of March, eighteen hundred and forty-nine. The following is a copy of this justly admired declaration of principles:

BATON ROUGE, April 12, 1848

DEAR SIR:—My opinions have so often been been misconceived and misrepresented, that I deem it due to myself, if not to my friends, to make a brief exposition of them upon the topics to which you have called my attention.

I have consented to the use of my name as a candidate for the Presidency. I have frankly avowed my own distrust of my fitness for this high station; but having, at the solicitation of many of my countrymen, taken my position as a candidate, I do not feel at liberty to surrender that position until my friends manifest a wish that I should retire from it. I will then most gladly do so. I have no private purposes to accomplish, no party projects to build up, no enemies to punish—nothing to serve but my country.

I have been very often addressed by letter, and my opinions have been asked upon almost every question that might occur to the writers, as affecting the interest of their country or their party. I have not always responded to these inquiries, for various reasons.

I confess, while I have great cardinal principles which will regulate my political life, I am not sufficienly familiar with all the minute details of political legislation to give solemn pledges to exert myself to carry out this, or defeat that measure. I have no concealment. I hold no opinion which I would not readily proclaim to my assembled countrymen; but crude impressions upon matters of policy, which may be right to-day and wrong to-morrow, are perhaps not the best tests of fitness for office. One who cannot be trusted without pledges, cannot be confided in merely on account of them.

I will proceed, however, now to respond to your inquiries.

First—I reiterate what I have so often said: I am a Whig. If elected, I would not be the mere President of a party. I would endeavor to act independent of party domination. I should feel bound to administer the government untrammelled by party schemes.

Second—The veto power. The power given by the Constitution to the Executive to interpose his veto, is a high conservative power; but in my opinion should never be exercised, except in cases of clear violation of the Constitution, or manifest haste and want of consideration by Congress. Indeed, I have thought that for many years past, the known opinions and wishes of the Executive have exercised an undue and injurious influence upon the legislative department of the government; and for this cause I have thought our system was in danger of undergoing a great change from its true theory. The personal opinions of the individual who may happen to occupy the Executive chair, ought not to control the action of Congress upon questions of domestic policy; nor ought his objections to be interposed where questions of constitutional power have been settled by the various departments of government, and acquiesced in by the people.

Third—Upon the subject of the tariff, the currency, the improvement of our great highways, rivers, lakes, and harbors, the will of the people, as expressed through their representatives in Congress, ought to be respected and carried out by the Executive.

Fourth—The Mexican war. I sincerely rejoice at the prospect of peace. My life has been devoted to arms, yet I look upon war, at all times and under all circumstances, as a national calamity, to be avoided if compatible with the national honor. The principles of our government, as well as its true policy, is opposed to the subjugation of other nations and the dismemberment of other countries by conquest. In the language of the great Washington, "Why should we quit our own to stand on foreign ground? In the Mexican war our national honor has been vindicated; and in dictating terms of peace, we may well afford to be forbearing and magnanimous to a fallen foe.

These are my opinions on the subjects referred to by you, and any reports or publications, written or verbal, from any source, differing in any essential particular from what is here written, are unauthorized and untrue.

I do not know that I shall again write upon the subject of national politics. I shall engage in no schemes, no combinations, no intrigues. If the American people have not confidence in me, they ought not to give me their suffrages. If they do not, you know me well enough to believe me, when I declare I shall be content. I am too old a soldier to murmur against such high authority.

Z. TAYLOR.

To Capt. J. S. Allison.

CHAPTER X.

Meeting of the Whig National Convention—Judge Saunders' Statement —Gen. Taylor's Nomination—The Vote in the Convention—His Letter of Acceptance—His Nomination by the Charleston Meeting—His Second Allison Letter—His Election—Vote of the different States—His Departure for Washington—Order announcing his final Withdrawal from the Military Service—His Reception during his Journey —Conclusion.

It had become the settled policy of the Whig, as well as the Democratic party, since 1839, when the first Whig National Convention was held at Harrisburgh, to decide the claims of the different candidates for the Presidency by that agency. In the opinion of many of General Taylor's friends, however, it was believed that the necessity for a National Convention had been obviated by the nominations he had received from the people in primary meetings, and through county, State and Legislative conventions and caucuses. But it was contended, on the other hand, that the usual mode of selecting a candidate should be observed, even though it should be conceded that General Taylor was the choice of a large portion of the Whig party, and had virtually been nominated by the people in their primary capacity. It was claimed that the unity of the Whig party would thus be preserved, and all cause for declining to yield to him a cordial support by those who preferred another candidate, effectually removed.

The Whig members of Congress, upon whom custom had imposed the duty of deciding on the propriety of designating a Presidential candidate to be supported by that party, in the usual mode, adopted this view of the question; and in pursuance with this determination they adopted a resolution during the session of 1847–8, with much unanimity, that a National Convention should be held at Philadelphia on the 7th day of June, 1848, for the purpose of nominating a candidate to be supported by the Whig party for the Presidency. To this decision the Whigs in every part of the Union yielded their ready consent. Accordingly, on the day designated, representatives of the Whig party from every State in the Union, assembled at Philadelphia, for the purpose of nominating a candidate for President.

Coming, as these Representatives did, from every part of our vast Confederacy, and representing, as they were bound to do, the varied interests, views and feelings of the whole Whig people of the nation, it was no more to be expected that there should have been entire harmony and unanimity of sentiment amongst them, upon the question for which they had assembled, than it was that there should be no difference of opinion amongst the people themselves upon the same subject. Nor is it desirable that it should be otherwise. However pure may be the character, and lofty the patriotism of any man, it is far better that his claims and qualifications for the position to which he aspires, or to which his friends would elevate him, should be closely scrutinized and rigidly canvassed. This peculiar characteristic of our social and political organization, is, perhaps, the surest guaranty of the perpetuity of our institutions. As long as the freedom with which the characters of candidates for public favor is criticised, does not degenerate into licentiousness, its effect will be salutary to the public morals.

It cannot be regretted, therefore, that no man in this Republic should ever obtain so unlimited a hold upon the popular feeling as to place him beyond the reach of all competition, either for the Presidency or any other office under our government. That even the popularity of General Taylor, unbounded as it was, did not leave him without a rival in the Presidential contest, should be a source of congratulation, as it illustrated the independent character of the American people.

Besides General Taylor's, the names of General Scott, Mr. Clay and Mr. Webster were submitted to the Convention. Each of them had ardent, influential, and numerous friends in every part of the Union. Their claims had been warmly urged during the progress of the canvass. Their long-tried, patriotic and faithful public services, the one in a military and the others in civil capacities, had inspired public confidence, and attached to them a strong body of zealous and enthusiastic personal and political friends, who adhered to them through every change of fortune. Each of these gentlemen had a large number of delegates in the Convention, who pressed their claims with zeal and ability. On the first ballot Mr. Clay had 97 votes, General Scott 43 votes, Mr. Webster 22 votes, and 6 scattering, against 111 for General Taylor; and it was not until the fourth ballot that he received the nomination, though it was well understood from the organization of the Convention that he must ultimately be its choice. The vote on the fourth ballot was for General Taylor 171, for Mr. Clay 32, for General Scott

63, and for Mr. Webster 13; the whole number of votes cast being 279, and necessary for a choice 140. The several States on the final ballot stood as follows:

Maine—Taylor 5, Scott 3.
N. Hamp.—Taylor 2, Webster, 4.
Verm.—Taylor 2, Clay 2, Scott 2.
Massachusetts—Taylor 1, Scott 2, Webster 9.
Rhode Island—Taylor 4.
Connecticut—Taylor 3, Clay 3.
New York—Taylor 6, Clay 13, Scott 17.
New Jersey—Taylor 4, Clay 3.
Pennsylvania—Taylor 12, Clay 4, Scott 10.
Delaware—Taylor 2, Scott 1.
Maryland—Taylor 8.
Virginia—Taylor 16, Clay 1.
N. Carolina—Taylor 10, Clay 1.
S. Carolina—Taylor 1, Clay 1.
Georgia—Taylor 10.
Alabama—Taylor 6, Clay 1.
Mississippi—Taylor 6.
Louisiana—Taylor 6.
Texas—Taylor 4.
Tennessee—Taylor 13.
Kentucky—Taylor 11, Clay 1.
Missouri—Taylor 7.
Ohio—Taylor 1, Clay 1, Scott 21.
Ind.—Taylor 7, Clay 1, Scott 4.
Illinois—Taylor 8.
Michigan—Taylor 2, Scott 3.
Florida—Taylor 3.
Arkansas—Taylor 3.
Wisconsin—Taylor 4.
Iowa—Taylor 4.

General Taylor's nomination had been opposed by a respectable minority of the Convention, under the apprehension or misapprehension that he had avowed his determination to remain a candidate for the Presidency, without regard to the action of a Whig National Convention. This consideration influenced the conduct of a considerable number of the delegates in the Convention, with whom otherwise he would have been the first choice, besides rendering more determined the opposition of those whose preferences were in favor of other gentlemen. This error in regard to Gen. Taylor's intentions was used against him with much force; and notwithstanding the proof that he should cheerfully acquiesce in the decision of the Convention, was in the hands of one of its members, it was not publicly used to disabuse the minds of the delegates until after the third ballot. Then, however, Judge Saunders, one of the delegates from Louisiana, who had in his possession the evidence referred to, submitted to the Convention, on behalf of the delegation from that State, the following satisfactory and authentic statement:

"The position occupied by General Taylor in relation to the Presidency, does not seem to be correctly understood by many persons, and for that reason it is deemed proper, by the delegation of Louisiana, to make such explanation and statements in relation to that statesman as may effectually remove all doubt, in the efforts at misrepresentation and misapprehension on that point. General Taylor has taken no part in bringing his name before the American people, in connection with the Presidency, nor does he present his name to this Convention as a candidate. His friends throughout the country, rather discouraged than encouraged by him, have placed him prominently before the nation, for the place once occupied by the illustrious father of his country; and Gen. Taylor consents to the nomination. He considers himself in the hands of his friends, who have honored him with their choice. He has publicly and repeatedly stated that they might withdraw him whenever they thought that the interests of the country required it. He does not consider that, under the circumstances in which his name had been brought forward, it would be proper in him to withdraw himself. Such has been his position since he assented to the use of his name subsequent to the capture of Monterey, and such is his position now. On the part of the delegation from Louisiana, I will further state, that General Taylor desires it to be understood, that in his opinion, his friends who came into the Convention are bound to abide by its decision, and to sustain the nominee, heart and soul; that General Taylor recognizes, in his friends in this Convention, the right to withdraw his name, and he will cheerfully acquiesce in such withdrawal.

"General Taylor, we are also authorized to say, will hail with entire satisfaction any nomination besides himself, being persuaded that the welfare of our country requires a change of men and measures, in order to arrest the downward tendency of our national affairs. On making this announcement, the delegates of Louisiana wish it to be distinctly understood that it involves no inconsistency on the part of General Taylor, in case the choice of this Convention should fall on another. If General Taylor's friends in this Convention withdraw him, it will be their act, and not his; and by the act of uniting with this Convention, his friends withdraw his name from the canvass, unless he be the nominee of this Convention; and we deem it proper to assure the Whigs of the Union, that we desire the nomination and election of General Taylor to the Presidency, on no other than national grounds."

This statement mainly removed the doubts that had, up to that time, existed, in some quarters, as to the policy of nominating General Taylor, and relieved those who had honestly opposed him, under the conviction that whatever might be the conclusion of the members of the Convention, he would still continue a candidate, from much of the embarrassment in which they were placed. And as it was fully and unequivocally sanctioned and approved by General Taylor himself shortly after, all candid members of the Whig party, in every section of the Union, ceased any longer to urge this objection against him.

To the communication of the Hon. John Morehead, President of the National Convention, officially informing him of his nomination for the office of President, General Taylor returned the following reply. It will be seen, that after expressing his gratitude for the honor conferred upon him by the Convention, he declared his willingness cordially to accept the nomination tendered him by the Whig party, as their candidate in the coming contest, though he modestly expressed his distrust of his ability properly to discharge the duties of the office for which he had been nominated. But should he be elected, he pledged himself to use his best efforts to perform the duties of the high trust conferred upon him, in a manner that should meet the expectations of the people, and so as to preserve undiminished the prosperity and reputation of the country. There were undoubtedly those who preferred that he should have laid down in it a platform of Whig principles. But to a large majority of the Whig party it was received with cordial approval.

BATON ROUGE, July 15th.

HON. JOHN M. MOREHEAD, Greensborough, N. C.

SIR :—I had the honor to receive your communication of June 10th, announcing that the Whig Convention which assembled at Philadelphia on the 7th of that month, of which you were the presiding officer, has nominated me for the office of President of the United States.

Looking to the composition of the Convention, and its numbers and patriotic constituents, I feel duly grateful for the honor bestowed on me, and for the distinguished confidence implied in my nomination to the highest office in the gift of the American people.

I cordially accept that nomination, but with the sincere distrust of my fitness to fulfil the duties of an office which demands for its exercise the most exalted abilities and patriotism, and which has been rendered illustrious by the greatest names in our history.

But should the selection of the Whig Convention be confirmed by the people, I shall endeavor to discharge the new duties then devolving upon me, so as to meet the expectations of my fellow-citizens, and preserve undiminished the prosperity and reputation of our common country.

I have the honor to remain, with the highest respect, your obedient servant, Z. TAYLOR.

The triumphant nomination of General Taylor, however, did not wholly quiet the murmurs of all the friends of other candidates. There were those who still entertained doubts in regard to the soundness of his political opinions, and who feared that with a change of men, the Whig party would fail to secure a change of measures. The opposition of this class was strengthened by his continued determination to accept the nomination of all parties, though he never failed to accompany such acceptances with a positive refusal to make them any pledges, or hold out to them the slightest encouragement that he would in any measure favor their views. None of these letters of acceptance, however, was so warmly discussed, or added so much to the latent opposition that already existed, and to which reference has frequently been made, as one in reply to the Resolutions of a meeting of the Democratic citizens of Charleston, South Carolina, nominating him for the Presidency. The first version of this letter which reached the North, represented that he had ac-

17*

cepted the nomination of a Whig meeting which had rejected the name of Mr. Fillmore as the Whig candidate for Vice President. As was not unnatural, this produced a feverish state of excitement amongst the Whigs, especially of New York, and before the letter itself had arrived, a meeting was called at Albany, to consult upon the emergency which it seemed to have created. This was undoubtedly a crisis to the Whig party, and wise politicians foresaw that it had become necessary to take some measures for clearing the political atmosphere of the elements of disaffection that had so long existed, or abandon the hope of success. It was for this purpose that the Albany meeting was called, and though, at the time, strong fears were entertained that it would lead to a disruption of the Whig party, yet by the discretion and wisdom of those at whose suggestion it had been called, the very alarm which it created was made the means of accomplishing an object that before seemed hopeless; and the meeting, instead of repudiating General Taylor, was turned to his advantage. From that day, the idea of nominating another Whig candidate was abandoned. His letter to the Charleston meeting was made to have so important an influence upon the result of the campaign, that it is inserted.

BATON ROUGE, La., Aug. 9, 1848.

SIR :—I have the honor to acknowledge the receipt of your communication of the 26th ultimo, officially announcing to me my nomination for the Presidency by a large meeting of the Democratic citizens of Charleston, S. C., held at that city on the 26th ult., and over which you were the presiding officer.

This deliberate expression of the friendly feelings

existing toward me among a large and respectable portion of the citizens of your distinguished State, has been received by me with emotions of profound gratitude; and though it be but a poor return for such a high and unmerited honor, I beg them to accept my heartfelt thanks.

Concluding that this nomination, like all others which I have had the honor of receiving from assemblages of my fellow-citizens in various parts of the Union, has been generously offered, without pledges or conditions, it is thankfully accepted; and I beg you to assure my friends, in whose behalf you are acting, that should it be my lot to fill the office for which I have been nominated, it shall be my unceasing effort, in the discharge of its responsible duties, to give satisfaction to my countrymen.

With the assurance of my high esteem, I have the honor to be, your obedient servant,

Z. TAYLOR.

To W. B. PRINGLE, ESQ.

These misconceptions and misconstructions of his published letters had become so general, and so much ingenuity had been expended in giving them a false coloring, that General Taylor again found it necessary to correct the impressions and prejudices thus sought to be created. This he did in another letter to Captain J. S. Allison, in which he gave a connected narrative of a series of circumstances which resulted in his becoming a candidate for the Presidency. It presents in a compact form, and with a comprehensiveness that left no room for cavil, all the matters bearing upon the subject, and exhibits him in his proper character, true to himself, his friends and his country. The few who had still withheld from him their confidence and support, and who had not yet determined to relinquish their old party associations, were satisfied with its manly explanation of his sentiments.

East Pascagoula, Sept. 4, 1848.

Dear Sir:—On the 22d of May last I addressed you a letter, explaining my views in regard to various matters of public policy, lest my fellow-citizens might be misled by the many contradictory and conflicting statements in respect to them which appeared in the journals of the day, and were circulated throughout the country. I now find myself misrepresented and misunderstood upon another point, of such importance to myself personally, if not to the country at large, as to claim from me a candid and connected exposition of my relations to the public in regard to the pending Presidential canvass.

The utmost ingenuity has been expended upon several letters, and detached sentences of letters, which have recently appeared over my signature, to show that I occupy an equivocal attitude towards the various parties into which the people are divided, and especially towards the Whig party, as represented by the National Convention which assembled at Philadelphia in June last. Had these letters and scraps of letters been published or construed in connection with what I have heretofore said upon this subject, I should not now have to complain of the speed with which my answers to isolated questions have been given up to the captious criticism of those who have been made my enemies by a nomination which has been tendered me without solicitation or arrangement of mine, or of the manner in which selected passages in some of my letters, written in the freedom and carelessness of a confidential correspondence, have been communicated to the public press. But riven from the context, and separated from a series of explanatory facts and circumstances which are, so far as this canvass is concerned, historical, they are as deceptive as though they were positive fabrications. I address you this letter to correct the injustice that has been done me, and the public—to the extent that I am an object of interest to them—by this illiberal process.

I shall not weary you by an elaborate recital of every incident connected with the first presentation of my name as a candidate for the Presidency. I was then at the head of the American army in the valley of the Rio Grande. I was surrounded by Whigs and Democrats, who had stood by me in the trying hours of my life, and whom it was my destiny to conduct through scenes of still greater trial. My duty to that army, and to the Republic whose battles we were waging, forbade my assuming a position of seeming hostility to any portion of the brave men under my command—all of whom knew I was a Whig in principle, for I made no concealment of my political sentiments or predilections.

Such has been the violence of party struggles during our late Presidential elections, that the acceptance of a nomination, under the various interpretations given to the obligations of a candidate presented to the public with a formulary of political principles, was equivalent almost to a declaration of uncompromising enmity to all who did not subscribe to its tenets. I was unwilling to hazard the effect of such relationship towards any of the soldiers under my command, when in front of the enemy common to us all. It would have been unjust in itself; and it was as repugnant to my own feelings as it was to my duty. I wanted unity in the army, and forbore any act that might sow the seeds of distrust and discord in its ranks. I have not my letters written at the time before me, but they are all of one import, and in conformity with the views herein expressed.

Meanwhile I was solicited by my personal friends and by strangers, by Whigs and Democrats, to consent to become a candidate. I was nominated by the people in primary assemblies—by Whigs, Democrats and Natives, in separate and mixed meetings. I resisted them all, and continued to do so till led to believe that my opposition was assuming the aspect of a defiance of the popular wishes. I yielded only when it looked like presumption to resist longer, and even then I should not have done so had not the nomination been presented to me in a form unlikely to awaken acrimony, or re-produce the bitterness of feeling which attends popular elections. I say it in sincerity and truth, that a part of the inducement to my consent was the hope that by going into the canvass, it would be conducted with candor, if not with kindness. It has been no fault of mine that this anticipation has proved a vain one.

After I permitted myself to be announced for the Presidency, under the circumstances above noticed, I accepted nomination after nomination in the spirit in which they were tendered. They were made irrespective of party, and so acknowledged. No one who joined in those nominations, could have been deceived as to my political views. From the beginning till now I have declared myself to be a Whig, on all proper occasions. With this distinct avowal published to the world, I did not think that I had a right to repel nominations from political opponents, any more than I had a right to refuse the vote of a Democrat at the polls; and I proclaimed it abroad, that I should not reject the proffered support of any body of my fellow-citizens. This was my position when, in November last, I returned to the United States, long before either of the great divisions of the people had held a National Convention, and when it was thought doubtful if one of them would hold any.

Matters stood in this attitude till spring, when there were so many statements in circulation concerning my views upon questions of national policy, that I felt constrained to correct the errors into which the public mind was falling, by a more explicit enunciation of principles, which I did in my letter to you of April last. That letter, and the facts which I have detailed as briefly as a proper understanding of them would permit, developed my whole position in relation to the Presidency, at the time.

The Democratic Convention met in May, and composed their ticket to suit them. This they had a right to do. The National Whig Convention met in June, and selected me as their candidate. I accepted the nomination with gratitude and with pride. I was proud of the confidence of such a body of men, representing such a constituency as the Whig party of the United States—a manifestation the more grateful, because it was not encumbered with exactions incompatible with the dignity of the Presidential office, and the responsibilities of its incumbent to the whole people of the nation. And I may add, that these emotions were increased by associating my name with that of the distinguished citizen of New York, whose acknowledged abilities and sound conservative opinions might have justly entitled him to the first place on the ticket.

The Convention adopted me as it found me—a Whig, decided, but not ultra, in my opinions; and I would be without excuse, if I were to shift the relationships which subsisted at the time. They took me with the declaration of principles I had published to the world, and I would be without defence, if I were to say or do anything to impair the force of that declaration.

I have said that I would accept a nomination from Democrats; but in so doing, I would not abate one jot or tittle of my opinions as written down. Such a nomination, as indicating a coincidence of opinion on the part of those making it, should not be regarded with disfavor by those who think with me; as a compliment personal to myself, it should not be expected that I would repulse them with insult. I shall not modify my views, to entice them to my side; I shall not reject their aid, when they join my friends voluntarily.

I have said I was not a party candidate, nor am I, in that straitened and sectarian sense which would prevent my being President of the whole people, in case of my election. I did not regard myself as one, before the Convention met, and that body did not seek to make me different from what I was. They did not fetter me down to a series of pledges which were to be an iron rule of action in all, and in despite of all, the contingencies that might arise in the course of a Presidential term. I am not engaged to lay violent hands indiscriminately upon public officers, good or bad, who may differ in opinion with me; I am not expected to force Congress, by the coercion of the Veto, to pass laws to suit me, or pass none. This is what I mean by not being a party candidate. And I understand this is good Whig doctrine—I would not be a partisan President, and hence should not be a party candidate in the sense that would make me. This is the sum and substance of my meaning, and this is the purport of the facts and circumstances attending my nomination, when considered in their connection with, and dependence upon one another.

I refer all persons who are anxious on the subject, to this statement, for the proper understanding of my position towards the Presidency and the people. If it is not intelligible, I cannot make it so, and shall cease to attempt it.

In taking leave of the subject, I have only to add, that my two letters to you embrace all the topics I design to speak of, pending this canvass. If I am elected, I shall do all that an honest zeal may effect, to cement the bonds of our Union, and establish the happiness and prosperity of my country upon an enduring basis.

Z. TAYLOR.

To Capt. J. S. Allison.

The election for President and Vice-President took place on the 7th day of November, and resulted in the election of General Taylor and Millard Fillmore, for the offices of President and Vice President. They received 163 electoral votes; and General Cass and General Butler, the Democratic candidates for the same offices, received 127 votes. The states of Vermont, Massachusetts, Rhode Island, Connecticut, New York, New Jersey, Pennsylvania, Delaware, Maryland, North Carolina, Georgia, Louisiana, Florida, Kentucky and Tennessee, seven free and eight slave States, voted for the Whig candidates; and Maine, New Hampshire, Ohio, Indiana, Illinois, Michigan, Wisconsin, Iowa,

Virginia, South Carolina, Alabama, Mississippi, Texas, Arkansas and Missouri, eight free and seven slave States, voted for the Democratic candidates.

The result of the election, though confidently anticipated by those who closely scrutinized the condition of parties, was hailed with unbounded satisfaction by the successful party, and was looked upon by the moderate and good men of all parties as a signal triumph of the conservative principles of the country, over that spirit of radicalism and centralization towards which the government had been verging during the last twenty years. However zealously General Taylor's election had been opposed, all candid and intelligent men conceded to him abilities of the highest order, unimpeachable integrity and inflexible firmness of purpose. In these respects, as well as in many other traits of character, he was believed more nearly to resemble WASHINGTON than any other public man since the organization of our government. The purity of his life, and the wisdom that had ever governed his conduct, had inspired unbounded confidence in his disposition and ability to carry out the true principles of the constitution in the spirit of its illustrious framers.

On the 24th of January, General Taylor took his departure from Baton Rouge, for Washington, to enter upon the duties of the high office to which he had been elected by the suffrages of the people. On the day previous to his taking leave of his home, and his old and tried friends, the citizens of Baton Rouge, irrespective of party differences, assembled spontaneously, and in large numbers, to pay him their respects and bid him farewell. A large procession was formed, which proceeded to his residence at the United States Barracks, where he was appropriately addressed on behalf of the citizens by one of their number. To this address he made a brief but touching reply, in which he assured them that it was with feelings of no ordinary character that he met with his fellow-citizens on such an occasion, many of whom he had been associated with more than a quarter of a century. Had he consulted his own wishes, he said, he should have preferred the office he was then about to vacate, and have remained among his old friends, but that as the people had, without his solicitation, seen fit to elevate him to another, though he distrusted his abilities satisfactorily to discharge the great and important duties thus imposed upon him, yet he assured them that he should endeavor to fulfil them without regard to fear, favor or affection from any one. In conclusion, he feelingly invoked God's blessing upon his fellow-citizens, and prayed that He might grant them all, and their families, long life, health and prosperity; and bid them an affectionate farewell.

The day succeeding General Taylor's departure, Major Bliss, his accomplished Adjutant General, issued an order announcing his final withdrawal from the military service of the country. In resigning his command, General Taylor expressed his regret at his separation from a service to which he was attached by so many pleasing and proud associations. To the officers and men who had served his immediate orders, he warmly expressed his parting thanks for their zealous and cordial support in the execution of the duties confided to him during a long and eventful service. To them, and to all, he extended a heartfelt farewell, and his warmest wishes for their continued happiness and success in the arduous and honorable career which they had chosen.

Everywhere on his journey to the Capital he was met with the liveliest expression of gratitude by the people along his route. The demonstrations of popular favor which were displayed, were the cordial and unaffected offerings of the people to his eminent public services, his acknowledged moral worth, and his great abilities. They were tributes from the heart, and to a man of General Taylor's unambitious character they were undoubtedly far more gratifying than the high political honors they had just bestowed upon him. It was only in this light that, to a mind so admirably constituted as his is, these popular demonstrations were valuable. That popularity which is raised without merit and lost without a crime, that always follows those in power, was neither courted nor desired by him. But that applause which should only be bestowed for good and virtuous actions, he was not insensible to. This is the popularity which he had so richly won by his good deeds and pure life, and the evidences of it were now freely offered to him. It is the only applause which is prized by the great and bestowed by the good.

In the latter part of February Gen. Taylor arrived at the Capital, and on the fifth day of March was inaugurated as twefth President of the United States. He entered upon the duties of that high office under as favorable circumstances as were ever enjoyed by a Chief Magistrate of this nation. Added to a strong and well-disciplined mind, and abilities of the highest order, he possesses a reputation above reproach, unimpeachable integrity, and firmness and energy of character. From the nature of his pursuits, he is necessarily free from those prejudices and entangling alliances which are so apt to warp the judgment and embarrass the action of all men, however honest their intentions, and he therefore has "no private purposes to accomplish, no party projects to build up, no enemies to punish—nothing to serve but his country." That he will act from the highest and purest motives, the country has full confidence; and whatever errors he may commit,—and no man was ever yet free from them,—he has given assurance by his past life, that they will arise from a mistaken judgment, and not from a perverted heart.

INAUGURAL ADDRESS.

Elected by the American people to the highest office known to our laws, I appear here to take the oath prescribed by the Constitution, and in compliance with a time-honored custom, to witness which you are now assembled. The confidence and respect shown by my countrymen, in calling me to be the Chief Magistrate of a Republic holding a high rank among the nations of the earth, has inspired me with feelings of the most profound gratitude. But when I reflect that the acceptance of the office which their partiality has bestowed, imposes the discharge of the most arduous duties, and involves the weightiest obligation, I am conscious that the station which I have been called to fill, though sufficient to satisfy the loftiest ambition, is surrounded by fearful responsibilities.

Happily, however, in the performance of my new duties, I shall not be without able co-operation. The legislative and judicial branches of the government present prominent examples of distinguished civil attainments and matured experience; and it shall be my endeavor to call to my assistance, in the executive departments, individuals whose integrity and purity of character will furnish ample guarantees for the faithful and honorable performance of the trusts to be committed to their charge. With such aids, and an honest purpose to do what is right, I hope to execute diligently, impartially, and for the best interests of the country, the manifold duties devolving upon me.

In the discharge of these duties, my guide will be the Constitution I this day swear to preserve, protect, and defend.

For the interpretation of that instrument, I shall look to the decisions of judicial tribunals established by its authority, and to the practice of government under the earliest Presidents, who had so large a share in its formation. To the example of those illustrious patriots I shall always refer with deference, and especially to his example who won the title of the Father of his Country.

To command the army and navy of the United States, with the advice and consent of the Senate to make treaties and to appoint ambassadors and other officers, to give to Congress information of the state of the Union, and recommend such means as he shall judge to be necessary, and to take care that the laws shall be faithfully executed—these are

CHAPTER XI.

General Taylor's Inauguration.—His Inaugural Address.—His first Annual Message.—His Proposition for adjusting the Slavery Question.—His illness and death.—Sensation created by the event.—Obituary Addresses, and the funeral.—Conclusion.

On the 23d of February General Taylor arrived at the Capital, where he was received with demonstrations of respect and confidence, due alike to his many private virtues and his eminent and brilliant public services; and with military and civic honors, such as became the high position to which he had been elevated by the free choice of a grateful nation.

In the meantime, extensive and appropriate arrangements were being made for his approaching inauguration. The enthusiastic attachment which every loyal American citizen felt for his character as a man, and the anxiety that pervaded all hearts to behold one, the splendor of whose military deeds had filled, not only the nation, but the world, with his fame, had drawn together, from all quarters of the Republic, an immense number of his ardent admirers and others, desirous of witnessing the imposing, and it may be truly said, the sublime spectacle of inducting into office an American President.

The ceremony of the inauguration of General Taylor as President of the United States, took place in front of the great portico of the Capitol, on Monday the 5th day of March, at 12 o'clock, the day prescribed by the Constitution (March 4th) falling on Sunday. The multitude of people assembled on the occasion, from every part of the Union, to witness the spectacle, is supposed to have been much larger than was ever before collected in Washington.

At the break of day the strains of martial music resounded along every avenue of the city, and the star-spangled banner was everywhere to be seen unfolded to the breeze. The bells of the city rang out a stirring peal, and everything gave signs of the universal interest the occasion had excited. Long before the usual breakfast hour, the people were wending their way to the Capitol.

The procession, which had been formed under the direction of a marshal, took up its line of march, from Willard's hotel, down Pennsylvania Avenue, to the Capitol, at half-past 11 o'clock. General Taylor was accompanied in his carriage by Ex-President Polk, the Speaker of the late House of Representatives, and the Mayor of Washington. Upon reaching the Capitol, General Taylor entered the Senate Chamber, in company with Ex-President Polk, and took the seat prepared for him, Mr. Polk occupying another on his left. After a brief pause, the order of procession was announced, and the company retired from the Senate-Chamber to the eastern portico of the Capitol, when the following admirable inaugural address was delivered by the President elect:—

"FELLOW-CITIZENS:—Elected by the American people to the highest office known to our laws, I appear here to take the oath prescribed by the Constitution; and, in compliance with a time-honored custom, to address those who are now assembled.

the most important functions entrusted by the Constitution, and it may be expected that I shall briefly indicate the principles which will control me in their execution.

Chosen by the body of the people, under the assurance that my administration should be devoted to the welfare of the whole country, and not to the support of any particular section of merely local interest, I this day renew the declarations I have heretofore made, and proclaim my fixed determination to maintain, to the extent of my ability, the government in its original purity, and to adopt, as the basis of my public policy, those great republican doctrines which constitute the strength of our national existence.

In reference to the army and navy, lately employed with so much distinction in active service, care should be taken to insure the highest condition of efficacy; and in furtherance of that object, the military and naval schools sustained by the liberality of Congress, shall receive the most special attention of the Executive.

As American freemen, we cannot but sympathize with all efforts to extend the blessings of civil and political liberty; but at the same time, we are warned, by the admonition of history, and the voice of our own beloved Washington, to abstain from entangling alliances with foreign nations, on all disputes between conflicting governments. It is our interest, no less than our duty, to remain strictly neutral; while our geographical position, the genius of our institutions and our people, the advancing spirit of civilization, and above all, the dictates of religion, direct us to the cultivation of peaceful and friendly relations with all other powers.

It is to be hoped that no international questions can now arise, which a government confident in its own strength, and resolved to protect its own just rights, may not settle by wise negotiation; and it eminently becomes a government like our own, founded on the morality and intelligence of its citizens, and upheld by their affections, to exhaust every resort of honorable diplomacy, before appealing to arms. In the conduct of our foreign relations, I shall conform to these views, as I believe them essential to the best interests and honor of our country.

The appointing power vested in the President, imposes delicate and onerous duties. So far as it is possible to be informed, I shall make honesty, capacity, and fidelity, indispensable pre-requisites to the bestowal of offices, and absence of either of these qualities shall be deemed sufficient cause for removal.

It shall be my study to recommend such constitutional measures to Congress, as may be necessary and proper to secure encouragement and protection to the great interests of agriculture, commerce, and manufactures; to improve our rivers and harbors; to provide for the speedy extinguishing of the public debt; to enforce a strict accountability on the part of all officers of the government, and the utmost economy in all public expenditures.

It is for the wisdom of Congress itself, in which all legislative powers are vested by the Constitution, to regulate these and other matters of domestic policy.

I shall look with confidence to the enlightened patriotism of that body, to adopt such measures of conciliation as may harmonize conflicting interests, and tend to perpetuate that Union which should be the paramount object of our hopes and affections.

Any action calculated to promote an object so near the heart of every one who truly loves his country, I will zealously unite with the co-ordinate branches of government to promote.

In conclusion, I congratulate you much, fellow-citizens, upon the high state of prosperity to which the goodness of Divine Providence has conducted our common country. Let us invoke a continuance of the same protecting care, which has led from small beginnings to the eminence to which we have this day arrived; and let us seek to desire, that by prudence and moderation in our counsels, by well-directed attempts to assuage the bitterness which too often marks differences of opinion, the promulgation and practice of just and liberal principles and enlarged patriotism, which shall acknowledge no limits but those of our own wide Republic.

ZACHARY TAYLOR.

WASHINGTON, March 5th, 1849.

conflicting governments, it is our interest, not less than our duty, to remain strictly neutral; while our geographical position, the genius of our institutions and our people, the advancing spirit of civilization, and, above all, the dictates of religion, direct us to the cultivation of peaceful and friendly relations with all other powers. It is to be hoped that no international question can now arise which a government, confident in its own strength, and resolved to protect its own just rights, may not settle by wise negotiation; and it eminently becomes a government like our own, founded on the morality and intelligence of its citizens, and upheld by their affections, to exhaust every resort of honorable diplomacy before appealing to arms. In the conduct of our foreign relations, I shall conform to these views, as I believe them essential to the best interests and the true honor of the country.

"The appointing power vested in the President, imposes delicate and onerous duties. So far as it is possible to be informed, I shall make honesty, capacity, and fidelity, indispensable pre-requisites to the bestowal of office, and the absence of either of these qualities shall be deemed sufficient cause for removal.

"It shall be my study to recommend such Constitutional measures to Congress as may be necessary and proper to secure encouragement and protection to the great interests of Agriculture, Commerce, and Manufactures; to improve our rivers and harbors; to provide for the speedy extinguishment of the public debt; to enforce a strict accountability on the part of all officers of the Government, and the utmost economy in all public expenditures. But it is for the wisdom of Congress itself, in which all legislative powers are vested by the Constitution, to regulate these and other matters of domestic policy. I shall look with confidence to the enlightened patriotism of that body to adopt such measures of conciliation as may harmonize conflicting interests, and tend to perpetuate that Union which should be the paramount object of our hopes and affections. In any action calculated to promote an object so near the heart of every one who truly loves his country, I will zealously unite with the co-ordinate branches of the Government.

"In conclusion, I congratulate you, my fellow-citizens, upon the high state of prosperity to which the goodness of Divine Providence has conducted our common country. Let us invoke a continuance of the same protecting care, which has led us from small beginnings to the eminence we this day occupy, and let us seek to deserve that continuance by prudence and moderation in our councils; by well-directed attempts to assuage the bitterness which too often marks unavoidable differences of opinion; by the promulgation and practice of just and liberal principles; and by an enlarged patriotism, which shall acknowledge no limits but those of our own wide-spread Republic."

As soon as the applause which marked the conclusion of this address had subsided, the oath to execute the office of President of the United States, and to the best of his ability to preserve, protect, and defend the Constitution, was administered by Chief Justice Taney. The ceremony at the Capitol was terminated by peals of artillery, when the President retraced his steps, and soon after entered the White House as the twelfth President of this great Republic.

Having thus complied with the provision of the Constitution necessary to qualify him for the discharge of the high and responsible duties he had assumed, all the faculties of a great mind, the wisdom of a sound head, and the patriotism of a noble heart, were brought into requisition. The many admirable traits of character which had been claimed for him previous to his election to the Presidency, soon began to develop themselves more fully to the public, and every day added to the evidence, that he possessed no less the elements of a statesman than he had already proved to the world that he did those of a soldier. He seemed almost by intuition to grasp every question of national policy, and by his sound discriminating common sense, to unriddle what had puzzled the heads of our most experienced statesmen. His course was always straight to his object by the most direct path. He pursued no devious or winding way to reach the end his mind told him was right. None of the subtilties which sometimes mark the course of politicians and of statesmen, ever found favor with him. Having declared to the public, previous to his elevation to the Presidency, the policy he should pursue, and sworn to "preserve, protect, and defend" the Constitution, his sole aim seemed to be, an earnest desire faithfully to observe the oath, and to comply with the pledges he had made to the people.

It was not to have been expected that, in the discharge of the delicate and responsible trust which he was called upon to execute, of equalizing the offices of the Government, which for twenty years had been in the hands of the party opposed to his election, he should not have incurred the opposition of those upon whom the hand of reform was compelled to fall. It was, indeed, the inevitable result of measures a new administration was expected and required to adopt. But, however indiscriminately party fidelity required the Press opposed to his administration to denounce him, a spirit of candor will force all to admit, that he exercised the delicate power of removal, with no feeling of party malice, and no love for political proscription. No President ever exercised it more sparingly, or with a more scrupulous regard for the public interests and individual justice. The principle he had avowed of removing no man for a mere difference of political opinion, was religiously adhered to, so far as it was in the power of man to do so; and if he ever departed from it, it was upon erroneous information.

Strong as was the confidence of the public in General Taylor's wisdom, patriotism, and honesty, and warmly as the Whig party were attached to him, no opportunity had presented itself for an avowal of his views upon the various local questions which had divided the people of the country; and accordingly the meeting of Congress, and his first annual message to that body, were looked to with deep anxiety, not only by his political friends, but by the whole American people. And above all, was there a painful solicitude in the public mind, both north and south, to know more explicitly than he had yet been called upon to declare them, his views upon the all-absorbing and most embarrassing subject of slavery. Though he had, on more than one occasion, declared the general principles that would govern him, with sufficient distinctness to satisfy all who were familiar with his frank and noble nature, as well as a very large portion of the party whose suffrages had elevated him to the Presidency; yet it need not be concealed that there was still a large class, even of his political friends, who did not give him their whole confidence. They feared that, being a southern man, reared under southern institutions, and his *interests* closely identified with slavery, that an undue share of the influence of his administration would be exerted to extend and strengthen that institution; but, all such had yet to learn, as they did learn, that they did not understand General Taylor's true character, his enlarged patriotism, and his comprehensive and truly national views. This they discovered before his death, as they then and now frankly admit.

During the progress of the campaign, which resulted in placing him in the executive chair of the nation, he had, on various occasions, as has already been stated, avowed in general, but very explicit and manly terms, the leading features of the policy he should pursue. But he expressly declined, for reasons deemed generally satisfactory, in consideration of the peculiar and delicate position in which he was placed, to enter into a detailed exposition of his views upon the various questions of local and domestic policy, which were before the country. Hence the anxiety, to which reference has been made, to know the opinions he would advance and the recommendations he would make, in his first message to Congress.

The two houses of Congress assembled on Monday, the third day of December; but in consequence of the failure of the House of Representatives to effect an organization, its delivery was delayed until the twenty-fourth. On that day it was sent to both branches of Congress.

After invoking in appropriate and feeling terms, the guidance of the Almighty, and expressing the obligations of gratitude and thankfulness we were under to Him, for having stayed the ravages of the dreadful pestilence which had visited portions of our country, he briefly, but succinctly recapitulated the condition of our relations with foreign countries;—paid a feeling and eloquent tribute to the noble but unsuccessful struggle of the Hungarians for a national existence and independence, and expressed his deep sympathy for their cause; —referred to the projects of a ship canal through the State of Nicaragua, to connect the Atlantic and Pacific, and of a railroad across the Isthmus of Panama; and recommended them as worthy the consideration of Congress;—gave a statement of the condition of the finances of the government;—recommended a reduction of postage to a uniform rate, and the abolition of the franking privilege;—reiterated his views upon the exercise of the veto power, declaring that he should never resort to it except in extreme cases, such as were evidently contemplated by the framers of the Constitution, and the fathers of the Republic—to prevent the encroachment of the legislative power, for instance, or, hasty and inconsiderate or unconstitutional legislation, and closed by thus declaring his opinion of the value of the Union, his warm attachment to it, and his firm determination to defend and preserve it:—

"But attachment to the union of the States should be habitually fostered in every American heart. For more than half a century, during which kingdoms and empires have fallen, this Union has stood unshaken. The patriots who formed it have long since descended to the grave; yet still it remains the proudest monument to their memory, and the object of affection and admiration with every one *worthy to bear the American name.* In my judgment, its dissolution would be the greatest of calamities; and to avert that, should be the study of every American. Upon its preservation must depend our happiness and that of countless generations to come. Whatever dangers may threaten it, I SHALL STAND BY IT AND MAINTAIN IT,

IN ITS INTEGRITY, TO THE FULL EXTENT OF THE OBLIGATIONS IMPOSED, AND THE POWER CONFERRED UPON ME BY THE CONSTITUTION."

If there were nothing else in this first message of General Taylor to commend him to the favor of the American people, and it had been the last sentiment that ever fell from his lips, it would have endeared his memory to every American heart while the Republic stands. It was such a sentiment as was worthy the pure patriot, the illustrious soldier, and the incorruptible statesman who uttered it. It was such a declaration of determination to stand by and *defend* the Constitution, made by a man with hands so able, and a heart so willing, and a mind so resolute to carry them out, that has kept from breaking into an open flame the now inert spirit of treason to the country, that is known to exist in certain States of the Union. And it is only by a similar determined disposition to nip in the bud the first overt act, that that insane spirit of disunion will be kept confined to empty threats.

But this patriotic avowal of his determination to save the nation from the calamity with which it had then been threatened, as it is now, was not the only merit of the message. It was almost universally conceded to be a model document in its style and character, and to have conformed more literally to the design of the Constitution, in requiring the Executive simply to *recommend* measures to Congress, than any similar paper since the founders of the Republic. The variety of subjects touched upon, the simple brevity, yet perspicuity and directness with which they are presented, its freedom from that air of assumed superiority and arrogance, which form so offensive a feature in the official communications of many public functionaries—the very absence, indeed, of all rhetorical flourish and studied straining for fine turned periods, as well as the entire reliance of its author on the ability of Congress to comprehend its duty, without the aid of a labored and tedious argument appended to each distinct "recommendation;"—all these served but to commend it to the popular mind, and to strengthen the confidence which had already begun to take so deep a root in the hearts of the people.

The message, it is true, contained no distinct avowal of the policy he should pursue in regard to one of the cardinal principles of the party to whom he owed his election,—that of protection to American industry, nor upon the slavery question, the two principal topics that occupied public attention. But his Secretary of the Treasury, within the sphere of whose legitimate duty it was, presented the first of these subjects to Congress with a force of reasoning, strengthened by an array of facts that exhausted the whole subject, and left no more to be said in favor of the principle, and little room for controverting his positions. In regard to the other, the time had not come for him to present his views to Congress. He was not then called upon, either by the Constitution or his obligation to the country, to submit to Congress any recommendations on the subject of slavery, as it could only serve to increase the bitter and angry dissensions that already existed to so great an extent among the people of the United States.

But an occasion was soon presented, when it became the duty of the President to express his opinions upon the agitating question of the extension, or non extension of slavery in the territory acquired from Mexico, and when he could do so without violating the principle of action he had marked out, or adding to the existing excitement. It had been well understood that the people of California had organized a State government, and that they would soon be applying to Congress, through her chosen Representatives, for admission into the Union. This had created no small commotion amongst many southern members of Congress, on the ground that it would destroy the "equilibrium" which they contended should exist between the free and slave States. The President was freely charged with exercising an improper influence upon the people of California, through the United States troops stationed there, with a view to coerce them into the adoption of a State government. A resolution was introduced into the House of Representatives, and adopted, calling upon him for all orders and correspondence, and all official information in his possession in relation to California. In accordance with this resolution, the President transmitted to the House, on the 21st of January, the information called for, with the following message, embracing his views upon the subject in dispute, and recommending what he conceived to be the wisest plan for settling the territorial difficulty. This message is so admirable in tone and temper, and contains sentiments so much in harmony with the intelligent public opinion, that it is here placed on record as the most striking evidence of the foresight, wisdom, and patriotism of General Taylor:—

"I transmit to the House of Representatives, in answer to a resolution of that body, passed on the 31st of December last, the accompanying reports of Heads of Departments, which contain all the official information in the possession of the Executive asked for by the resolutions.

"On coming into office I found the military commandant of the department of California exercising the functions of civil governor in that Territory; and left as I was to act under the treaty of Guadalupe Hidalgo without *the aid of any legislative* provision in establishing a government in that Territory, I thought it best not to disturb that arrangement, made under my predecessor, until Congress should take some action on that subject. I therefore did not interfere with the powers of the military commandant, who continued to exercise the functions of civil governor as before, but I made no such appointment, conferred no such authority, and have allowed no increased compensation to the commandant for his services.

"With a view to the faithful execution of the treaty, so far as lay in the power of the Executive, and to enable Congress to act at the present session with as full knowledge and as little difficulty as possible on all matters of interest in these Territories, I sent the Hon. Thomas Butler King as bearer of dispatches to California, and certain officers to California and New Mexico, whose duties are particularly defined in the accompanying letters of instruction addressed to them severally by the proper Department.

"I did not hesitate to express to the people of those Territories my desire that each Territory should, if prepared to comply with the requisitions of the Constitution of the United States, form a plan of State constitution, and submit the same to Congress, with a prayer for admission into the Union as a State; but I did not anticipate, suggest, or authorize the establishment of any such government without the assent of Congress, nor did I authorize any government agent or officer to interfere with, or exercise any influence or control over the election of delegates, or over any convention, in making or modifying their domestic institutions, or any of the provisions of their proposed constitution. On the contrary, the instructions given by my orders were, that all measures of domestic policy adopted by the people of California must originate solely with themselves; that while the Executive of the United States was desirous to protect them in the formation of any government republican in its character, to be at the proper time submitted to Congress, yet it was to be distinctly understood that the plan of such a government must at the same time be the result of their own deliberate choice, and originate with themselves, without the interference of the Executive.

"I am unable to give any information as to laws passed by any supposed government in California, or of any census taken in either of the Territories mentioned in the resolution, as I have no information on those subjects.

"As already stated, I have not disturbed the arrangements which I found had existed under my predecessor.

"In advising an early application by the people of the Territories for admission as States, I was actuated principally by an earnest desire to afford to the wisdom and patriotism of Congress the opportunity of avoiding occasions of bitter and angry dissensions among the people of the United States.

"Under the Constitution every State has the right of establishing, and from time to time altering, its municipal laws and domestic institutions, independently of every other State and of the General Government, subject only to the prohibitions and guarantees expressly set forth in the Constitution of the United States. The subjects thus left exclusively to the respective States were not designed or expected to become topics of national agitation. Still, as under the Constitution Congress has power to make all needful rules and regulations respecting the Territories of the United States, every new acquisition of territory has led to discussions on the question whether the system of involuntary servitude which prevails in many of the States should or should not be prohibited in that Territory. The periods of excitement from this cause which have heretofore occurred have been safely passed, but during the interval of whatever length which may elapse before the admission of the Territories ceded by Mexico as States, it appears probable that similar excitement will prevail to an undue extent.

"Under these circumstances I thought, and still think, that it was my duty to endeavor to put it in the power of Congress, by the admission of California and New Mexico as States, to remove all occasion for the unnecessary agitation of the public mind.

"It is understood that the people of the western part of California have formed a plan of a State constitution, and will soon submit the same to the judgment of Congress, and apply for admission as a State. This course on their part, though in accordance with, was not adopted exclusively in consequence of, any expression of my wishes, inasmuch as measures tending to this end had been promoted by the officers sent there by my predecessor, and were already in active progress of execution before any communication from me reached California. If the proposed constitution shall, when submitted to Congress, be found to be in compliance with the requisitions of the Constitution of the United States, I earnestly recommend that it may receive the sanction of Congress.

"The part of California not included in the proposed State of that name is believed to be uninhabited, except in a settlement of our countrymen in the vicinity of Salt lake.

"A claim has been advanced by the State of Texas to a very large portion of the most populous district of the Territory commonly designated by the name of New Mexico. If the people of New Mexico had formed a plan of a State government for that Territory as ceded by the treaty of Gaudalupe Hidalgo, and had been admitted by Congress as a State, our Constitution would have afforded the means of obtaining an adjustment of the question of boundary with Texas by a judicial decision. At present, however, no judicial tribunal has the power of deciding that question, and it remains for Congress to devise some mode for its adjustment. Meanwhile I submit to Congress the question, whether it would be expedient before such adjustment to establish a Territorial government, which, by including the district so claimed, would practically decide the question adversely to the State of Texas, or, by excluding it, would decide it in her favor. In my opinion such a course would not be expedient, especially as the people of this Territory still enjoy the benefit and protection of their municipal laws, originally derived from Mexico, and have a military force stationed there to protect them against the Indians. It is undoubtedly true that the property, lives, liberties, and religion of the people of New Mexico, are better protected than they ever were before the treaty of cession.

"Should Congress, when California shall present herself for incorporation into the Union, annex a condition to her admission as a State, affecting her domestic institutions, contrary to the wishes of her people, and even compel her temporarily to comply with it, yet the State could change her constitution at any time after admission, when to her it should seem expedient. Any attempt to deny to the people of the State the right of self-government in a matter which peculiarly affects themselves, will infallibly be regarded by them as an invasion of their rights; and, upon the principles laid down in our own Declaration of Independence, they will certainly be sustained by the great mass of the American people. To assert that they are a conquered people, and must as a State submit to the will of their conquerors, in this regard, will meet with no cordial response among American freemen. Great numbers of them are native citizens of the United States, not inferior to the rest of our countrymen in intelligence and patriotism; and no language of menace to restrain them in the exercise of an undoubted right, substantially guarantied to them by the treaty of cession itself, shall ever be uttered by me, or encouraged and sustained by persons acting under my authority. It is to be expected that in the residue of the territory ceded to us by Mexico, the people residing there will, at the time of their incorporation into the Union as a State, settle all questions of domestic policy to suit themselves.

"No material inconvenience will result from the want, for a short period, of a government established by Congress over that part of the territory which lies eastward of the new State of California; and the reasons for my opinion that New Mexico will at no very distant period ask for admission into the Union, are founded on unofficial information, which I suppose is common to all who have cared to make inquiries on that subject.

"Seeing, then, that the question which now excites such painful sensations in the country will, in the end, certainly be settled by the silent effect of causes independent of the action of Congress, I again submit to your wisdom the policy recommended in my annual message of awaiting the salutary operation of those causes, believing that we shall thus avoid the creation of geographical parties, and secure the harmony of feeling so necessary to the beneficial action of our political system. Connected as the Union is with the remembrance of past happiness, the sense of present blessings, and the hope of future peace and prosperity, every dictate of wisdom, every feeling of duty, and every emotion of patriotism tend to inspire fidelity and devotion to it, and admonish us cautiously to avoid any unnecessary controversy which can either endanger it or impair its strength, the chief element of which is to be found in the regard and affection of the people for each other."

Though the recommendation in regard to the proper mode of settling the question to which it more particularly referred, met the cordial approbation of many of the wisest and most considerate men in every part of the Union, yet it cannot be denied that it received either a cold support or the open opposition of many others, both in and out of Congress. But this opposition arose principally from a misapprehension of the real nature of the President's proposition, and a mistaken view of its operation upon the territorial question. And the more the suggestions of the Executive were discussed and reflected upon, the more they commended themselves to the people. So evidently was this the case, that all moderate and reasonable men everywhere and of every party were becoming to look upon it as the means of deliverance from the dangers that threaten the Union, and were rallying to its support. And if General Taylor had lived but a few weeks longer, there can be little doubt that it would have been adopted by Congress, and sanctioned by the people. The subject is still before Congress, and whether the spirit of the President's recommendation will be carried out, or some other plan thought to be wiser, and better adapted to the end proposed, is yet for time to reveal.

Indeed, it may be said of General Taylor's policy as Executive, as of his character, that the more it was developed to the public, and the better it was understood, the more warmly was it commended, and the more evidently approved. Every act of his official life, seemed to have been dictated by a spirit of profound wisdom, enlarged statesmanship, and pure patriotism, that went right home to the American heart; and that sooner or later must meet a cordial response from the people everywhere. His intercourse with foreign nations, his recommendations to Congress, his whole domestic policy, were prompted by so clear a regard for the interests as well as the honor of the country, that an unwilling approval was wrung from even the bitterest of his opponents. He proved to the world by his treatment of the expedition against Cuba that he was as prompt to do justice to foreign nations as he was to defend the honor of his own; and he has shown by the various advantageous treaties negotiated under his direction that his abilities as a statesman were not excelled by his merits as a soldier.

But great, and wise, and good as General Taylor had shown himself to be, no less as President of the United States than as commander of our armies abroad; and as necessary as he was almost universally believed to be, to the harmony and welfare of the Union, an All-wise Providence had in store a far different destiny for him. The Ruler of the affairs of men and nations had decreed that the Patriot, Statesman, and Sage, whom all so revered and loved, was not to fulfil the career of honor and usefulness which others had assigned him.

On the morning of the Fourth of July,* the President, in company with his family and several of the Heads of Departments, attended the celebration of the anniversary of American Independence of the Washington National Monument Association, and listened to the oration of the Hon. H. S. Foote, in apparently as good health and as fine spirits as he had exhibited for months. And even up to five o'clock of that day he had shown no symptoms of illness. However, while upon the ground, he partook freely of water; and then, after considerable exercise in walking, and exposure to the sun, he drove home. Arrived at the mansion, he "felt," as he expressed himself to Dr. Weatherspoon, "very hungry;" and without reflecting that he was in an unfit condition to indulge freely in fruits, &c., he called for some refreshments, and ate heartily of cherries and wild berries, which he washed down with copious draughts of iced milk and water. At dinner he applied himself again to the cherries, against the remonstrances of Dr. Weatherspoon, and in an hour was seized by cramps, which

* The principal facts connected with Gen. Taylor's last illness, are taken from the Philadelphia Bulletin, and are no doubt nearly correct.

soon took the form of violent cholera morbus. His physician presciibed the usual remedies, but for a time he resisted, deeming the attack only temporary, and that it would yield finally to his naturally strong constitution. Toward midnight, instead of relief, the attack increased in violence and threatened desperate results, if not speedily arrested. He continued in this condition, without much change, until the evening of the 6th. It was then deemed advisable to call in other physicians. Accordingly, Messrs. Hall and Coolidge were invited, and promptly responded; but they thought it further advisable to send for the assistance of Dr. Wood of Baltimore. That gentleman attended immediately, and in the same cars came Colonel Taylor, the brother of the General, and his family, who had likewise been telegraphed for. By this time (the morning of the 8th), the disease had made rapid encroachments on his frame; but by the united skill of these eminent practitioners the visible stages of the cholera morbus were soon after checked. However, fever ensued, and from a remittent character, it took the form of typhoid. Anxiety now began to manifest itself, not only among the exalted patient's family, but among the physicians themselves. His chances of life hung upon a thread.

Meanwhile, there were other causes, beside merely eating and drinking, that operated fatally upon his system. To his medical attendant on the 8th, he said :—"I should not be surprised if this were to terminate in my death. I did not expect to encounter what has beset me since my elevation to the Presidency. God knows that I have endeavored to fulfil what I conceived to be an honest duty. But I have been mistaken. My motives have been misconstrued, and my feelings most grossly outraged." He alluded doubtless to the slavery question, and the manner in which he had been variously assailed.

Toward the evening of the 8th, the chronic type of dysentery which had set in disappeared, and vomiting ensued. Dr. Joubron of Philadelphia, who is eminent in these branches of treatment, was telegraphed, and a reply received from him that he would arrive that evening; but, alas! too late to be of service.

The condition of the patient was now at its critical point. The sick chamber was restored to solemn silence, attendance placed on the outside, and none permitted to enter except the physicians. The family of the President, with Col. Bliss, and other relatives of the deceased, occupied a room adjoining, where they remained, overwhelmed with grief, and refusing even the indulgences of necessary repose. Bulletins were hourly sent out, to inform the masses of the changes observable in the patient; but these so slightly varied for the better, that all hope of his safety was dispelled at 11 o'clock. From that period until daylight the utmost anxiety prevailed.

The 9th dawned, but gloom still surrounded the Executive mansion. Thousands began to flood the avenues leading thither, and throughout the day a messenger was kept posted at the main door to answer the interrogatories that were incessantly poured upon him. At 10 o'clock A. M. a report circulated that the President had rallied—at 1 P. M. that he was dead. The consternation created by the latter rumor was happily relieved by an official bulletin at 3½, that the crisis had been passed, and that he was then beyond immediate danger. Bells rang for joy, and even the boys in the streets lit bonfires, and shouted in childish gratulation.

The stream now to the White House was greater than ever, but about seven in the evening the pall of gloom again shrouded all faces, for it was announced that the illustrious hero was dying.

At 5—two hours previous—the physicians refused to administer any more medicine, considering his case hopeless and in the hands of God. The heads of Department, corporate authorities of the city, diplomatic body, and officers of the army and navy, paid their respects often during the day, and seemed to entertain lively feelings of solicitude for his safety. Everything that could contribute to the comfort of the sick, thenceforward, was extended; but the sands of life had run out, and his hours were numbered.

At nine the vomiting partially ceased, as all pain had disappeared about four in the afternoon. But the system had wasted under the shock, and gradually sunk beyond recovery. Green matter was thrown from his stomach at intervals until twenty minutes past 10—that peculiar coloration of bile that indicates the dissolution of patients thus seized. At 35 minutes past 10 his wife, and other members of his family, were called to his bedside, to receive his last earthly adieu—a farewell that the stoutest could not gaze upon without a tear. It must be remembered that his was a domestic life; and his beloved partner felt for the first time the loneliness of a bereaved heart, and understood nothing of that rigid discipline that would have dictated to her, "Go and weep in solitude—society decrees it." Her abandonment and grief were truly heart-piercing.

At a few minutes past ten, as already stated, it became apparent that the soul of the hero and conqueror was about taking its rest. The medical yielded to the spiritual agent, whose office it was to prepare for the approach of the King of Terrors. But there was nothing in the conduct of the sufferer to indicate that he feared the mortal leap. In the secret communion of his heart with Heaven, who can say that he died not a Christian? After prayer he seemed refreshed, and called for a glass of water. It was given him, and he drank sparingly. He then inquired of Dr. Weatherspoon, how long he thought he would live, to which the latter replied, "I hope, General, for many years;" but thinking this a useless deception, he added, "I fear not many hours." "I know it," was the response; then, after musing a moment, he asked for his family. They were sent for, and soon entered. The interview was indescribably affecting. The pain, which had afflicted the patient in the side of his chest, ceased; and attended by other symptoms of ease, it was thought he might endure till morning. But he himself knew better, and so declared in a quite audible voice. He was asked whether he was comfortable. "Very," he replied, "But the storm in passing, has swept away the trunk." Immediately after he added, with the consciousness of an upright and pure life, and an honest heart, "I HAVE ENDEAVORED TO DO MY DUTY, I AM PREPARED TO DIE. MY ONLY REGRET IS IN LEAVING BEHIND ME THE FRIENDS I LOVE." These were the last words of the great and good man, and they were characteristic of his whole life and of his noble mind. They are the words of a Hero, a Patriot, and a Sage. They show the ruling *principle,* strong in death. At his closing hour, as in his early manhood, and through his whole life, *duty* was the ever-active and controlling principle of ZACHARY TAYLOR. *Ready and Faithful,* had been the motto blazened upon the arms of General Taylor's ancestors.

With *Ready and Faithful* on his lips, he was gathered to his fathers.

"I am prepared to die—I have faithfully *endeavored* to do my duty!" These words, spoken by an aged patriot on the borders of the grave, are simple and sublime, and suggest to the mind the affecting declaration of the apostle Paul: "For I am ready to be offered, and the time of my departure is at hand. I have fought the good fight, I have finished my course, I have kept the faith." The solemn sentence with which General Taylor closed his eyes upon the world, deserve to be engraven upon his monument, as an illustration of his character and a history of his life. It ought to studied and imitated by all living men, that they may live so as to know how so well to die.

Every American will earnestly respond to the modest declaration of the departed hero—"I have faithfully endeavored to do my duty," and affirm that it is *true.* Amid the snows of the northwest, in the swamps of Florida, upon the fields of Palo Alto, Resaca de la Palma, and Monterey; amid the red ravines of Buena Vista, and in the lofty elevation of the Presidential chair, *duty* was the polar star of Zachary Taylor. Ordered to the Rio Grande with an insufficient force, he *obeyed* with alacrity, declaring, "Should the enemy obstruct my way, in whatever numbers, I will fight him." Stripped of his veteran regulars at Saltillo, he advanced at the head of *five thousand militia,* with a firm and cheerful front, to meet *twenty thousand* picked troops of Mexico, ready to sacrifice his life rather than abandon his *duty.* Called by a grateful people to the Presidential chair, he honestly sought to decline a station, for the responsibilities of which he repeatedly declared that he felt himself incapable. But finding that the popular mandate would not be withdrawn, he yielded, solely from his constant principle of *obedience* to the voice of his country. Occupying the presidential chair, he called around him counsellors, in whose ability and experience he confided, and honestly and industriously sought "according to the best lights before him," to perform the obligations of his new and most responsible position. He came to the government at a period more perilous to its stability and peace than any which has occurred since its foundation, and he has fallen a victim to the harrassing and terrible anxieties which a man must suffer, who, under such circumstances, "faithfully endeavors to discharge his duty." At the shrine of *duty* he was a worshipper in life, and a martyr in death.

Generous, intrepid Old Chief! Enviable indeed is a remorse like thine! Illustrious thy lot, to do such brave and noble deeds as shall gild the pages of thy country's history for ages after thy sun has set! Glorious to sleep on a hero's couch, wrapped in thy country's flag, and followed to the grave by a nation's notes of lamentation. But better far than these—better than brilliant plume and gleaming sword—better than all earthly recompense and honor, to stand at the gate-way of the tomb with hoary locks clothed with a crown of righteousness, and to be able to declare, with expiring lips—"I AM READY TO DIE. I HAVE FAITHFULLY ENDEAVORED TO DO MY DUTY."

Equally characteristic of his brave and firm heart, were the words spoken to one of his physicians shortly before, and after he had himself abandoned all hope of life. "*You have fought a good fight*," he calmly remarked, "*but you cannot make a stand.*"

He essayed to speak to his wife a few moments before his demise, but his voice failed him. Dr. Weatherspoon administered a stimulus, but it was powerless in reviving the functions. The soul of the hero had fled.

> "The lightnings may flash, and the thunder may rattle,
> He heeds not, he hears not, he's free from all pain;
> He sleeps his last sleep, he has fought his last battle,
> No sound can awake him to glory again."

Congestion of the brain and stomach began at half-past 8 o'clock, so that no earthly power could stay the fatal result which has plunged the nation in mourning. The unwearied attentions of his medical advisers deserved credit, and their skill is unquestionable. It is believed, however, that had the mind of the President not been laboring under embarrassment and affliction, proceeding from causes named, the disease could have been checked and his life saved. But now that he is gone, it is vain to speculate. One succeeds him whose sensitiveness is not quite so keen, because intimate with all the trials of politics, and therefore possessing fortitude sufficient to withstand them.

Those surrounding the dying President at the moment, were his own family, including Col. Bliss, Col. Taylor and family, Jefferson Davis and family, Vice President Fillmore, several Senators and Members, several members of the diplomatic corps, the Cabinet, Benton, Hale, Wood, Coolidge, and Weatherspoon, and a number of intimate friends. Without the mansion, the grounds were literally covered with an immense multitude, who continued to linger in groups until after midnight, scarcely crediting the intelligence, though officially announced.

General Taylor died without a struggle. It was a

kind of sinking into eternity, without feeling its pain, or experiencing its horrors. When all was over, the chamber was cleared, until the undertakers had concluded their duties. The body was encased in ice, and ordered to remain where it was until morning, when it was finally robed for the grave, and laid out in state in the east room. Thus ended the melancholy siege of disease against a strong bulwark of nature.

The Cabinet immediately after the death of the President, held an informal meeting, at which a paper was drawn up, and signed by the members, in which his decease was set forth, and officially communicated to Mr. Fillmore, as his constitutional successor. Mr. F. in return thanked them for their courtesy, and in a brief epistle, deplored the event that had just taken place. He further invited them to a council this morning, for the purpose of executing such measures, as under the circumstances appeared advisable. These proceedings terminated the night.

As soon as the death of General Taylor was announced, several of the bells of the city were tolled, and the solemn concert was kept up through the night and next day; and late as the hour of his death was, the melancholy intelligence was known that night to almost every citizen of the Capital, and was on its way with lightning speed to the remotest section of the Union.

At sunrise the next morning the national colors, shrouded in black, were disclosed at half mast. All the public offices were closed and arrayed in the same sable colors, even to the National Monument. The Executive mansion was literally covered with black, and the badge was worn on the housings of the horses attached to the Secretaries' carriages. Business of all kinds was suspended, and a stream of living objects kept pouring into the President's grounds, and besieging the edifice until as late as 11 o'clock. • From the War and Navy and State Departments, orders were transmitted to stations abroad, communicating the awful tidings and directing appropriate honors in consequence. The Executive mansion was open until 2 P. M. during which time the public availed themselves of the opportunity to visit the remains. They were contained in one of Fisk and Raymond's metallic coffins, and exposed on a bier in the East Room. The body is greatly emaciated, but the lineaments of the face are preserved tolerably perfect. Perhaps the death of Washington did not inspire more real sorrow and regret than that of President Taylor. Every face wore a mournful shade, and none are so poor in charity as to deny him the tribute of a sigh. Groups beset the corners of the streets, and not a passing vehicle but what contains a countenance of grief. The Mayor of the city ordered appropriate honors, and, truly, it may be said, we live "with the willow and cypress waving around us."

The chief incidents that transpired during his illness, are those embodied in the above. He regretted in plain language, and so many words, the crusade waged against him, and thought that parties failed to do him justice. The course pursued, by Southern ultraists irritated him, but only because they made him responsible for conduct with which he had nothing to do. He deplored the strife which prevails, but did not hesitate to ascribe the cause to sectional demagogues. The dictatorial license assumed by his opponents displeased him; but when it was hinted that his own friends would move a vote of censure, he sunk under the blow and conceived that to be the most fatal stab of all. He was resolved, however, to pursue the line of policy to which he had thus long adhered, though convinced that gentlemen of the South meditated his ruin. This, while it preyed upon his mind, only determined him the more to stand by his doctrines.

The news of General Taylor's death was received with overwhelming regret everywhere by all classes and parties and sects, as it became disseminated over the country. It fell with almost stunning effect upon the public mind. North and South, East and West, it was viewed as a dire national calamity. The first report of his death was so alarming, and so wholly unexpected, that it was received with general incredulity, and the telegraph stations, newspaper offices, and every place where there was a hope of obtaining information, were literally besieged for days by people for miles around, anxiously inquiring into the truth of the painful and startling rumor. The people seemed determined not to believe the afflicting report until confirmed by the most positive and direct authority. When there was no longer any room to doubt its sad reality, they begun to exhibit the evidence of the deep sorrow the event was so well calculated to inspire; and the same tokens of hearfelt grief that pervaded the Capital were visible throughout the length and breadth of the entire Union.

The melancholy calamity was officially communicated to both Houses of Congress by the Hon. Millard Fillmore, now President of the United States, in the following appropriate and feeling message:—

WASHINGTON, July 10, 1850.

FELLOW-CITIZENS OF THE SENATE
AND OF THE HOUSE OF REPRESENTATIVES;

I have to perform the melancholy duty of announcing to you that it has pleased Almighty God to remove from this life ZACHARY TAYLOR, late President of the United States. He deceased last evening, at the hour of half-past ten o'clock, in the midst of his family, and surrounded by affectionate friends, calmly, and in the full possession of all his faculties. Among his last words were these, which he uttered with emphatic distinctness: "I have always done my duty—I am ready to die; my only regret is for the friends I leave behind me."

Having announced to you, fellow-citizens, this most afflicting bereavement, and assuring you that it has penetrated no heart with deeper grief than mine, it remains for me to say that I propose, this day, at 12 o'clock, in the hall of the House of Representatives, in the presence of both Houses of Congress, to take the oath prescribed by the Constitution, to enable me to enter on the execution of the office which this event has devolved on me.

MILLARD FILLMORE.

Resolutions were adopted in both Houses to meet in the Hall of the House of Representatives to be present at the administration of the oath of office required by the Constitution to Mr. Fillmore. The interesting ceremony having been performed, the Senators returned to their Chamber, when resolutions were offered by Mr. Downs, of Louisiana, for making suitable arrangements for the funeral ceremonies, prefaced by an eloquent, chaste, and worthy tribute to the memory of the deceased patriot and hero. Beautiful and touching tributes of respect and veneration were also paid to his memory by Mr. Webster, Mr. Cass, Mr. Pearce, Mr. King, and Mr. Berrien. The remarks of Mr. Webster are given below as portraying in true and glowing colors the many admirable and remarkable traits of General Taylor's life and character. Those of other Senators were equally appropriate and eloquent, but they are necessarily omitted.

Mr. WEBSTER said: Mr. Secretary, at a time when the general mass of our fellow-citizens enjoy remarkable health and happiness throughout the whole country, it has pleased Divine Providence to visit the two Houses of Congress, and especially this House, with repeated occasions for mourning and lamentation. Since the commencement of the session, we have followed two of our own members to their last home; and we are now called upon, in conjunction with the other branch of legislature, and in full sympathy with that deep tone of affliction which I am sure is felt throughout all the country, to take part in the last and due solemnities of the late President of the United States.

Truly, sir, was it said in the communication read to us, that a "great man has fallen among us." The late President of the United States, originally a soldier by profession, having gone through a long and splendid career of military service, had at the close of the late war with Mexico, become so much endeared to the people of the United States, and had inspired them with so high a degree of regard and confidence, that without solicitations or application, without pursuing any devious paths of policy, or turning a hair's breadth to the right or the left from the path of duty, a great, and powerful, and generous people saw fit, by popular vote and voice, to confer upon him the highest civil authority in the nation. We cannot forget that, as in other instances so in this, the public feeling was won and carried away, in some degree, by the eclat of military renown. So it has been always; and so it always will be, because high respect for noble feats in arms has been, and always will be outpoured from the hearts of the members of a popular Government. But it will be a great mistake to suppose that the late President of the United States owed his advancement to high civil trust, or his great acceptability with the peeple, to military talent or ability alone. I believe, sir, that associated with the highest admiration for those qualities possessed by him, there was spread throughout the community a high degree of confidence and faith in his integrity and honor and uprightness as a man. I believe he was especially regarded as both a firm and a mild man in the exercise of authority. And I have observed more than once in this and in other popular Governments that the prevalent motive with the masses of mankind for conferring high power on individuals, is a confidence in their mildness, their paternal, protecting, secure, and safe character. The people naturally feel safe where they feel themselves to be under the control and protection of sober counsel, of impartial minds, and a general paternal superintendence.

I suppose, sir, that no case ever happened in the very best days of the Roman republic, when any man found himself clothed in the highest authority in the State, under circumstances more repelling all suspicion of personal application, all suspicion of pursuing any crooked path in politics, or all suspicion of having been actuated by sinister views and purposes, than in the case of the worthy, and eminent, and distinguished, and good man whose death we now deplore.

He has left to the people of his country a legacy in this. He has left them a bright example, which addresses itself with peculiar force to the young and rising generation; for it tells them that there is a path to the highest degree of renown—straight, onward, steady, without change or deviation.

Mr. Secretary, my friend from Louisiana (Mr. Downs) has detailed briefly the events in the military career of General Taylor. His service through life was mostly on the frontier, and always a hard service—often in combat with the tribes of Indians all along the frontier for so many thousands of miles. It has been justly remarked by one of the most eloquent men whose voice was ever heard in these houses, that it is not in Indian wars that heroes are celebrated, but it is there that they are formed. The hard service, the stern discipline, devolving upon all those who have a great extent of frontier to defend, and often with irregular troops of their own, being called on suddenly to enter into contest with savages, to study the habits of savage life and savage war, in order to foresee and overcome their stratagems—all these things tend to make hardy military character.

For a very short time, sir, I had a connexion with the Executive government of this country; and at that time very perilous, embarrassing circumstances existed between the United States and the Indians on the borders, and war was actually raging between the United States, and the Florida tribes, and I very well remember that those who took counsel together on that occasion officially, and who were desirous of placing the military command in the safest hands, came to the conclusion that there was no man in the service more fully uniting the qualities of military ability and great personal prudence than ZACHARY TAYLOR; and he was, of course, appointed to the command.

Unfortunately, his career at the head of this Government was short. For my part, in all that I have seen of him, I have found much to repect and nothing to condemn. The circumstances under which he conducted the Government for the few months he was at the head of it, have been such as perhaps not to give to him a very favorable, certainly not a long opportunity of developing his principles and his policy, and to carry them out; but I believe he has left on the minds of the country a strong impression, first, of his absolute honesty and integrity of character; next, of his sound practical good sense; and, lastly, of the mildness, kindness, and friendliness of his temper towards all his countrymen.

But he is gone. He is ours no more, except in the force of his example. Sir, I heard with infinite delight the sentiments expressed by my honorable friend from Louisiana, (Mr. DOWNS,) who has just resumed his seat, when he earnestly prayed that this event might be used to soften animosities, to allay party criminations and recriminations, and to restore fellowship and good feeling among the various sections of the Union. Mr. Secretary, great as is our loss to-day, if these inestimable and inappreciable blessings shall have been secured to us, even by the death of ZACHARY TAYLOR, they have not been purchased at too high a price; and if his spirit, from the regions to which he has ascended, could see these results flowing from his unexpected and untimely end—if he could see that he had entwined a soldier's laurel around a martyr's crown, he would say exultingly, 'Happy am I, that by my death I have done more for that country which I loved and served, than I did or could do by all the devotion and all the efforts that I could make in her behalf during the short span of my earthly existence.'

Mr. Secretary, great as this calamity is, we mourn, but not as those without hope. We have seen one eminent man, and at last a man in the most eminent station, fall away from the midst of us. But I doubt not there is a power above us exercising over us that parental care that has marked our progress for so many years. I have confidence still that the place of the departed will be supplied; that the kind, beneficent favor of Almighty God will still be with us, and that we shall be borne along, and born upward and upward, on the wings of His sustaining Providence. May God grant that in the time that is before us, there may not be wanting to us as wise men, as good men for our counsellors, as he was whose funeral obsequies we now propose to celebrate!

In the House, resolutions in regard to the funeral, corresponding with those in the Senate, were adopted.

After the oath of office had been administered to Mr. Fillmore, the following message from him was read. as it was also in the Senate:—

FELLOW-CITIZENS OF THE SENATE
AND OF THE HOUSE OF REPRESENTATIVES;

I recommend to the two houses of Congress to adopt such measures as in their discretion may seem proper, to perform with due solemnities the funeral obsequies of ZACHARY TAYLOR, late President of the United States; and thereby to signify the great and affectionate regard of the American people for the memory of one whose life has been devoted to the public service, whose career in arms has not been surpassed in usefulness or brilliancy: who has been so recently raised by the unsolicited voice of the people to the highest civil authority in the government, which he administered with so much honor and advantage to his country; and by whose sudden death so many hopes of future usefulness have been blighted forever.

To you, Senators and Representatives of a nation in tears, I can say nothing which can alleviate the sorrow with which you are oppressed.

I appeal to you to aid me, under the trying circumstances which surround me, in the discharge of the duties, from which, however much I may be oppressed by them, I dare not shrink; and I rely upon Him, who holds in his hands the destinies of nations, to endow me with the requisite strength for the task, and to avert from our country the evils apprehended from the heavy calamity which has befallen us.

I shall most readily concur in whatever measures the wisdom of the two Houses may suggest, as befitting this deeply melancholy occasion.

MILLARD FILLMORE.

WASHINGTON, July 10, 1850.

Eloquent addresses graphically describing General Taylor's public and private character, and his many eminent services were then delivered by Mr. Conrad, of Louisiana, Mr. Winthrop, of Massachusetts, Mr. Baker, of Illinois, Mr. Bagby, of Virginia, Mr. Hilliard, of Alabama, Mr. John A. King, of New York, Mr. McLane, of Maryland, and Mr. Marshall, of Kentucky. From these equally heartfelt and touching outpourings of grief, that of Mr. Baker, of Illinois, is selected, only because a choice must be made :—

Mr. BAKER said:

Mr. SPEAKER: It is often said of sorrow, that, like death, it levels all distinctions. The humblest heart can heave a sigh as deep as the proudest; and I avail myself of this mournful privilege to swell the accents of grief which have been poured forth to-day with a larger though not more sincere utterance. A second time since the formation of this Government, a President of the United States has been stricken by death in the performance of his great duties. The blow which strikes the man falls upon a nation's heart, and the words of saddened praise which fall upon our ears to-day, and here, are but echoes of the thoughts that throng in the hearts of the millions that mourn him *everywhere*. You have no doubt observed, sir, that in the first moments of a great loss the instincts of affection prompt us to summon up the good and great qualities of those for whom we weep. It is a wise ordination of Divine Providence; a generous pride tempers and restrains the *bitterness* of grief, and noble deeds and heroic virtues shed a consoling light upon the tomb. It is in this spirit that I recur for an instant, and for an instant *only*, to the events of a history fresh in the remembrance of the nation and the world.

The late President of the United States has devoted his whole life to the service of his country. Of a nature singularly unambitious, he seems to have combined the utmost gentleness of manner with the greatest firmness of purpose. For more than thirty years the duties of his station confined him to a sphere where only those who knew him most intimately could perceive the qualities which danger quickened and brightened into sublimity and grandeur. In the late war with Great Britain he was but a captain; yet the little band who defended Fort Harrison saw amid the smoke of battle that they were commanded by a man fit for his station. In the Florida campaign he commanded but a brigade; yet his leadership not only evinced courage and conduct, but inspired these qualities in the meanest soldier in his ranks. He began the Mexican campaign at the head of only a division; yet as the events of the war swelled that division into an army, so the crisis kindled him into higher resolves and nobler actions, till the successive steps of advance became the assured march of victory.

Mr. Speaker, as we review the brilliant and stirring passages of the events to which I refer, it is not in the power even of sudden grief to suppress the admiration which thrills our hearts. When, sir, has there been such a campaign—when such soldiers to be led—and when such qualities of leadership so variously combined? How simple, but yet how grand, was the announcement, "in whatever force the enemy may be, I shall fight him." It gave Palo Alto and Resaca to our banner. How steadfast the resolution that impelled the advance to Monterey! How stirring the courage which beleaguered the frowning city—which stormed the barricaded street—which carried the embattled heights, and won and kept the whole! Nor, sir, can we forget that in the flush of victory, the gentle heart stayed the bold hand, while the conquering soldier offered sacrifices on the altar of *pity*, amid all the exultations of triumph.

Sir, I may not stop to speak of the achievements of Buena Vista; they are deeds that will never die—it was the great event of the age, a contest of races and institutions. An army of volunteers, engaged not in an impetuous advance, but in a stern defence of chosen ground against superior force, and in a last extremity,—men who had never seen fire faced the foe with the steadiness of veterans. Sir, as long as those frowning heights and bloody ravines shall remain, these recollections will endure, and with them the name of the man who steadied every rank, and kindled every eye, by the indomitable resolution which would not yield, and the exalted spirit which rose highest amid the greatest perils. It was from scenes like these he was called to the Chief Magistracy. It was a summons unexpected and unsought—the spontaneous expression of a noble confidence, the just reward of great actions. It may not be proper to speak here and now of the manner in which these new duties were executed; but I may say that here, as every where else, he exhibited the same firmness and decision which had marked his life. He was honest and unostentatious; he obeyed the law and loved the Constitution; he dealt with difficult questions with a singleness of purpose which is the truest pilot amid storms. Nor can it be doubted that when impartial history shall record the events of his Administration, they will be found worthy of his past life, and a firm foundation for his future renown.

You remember, Mr. Speaker, that when the great Athenian philosopher was inquired of by the Lydian king as to who was the happiest among men, he declared that no man should be pronounced happy till his death. The President of the United States has so finished a noble life, as to justify the pride and admiration of his countrymen—he has faced the last enemy with a manly firmness and a becoming resolution. He died where an American citizen would most desire to die—not amid embattled hosts and charging squadrons, but amid weeping friends and an anxious nation—in the house provided by its gratitude, only to be taken thence to a "house not made with hands, eternal in the heavens."

Sir, in the death which has caused so much dismay there is a becoming resemblance to the life which has created so much confidence. His closing hours were marked with a beautiful calmness; his last expressions indicated a manly sense of his own worth, and a consciousness that he had done his duty. Nor can I omit to remark, that it is this sense of the obligation of duty which appears to have been the true basis of his character. In boyhood and in age—as captain and as general—whether defending a fort against savages, or exercising the functions of the Chief Magistracy, duty, rather than glory—self-approval, rather than renown—have prompted the deeds which have made him immortal.

Mr. Speaker, the character upon which death has just set his seal, is filled with beautiful and impressive contrasts; a warrior, he loved peace; a man of action, he sighed for retirement. Amid the events which crowned him with fame, he counselled a withdrawal of our troops. And, whether at the head of armies, or in the Chair of State, he appeared as utterly unconscious of his great renown as if no banners had drooped at his word, or as if no gleam of glory shone through his whitened hair. It is related of Epaminondas, that when fatally wounded at the battle of Mantinea, they bore him to a height from whence, with fading glance, he surveyed the fortunes of the fight, and when the field was won, laid himself down to die; the friends who gathered around him wept his early fall, and passionately expressed their sorrow that he died childless. "Not so," said the hero with his last breath, "for do I not leave two fair daughters, Leuctra and Mantinea?" General TAYLOR is more fortunate, since he leaves an excellent and most worthy family to deplore his loss and inherit his glory. Nor is he fortunate in this only, since, like Epaminondas, he leaves not only two battles, but four—Palo Alto, Resaca, Monterey, Buena Vista—the grand creations of his genius and valor, to be remembered as long as truth and courage appeal to the human heart.

Mr. Speaker, the occasion and the scene impress upon us a deep sense of the instability of all human concerns, so beautifully alluded to by my friend from Massachusetts, (Mr. WINTHROP.) The great southern Senator is no longer among us. The President, during whose administration the war commenced, sleeps in "the house appointed for all the living;" and the great soldier who led the advance and assured the triumph, "lies like a warrior taking his rest." Ah! sir, if in this assemblage there is a man whose heart beats with a tumultuous and unrestrained ambition, let him to-day stand by the bier upon which that lifeless body is laid, and learn how much of human greatness fades in an hour; but if there be another man here whose fainting heart shrinks from a noble purpose, let him, too, visit these sacred remains, to be reminded how much there is in true glory that can never die.

The joint committee of Congress which had been appointed to make the necessary and appropriate arrangements for the funeral, immediately set about that melancholy duty with becoming zeal and energy, and fixed upon Saturday, the 13th day of July, for the solemn ceremony. On that day, accordingly, the mortal remains of the illustrious and eminent deceased were consigned to the tomb.

The deep-toned artillery gave early note of preparation, and the avenues were soon alive with thronging multitudes, dressed in decent apparel, and evidently impressed with the seriousness of the occasion. All places of business were closed, and the drapery of mourning hung in graceful festoons upon the walls of almost every house throughout the long route the procession was to traverse.

Vast numbers from abroad had already arrived in the city, and every hotel and house of entertainment was full; yet the arrivals on this morning followed each other in rapid succession. More than forty passenger-cars arrived from Baltimore during the forenoon, bringing military companies and citizens. Many came in the steamboats from Alexandria, Fredericksburg, and Richmond, and from the adjacent country every description of vehicle had been put in requisition.

The morning had not far advanced before every advantageous position from the President's house, to the Capitol was occupied—every window, every elevated place along the avenue, and every favorable position on the sidewalks; and yet from all directions the multitudes pressed onward to the avenue and toward the President's house. And the deep voice of the cannon boomed heavily at intervals, and its echoes died away with an undulating murmur.

The military now approached to take position on the avenue in front of the President's house. The Flying Artillery, from Fort McHenry, commanded by Major Sedgwick, presented a most magnificent appearance. This company, with four others of the regular service, constituted a battalion under the command of Major S. The others were as follows, viz., one company from Fort Mifflin, of artillery serving as Infantry, commanded by Capt. Bowen; two companies from Governor's Island, New York; and one company from Fort Washington. There was with these a very beautiful band from Governor's Island.

There was also a battalion of Marines, commanded by Captain Tansil. This consisted of two companies, commanded by Lieutenant Graham and Sergeant-Major Pulizzi respectively. With them was the excellent band attached to the Marine Barracks led by Mr. Treioy. The martial music of this corps, always so much admired, was led by McGrery.

From the city of Alexandria there were two volunteer companies; the Mechanical Artillery, Capt. Duffie, and the Mount Vernon Guards, Captain Fields. The latter was accompanied by Little's excellent band.

The Georgetown Grays, Capt. Goddard, were in new and very handsome uniform.

The Fredericksburg Guards, commanded by Capt. W. S. Barton, were also accompanied by a find band.

From Richmond there was a large and fine company of Blues, of which Capt. Lawrence is commander; but we believe it was at this time under the command of Lieutenant Regnault. There was also a small company from Richmond, composed of officers of the 179th Regiment. A band of music accompanied the former.

From Baltimore there were the following, viz: The Independent Grays, Captain Hall, with a fine band; the Independent Blues, Captain Schutt; the First Baltimore Sharpshooters, Captain Lilley; the Eagle Artillerists, Captain Phillips; the Junior Artillerists, Captain Marshall; the Patapsco Rifles, Captain Swaim, with a band led by Mr. Wagoner; the Maryland Cadets, Captain Poor; the Baltimore Mounted Carbineers, Captain Owens; a battalion of Germans, consisting of two fine companies of infantry, and a large and excellent company of youths, from the academy at St. Timothy's Hall, (near Baltimore,) commanded by Captain Brown.

There was also a portion of a company from Philadelphia—the National Guards—commanded by Captain Lyle.

The volunteers of Washington consisted of the Washington Light Infantry, Captain Tate; the National Greys, Captain Bacon; and the Walker Sharpshooters, Captain Bryant, Lieutenant Birkhead, commanding.

Accompanying the Baltimore volunteers were a number of aged men who had aided in the defence of that city in 1814. They are known by the honored name of the "Old Defenders."

The number of vehicles in the line of the procession was one hundred and five. The line was one mile and a half in length. At one point on the avenue it occupied forty-five minutes in passing; at another, moving less steadily, it occupied an hour.

The President's house was, throughout the morning, guarded by Captain Goddard and the Auxiliary Guard, wearing badges and having batons in their hands.

The persons entitled to admission here were those designated in the following extract from the printed programme, viz.:

The United States' Marshal of the District of Columbia and his Aids.

The Mayors of Washington and Georgetown.

The Committee of Arrangements of the two Houses of Congress.

The Chaplains of the two Houses of Congress, and the officiating Clergyman of the occasion.

Attending Physicians to the late President.

PALL BEARERS.

Hon. Henry Clay,	Hon. T. H. Benton,
Hon. Lewis Cass,	Hon. Daniel Webster,

Hon. J. M. Berrien,	Hon. Truman Smith,
Hon. R. C. Winthrop,	Hon. Linn Boyd,
Hon. Jas. McDowell,	Hon. S. F. Vinton,
Hon. Hugh White,	Hon. Isaac E. Holmes,
G. W. P. Custis, Esq.,	Hon. R. J. Walker,
Chief Justice Cranch,	Joseph Gales, Esq.,
Maj. Gen. Jesup,	Maj. Gen. Gibson,
Com. Ballard,	Brig. Gen. Henderson.

Family and relatives of the late President.

The President of the United States and the Heads of Departments.

The Sergeant-at-Arms of the Senate.

The Senate of the United States, preceded by their President, *pro tempore*, and Secretary.

The Sergeant-at-Arms of the House of Representatives.

The House of Representatives, preceded by their Speaker and Clerk.

The Chief Justice and Associate Justices of the Supreme Court of the United States and its officers.

The Diplomatic Corps.

Governors of States and Territories.

Ex-members of Congress.

Members of State Legislatures.

District Judges of the United States.

Judges of the Circuit and Criminal Courts of the District of Columbia, with the members of the bar and officers of the courts.

The Judges of the several States.

The Comptrollers of the Treasury, Auditors, Treasurer, Register, Solicitor, and Commissioners of Land Office, Pensions, Indian Affairs, Patents, and Public Buildings.

At a little after 12 o'clock the services were commenced by singing the following anthem, under the direction of Professor Berlin:

"I heard a voice from heaven, saying unto me: Write, from henceforth blessed are the dead who die in the Lord; even so saith the spirit, for they rest from their labors. Amen."

The funeral service, as prescribed by the book of common prayer, was then read by the Rev. Dr. Pyne, assisted by the Rev. Dr. Butler.

The following impressive address was then delivered by the Rev. Dr. Pyne, Rector of St. John's Church, where General Taylor attended public worship:—

In other lands, where there prevails a class of political and social relations essentially different from our own, there is a word often used which, important and expressive as may be its import to the people of those lands, seems with us, under ordinary circumstances, scarcely to find a place or an application; I mean the word *august*. It may appear strange, speaking as an American to Americans, to employ such an expression as an august person, or an august presence; and yet, whatever there be in that word that conveys the associations and attributes of majesty, of all that can impress a human creature with reverence and awe, I find it in this audience and this presence; for I speak in an assemblage which is but the type and symbol of a mourning *nation*—appropriate symbol of its dignity and power. The Chief Magistrate of this republic, the members of its legislative councils, the honorable heads of its Executive Departments, the honored chiefs of the two great arms of the public service—this is a presence which to me, as a citizen of this republic, is indeed *august*.

And not less imposing to me is the representation of the dignity of other lands in peace and harmony with our own; for that presence tells me not only that they are here among us great agents for the interests of great nations, and therefore for the interests of the civilized world, but I believe they are here this day, in this place of the mourning obsequies of the honored dead, giving a tribute of not mere official reverence, but personal regret; yes! as ministers of this world's rulers, to whom the *peace* of the world is all important, well may they regret him who, as long as he filled his great place, was a guarantee for one element in that world-wide security—*the stern, impartial neutrality of these United States.* I am sure I do them no more than justice in believing that a tenderer feeling is blended with this: the warm grasp of the hand, the cordial address, the true, honest words of welcome, and the homely but affectionate farewell, are present, I doubt not, at this moment to the memory of many a heart that beats beneath those insignia of official station. I remember well the impression made on me by his parting speech to the minister of a great empire: "God bless you, come back to us again"—a strange farewell, according to the vocabulary of diplomatic etiquette—a noble and characteristic one from General TAYLOR to the man he was really sorry to part with, and whom he honestly wished to see again. I feel, then, that I speak in the presence of not mere official representatives of courts and countries, but of men whose sympathies accompany that presence, making it all the more impressive to me as it is honorable to them.

There is another presence here, to me the most august of all—the presence of that relic of the mighty dead! When living, he never heard from my lips one word of adulation, and now, if in that light and life of truth to which that true soul has been taken, he is conscious of aught that passes here, he sees that I am doing for him when dead, that which would most have pleased him in life. I will speak the *truth*, utter no single word which my conscience does not avouch, which is not an index of the feelings of my heart.

And oh! may I, the minister of God, not lose for one moment the conscious sense of that Presence—the "discerner of the thoughts and intents of the heart!" May these few poor words of mine perform the best office for the dead, by doing good to the living who in their turn must die!

In their appropriate time and place words have been spoken, the record of this great man's life, the tribute to his multiplied claims upon the country—words worthy of those who uttered them, worthy of him whom they commemorated. Had this, then, been the fit occasion, or mine the proper voice, to expatiate on such themes, I could only have reiterated what has been far better and more effectively said. Of his glorious history, then, as the leader of armies—of his measures as the Chief Magistrate of a great nation, I shall say nothing. I shall advert to one point alone, a subject of contemplation as useful as it is beautiful.

I have been struck with the coincidence, not merely in feeling, but in the very expression of that feeling, which has marked the reception, throughout the country, of the late heavy tidings. Simultaneously, from our halls of Congress, in every form of official announcement, in every private letter I have received or seen, there was one phrase, as though it were the only possible, the instinctive expression of one universal feeling: "*the great man!*" It is evidently no mere form of speech, nor is it employed in that conventional acceptation by which any man who had died in that great office might be called great. No, it is plain that in that individual man there were elements of character which have impressed upon the common sense and judgment of this country the indelible conviction that he was a great man. It is worth while for us to pause a moment to consider what those qualities were, which elicited an acknowledgment so unusually, so universally accordant. It was not his military prowess or success. "Vixere fortes ante Agamemnona." The civic and the mural crowns adorn too many brows to have made this man, as by emphasis, great. That wonderful campaign was indeed the lever which raised him up to show the world, not what *it* had made him, but what he was in himself, *the man* —the man to do the right thing at the right time; the man who would not leave his wounded behind him, and would have encountered any personal hazard or sacrifice to abide by that which his heart told him was right; the man quiet in expression, strong in action, firm in purpose; and whether in expression, action, or purpose, that transparent honesty and simple integrity forming, as it were, the atmosphere in which he lived and moved—which so happily for himself and for us not only enabled him to see clearly and do resolutely what became a a true and brave man, but enabled the world to see how bravely and how honestly it was done. A rare gift! Let us honor it; and, above all, let us try to learn a lesson from it.

The secret of this illustrious man's strength and greatness lay in his being honest, true, right-minded. He might have possessed the same clearness of judgment in discerning any practicable or desirable end, the same determination of purpose in adhering to his maturely adopted plan for working it out. Would these things alone have made him what this nation has so universally called him? A man may see very clearly a *bad* end, work with astonishing vigor and perseverance to accomplish it. Can such a man be really great—can he be really strong? It is true that, without these more active qualities, mere rectitude of intention and goodness of heart might constitute a good but not a great man. And yet even in those elements of *goodness* lie the essential elements of *greatness*. The working powers of energy and will, of what avail are they if they have not the true material to work withal?—*reliability!* If a man have not that, who will trust him? Though he had the energy and intelligence of the arch fiend himself, who will let him work with them or for them? And where is that reliability to be sought? In the fickle changes of a man's self-interest, in the declared submission to popular will, so that a man is perpetually looking without and never within for his rule of right? No! To give real body and strength to human character, there must be the strong mind, indeed, but it must be the strong mind acting responsively to the teachings of the *right* mind. "If the eye be single, then shall the whole body be full of light." *Goodness* and *power*—that is *greatness*. The people of this land saw it *there*, and therefore have they called him great. It is an honor to them to have seen him as they did, and to have placed him where they did.

There is, then, a great lesson to be learned here this day. I will not suffer myself to suppose that there is a public man who hears me, who does not covet that which is high in honor, bright in fame, and which will last in the memory of man. We have had a great living example of what there must be in a man to win from the world these noble appliances of honor and fame. Being dead, he yet speaketh a lesson, which will be read and treasured by the generation who shall follow us.

Permit me, now, to pass to the yet higher teachings of this great event.

There is a series of commonplaces respecting death, judgment, eternity, which, awful and true as they are admitted to be, still whether it be from the familiarity of our minds with them in consequence of frequent repetition, or that the overwhelming interests of the solid, tangible present, veil the equally certain, but, as we think, far-removed realities of the future; from some cause or other, I repeat, these admitted, awful truths fail to exercise any influence on human conduct or character at all commensurate with their importance. The great reason of this is probably the practical ignorance or the forgetfulness of the great fact that, in the revelation of Christianity, judgment is not a thing which is to come, but is *now;* that we are actually in the kingdom of the Great Judge, the God man, who is near to us, and we to him,—near, with his supplies of grace to help in time of need—near, knowing from His human experience what man can do as well as what he ought to do, knowing from His divine omniscience every thought and intent of the heart. It is not, then, a remote judge and a remote judgment with which we have to do, but one at the door. The judgment of the great day is, in fact, only the sentence educed by the sum of those judgments which have gone up day by day from the thoughts, and words, and works. Alas! even in Christian people who are not insensible to the fact of their religion, who feel its restraining and guiding influence is great in many of the circumstances of life, there is great hazard of their losing the practical conviction that there is only one judge in the world with whom they have anything really to do—that they should suffer questions of expediency or policy, or the opinions of men, to take the place of this simple accountability of the Christian conscience to the Christian Judge; so that any course of action for which we can adduce such plausible reasons as will satisfy the world, we take for granted as fit to stand before the bar of conscience. "If our heart condemn us not, then have we confidence towards God," saith an apostle. But when, by any process of reasoning, we have so justified our conduct, that, before the tribunal of man's judgment, we pass free, we may infer, as a necessary consequence, that our hearts should not condemn us; from this the step is easy to the conclusion that it does not. Seeing, then, how easily and insensibly we may fall into practical forgetfulness of the great judgment which standeth ever at the door, whose final award we shall all assuredly meet, it is the business of reasonable men, it is the solemn duty of responsible Christian men, whenever in God's providence, any event occurs which teaches a great lesson on this very point, to study it devoutly, reverently. It is the great purpose of God, in troubling the still waters of common life, that we should note the descent of the angel and gather health from the perturbed element. Such a visitation has now been made. It weakens the effect of such an event to multiply words respecting it. It is a world-speaking sermon—to the world more immediately around us, among whom this illustrious person so lately and so conspicuously moved—speaking with especial emphasis. May God teach our hearts all its lessons. I shall not pretend to present them all, but will endeavor, by His grace, to awake your attention and my own to that lesson at least which comes home to the great business and wants of our daily life, and may make us wise unto salvation.

I would remark, then, that in the sudden removal of this distinguished person from the cares, activities, and responsibilities of life, taking him (to use a common phrase) *to his account*, God was only doing in a way which men in a sense see, and therefore more fully realize, what He was just as really doing at every moment of his previous existence. Before he came to that great office, at every instant of that momentous period of his life, up to the very time when the Great Judge gave visible note of what He had never ceased to do—it is not one whit more true that he has now gone to his account, that his Great Judge will one day pronounce his final award, than that every day he lived he was going to it—the Judge just as near to him, the account going on, the award made.

This is true of every human creature, but its great and startling truth is unquestionably brought more home to us when we have before us some noted instance like the present.

Let us suppose that on that memorable fifth of March, sixteen months ago, a message from God had revealed to the departed President, that which we now know!—that he had said to him, "I have brought you to this great office; in the full career of its duties you shall die." It is not for any human creature to say whether it would have changed or modified any of the acts of his Presidential career; perhaps I cannot express in stronger terms my individual estimation of the man than to declare my strong personal impression that it would not. I do in my heart believe that every act of his official life was done under the sense of personal and official responsibility. But, unquestionably, such a revelation would have given awful solemnity to every decision—it would have suffered no veil to interpose to conceal motive, no conflict or combination of interests to modify the one great motive and purpose, to repress the abiding conviction, "I am making up my own judgment—the judgment of man is nothing to me except as it responds to the judgment of my conscience and my God. I must do my work—the messenger stands at the door and knocks—the grave is waiting—it is my work—the instruments I use to do it, must not be those which others like the best, but such as I believe will do the work the best."

Now, I am not preaching to *official* people simply—be the office high or low; I am preaching, and this great event is preaching to all. We are all in office!—an office before which the government of the world itself sinks into insignificance; the dignity of which was fully realized by Him who, when the world and its glories were proffered to Him, saw their comparative *nothingness—the great realm of conscience, the kingdom of God within us.* To the administration of this government all the powers of nature and of grace are made subordinate; we may use them or abuse them; for that use or abuse we know that we shall be held accountable. But we know it and admit it in a general way; and we know that were such a revelation made to us as that I have intimated, the whole character and tenor of life would be affected by it. If you and I knew beyond the possibility of doubt that on the ninth of next July we should die, I say to you unhesitatingly that we would not live the coming year as we have lived the last. The world would assume a different character and relation to us; the opinions and associations of men would possess a widely different influence. Things which we think of very little importance because the rest of the world think them so, would be weighed in a very different balance—things that occupy a large portion of our attention and affection, because other men value or love them, would sink immeasurably in the scale. Oh! it is in the light of such a revelation that we should learn the full force of that apostolic injunction: "Love not the world, nor the things that are in the world," for we should find, amid all our imagined love of God, and of His truth, what deep-seated care, and love, and worship of the world there is in the best of us; ay, and even in the best moods and movements of the best of us. Well, such a revelation has been made—not of the hour of death, but the hour of judgment—not of years in perspective, but in the awful *present.* The *eternal now* is judging us *now.* The hour of death, indeed, is not revealed; but come when it will, it comes not as the hour of judgment, but the hour which tells us that all judgment is *at an end*—the balance struck, the account made up, the recording angel's function ended. No more make-weights of faith, and prayer, and repentance, and sanctity! The blood of the covenant has sealed the soul for its final passage in the great audit!—that blood which tells, *that it has paid the debt, or doubled it.* And as for that hour of death, we are not, indeed, told that it shall come in one, or ten, or fifty years, but we are told that *it shall come.* Told! There is not a day we live that we are not told it by that which moves men's minds more than God's own revelation. We see infancy and age, wisdom and folly, poverty and riches, lie down in that common bed. "But when? If we knew when! It would make us thoughtful, serious; the great business of life would be to make ready."

Do you think so? I believe that it would make you *mad*—I believe that reason would reel before the dreadful assurance, or that men's hearts would run into desperate recklessness. God, in his mercy, has concealed the *when.* He has not said "this night thy soul shall be required of thee." But he has said, this *hour it may, some hour it will.* In the construction of human language, the potential and the imperative are separate things. In the divine vocabulary this distinction exists not. Whatever he has said *may* be, is not only within his potentiality, but at every moment is at his fiat, when what *may be, is.* It is the business of the children of God to view all those things which God, in reference to our condition, has pronounced contingencies, as realities. This contingency above all. And yet, upon this simple difference of the *may* and the *shall*—creatures of intelligence and observation, as we boast ourselves—how absolutely does the whole tenor of our lives and actions often turn; we act as though the only revelation made to us were that of the Psalmist: "A thousand shall fall beside thee, and ten thousand at thy right hand, but it shall not come nigh thee."

Oh! may God's message now awake us from this delusion; making us feel that, as in the startling case before us, revelation itself could not make the event more certain. So there is a revelation always speaking to us its message, but now echoed by heaven's own angel, sounded abroad on the wide surface of our land; "Behold I stand at the door and knock. Thy soul shall be required of thee." I have now performed this function allotted me with such ability as God has given me. I trust that the humble but very sincere tribute to one who held so high a place among us, is not unsuited to the time or place. It is indeed a high office; and for our own sake we should honor all who hold it—honor them living, honor them dead. We should show that those whom a great people place in such a station of eminence are, by that single act, taken out of the category of common men. While they live we should respect them, and when they go the way of all flesh, I would still have them honored in such a way as will do good to the living. There is a monument even now in progress to the memory of the first President of this country, but how utterly inadequate must that or any other monument be, as an expression of the veneration of this country or of the world itself. I can imagine a monument more worthy of the country and of him; one that would preach a great lesson to generations yet to come. Let the spot where the great Father of his Country reposes become national soil. Let there arise on the bank of his own river, beneath the shade of his own trees, a great mausoleum—there, around his mortal remains, let the bodies of all be gathered who have ever been chosen or shall ever be chosen by the American people to bear that office which Washington dignified and adorned. I believe that such a monument might do much to secure the best succession in the world, the succession of virtues and patriotism like his own. I am very sure that it would be visited like a shrine; that many a heart would beat with nobler pulses when looking on that assemblage of the mighty dead. And, if the day must come when the fate of the great nations that have gone shall be ours; when strangers of some newer race and name shall come hither to visit the relics of a people once mighty and free—the very memory of other places, other names may have vanished, but that will remain; and the world will never cease to bear record that that must indeed have been a great nation which had such honorable sons, and so honored them.

In concluding his address, it will be seen that Dr. Pyne presented an important suggestion to the minds of his hearers, one that will be welcomed by the American people. It is that the home of Washington be purchased by the nation, and adorned as the Mausoleum of the departed Presidents. How appropriately chosen! What depository so fitting for the remains of the honored and illustrious of our land, as the home in which Washington lived—as the earth where his body reposes.

The following dirge (by B. F. Niles, Esq.) was then sung by Professor Berlin and three of the Eberbach family, Professor B. accompanying on the seraphina:—

His triumphs are over—he's gone to his rest,
To the throne of his Maker, the home of the blest,
How peaceful and calm he now rests on the bier,
Each heart droops in sadness, and each eye sheds a tear.
The Hero, the Statesman—his journey is done;
All his cares now are over, his last battle won.
Now sweetly he rests from his sorrows and fears,
And left a proud nation in sadness and tears.

Oh! bear him full gently—disturb not his rest,
And let the turf lightly, be heap'd on his breast;
For oh! he was noble, and gentle, and kind—
And was deep in the hearts of the people enshrined.
Let the flag which he loved envelope his form,
Which often streamed o'er him in the battle's fierce storm.
Oh! calm let him rest with his deeds and his fame,
And halos of glory encircle his name.

It was near two o'clock when the procession commenced to move. The rich yet simple coffin was borne through the great hall door, before which stood the funeral car. This was a very imposing vehicle. The wheels were black and massive, in imitation of those of the ancient Roman chariots. The main body of the car expanded over these to the length of eleven and a half feet, and width of six and a half. Upon this, the place on which the coffin was to rest was raised in the centre. A canopy, in form of an arch, extended from front to rear. All this was enveloped in fine black cloth, entwined with white satin, having large silver spangles in each rosette. The canopy was surmounted by a large golden eagle, covered with crape. At the four corners of the car were golden urns, also shrouded with crape. The coffin was covered with black silk velvet. Eight gray horses were attached to the car, each of them led by a youth, habited in a white frock with crape around the waist, and a white turban upon the head.

During the progress of the procession to the grave, a distance of about three miles, the bells of the city were tolled, and in the various public squares cannon were discharged. At the point of starting the crowds were immense. The grounds adjacent to the President's house, and the porticoes of the Departments, were literally alive. General Scott, the commander-in-chief of the military, presented a noble appearance on this occasion.

Behind the funeral car "Old Whitey" was led by Mr. Swartzman, a well-tried friend of the late President, who had served with him in the Indian wars. The service the old war-horse had rendered, and the association of his name with many of the great battles of Mexico, have rendered him an object of interest; but at this time it seemed only necessary to know that he was the object of the late President's kind regard, in order to rivet the interest of every one upon him.

It is a subject worthy of remark in this place, that although the multitude was vast, and the scenes presented of great novelty, the most perfect order prevailed throughout the whole city; and as the funeral car passed by, the heads of the people were, as it would appear, instinctively uncovered.

Arriving at the burial-ground, the remains were interred with no other ceremonies than the simple and impressive words pronounced by the minister, ending with the benediction, except that the soldier's farewell was poured forth in triple volleys by a portion of the infantry and light artillery.

It was late in the afternoon when the multitude returned to the city, and in a few hours more there was every where stillness and quiet, and the people in the capital of a republic owned a powerful control, and a motive for order and decorum, stronger than regal thrones and glittering bayonets could ever exercise and inspire.

Thus ended this day of sorrow and gloom, and thus terminated the last earthly honors paid to one of the greatest names that ever adorned our country's history, and one of the bravest hearts and *truest men* that ever honored and ennobled human nature. Most happily and aptly may the following beautiful lines of Willis be applied to the lamented soldier, and most heartily will it be responded to by every American:

Lay his sword on his breast! There's no spot on its blade,
In whose cankering breath his bright laurels will fade!
'Twas the first to lead on at humanity's call—
It was stayed with sweet mercy when "glory" was all!
As calm in the council as gallant in war
He fought for his country, and not its "hurrah!"
In the path of the hero with pity he trod—
Let him pass—with his sword—to the presence of God!
Follow now, as ye list! The mourner to-day
Is the nation—whose father is taken away!
Wife, children, and neighbor may mourn at his knell—
He was "lover and friend" to his country as well!
For the stars on our banner, grow suddenly dim,

Let us weep, in our darkness—but weep not for him!
Not for him—who, departing, leaves millions in tears!
Not for him—who has died full of honor and years!
Not for him—who ascended Fame's ladder so high
From the round at the top he has stepped to the sky!
It is blessed to go when so ready to die.

Never since the death of WASHINGTON, has any public man been called from the theatre of his usefulness, who was so universally and so sincerely mourned as General Taylor; nor whose death was so generally looked upon as a national disaster. There was an affectionate attachment felt for him which no other man except the Father of his country had ever inspired to so great a degree. Every American entertained towards him the warmest regard, and looked upon him as upon a dear and intimate *friend.* Even the thousands who had never seen him felt this affectionate regard for his character. His reputation was looked upon as the common property of every American, and they felt an equal pride in the honor his glorious public career and his pre-eminent public and private virtues had reflected upon the country. Long will his memory be remembered and venerated by his countrymen, and long will his deeds continue to fill one of the brightest pages of his country's history. Longer still may his noble deeds and his numerous virtues serve to stimulate and encourage to like deeds and like virtues those in whose hands the destinies of the nation may be placed!

The following letter written by General Taylor after the commencement of the attack which terminated his earthly career,—first published since his death, is probably the last one he ever wrote. As such, it will possess a melancholy interest. Its object will be gathered from its contents:

WASHINGTON, July 5, 1850.

E. P. Prentice, Esq., Albany, N. Y.

SIR:—I have duly received your favors of May 18, and June 25, the former wishing me to attend the Annual Fair of the N. Y. State Agricultural Society in September next, the latter kindly asking my company at your house on that occasion.

In the extreme uncertainty attending the adjournment of Congress, until which event I cannot leave the seat of Government, I find it quite impossible to give any assurance in regard to my presence at the State Fair. I was greatly disappointed when circumstances prevented my attendance at the Fair of last year, and it is my hope this season to have the gratification of witnessing a similar exhibition. Unless prevented by an extraordinary prolongation of the session of Congress, or by other circumstances not now foreseen, I shall certainly comply with the invitation which you have extended to me as President of the Agricultural Society.

I fear, however, that I shall be obliged to decline your very kind request that I should make your house my home during my attendance at the Fair. It will hardly be in my power to accept any private invitations, but should I do so, that of Gov. Fish, which I some time since received, would have the strongest claim upon my attention.

With many thanks for your hospitable offer, I remain, very truly, yours,

Z. TAYLOR.

To attempt a description of General Taylor's character after the elegant portrait of it drawn by WEB-

STER, and BAKER, and PYNE, to be found in the previous pages, and after the many illustrations of it found in every act of his life, as it has been attempted to be drawn in this volume, cannot be deemed necessary. Nor could anything more that might now be added, convey any clearer impression of its remarkable points to the reader than is to be found in the tributes of the men named above. It cannot fail to be seen from them that the leading features of his striking, and, it might almost be said, his sublime character, are its beautiful simplicity, its unyielding integrity, its remarkable firmness, and its open, manly frankness. He "carried his heart in his hand" before his friends, and indeed, before the whole world, and every one who would, could not fail to see the whole man. He had an unalterable abhorrence for everything that bore the slightest resemblance to trickery or management, and would not look with patience upon any deviation from the straight line of rectitude which he himself had ever pursued. To such as inspired his confidence by the exhibition of those traits which so eminently characterized him, he was a fast and unwavering friend. No man possessed warmer or stronger attachments. When he had once formed a friendship, or adopted a resolution after due deliberation, no earthly power could make him desert the one or abate the other. Of course, such a man, with such traits of character, was more at home and more happy in the domestic circle than in public life, or when surrounded by public men. His love of domestic life, and his amiable and kind heart, were often exhibited during his brief Presidential career, in the garden attached to the white house where he could be seen with a dozen children flocking round him, all receiving a shake of the hand and a kind word. They seemed at home with him, and he happy with them. These simple incidents, revealed General Taylor's whole character, and show him the kind-hearted and benevolent man, the devoted friend, and the affectionate father. Children love by instinct men who possess such traits; and every child who once came within his influence, loved General Taylor with the love of a child for its father.

THE END.

SEWARD'S LIFE OF JOHN Q. ADAMS.

* * We are glad to see a pretty full account of Mr. Adams' Anti-Slavery efforts in Congress have been given; for, great as his public services were during a long life, his greatest fame with the present and future generations, will rest upon his efforts to break down the Slave power. The great men who eulogized Mr. Adams in Congress and elsewhere, generally passed silently over this part of his life, as if it was something not very creditable to him, and to be talked about as little as possible. Mr. Seward has taken a better view of the subject. We can recommend this biography as being a clear and concise history of Mr. Adams' life. * * * *Lowell Republican, (Free Soil.)*

It is a work well written, prepared evidently with care, conveys an excellent idea of the life and services of that distinguished patriot and statesman. It is well adapted for popular reading, and comes within the means of every citizen. * * And possessing, as it does, a fund of historical and biographical information, of the most interesting description, it will be a desirable book for the library and a welcome companion to any man who cherishes a respect for the memory of Adams. * * * *Boston Journal.*

* * We have read it and are delighted with the good taste and discrimination with which facts and cotemporary events are brought in to show forth the noble and manly stand of John Quincy Adams. Next to our national pride, that we have such great and good men to adorn the pages of our history, we should glory in having authors like Wm. H. Seward, to chronicle their lives and their deeds. * * * *Massachusetts Eagle.*

The association of such names as Adams and Seward, one as the subject of the biography, and the other as the biographer, must give to this work an interest which rarely attaches to anything emanating from an American pen. * * * *Washington Advocate.*

We would recommend this work to every class of mind — to the vicious, that they may be benefited by the contrast — to the virtuous, that they may be incited to still higher attainments — to the patriot, that the love of country may be renewed in his bosom — to the Christian, that he may see how to honor God in exalted positions — to the young, that they may drink from the pure rill of patriotism, and learn to cherish and protect their privileges — and lastly to the old, that they may yet once more read the lessons of wisdom, as they distilled from the lips of him who was a Nestor among statesmen.— *Wisconsin Chronicle.*

This volume has been now but a few months before the public, during which we understand that some 20,000 copies have been circulated. The fact is sufficient to show that the deceased statesman has found a worthy biographer. Designed for popular use, and prepared from the materials existing in public documents and journals, it is a book, nevertheless, that cannot fail to be read with interest by the scholar as well as the masses. The writer seems imbued with a sincere reverence for the great man whose career he chronicles, and depicts its various eventful incidents with spirit and fidelity. There is no book that we now remember, which presents in the same compass so much that is interesting in our history, during the period of which it treats.— *Washington Republic.*

Headley's Women of the Bible: Historical and descriptive sketches of the Women of the Bible, as maidens, wives, and mothers; from Eve of the Old, to the Marys of the New Testament: by Rev. P. C. Headley, in one 12mo. volume, illustrated—uniform with "Headley's Sacred Mountains." $1,25.

The author of this work possesses enough traits of resemblance to the author of the Sacred Mountains, to leave no doubt of his right to the name of Headley. There is much of that spirited descriptive power, which has made the elder brother a popular favorite, and gives promise of a successful career on his own account. The sketches are brief, and embody all the historic incidents recorded of them.—*New York Evangelist.*

A younger brother of J. T. Headley is the author of this beautiful volume. It will probably have a larger circulation than the splendid work issued last fall by the Messrs. Appleton, being better adapted for the general reader, in form and price, while it is ornamental enough for the centre table. It contains nineteen descriptive biographical sketches, arranged in chronological order, including nearly all the distinguished women of the sacred annals, and forming an outline of Scripture history. The illustrations are from original designs, and are numerous and appropriate. No ordinary powers of imagination and expression are shown in the vivid and picturesque descriptions; and the fine portraitures of character rivet the interest, and set forth the Scripture delineations in a stronger light. In this respect the book has no rival, for no other is so complete, following so closely at the same time, the sacred narrative. We hope it is but an earnest of other works from the pen of its gifted author.—*Home Journal.*

We were so struck with the title of this work, and the prepossessing appearance of its typography, that we have so far departed from the usual course adopted in like cases, as to *read* carefully the work in hand, before recommending it to our readers. And we are prepared to say, that a more attractive volume has not fallen in our way for a long time. It is made up of brief historical and descriptive eulogies of the most remarkable females of a most extraordinary era in the world's history. The author has appropriated very much of the poetry and romance of the Bible, in the sketches he has given of *nineteen* women, who have come down to us through their peculiar merits, embalmed in sacred inspiration. Whoever reads the story of Sarah, the beautiful Hebrew maiden, the admiration of the Chaldean shepherds and the pride of her kindred; or of Rebecca, whom the "faithful steward of Abraham" journeyed to the land of Nahor and selected as the bride of Isaac, and who, it is said, "was *very fair to look upon;*" or of Rachel, the beautiful shepherdess who tended her father's flocks in the valley of Haran; or of Merriam, Deborah, Jeptha's Daughter, Delilah, Ruth, Queen of Sheba, the Shunamite, Esther, Elizabeth, Virgin Mary, Dorcas, and others — will read a story far more interesting and attractive than any romance or novel. Every young lady in town should read this work; and we will venture to say that they *will* do so if they but once get hold of it, for it is a book that cannot be laid aside.— *Oswego Times.*

The Lives of Mary and Martha, mother and wife of Washington: by Margaret C. Conkling, with a steel portrait, 18mo, scarlet cloth.

MISS CONKLING, who is a daughter ef Judge Conkling of Auburn, is favorably known as the author of Harper's translation of "Florian's History of the Moors of Spain." She also wrote "Isabel, or the Trials of the Heart." In the preparation of the pretty little volume she has done a praiseworthy deed, and we hope she will receive the reward she merits. She has taught us in the work

"how divine a thing
A woman may be made."

The mother and wife of Washington were, in many respects, model women, and the daughters of America will do well to study their character — which is finely drawn on these pages.— *Literary Messenger.*

This beautifully printed and elegantly bound little work, reflecting the highest credit upon the skill and task of the publishers, contains biographical sketches of Mary, the mother, and Martha, the wife of the Father of his country. It is a most valuable contribution to the history of the American people, embracing not only the great public events of the century during which the subjects lived, but those pictures of home life, and that exhibition of social manners and customs, which constitute the most important part of life, but which, from the fact of their apparent triviality and intangibility, the historian generally passes over. The authoress evidently sympathises earnestly with her subject, and feels that in the exhibition of those womanly virtues which characterized the heroines of her narrative, she makes the most eloquent plea in favor of the dignity of her sex. It is dedicated to Mrs. WM. H. SEWARD, and contains a finely executed engraving of the wife of Washington. We cordially commend it to the public, and most especially our lady readers.— *Syracuse Journal.*

This acceptable and well written volume goes forth upon a happy mission,

"To teach us how divine a thing
A woman may be made,"

by unfolding those charms of character which belong to the mother and wife of the hero of the Land of the Free; and in the companionship of which, while they illustrated the watchful tenderness of a mother, and the confiding affections of a wife, is shown those influences which made up the moral sentiments of a man, whose moral grandeur will be felt in all that is future in government or divine in philosophy; and one whose name is adored by all nations, as the leader of man in in the progress of government, to that perfection of human rights where all enjoy liberty and equality. To say that Miss Conkling has fulfilled the task she says a "too partial friendship has assigned her" faultlessly, would perhaps be too unmeasured praise, for perfection is seldom attained; but it will not be denied but that her biographies are traced in the chaste elegances that belong to the finished periods of a refined style, which fascinates the reader with what she has thus contributed to our national literature.

The design of the volume is, to picture a *mother* fitting the "Father of his Country" in a light full of the inexhaustible nobleness of woman's nature, and yet as possessing that subdued and quiet simplicity, where Truth becomes the Hope on which Faith looks at the future with a smile. The mother of Washington was tried in a school of practice where frugal habits and active industry were combined with the proverbial excellences of those Virginia matrons, who were worthy mothers of such men as Washington, Jefferson, Marshall, and Henry. Miss C. has pictured with fidelity and elegance, her views of this remarkable woman; not less beautifully has she sketched the character of Martha, the wife; following her from her brilliant manners as the Virginia belle, through the various phases of her life, she gives a rapid but comprehensive view of those characteristics which make up the quiet refinement of manners native to her, and which ever gave her the reputation of an accomplished wife and lady. And with peculiar delicacy Miss Conkling has portrayed the thousand virtues with which she embellished a home; her amiable disposition and winning manners made the happiest to the purest and best of all men fame has chosen for its noblest achievments.— *Syracuse Star.*

www.ingramcontent.com/pod-product-compliance
Lightning Source LLC
LaVergne TN
LVHW020916110826
845150LV00004B/692

9781425556181